Reviews for
Applied SAP® BI 7.0 Web Reports: Using BEx Web Analyzer and Web Application Designer

In my opinion, it is a must-read for anyone who wants to have an overview of SAP BOBJ reporting tools and how to implement them, virtually in any business, in a smooth way. This book is a great asset, whether you are planning for a SAP BW reporting career or are responsible for SAP BW BOBJ implementation in your company.

—*Thiagu Bala,* Independent SAP BW, IP, BOBJ, and BPC consultant

This book is insightful, straightforward, and practical, and includes a good balance of concepts, configuration tips, and best practices. *Applied SAP BI 7.0 Web Reports* enables the developer to get actionable information to business users in an intuitive format. That is what is needed most!

—*Thomas S. Eisenhart,* Independent SAP BI Consultant, Pro-Activity Technology Group, LLC

About the Author

Peter Jones is a Platinum Principal Business Applications Consultant with SAP Professional Services Consulting specializing in Controlling (CO), Enterprise Controlling (EC), Auditing, Business Warehouse (BW/BI), Strategic Enterprise Management (SEM), Business Planning and Consolidations (BPC), and BusinessObjects (BOBJ). He has over eleven years of consulting and educational experience in a variety of strategic and leadership roles, focused on Controlling, Profitability Analysis, Planning and Consolidations, Corporate Governance, Data Warehousing, Business Intelligence, and Business Analytics. Peter's diverse professional background includes not only consulting experience but participation in the academic areas of Finance, Controlling, Data Warehousing, Enterprise Management, and Corporate Governance. He is serving as an SAP Principal/Platinum Business Consultant for areas including CO, BW, and SEM. He has been involved with numerous implementations for BW and ECC, from the Blueprint phase through to the Go-Live Process. His responsibilities include being a Subject Material Expert (SME) in all of the areas listed above, active presenter at conferences including ASUG, SAPPHIRE, and BI conferences, and editor/writer for *FICO Expert* and *BI Expert*. Along with consulting and education at SAP, Peter has been involved with the academic world in developing and presenting numerous topics for the University Alliance, which included topics in the areas of CO, BI, Auditing, SEM, and now BPC. He has an MBA from Drexel University in Finance and is SAP certified in the areas of FI, CO, BW, SEM, BPC, and BOBJ. Prior to working for SAP, Peter was self-employed for 15 years in his own accounting and finance business.

About the Technical Editor

Charles Soper has worked in the industry at Eastman Kodak Company in Rochester, New York in a variety of finance and accounting roles. He has an undergraduate degree in Economics and an MBA in Finance from the University of Rochester. He is a Senior Applications Instructor with SAP Educational Services specializing in the areas of Controlling, Finance, Business Intelligence, Strategic Enterprise Management (SEM), and Business Planning and Consolidations (BPC). He has over nine years of experience in the Educational Group at SAP and is involved with the development of training material for areas such as BPC and BW/BI. He has taught in areas including Finance, Controlling, BI, SEM (CPM), and BPC. He is SAP certified in the areas of BW, SEM, and BPC.

Applied SAP® BI 7.0 Web Reports: Using BEx Web Analyzer and Web Application Designer

Peter Jones

This book contains references to the products of SAP AG,
Dietmar-Hopp-Allee 16, 69190 Walldorf, Germany. The
names of these products are registered and/or unregistered
trademarks of SAP AG. SAP AG is neither the author nor the
publisher of this book and is not responsible for its content.

New York   Chicago   San Francisco
Lisbon   London   Madrid   Mexico City
Milan   New Delhi   San Juan
Seoul   Singapore   Sydney   Toronto

The McGraw·Hill Companies

Cataloging-in-Publication Data is on file with the Library of Congress

McGraw-Hill books are available at special quantity discounts to use as premiums and sales promotions, or for use in corporate training programs. To contact a representative, please e-mail us at bulksales@mcgraw-hill.com.

**Applied SAP® BI 7.0 Web Reports: Using BEx Web Analyzer
and Web Application Designer**

1234567890   DOC DOC   109876543210

ISBN   978-0-07-164026-8
MHID   0-07-164026-6

Sponsoring Editor Wendy Rinaldi	**Technical Editor** Charles Soper	**Composition** Glyph International
Editorial Supervisor Janet Walden	**Copy Editor** William McManus	**Illustration** Glyph International
Project Manager Madhu Bhardwaj, Glyph International	**Proofreader** Claire Splan	**Art Director, Cover** Jeff Weeks
Acquisitions Coordinator Joya Anthony	**Indexer** Claire Splan	**Cover Designer** Pattie Lee
	Production Supervisor George Anderson	

Contents at a Glance

Contents

Acknowledgments

This endeavor has been an exciting and interesting process. Since this is a turning point for SAP Business Intelligence, moving from the BEx-driven components to the BusinessObjects (BOBJ) components, the approach in writing this book was a bit different, knowing that providing a blend of two different reporting components is necessary to satisfy everyone who is interested in both understanding the configuration details for the current BEx toolset and getting an idea of the roadmap of the current and future integration of BOBJ. Also the difference in my overall experience in configuration and implementation of the two toolsets presented a challenge. Knowing the BEx toolset inside and out versus having a good knowledge base but not as much configuration experience with BOBJ as with BEx made writing this book definitely different and more challenging from writing my previous BI books.

I would like to thank all the people at McGraw-Hill who were involved in this publication for their help, including Wendy Rinaldi, Joya Anthony, Janet Walden, Bill McManus, and Madhu Bhardwaj. Also thanks to Charles Soper for his helping to keep me focused on the straight and narrow with the functionality of both components.

Finally, to my wife, Lisa, for helping me along the way and giving me the time and opportunity to work on and finish this project.

Introduction

This book offers a combination of system functionality, configuration, and actual real-life examples of the use of SAP Web Reports in the corporate environment. It also incorporates an explanation of the newer components for reporting in BI—SAP BusinessObjects.

In the current economy, one of the most valuable assets of a corporation is information and the ability to deliver that information in a useable format, in a timely manner, and on numerous platforms. This book investigates the use of the Web-based functionality of SAP 7.0 BI systems to deliver a useful and viable alternative for these requirements. The ability to deliver huge amounts of data is a given with most data warehousing systems, but the ability to deliver the correct data in as flexible a format as possible and turn that into useful information is much more challenging. There are many instances of corporations having all the data they need to execute their corporate plans but not have the ability to deliver that information in a format that offers the C-level management (CEO, CFO, etc.) useful key performance indicators (KPIs).

This book offers both the basic setup of the components for BEx Web Analyzer and real-life examples of the uses and setup of the Web-based reporting component. We will investigate the configuration starting from a basic Web report and working up to some very complex dashboard functionality. With this book, you can easily work your way through the setup and configuration of Web-based reports in BW. You can use the information in this book to review basic settings and the functionality delivered by them, review completed reports and dashboards on the Web to understand the mechanics of configuration, as well as learn some tips and tricks to get started faster and more easily. One of the more frequently requested activities is to set up a prototype quickly and demo it for the initial analysis of the reporting components. With the information in this book, you can get through that process much faster so that you can focus on the actual project.

You can also use this book to review and work through the migration process from 3.x versions to BI 7.0. It gives you a step-by-step migration process for both Web-based reports and BEx-based reports.

In conjunction with the idea of migration or upgrades, this book offers a positional analysis of the SAP BusinessObjects reporting component. You can use this to review the functionality and enhancements offered by the SAP BusinessObjects reporting components during the selection phase of your process.

BEx Web Analyzer Reporting Functionality

A s mentioned in the introduction, this book focuses on the Web-based reporting components available in SAP BI. This chapter discusses the functionality, flexibility, and configuration of the BEx Web Analyzer. Most of this discussion will be directed to the actual business user, because the BEx Web Analyzer comes ready to use and all you need to do is create a query to use on the Web. However, instead of configuring a query from scratch, in this chapter we will take a query that has already been configured and use it within the Web-based components. Occasionally, we will have to open the Web Application Designer (WAD) template query to get through a specific discussion in this chapter, but we will do so only when necessary because Chapters 3 and 4 are dedicated to coverage of the WAD.

As we go through the information for the BEx Web Analyzer, you may notice some overlap in terms of capabilities and topics between the two frontend options available in SAP BI, the BEx Web Analyzer and the BEx Analyzer (the Excel-based component). This book assumes that you are familiar already with the BEx Analyzer, so I will attempt to minimize the amount of redundant information, but in some cases redundancy is important to highlight certain areas and to reinforce the functionality of the Web frontend. In this chapter, the discussion will be driven by the navigational functions within the BEx Web Analyzer and the WAD template query. Numerous activities can be executed on the Web via either the Web query or the WAD template query; the usability of this approach to reporting can't be understated. The Web is definitely a user-friendly interface within the SAP reporting strategy and enterprise reporting that should be reviewed and discussed as an interface of choice.

We will not review the functionality of the BEx portion of the Web Analyzer because that is an extension of the BEx Analyzer. If you need additional information about the BEx component, please refer to Chapter 3 of my book *SAP Business Information Warehouse Reporting*. Basically, the BEx Web Analyzer is the same as the BEx Analyzer except that it uses the Web as a distribution channel. So, all the functionality of the BEx Analyzer is also available via the Web using the workbook component found in the BEx Analyzer. For this to be useable, there will be some footprint on your company systems, so keep that in mind during the process of deciding what components to use. If you decide to use the BEx version on the Web and are already using the BEx Analyzer, then you don't have any additional work to do to use it on the Web.

Status of Reporting Tools in SAP BI

I know what some of you are asking right now: Why dedicate a book to the use of the BEx Web Analyzer and the WAD when SAP is pushing customers toward the new SAP BusinessObjects BI Tools? Well, there are a number of reasons, and we should address them before we head into the details of the BEx Web Analyzer and the WAD.

First, the BEx Web Analyzer and the WAD are not going away anytime soon. Yes, they are being assimilated into the BusinessObjects (BOBJ) components, but the actual reporting toolset covered in this book will be supported by SAP through 2014 and continue to be available past 2014—no plans are in the works to completely phase out these reporting components. So, companies that have this toolset do not need to start thinking about any changes immediately, but it's always good to be moving in the correct direction—which, according to SAP, is to start to transition over to using the BusinessObject components for reporting but realize that 2014 is only the time frame when SAP will stop support for this component set and not the final date that your reporting tools will work. Nothing will preclude your company from having support onsite for this product after 2014.

Second, with over 9500 BW implementations around the world, there will definitely be companies that are happy with the current reporting options and thus choose not to move to the BOBJ components. We will talk more about this in Chapter 9.

Finally, presently the BW (and therefore the BI reporting frontend) doesn't automatically include the BOBJ components. This is likely to change in the near future, but currently, even though the BOBJ components are fully integrated with the BW backend, they are not included with the Business Intelligence license based on the BW system. You will have to add these components and the license cost onto the base pricing for BW.

In short, not all companies will be moving immediately to the BOBJ suite of products but instead will use the current SAP BI reporting tools for several years. So, I'm confident that quite a bit of work will be available for support of and enhancements to the SAP BI Web Analyzer and the WAD for years to come, making this book a valuable tool.

I will defer a full discussion of the changes and transition within SAP's reporting components until Chapter 9 because that is where I will discuss some of the functionality of BOBJ within the SAP environment. In Chapter 9, I'll discuss the roadmap of SAP reporting tools and where they are going over the next several years. If your company is contemplating a move from another reporting component to SAP BusinessObjects, you might want to read that chapter before continuing here.

Introduction to the BEx Web Analyzer

The BEx Web Analyzer is the initial Web frontend tool offered as part of the Business Explorer reporting options. The entire navigational and analytical process within the Web Analyzer is structured to be business user friendly. Much of the functionality that is available in the BEx Query Designer is now available to the business user from the executed Web query. Thus, most of the functionality that can be configured when using the Query Designer can also be configured by the business user on the Web. For example, in addition to configuration capability, the capability to create exceptions and conditions is available to the business user.

Also, new to the most current Frontend Support Package (FEP) is the capability to create calculated key figures (CKFs) directly from the frontend of the BEx Web Analyzer (once CKFs are created, if you save your report, they will be saved for that specific version of the report). This offers a significant enhancement for the business user on the Web. One of the concerns I've heard over the past several years is that the capability to create any sort of additional columns or calculations is assigned specifically to the BW IT group rather than to the business user. Well, now business users can create any CKF they need on-the-fly and save it. The BEx Query Designer functionality is unavailable to the end user in only a few areas—the creation of variables, restricted key figures, and some cell editor functionality. Therefore, the business user now has a variety of options available at their fingertips.

This Web-based frontend has easy-to-use drag-and-drop functionality that allows the user to navigate intuitively through queries. The Web frontend holds a very important position in the architecture of the reporting strategy. A Web-based strategy increases the ability to distribute the information from a report twofold; it not only gives the business user access to information via a thin frontend—a Web screen—and thus obviates the need to have access to the GUI version of the workbook or query, it also allows them to access other, third-party systems via the Web. Figure 1-1 shows the positioning of the Web-based frontend in the BEx-specific reporting strategy of SAP.

The capability of a business user to save a query or query view directly is also available in the BI environment, but your company, depending on its policies regarding what a superuser versus a business user can do, might not allow this option. In other words, if your company has a standing requirement not to save anything in production, then saving a

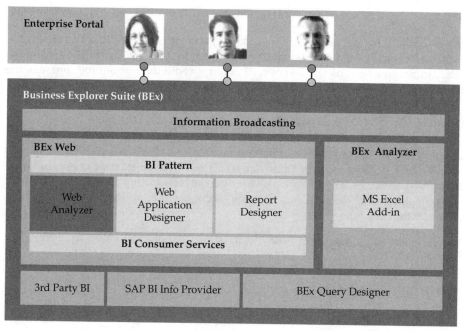

Copyright by SAP AG

FIGURE 1-1   Web Analyzer in the frontend architecture

query in the production system would not be allowed. I expand on this discussion of using the BEx Web Analyzer to help increase business user capabilities in the following sections.

The following illustration shows the final result of a save process in the BEx Query Designer. A query developed in the BEx Query Designer has a format available for both the BEx Analyzer frontend (Excel based) and the BEx Web Analyzer (Web based). As you can see, this query has been saved in the Favorites folder, but we also have the option to store the query in a menu role, which is another Folder option. Both options make the query available for publishing to the SAP NetWeaver Enterprise Portal once an iView is created.

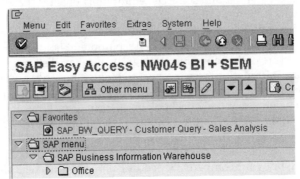

Copyright by SAP AG

NOTE *An iView is created so that the final report can be assigned to the BI portal and from that point can be used by assigning the BI portal to another company portal or a federated portal.*

Keep in mind that the purpose of this chapter is to introduce the BEx Web Analyzer reporting functionality and navigation in general, not to review each of the different options in detail. Individual options will be covered in more depth throughout the course of this book.

Accessing the BEx Web Analyzer

You can access the BEx Web Analyzer in a few different ways. As mentioned, any query that you create using the BEx Query Designer automatically is saved as a Web-based query and is available for reporting using the BEx Web Analyzer. From an existing query that has been executed, you can access any BI data provider via the New button, as discussed in more detail in the upcoming "Toolbar Functionality" section. Other options to access the BEx Web Analyzer include the following:

- From the BEx Analyzer, choose BEx Analyzer I Tools I BEx Web Analyzer:

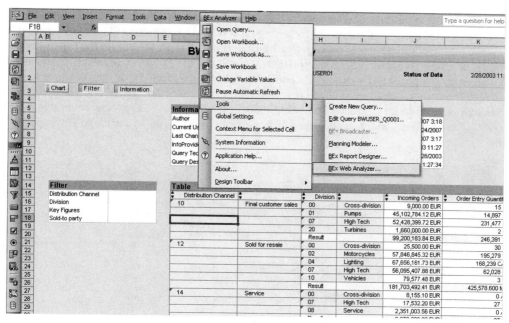

- From the BEx Query Designer, choose Query | Execute, as shown next. This executes the query directly to the Web. Alternatively, you can click the Execute icon directly on the Query Designer toolbar.

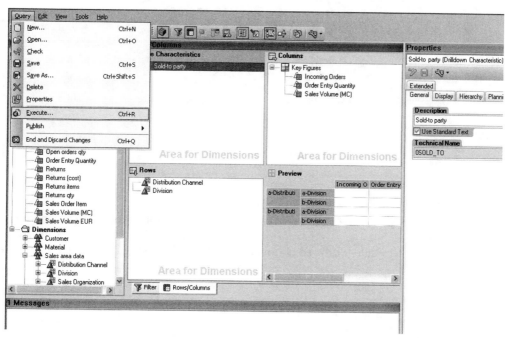

The following illustration shows the initial format of the query we will be using in this chapter. In terms of key figures, the Incoming Orders and Order Entry Quantity will work for the moment and allow us enough flexibility within the report to see all the functionality of the BEx Web Analyzer. For characteristics, we will use the Division, Material, Distribution Channel, and a time characteristic, Calendar Year/Month, as free characteristics, and in the rows use the characteristics Sold-to Party and Country for starters. There is a restriction on Sales Organization for characteristic value 1000. This will enable us to show several features within the BEx Web Analyzer that need to have a filter on the report results to emphasize the results.

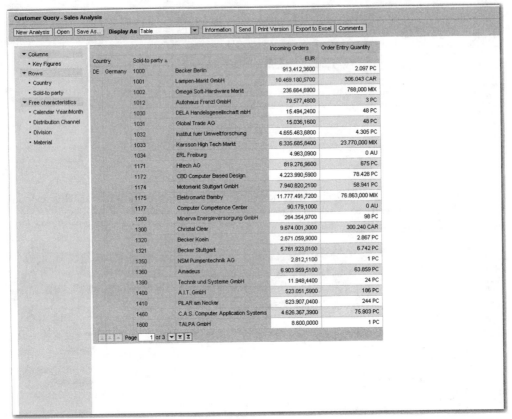

Once the query is displayed on the Web, it is embedded automatically into a standard Web template for ad hoc analysis that corresponds to the BEx Web Analyzer. You can call the standard Web template for the ad hoc analysis from the following BEx tools:

Tools	Path for Call
Query Designer	Click the Display Query on the Web button on the Query Designer toolbar.
Web Application Designer	Choose either Tools I BEx Web Analyzer or Web Template I Execute Use the Find function to search for 0ANALYSIS_PATTERN and then execute this template.

From a technical viewpoint, in BI 7.0 the standard Web template for ad hoc analysis and display of the BEx Web Analyzer is based on the template 0ANALYSIS_PATTERN. This template can be set by default for the ad hoc analysis in the SAP Reference IMG under SAP NetWeaver I Business Intelligence I Setting for Reporting and Analysis I BEx Web I Set Standard Web Templates. You can copy this Web template to make changes to it and set it as your new default Web template for the ad hoc analysis in the IMG. For example, if your company requires specific disclaimers or a company logo that the entire company will be using, this is a good approach to accommodating that change. The default Web template for the ad hoc analysis is delivered in the SAP delivery version (D version), so you can change it in the active version (A version) as required. However, I recommend that you make changes to and edit the template in a copy.

Many additional standard Web templates are included in 0ANALYSIS_PATTERN to support all the different Web items that you see on the 0ANALYSIS_PATTERN screen, such as the Save As and Information buttons on the toolbar across the top of the report. We will discuss the components found in the 0ANALYSIS_PATTERN template in Chapters 3 and 4 during the WAD conversation. At this point, just realize that some standard templates are required for the ad hoc display of the report to be available on the Web.

Navigation Options in the BEx Web Analyzer

Navigation in the BEx Web Analyzer is a bit different from navigation in its counterpart frontend, the BEx Analyzer. In the BEx Analyzer, the functionality of adding a characteristic or other component to the format is to use the context menu or dropdown and either insert the characteristic by drilling down or across with the options offered in the menu. This is a bit easier than using the drag and drop functionality in the BEx Analyzer. In contrast, with the BEx Web Analyzer, we can use either the ability to drag and drop characteristics into the query format or using the context menu and the functionality from the navigational pane to pick the item from the dropdown list of options. Both are very easy and quick to use in the Web toolsets. These are user-friendly options that allow you to navigate by using your cursor, from just about anywhere on the screen, and position the characteristic where you want it. In the BEx Analyzer, several navigational steps might be necessary before you get the characteristic in exactly the correct position. With the ability to drag and drop, you can format the report in one movement—and more intuitively. Most of the navigation and manipulation within the BEx Web Analyzer is accomplished using the toolbar functionality found in the standard Web template. As you will see, this is a combination of multiple standard templates grouped together to support user-friendly activities.

NOTE *Drag-and-drop functionality is also available in the BEx Analyzer but isn't as user friendly as it is in the BEx Web Analyzer.*

The following illustration shows the use of the Division within the rows of the query. Initially this characteristic was in the Free Characteristics section and we moved it to the rows of the query.

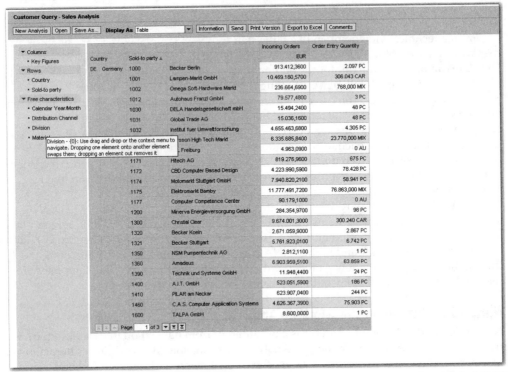

Again, this is done with a drag-and-drop operation and not via a context menu option, although both methods are available for use. Specifically, with drag and drop, the user can perform the following actions:

- Drag items from one section of the navigation pane to another, such as from the Rows to Columns, or from Rows or Columns to Free Characteristics.
- Drag items from the navigation pane directly to the rows or columns of the analysis results.
- Drag characteristics to the filter area to immediately perform the corresponding filtering of the results.
- Drag items out of the analysis grid to remove them from the analysis.

Using the navigation pane, you can do all the preceding actions without touching the actual report portion of the screen. Just by dragging and dropping from the navigation pane into the area/section that you require, you can adjust the display of the report.

Other differences exist between the BEx Analyzer and the BEx Web Analyzer, and they will become more apparent as we go through the list of navigation functions of the BEx Web Analyzer.

Toolbar Functionality

The best approach to reviewing all the BEx Web Analyzer toolbar options is to move from left to right across the toolbar. Following is the initial view of the toolbar on the Web-based query introduced earlier.

Each of the options in the toolbar will open a dialog box with its own specific components. The least conspicuous option in the toolbar is the most useful—the Settings option at the far right side of the toolbar. Note that this option and the Filter option are hyperlinks rather than buttons and thus are referred to as *link functions*. Whereas the functions of the buttons are reasonably straightforward to understand, the function of the Settings link is not too obvious, as you will discover later in the chapter. In any case, by using the buttons and link functions available in the BEx Web Analyzer toolbar, you can quickly navigate to important functions that perform convenient ad hoc analysis of your business data. (You can also use the navigation pane and context menu to access a variety of analysis functions, as discussed later in the chapter.)

New Analysis, Open, and Save As   The importance of each of these individual options is easier to grasp when they are considered as a group. The combination of these three components makes up a very important area of your overall reporting strategy. Before you make any decisions about how business users view and work with reports, you must define your long-term reporting strategy in terms of what business users can and can't do. You must decide as part of this strategy whether to give business users more independence and flexibility by allowing them to generate their own reporting options and components instead of depending on the BW IT team to create and develop all of the required reports.

I'm an advocate of giving business users some ability to create reports in production; I believe it is a very useful process and needs to be considered by every company. Sure, you must first address possible issues affecting performance, data modeling, consistency between levels in your BW system, and functionality before you allow business users to create queries in production. I recommend allowing business users to create temporary "Y" queries within production, and setting specific limits in terms of query creation and the length of time a temporary query exists before it is deleted. This enables business users to create a query on-the-fly, use it, discuss its importance and use with their business user group, validate it, and confirm the results. This facilitates the exchange of information and knowledge between analysts and gets that information out to the field faster, which in some cases is the only competitive edge that you might have. Once you reach a decision on these questions, you can discuss and review the functionality of these components and see how they can help you satisfy your reporting strategy needs.

The two leftmost buttons on the toolbar, New Analysis and Open, take us to very different servers and very different approaches to saving the queries. Clicking New Analysis takes us to the BW server, and clicking Open takes us to the portal server. You can see this difference in the following two illustrations, in the System field of the Open dialog box, which displays the specific server assignment. So, the initial question you must address before clicking one of these buttons is whether you want to save your report to the portal (by clicking Open) or to the BW system menu (by clicking New Analysis).

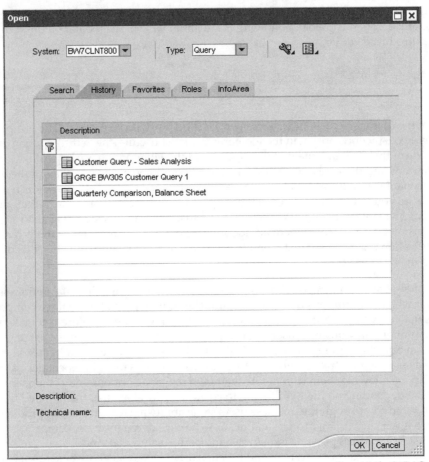

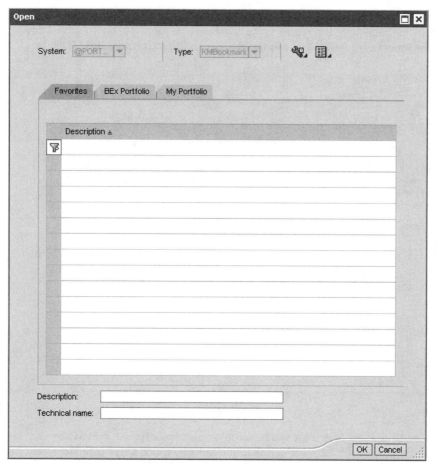

Copyright by SAP AG

Depending on which option you use, saving the report generates a different location that the report is available for viewing. With the New Analysis button, after closing the Open dialog box, the business user saves the report by right-clicking it and choosing Save View from the context menu, which generates a filtered view of the original report and saves it to the BW server. In the case of the Open button, after closing the Open dialog box, the business user clicks the Save As button and saves the report with this option, after which it is a query assigned to the portal and not available using the New Analysis button.

So, looking at these two approaches, we see that in the case of the New Analysis button, the BW team would be in charge of this process and the queries, and in the case of the Open button, the portal team would be responsible for the reports being set up and monitored. Either approach will deliver to your business users what they need, but the best approach for a particular company depends on whether it allows business users to "save" their work in the production environment.

I'll discuss the New Analysis approach first, which does allow business users to save their work, the query view, in the production environment to BW. As previously mentioned, when you begin with the New Analysis button, you save the report from the actual body of the report by right-clicking the report and choosing Save View, as shown next. I have adjusted the report a bit from earlier in the chapter to show Country and Division.

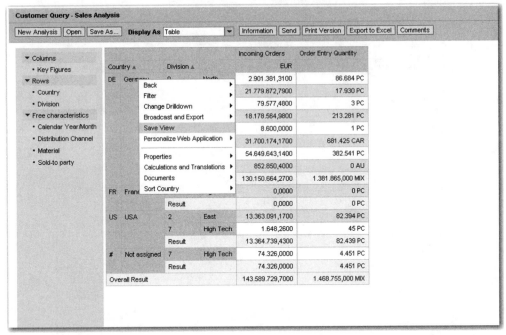

Copyright by SAP AG

Choosing Save View opens the Save As dialog box, shown next, which allows you to assign a description and a technical name to the report. Notice that the System field (upper-left corner) reflects the system number for BW and the Type field is grayed out to show that this object can be saved only as a query view.

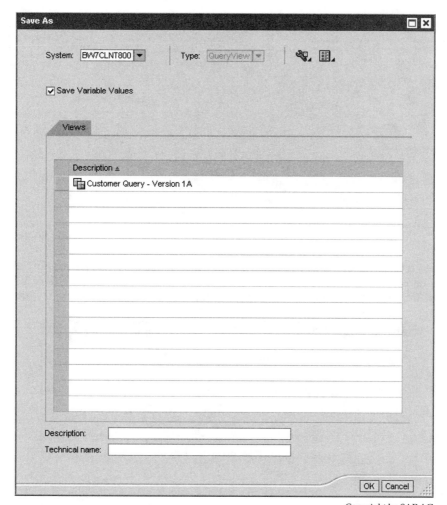

To view the Description and Technical Name fields, you may have to page down a bit. You can also use the icon to the right (looks like a wrench) to show the technical name and information about the query.

After you save the query view, you can access it again by clicking the New Analysis button, which opens a dialog box that allows you to either pick the query or search the list of existing queries. The initial step of clicking the New Analysis button is illustrated next.

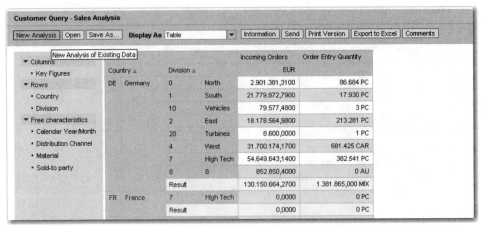

Once you execute this option, you will see an Open dialog box with the existing query views available, as shown next. You can also change the Type field from the Query View to Queries or InfoProviders (depending on your authorization and security).

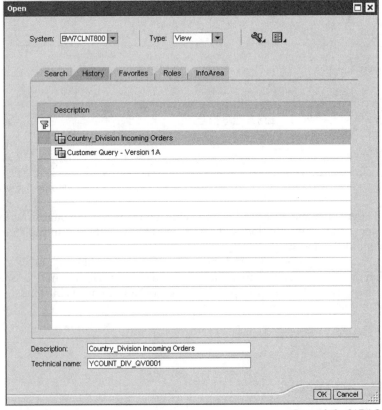

In terms of functionality and the decision of whether to use a query view or a query in this situation, it depends mostly on the configuration of the integration between the BI system and your portal. If the portal is set up to offer some components of the Knowledge Management (KM) system, then you should have the ability to use the Query option. This saves the query within the BI portal as the definition of the query, and no data is stored. If the portal is not set up to offer KM system components, then you should use the Query View option. The query view sits on the BI system and is a filtered version of the query. Since it's already filtered, it will execute faster and more efficiently.

You can also use the New Analysis button to create a new ad hoc analysis. To do so, you first select a data provider to form the basis of your analysis. You can select data providers from a BI system or from a non-SAP data source, depending on how your system is set up. You make this selection in the Type dropdown box of the Open dialog box. Data providers of this type can be queries, query views, or InfoProviders, which you can select from the History, Favorites, Roles, or InfoArea views (tabs). In one of these views, select the required data provider and click OK. (The display of the data is based on what you have selected in the Display As dropdown box, discussed in the next section.) Table 1-1 lists the tabs of the Open dialog box and describes their functionality.

Tab	Description	Use and Functionality
Search	Search process	Type in the technical name or description of the query, query view, or InfoProvider (based on the Type parameter at the top of the dialog box). Use either the technical name or description to search for the object.
History	List of queries, InfoProviders, or views	The queries, InfoProviders, or views that the business user has worked with in the past are listed here (based on the Type parameter at the top of the dialog box). This relies on the same functionality as the BEx Analyzer—namely the DataStore object that stores the historical activities of the business user. This stores and displays the last series of queries that you have worked with (normally the last 21 queries) and is an easy and straightforward approach to accessing the queries (versus having to find them each time you access this process).
Favorites	Favorites list	Any query or query view that is stored in the Favorites list during the save process is listed here. This option is available to help store the queries that you use on an ongoing basis.
Roles	Roles assigned to the business user	Any role that is attached to the business user can be viewed from here, which allows access to all the queries, query views, and other objects assigned to the role.
InfoArea	InfoArea list	This tab may not be available to all business users, depending on the authorization restrictions. If it's available, the user has access to all the InfoProviders and, in turn, all queries and query views in the system or for specific areas allowed.

TABLE 1-1 Functionality in the New Analysis Open Dialog Box for the BEx Web Analyzer

NOTE *A query view involves saving a specific view of a query and executing that view rather than executing the entire query. A query view is a version of a basic query and can be used in the BEx Analyzer, the BEx Web Analyzer, and the WAD. The query view is updated dynamically with new data at the time of execution, and the "saved view" refers to the structure of the display.*

On the InfoArea tab of the Open dialog box (accessed via the New Analysis button), you can double-click at each of the specific levels to navigate to the level with the InfoProvider that you are looking for, as shown in the following illustration. In this particular case, I used the options InfoArea | Financial Management & Controlling | Controlling | Overhead Cost Controlling | Cost Center Accounting to get to the level with the InfoProviders assigned.

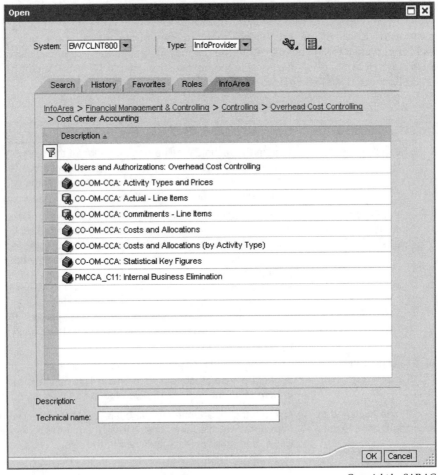

The alternative approach to clicking the New Analysis button is to click the Open button, which is the approach that allows business users to save their work in the production environment of the BI portal. The use of the Open button offers you the option to open saved ad hoc analyses from your favorites, the BEx Portfolio view, or the My BEx Portfolio view. This is similar functionality as the New Analysis button but not as robust. The following illustration shows a view of the initial execution of the Save As process (after closing the Open dialog box and then clicking the Save As button).

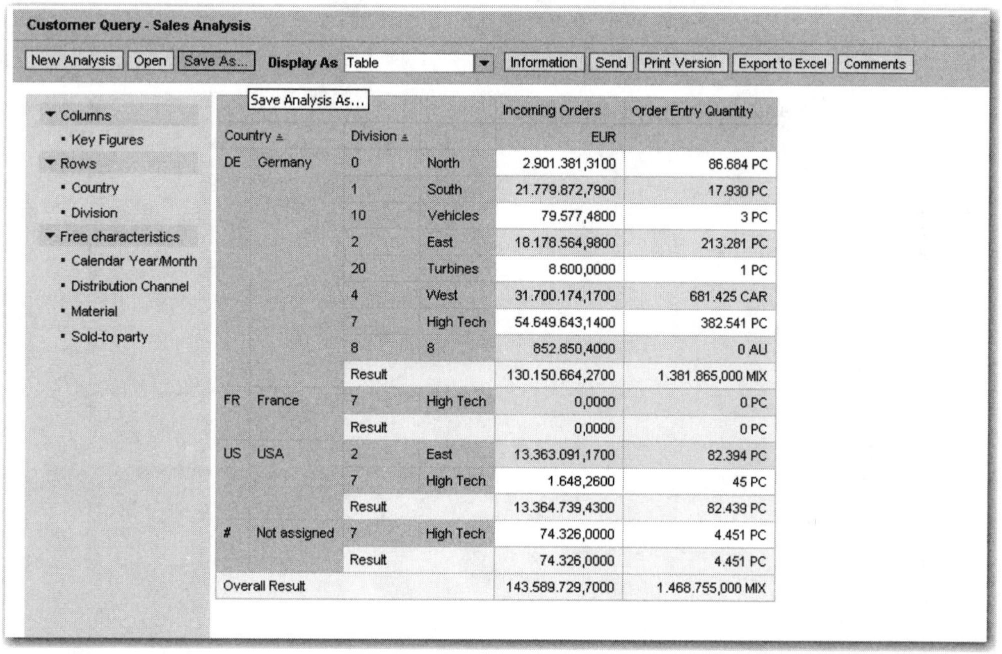

Customer Query - Sales Analysis

New Analysis | Open | Save As... | **Display As** Table | Information | Send | Print Version | Export to Excel | Comments

Save Analysis As...

	Country ≜	Division ≜		Incoming Orders EUR	Order Entry Quantity
	DE Germany	0	North	2.901.381,3100	86.684 PC
		1	South	21.779.872,7900	17.930 PC
		10	Vehicles	79.577,4800	3 PC
		2	East	18.178.564,9800	213.281 PC
		20	Turbines	8.600,0000	1 PC
		4	West	31.700.174,1700	681.425 CAR
		7	High Tech	54.649.643,1400	382.541 PC
		8	8	852.850,4000	0 AU
		Result		130.150.664,2700	1.381.865,000 MIX
	FR France	7	High Tech	0,0000	0 PC
		Result		0,0000	0 PC
	US USA	2	East	13.363.091,1700	82.394 PC
		7	High Tech	1.648,2600	45 PC
		Result		13.364.739,4300	82.439 PC
	# Not assigned	7	High Tech	74.326,0000	4.451 PC
		Result		74.326,0000	4.451 PC
	Overall Result			143.589.729,7000	1.468.755,000 MIX

Columns
 • Key Figures
 ▼ Rows
 • Country
 • Division
 ▼ Free characteristics
 • Calendar Year/Month
 • Distribution Channel
 • Material
 • Sold-to party

Using this process, you can save the result of your ad hoc analysis with an appropriate name in your portal favorites or in the BEx Portfolio. The following illustration shows this view of the process. Notice also that there is a bit of a difference in terms of saving. In this case, we can only assign a description to the saved version of the query, whereas in the option of saving a query view, we were required to provide both the technical name and the description to save the query to the BW system.

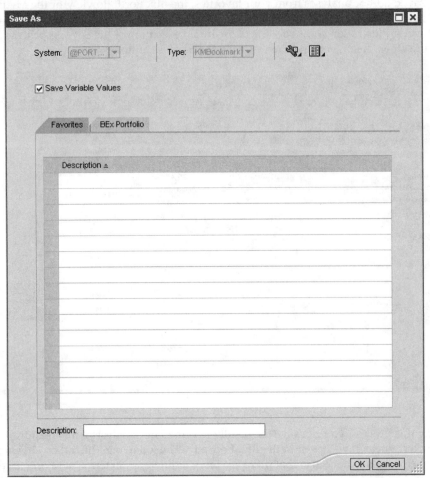

This saves the type of data display (table, chart, or table and graphic) in addition to the navigational state of the data. To access the saved result of your ad hoc analysis again, click Open, and the display of the portal query is available, as shown next.

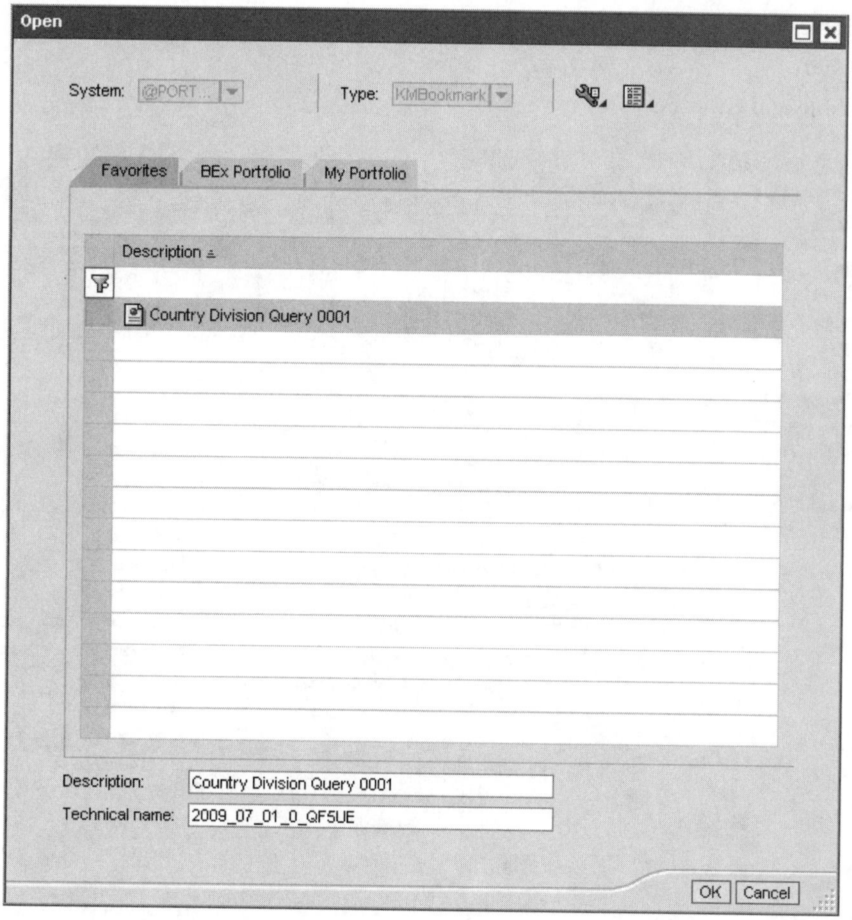

Copyright by SAP AG

Display As   You determine the type of display for the data using the Display As dropdown box, shown in the following illustration. You can choose from the following options for displaying the data:

- Table
- Chart
- Table and Graphic

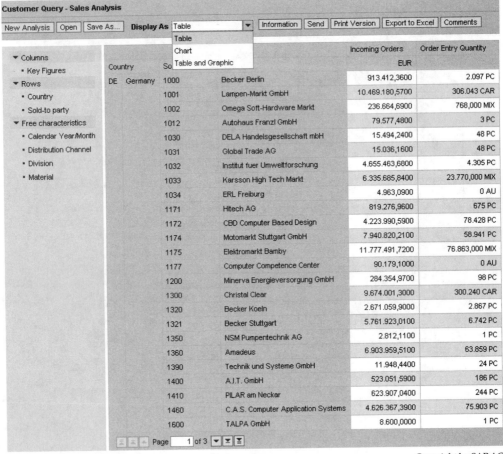

Depending on the amount of information in the table, the use of graphics can be very helpful. The following illustration shows the use of the Table and Graphic option with just the Country and Division information displayed.

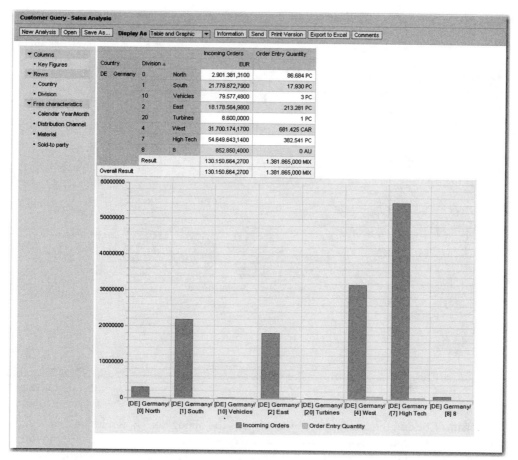

If you were to try to create a graphic with Sold-to Party and Division, too much information would be displayed and the graphic would be useless. This is where the use of the Web Application Designer (WAD) comes into play, with the additional functionality of managing the size and format of larger amounts of information. We will review that information and approach in Chapters 3 and 4, which cover the WAD. The following illustration shows some of the additional functionality in the Graphic display.

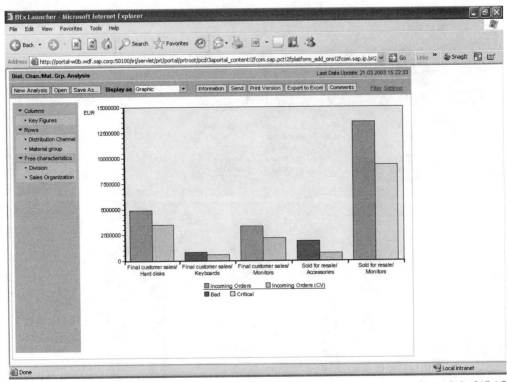

Information   Clicking the Information button opens the dialog box shown in the following illustration. Here, you can see information about the selected data provider, including the key date, the age of the data, the time of the last change, the person who last changed the query, and the date of the last refresh. This is critical information for the business user, who needs to know the last time data was refreshed or the actual report was changed. You also receive information about which static and dynamic filter values the query has and the variable values with which the query is filled. If needed, any of this information can easily be displayed directly on the report, though you need to use some of the functionality within the WAD to do so, which will be discussed in Chapter 4.

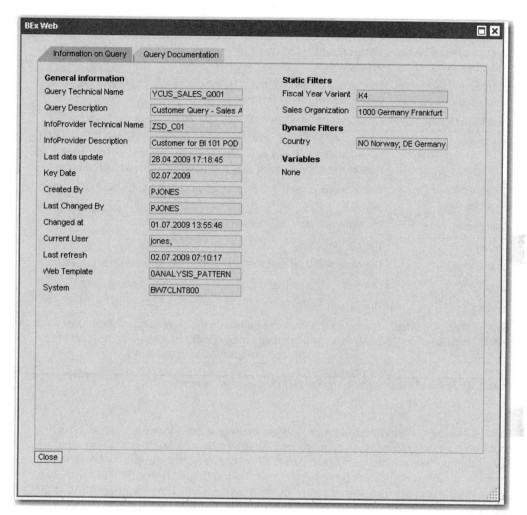

Table 1-2 shows all the fields available in the Information on Query tab. In the Query Documentation tab, any documentation or comments assigned to this Web query are available.

Field(s)	Description
Query Technical Name and Description	The saved technical name of the query and the current query description.
InfoProvider Technical Name and Description	The technical name of the InfoProvider of this query and the description of the InfoProvider.
Last Data Update	The date and time the data was last uploaded to the InfoProvider.
Key Date	The key date of the query. This controls the view of the characteristic values shown in the query. Depending on the time dependency of the master data, this setting may create different views of the data.
Created By and Last Changed By	The user who created the query and the user who last changed the query.
Changed At	The date and time that the change occurred.
Current User	The current user.
Last Refresh	The date and time that the query was last refreshed (executed).
Web Template	The technical name of the Web template that is being used.
System	The system identifier.
Static Filters, Dynamic Filters, Variables	The list of the static filters (within the Filter portion of the Query Designer), dynamic filters (free characteristics or other filters in the rows or columns), and variables used in the query.

TABLE 1-2   Fields of the Information on Query Tab of the Web Analyzer

Send   Clicking the Send button on the toolbar opens the Broadcasting Wizard, which enables you to use information broadcasting functions to broadcast your ad hoc analysis. The option in this case offers only some of the functionality. You can find and use the complete distribution process by using the Information Broadcaster (IB), which you can access via the Broadcasting Wizard from the initial step by clicking the "here" link at the end of the description of this step. The following illustration shows the initial step to complete the setup process. The setup involves a series of four steps, all of which are self-explanatory. The IB offers some excellent options for alerts and proactive reporting.

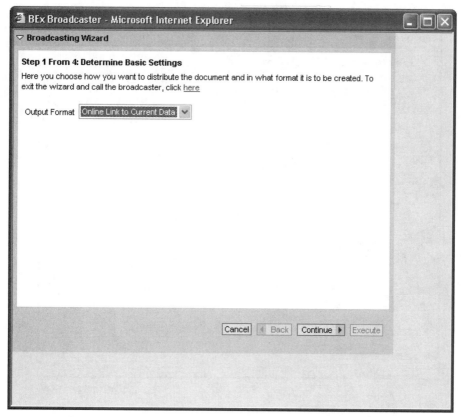

NOTE *For more information on the functionality of the Broadcasting Wizard, check out my previous book,* SAP Business Information Warehouse Reporting, *the SAP Help Portal (http://help.sap.com), or BI Expert Online (www.bi-expertonline.com).*

Print Version   By clicking the Print Version button, you can configure settings for a print version of your ad hoc analysis. For example, you can set the format for the print version and define whether a header appears on the pages printed. After you choose your settings and click OK, a PDF document is generated, which you can then print. The following illustration shows the dialog box with all the settings available.

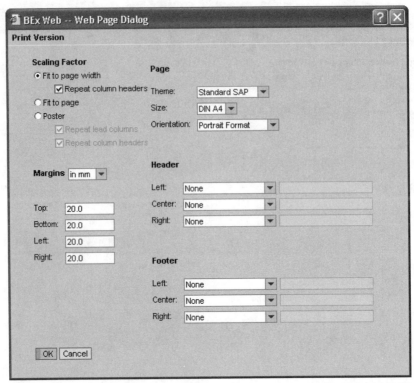

As you can see, the settings are basic: margins for the pages, scaling factors, page sizing, header information and format, and footer information and format. You can use the print functionality of your printer to gain additional functionality. If you want to set up standard or default settings for your business users from this screen and option, you're out of luck. You can't assign an object to store your personal parameters as a report will do based on your user entries against the variables in your reports (report variants). Therefore, you will have to set these parameters every time you are going to print something. This can be a bit cumbersome, especially for information such as a disclaimer, because you would have to type in the parameters every time you execute a print process. One option would be to create a template in the WAD for some of these settings and then assign it to the Web report as a selection option so the person building the report can select the template with the appropriate print functions already set. Some components can be managed by the WAD, but not all of them, and we will review these in Chapters 3 and 4. Again, this can be a bit cumbersome since you need to decide on just how many of these different templates you are willing to support and create. So, review the functionality and position these types of tasks in the best component for the print process.

Export to Excel   By clicking the Export to Excel button on the toolbar, you can export the query result to Microsoft Excel. The query data is displayed in the same way as queries are displayed in the BEx Analyzer. The filter restrictions and the data in the table are the same as in the Web Analyzer. Exceptions are highlighted in color in the same way as they are on the Web. This allows you to continue to edit the data using the Microsoft Excel functions. This definitely comes in handy with all the different Excel workbooks that a company may have and use to manipulate and homogenize data from different systems using some Excel functionality such as VBA or basic Excel formulas. Just download the information from the BEx Web Analyzer into Excel and you can set up standard V lookups in your Company Workbooks to link directly to the information downloaded from the BEx Web. As the following illustration shows, when the Export to Excel option is executed, the initial prompt is to Open, Save, or Cancel the download to Excel.

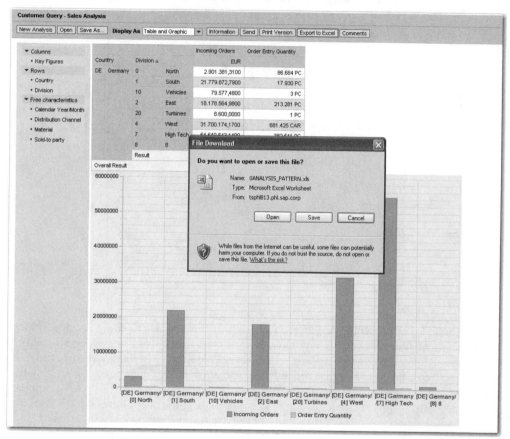

Copyright by SAP AG

NOTE *In the current Support Package for the Web Analyzer, the Excel version needs to be later than Excel 2000. Although you can use this or earlier versions of Excel with some additional configuration, doing so is not best business practice.*

Comments   Click the Comments button to create comments to assign to the data provider. This comes in handy during the budgeting and planning process. The options available in the resulting dialog box, shown next, are Comment (to create a comment), Formatted Text (to create a formatted text document), and Upload (to upload a document from another source). Approximately 25 to 30 different types of documents are supported for the Formatted Text option. You can upload just about any type of document that is available, and definitely all Microsoft document types.

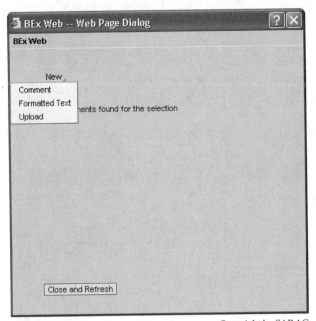

Copyright by SAP AG

Filter   The Filter option is located on the right side of the report screen. Again, depending on the sizing of your report, you may have to scroll over to see this link. You use this link to display the Filter pane. Basically, all the characteristics you have in the query are available via this pane to adjust the filtering process. You can enter values to be used for filtering for each characteristic used in the data provider. You can also filter the key figures that appear in the query. This is an excellent approach to manipulating the data all from one screen, rather than having to use the context menu or the drag-and-drop process. In terms of performance and processing, this is a very good option. Instead of having to drag and drop one characteristic or having to filter one characteristic at a time and wait for the system processing of each individually, you can change all the filter settings you need and then execute the query. You have to execute a process against the database only once to retrieve the data that is required. The following illustration shows the screen that appears once the Filter prompt is executed. If any variables are in the query, they will also be available from this view by clicking the Variable Screen button.

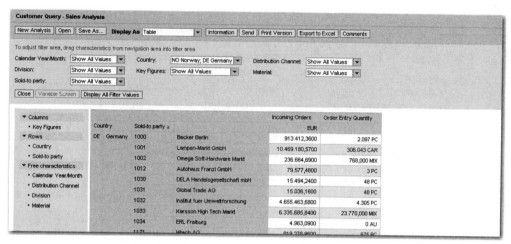

Settings   The Settings link is an important and useful option in adjusting the initial format of the report. It allows the business user to not only adjust the format and then save it as either a query view or a query, but also to retrieve their personal settings in the future. Using this link, you can access numerous functions. You can make settings for the table, chart, and data provider used for the ad hoc analysis. Settings are available for the table layout (display alternating styles for table rows) and data cells (such as display icons for existing InfoProvider documents). You can also use data-specific settings (such as display scaling factors) for the table. For the chart, settings are available for the Chart Web item on which the chart is based (such as chart type selections) and for the chart texts (such as overwrite axis labels), as well as data-specific settings (such as swap display axes).

You can also make various settings for the data provider at runtime. For example, you can define where the results are to be displayed in the table. You can also display existing exceptions and conditions for the data provider or define new exceptions and conditions in a step-by-step process. When you choose Insert on the Exceptions tab, you navigate to a new browser window in which you are guided through the process of creating new exceptions step by step. You can display details for existing exceptions, change their status, or delete them. When you choose Add on the Conditions tab, you navigate to a new browser window in which you are guided through the process of creating new conditions step by step. You can display details for existing conditions, change their status, or delete them.

NOTE   *The conditions or exceptions that you create are good only for the current session and will be deleted when you leave the report unless you decide to save your query or query view. This will allow you to go back and see the condition or exception that you created.*

Table 1-3 outlines all the options that are available by clicking the Settings link.

Tab	Option(s)	Use and Functionality
Table (see Figure 1-2)	Layout: Alternative Table Row Styles	Check this box if alternative table row colors are required. This will generate the blue/white format of the rows.
	Cell-Specific Settings: Exception Visualization	Settings include Color, Symbol, Symbol and Text, and Text and Symbol. This option affects the use of the Exception function and manages the format of the exception in the query.
	Cell-Specific Settings: Document Icons for Data, for Metadata, and for Masterdata	Check the respective boxes to display the document icon in the Web query for the data, metadata, and/or masterdata.
	Data-Specific Settings: Display Repeated Texts	Check this box if repeated text is needed in the query.
	Data-Specific Settings: Scaling Factors Visible	Allows the display of the scaling factor for the key figures.
Chart (see Figure 1-3)	Chart Settings: Chart Type	Use this option to adjust the display of the chart type. BEx Web Analyzer supports approximately 30 different chart types, including columns, pie, stacked lines, and bar charts (most of the chart types typically found in Excel).
	Chart Settings: Legend Type	In addition to None (no legend), the following settings are available: **DataTable** Displays the information in the legend directly from the database table information from the InfoProvider (for example, the values of the pointers of a tachometer chart). **Chart Legend Position** Uses the legend position for the information display. Also generates the view of only the naming convention for the legend. **Legend Only** Displays only the legend, sans the chart.
	Chart Settings: Chart Legend Position	When Legend Type is set to Chart Legend Position, this option positions the legend on the screen relative to the chart: North, South, East, or West.
	Chart Texts: Manual Axis Description	This option is used to assign the text manually for the primary category and value axes and the secondary category and value axes.
	Chart Texts: Manual Axis Label	This option is used to assign the label for the primary and secondary category and value axes.
	Data-Specific Settings: Swap Display Axes	Swaps the characteristic format for the X-axis. For example, rather than the data being displayed by division, the display would use the key figures for the X-axis and the divisions as columns.

TABLE 1-3   Functionality Available via the Settings Link for the Web Analyzer

Tab	Option(s)	Use and Functionality
	Data-Specific Settings: Result Visible	The results for each column are displayed while the user scrolls across them with the cursor.
	Data-Specific Settings: Show Expanded Hierarchy Nodes	If a hierarchy is used with the Web Analyzer, this option allows the user to manage the display of the levels of the hierarchy nodes.
Exceptions	(See the discussion following this table.)	Provides access to the Exception Wizard, described following this table.
Conditions	(See the discussion following this table.)	Provides access to the Condition Wizard, described following this table.
Data Provider (see Figure 1-4)	Data Formatting: Result Position	Displays the results using one of the following settings: Bottom/Right, Top/Left, Bottom/Left, Top/Left.
	Data Formatting: Display Columns Hierarchically and Drilldown to	This option offers the business user the ability to manipulate the data at the column level of the initial drilldown for display. If checked, the additional field to complete the drilldown is no longer grayed out and you can choose what level to drilldown to.
	Data Formatting: Display Rows Hierarchically and Drilldown to	This option offers the business user the ability to manipulate the data at the row level of the initial drilldown for display. If checked, the additional field to complete the drilldown is no longer grayed out and you choose what level to drilldown to. This allows the user to display a hierarchy level that is specific to their needs.
	Size Restriction for Result Sets: Maximum No. of Cells for Result Set	Set the total number of rows available (either 100,000; 500,000; or a user-defined number). Do not exceed approximately 750,000, for performance reasons.
	Number Format: Display of +/− Signs	Displays the format of the numbers as −5, 5−, or (5).
	Number Format: Display of Zeros	Displays zeros with currency/unit, without currency/unit, as empty cells, or as a custom string (with this option, an additional field appears, allowing the business user to enter a symbol or text, which can be critical if the business user needs a comment rather than just a value in this cell).
	Zero Suppression: Apply Suppression to Columns, Apply Suppression to Rows	Define the display of zeros to the columns and rows (the view with zeros or without).
	Zero Suppression: "Key Figures" As Group: Apply Zero Suppression Only if All Elements Are 0	Determines whether zero suppression is applied for key figures within a structure.

TABLE 1-3 Functionality Available via the Settings Link for the Web Analyzer (*continued*)

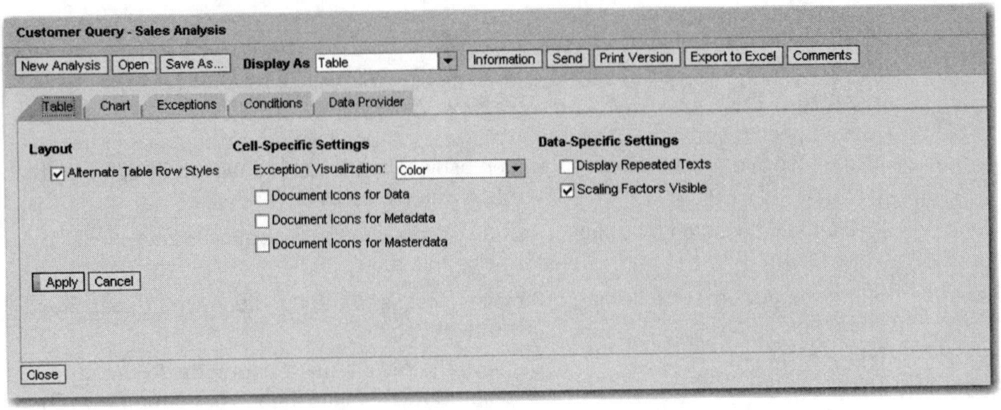

FIGURE 1-2 The Table component with parameters

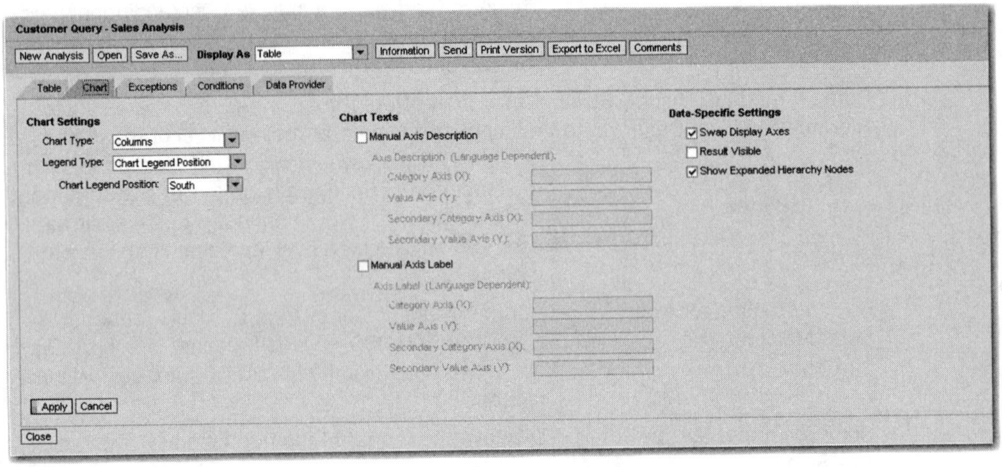

FIGURE 1-3 The Chart component with parameters

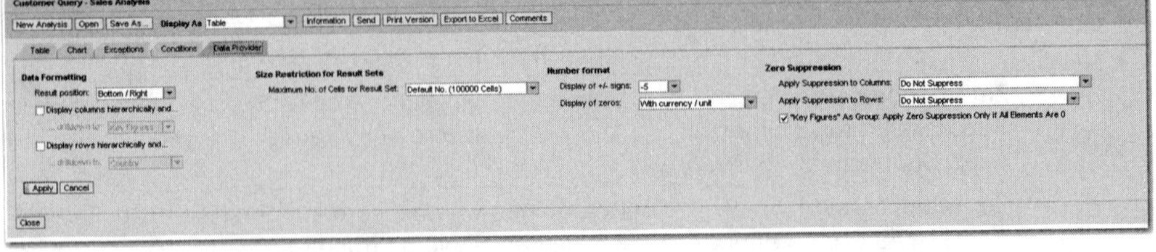

FIGURE 1-4 The Data Provider component with parameters

The two tabs that are not explained in detail in Table 1-3 are Conditions and Exceptions. Interesting differences exist between the display of exceptions and conditions in the BEx Analyzer and in the BEx Web Analyzer, so a more detailed discussion of the options and components of these two wizards is in order. The concepts behind each of these functions will not be discussed. (If you are not familiar with these concepts, they are covered in depth in my previous book, *SAP Business Information Warehouse Reporting*.) As you can see, both wizards can be launched from their associated tabs in the Settings area. Also, both wizards lead the user through their various steps, and the user can move back and forth in this process to adjust or correct a previous step.

Let's look at the Exception Wizard first. It has six steps. To create an exception in the BEx Web Analyzer, click the Settings link on the toolbar and then click the Add button on the Exceptions tab to start the process. The following illustration shows the initial wizard step, which is to choose an exception type—either Status or Trend.

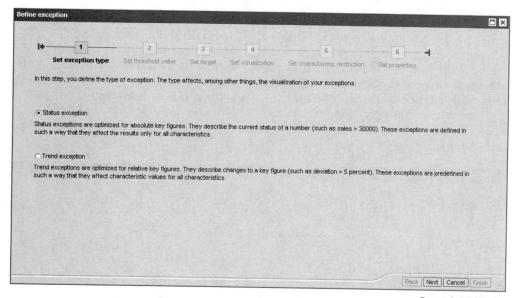

NOTE *Exceptions created via the Exception Wizard can be saved in the KM folder in the portal or can be broadcast to other parties. However, exceptions created with the Exception Wizard in the Web Analyzer do not become a part of the actual query. The only way to make the exception permanent is to save it as a part of the portal query using the Save As button or as part of the query view definition using the Save View context menu option. This allows the exception (or condition) to be saved but assigns it only to that specific object (the query view or query) and not to the query itself. Therefore, you would not see the new exception or condition using the BEx Query Designer.*

A status exception operates on absolute key figures. For example, a status exception is similar to a benchmark identified for Sales Volume – Sales Volume of Greater Than $1,000,000.00. A trend exception operates on relative key figures. For example, a key figure might be considered a trend exception if the deviation of the key figure is greater than a 5 percent variance. Both are good indicators; the choice depends on what the business user is looking to review or display—current information or comparison information over time.

When you choose the exception type, the subsequent wizard screens adapt to that choice. For example, in Step 4 of the wizard, Set Visualization, the choice for a status exception is a traffic light icon (normal view), whereas the choice for a trend exception is an arrow icon. This arrow icon is very similar to some of the functionality available in either the SEM-CPM (Strategic Enterprise Management–Corporate Performance Monitor) component of the Balanced Scorecard or the Strategy Management component of EPM (Enterprise Performance Management), where the trend of the analysis can be highlighted rather than just the position of the process. Therefore, the report analysis can be focused on the trending process of the key performance indicator and additional information is incorporated into the comparisons. Using this indicator rather than the absolute position of a specific value adds even more value to the delivered information that the business user will analyze.

Step 2 of the wizard is where the setup of the threshold values takes place. The user makes the settings for the key figure threshold values. A key figure is chosen for the exception definition, or all the key figures are involved in the exception. In addition, the timing of the exception evaluation can be either before or after any local calculations, such as formulas in queries or local calculations created in the BEx Web query. The additional setup of the threshold values for the alert levels and the operators is exactly the same as if you were creating the exception in the BEx Query Designer. There are nine alert levels: three in the Good alert, three in the Critical alert, and three in the Defective alert. The following illustration shows the details in Step 2.

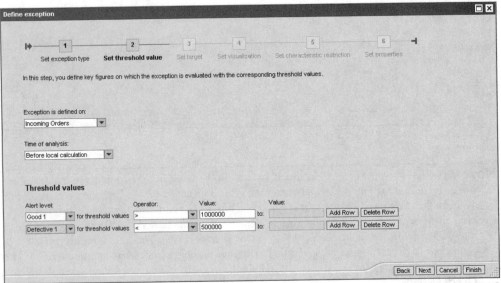

Copyright by SAP AG

In Step 3 of the Exception Wizard, the user first can choose whether the result of the exception is applied to the data cells of an analysis or to the column/row header information. If this option is checked, the user can make a subsequent choice of which data cells are affected. The choices are described in Table 1-4.

Step 3 is shown in the following illustration, and examples of the three options listed in Table 1-4 are shown in the second illustration. This is for the initial setting in Step 3.

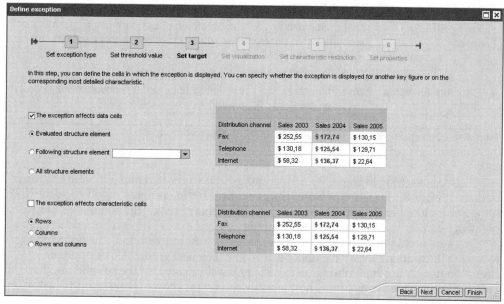

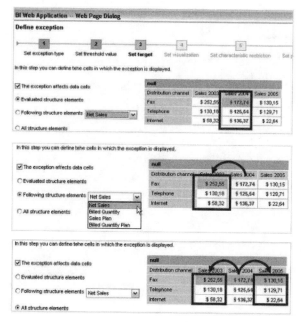

The exception affects the data cells only for the evaluated structure element chosen in step 2 of the wizard.

The exception will be determined from the structure element chosen in step 2 but affects the data cells of another key figure (e.g. the exception will be determined from a deviation but applied for the absolute key figure "Revenue").

The exception will be applied to the data cells for all available key figures.

Exception Option	Description and Functionality
Evaluated Structure Element	The Exception will apply to the key figures chosen for a specific exception in the prior step of the wizard (Step 2).
Following Structure Element	This option allows you to evaluate one key figure but apply the color emphasis to a different key figure. Therefore in this case, you can apply the actual calculation for the exception to one key figure but show the color emphasis on another key figure.
All Structure Elements	With this option, the color highlighting from an exception will be reflected on all key figures in the analysis.

TABLE 1-4   Options for Step 3, Setting Targets, in the Exception Wizard

The second setting in Step 3, The Exception Affects Characteristic Cells, also has three options: Rows, Columns, or Rows and Columns. This setting is not as involved as the first setting but is also very useful. Depending on what characteristic cells you would like to highlight, you can use either Rows or Columns.

Step 4 involves setting the visualization properties of the exception. The first of the following illustrations shows the options available. The Background Color option is displayed here. The other options are to display just the symbol in the cell and not the value, to display the symbol first and the value second (as shown in the second illustration), or to display the value first and the symbol second.

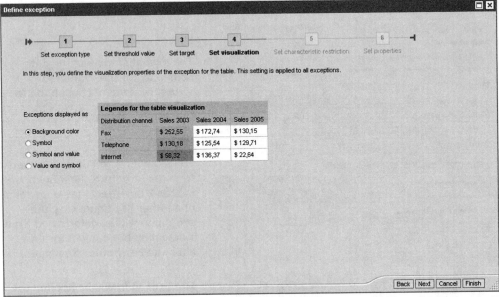

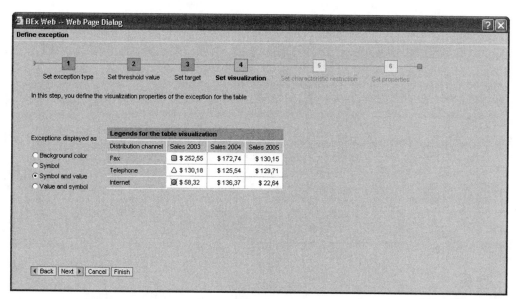

NOTE *As previously mentioned, if the setting in Step 2 is Static, the traffic light icon is displayed, and if Trend is chosen, the symbol is an arrow.*

Step 5 is for setting the characteristic restriction against the characteristics in the analysis. This step has several options (in the dropdown boxes) for the characteristic restriction:

- All Values
- Standard
- Only the Results
- Everything Except Results
- A Fixed Value (specify the value that will be used in the exception)
- A Fixed Hierarchy Level (specify the level that will be used in the exception)

The following illustration shows Step 5.

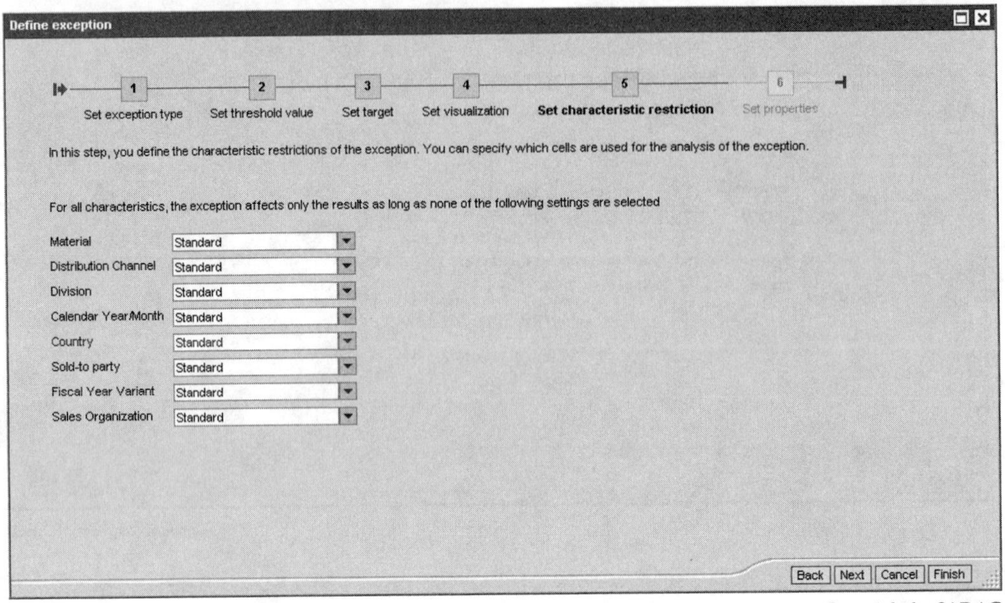

Copyright by SAP AG

Finally, in Step 6, the properties of the exception are assigned. The two settings in this screen are for the Exception Is Active option; therefore, the exception will be immediately applied before the display of the results and the description of the exception.

The following illustration shows an example of applying the exception generated by the Exception Wizard. Here, we defined the exception against the Incoming Orders, set the Good setting for anything above 1,000,000, and set the Defective/Bad setting for anything less than 500,000; the values between those two benchmarks are displayed as the normal color (colorless) in the background.

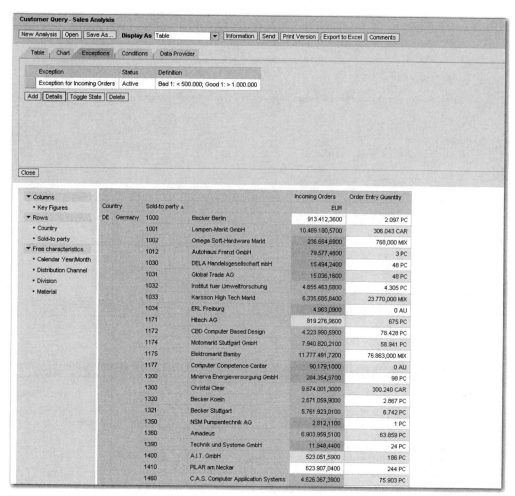

The second wizard available in the Settings area, the Condition Wizard, has only four steps. The first step is to set the condition type—either Ranked List Criterion, Threshold Value Condition, or Mixed Condition. These condition types cover most of the common filters required by business users and can be very useful to focus the business users' attention on the critical list of values. Table 1-5 provides the description and functionality of each setting. As in the Exception Wizard, depending on the setting in this step, other information will change. For example, Step 2, Set Condition Parameter, will change to fit the requirements.

The following illustration shows Step 1 of the Condition Wizard, with Ranked List Criterion being chosen. The second illustration shows Step 2, with the condition set to the top 10 based on incoming orders.

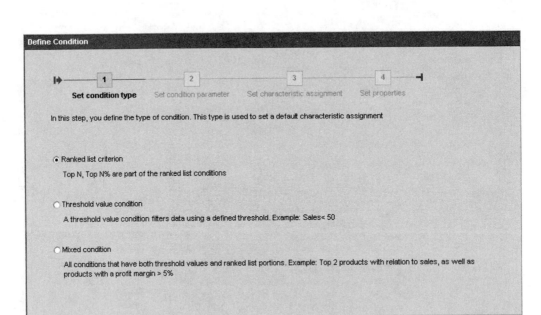

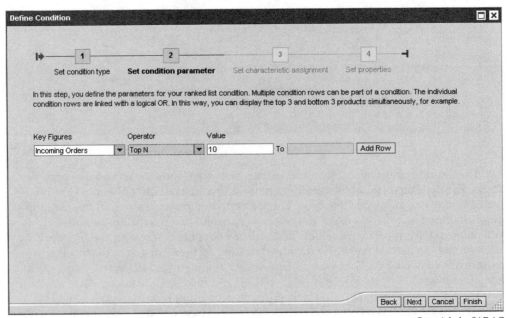

Condition Type	Description	Functionality Required in the Set Condition Parameter Step (Step 2)
Ranked List Criterion	Use this option to define conditions such as Top %, Top N, Bottom %, and Bottom N.	Identify the key figure to be affected. Operators are limited to Top and Bottom for %, N, and Total. The Value field requires a value for this option.
Threshold Value Condition	Use this option to define threshold values; for example, sales volume between 100,000 and 1,000,000.	Identify the key figure to be affected. Operators are limited to =, <>, >=, >, <=, <, [], and][. The Value field requires a set of values for each option.
Mixed Condition	Use this option to allow the combinations of multiple conditions to be applied using one setting activity. For example, apply two conditions at the same time—Top 10 Productions by Revenue and top 10 Productions by Net Income. This results in an intersection of the two conditions.	Identify the key figure to be affected. Operators available include all the operators for both of the other options. The Value field requires a set of values for each option.

TABLE 1-5   Settings for the Condition Wizard in the BEx Web Analyzer

Step 3 involves setting the characteristic assignment. The following options are available, as shown in the next illustration:

- **All Characteristics in Drilldown Independent**   This option is optimized for range list conditions, but can be used for threshold values with relevant values.

- **Detailed Characteristic Along the Rows or Columns**   This option is optimized for threshold conditions. The characteristic is applied to the most detailed characteristic of the specified axis.

- **Individual Characteristics and Characteristic Combinations**   This option is used to select any characteristic or characteristic combination.

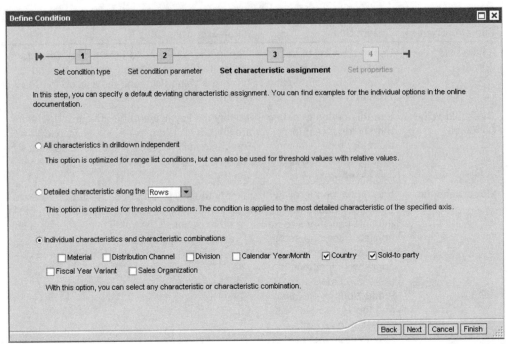

With the combination of options within Steps 2 and 3, you can set up a condition so that you can track a particular division, plant, or other characteristic and measure its performance on specific conditions. This is a very good approach to monitoring the performance or progress of a particular region, division, or other critical entity.

Finally, in Step 4, you identify whether the condition will be immediately active, identify whether the business user will activate it after execution of the query, and provide a description of the condition. I suggest choosing that the business user activates the condition after they have executed the query. That way, they will be able to see the entire picture, and then drilldown to the condition option.

NOTE *The Toggle State button can be used to switch from an active to inactive state of a condition or exception.*

The following illustration shows an example of applying the condition generated by the Condition Wizard. Here, the condition for the Top 10 by Incoming Orders generates a report with only ten sold-to parties. You have to be careful with these types of processes when the rows have more than one characteristic; make sure that you are getting the appropriate result set and not filtering on just one country but getting the top ten sold-to parties for all countries (as in this scenario).

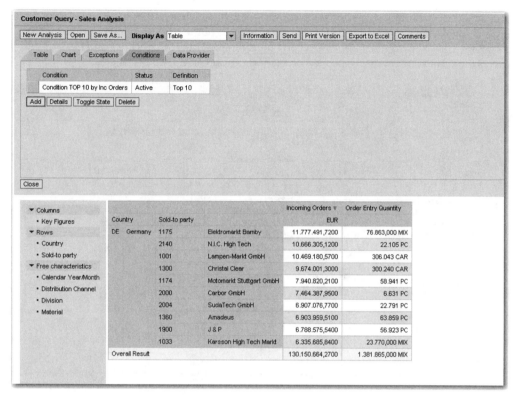

Copyright by SAP AG

Options and Functionality for Navigating in the Report Environment

As mentioned earlier in the chapter, several different options and approaches are available to navigate in the BEx Web Analyzer. Often, numerous ways exist to do the same thing, and it's handy to know all the options you have available to do the same activity. This section discusses the context menus available in several locations in the query. The functionality in these context menus overlaps the functionality in the toolbar, discussed in the previous section, although using the toolbar's Filter and Setting options is normally easier and faster than using the context menus. If the business user doesn't want to have the Filter and Settings options, then the context menu is the only other choice. The context menus discussed here are those available by right-clicking in the navigation pane (to the left of the query), by right-clicking the headings of the columns and rows, and by right-clicking the actual values within the report.

The navigation pane displays the navigational state of the data provider. All the characteristics and structures of the data provider are listed. You can alter the navigational state to analyze your data by dragging characteristics or structures to an axis (rows or columns) of the table (or you can remove them). You can swap axes in the navigation pane using drag and drop, and the table changes accordingly. You can also drag characteristics to the filter pane using drag and drop. Because much of the functionality and activities in this section are consistent with the processes used with the BEx Analyzer as well as with numerous other reporting systems, I will not cover them in depth, under the assumption that you probably have already worked with many of the same features. You can also perform the functionality of drag and drop with the navigation pane context menus, which is part of the focus of this section. The following two illustrations show the details of the context menu options; the first shows the context menu that appears when you right-click in the Rows area, and the second shows the context menu that appears when you right-click in the Columns area.

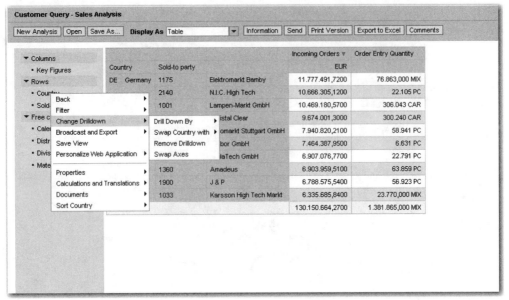

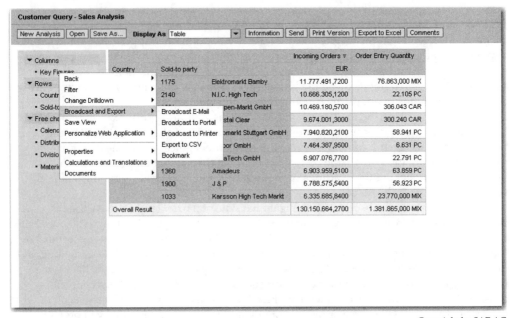

Table 1-6 lists and describes the options available in the context menus under Rows and Columns.

The context menu selections listed in Table 1-6 are the same as the selections available from the context menu accessed by right-clicking the characteristics within the body of the query.

Context Menu Option(s) in the Navigation Pane	Description and Functionality
Back	Back I Back undoes the last navigational step. Back I Back to Start restores the query to the initial view of the data at the time of execution.
Filter	Filter I Select Filter Value displays a dialog box that allows you to identify a single value, range of values, or other combination to show specific information. Filter I Remove Filter Value removes the filter value and shows all values in the query. Filter I Variable Screen displays the variable screen.
Change Drilldown	Offers the ability to drilldown vertically or horizontally (depending on whether you accessed this via the key figures or characteristics); swap characteristics or key figures with others within the report; remove drilldown; or swap axes, which switches the characteristics and key figures from one axis to the other.
Broadcast and Export	Offers the ability to broadcast using the IB functionality, export to a CSV file, or bookmark the view of the report.
Save View	Saves the view of the query as displayed to the BW server.
Personalize Web Application	Offers the ability to assign personalized settings to the query display. These settings will show up the next time you execute the query as default characteristic values in the variable screen or directly on the report.
Properties	Lists properties of characteristics and key figures. Additional details of this option are discussed following this table. Properties can also be set for all data cells and for all axes from here.
Calculations and Translations	Allows the use of currency translation for key figures. You can generate a dynamic calculation using currency translation exchange rates.
Documents	Allows you to display, create, or upload documents to the query. These documents will be assigned to the query and available to anyone that has authorization to see the query information.
Sort Characteristic I Sort Ascending by Text; Sort Ascending by Key; Sort Descending by Text; Sort Descending by Key (characteristics only)	Sorts the characteristic or key figure by either the key or text in either ascending or descending order.

TABLE 1-6   Navigation Pane Context Menu Options for Characteristics and Key Figures

As indicated in Table 1-6, the Properties context menu option requires further discussion. As previously mentioned, some functions are found in many areas, but the Properties options are unique in some ways. Properties can be accessed via the context menu either from the navigation pane (navigational filter) or from the analysis grid (body of the query). With your cursor on either the characteristic or the characteristic value, right-click and choose Properties from the context menu. The Properties attributes are the same parameters from either of these areas—characteristic or characteristic value. Table 1-7 lists and describes the fields and the options to fill those fields, and the results that you would view in the query. The following illustration shows the initial screen of the Properties dialog box for the characteristic Sold-to Party. In addition to these parameters, you also have an icon at the very bottom of the screen to turn on the technical names for the objects.

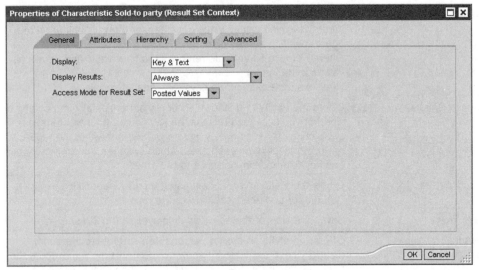

Copyright by SAP AG

Properties Field Name	Description and Functionality
General Tab	**General Information and Sorting Options**
Display	Options are None, Key & Text, Key, Text & Key, and Text. This setting adjusts the view of the values for this characteristic based on the option that is chosen. Thus, if Key & Text is chosen, the value shows the key and then the text. You can also change the use of the Compound/Text display if a compound characteristic is involved.
Display Results	Options are Always, Never, With More Than One Value. This setting affects the display of the results row on the query. The last option is the one that may be a bit confusing—With More than One Value. If you chose this option the results row will only show up if there is more than one row of data. If there is only one row of data then there will be no results row since the one row is the actual summary.

TABLE 1-7   Options for Each Tab for the Properties of the Characteristic

Properties Field Name	Description and Functionality
General Tab	**General Information and Sorting Options**
Access Mode for Result Set	Options are Master Data, Posted Values, Standard. This setting determines whether the result set shows the characteristic values from the master data table (all values even though no transactional data is assigned), posted values (only those that have transactional data assigned), or standard values (settings from the Query Designer or InfoObject itself).
Attributes Tab	**Display of Attributes of the Characteristic**
Available Attributes	Choose the display attributes that are required to be displayed in the report. Move them to the Selected Attributes columns to the right. This will allow the identified attributes to be available in the report.
Hierarchy Tab	**Display of the Hierarchies**
Hierarchy (if applicable)	Select the hierarchy, if available, that will be used in the display.
Attributes of the Hierarchy	Once the hierarchy is identified, additional settings are available: **Hierarchy Active** Determines whether the hierarchy is to be active at the time the report is executed. **Expansion Level** Determines to what level the hierarchy will be opened at the time of execution of the report. If the requirement is to have the hierarchy displayed to the second level at the time of execution of the query, choose Level 2 for this setting. **Position of Lower-Level Nodes** Determines whether the hierarchy will be displayed from top to bottom or from bottom to top. This will adjust the flow of the hierarchy for display to the end user. **Condensation of Nodes with Only One Lower-Level Node** If the node has only one lower-level value assigned, this parameter defines if a Text node will be shown in the report or only the actual value at that level. **Show Values of Posted Nodes** Only show characteristic values that have postings rather than all values of the characteristic which would include any values that have no postings or are blanks. This will eliminate any node that doesn't have posted amounts or values assigned. Therefore, the display of the hierarchy nodes can be affected and could show only postings that are in the InfoCube. **Display/Text** Adjusts the display of the Key and/or Text for each characteristic in the hierarchy.
Sorting Tab	**Sort Direction and By**
Sort Direction	Choose ascending or descending order.
Sort By	Choose default view, text, members, or key figure values.
Advanced Tab	**Binding Display**
Bind Display of Text/Attributes in Data Provider Result and in Value Help	Activating this setting shows both text and values in the Results and Value Help areas in the query.
Bind Display of Text/Attributes in Data Provider Result and in Filter Values (dropdown boxes, text elements, and so on)	Activating this setting shows both text and values in the results and in the filter values for the dropdown boxes and other components.

TABLE 1-7   Options for Each Tab for the Properties of the Characteristic (*continued*)

The other two options within the Properties option—All Data Cells and Axis—are very similar to the context menu options available on the key figures themselves, so we'll review the components of these from the point of view of a key figure property. These options are the only components in the context menu that are different between the BEx Web Analyzer and the BEx Analyzer. You can find these by right-clicking the heading of the key figure columns. The following illustration displays a basic list of activities available in a context menu for the header of the key figures column. As indicated in the illustration, we are going to focus first on the options under Calculations and Translations.

One option that is available is Cumulate After Applying Single Value Calculations and Result Calculations and is a fairly straightforward calculation. It generates a cumulative result rather than a specific value for that transaction. So, in this case, if you were to turn this on and have a list of values, each row would be a cumulative total of the complete list. This can be very handy for tasks such as reviewing the To Date values of a period of time. If you use this component, the system will automatically roll these values up for you. The newest option to the business user is Formulas | New Formula, which allows the business user to create CKFs on-the-fly directly within the report. Once this is complete, save it as a query view or portal query and you have your unique calculation. Again, remember that this is unique to your query. In addition a number of options are available in the key figure context menu under Calculate Single Values As and Calculate Results As, as outlined in Tables 1-8 and 1-9. They are shown in the following illustration from the query point of view. Another option that you may notice in the above illustration is Global Currency Translation. This option accesses the dialog box for currency translation on the fly within the query navigation. If the BW IT team has set up the appropriate currency translation components then this option will allow you to generate a display of all of the data using a Global currency. This allows the business user to see all of the information in their currency of choice—EURs, Canadian Dollars, Pounds, or US Dollars. The nice option included in this parameter is the ability to set up a series of currency translation keys that will allow you to see the information based on different currency views or exchange rates. For example, if you want to use this for the calculation of changes in inventory values based on currency fluctuation or currency fluctuation for exported material or any of the other multiple scenarios involving currency exchange rates, this will help you display the results as you need to in the appropriate currencies. In terms of the other options available in this context menu, we will review the basics here and then go into more detail in a subsequent chapter. The following illustration shows the options found using the context menu from the executed query.

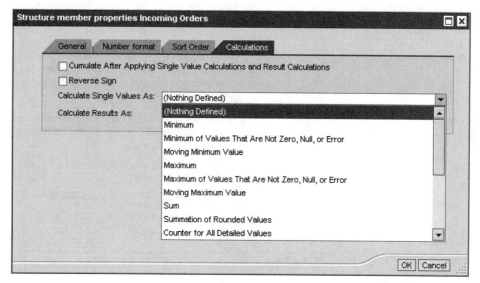

Calculate Results As Option	Description
Minimum	This option will display the Minimum value in the results row based on the values generated against the characteristic values.
Maximum	This option will display the Maximum value in the results row based on the values generated against the characteristic values.
Sum	This option is automatically defaulted into the results row for the query result.
Summation of Rounded Values	This option is available if scaling is turned on. This will generate the results row based on any rounding occurring due to scaling activities.
Counter for All Detailed Values/That are not Zero, Null or Error	This option counts up the number of values in the list/and can ignore the values that are Zero, Null or Errors.

TABLE 1-8   Options Available from the Calculate Results Values Context Menu (*continued*)

Calculate Results As Option	Description
First Value/That are not Zero, Null or Error	This option displays the First Value in the list/and can ignore the values that are Zero, Null or Errors.
Last Value/That are not Zero, Null or Error	This option displays the Last Value in the list/and can ignore the values that are Zero, Null or Errors.
Average/of Detailed Values that are not Zero, Null or Error	This option generates the Average of the values in the list/and can ignore the values that are Zero, Null or Errors.
Standard Deviation	This calculates the Standard Deviation based on the amounts generated from the characteristic combinations and displays this deviation in the results row.
Median/of Detailed Values that are not Zero, Null or Error	This option calculates the Median of the values in the list/and can ignore the values that are Zero, Null or Errors.
Variance	This option calculates the total variance of the amounts based on the characteristic combinations and displays this amount in the results row.
Hide	This option will Hide the values in this column— either for the single values or results.

TABLE 1-8 Options Available from the Calculate Results Values Context Menu (*continued*)

Calculate Single Values As Option	Description
Minimum/That are not Zero, Null or Error	This option will display the Minimum value in the amount row based on the values generated against the characteristic values.
Moving Minimum Value	This option calculates the minimum value using a moving average calculation based on the minimum values.
Maximum/That are not Zero, Null or Error	This option will display the Maximum value in the amount row based on the values generated against the characteristic values.
Moving Maximum Value	This option calculates the maximum value using a moving average calculation based on the minimum values.

TABLE 1-9 Options Available from the Calculate Single Values Context Menu

Calculate Single Values As Option	Description
Sum	This option is automatically defaulted into the amount row for the characteristic values.
Summation of Rounded Values	This option is available if scaling is turned on. This will generate the summation of the rounded values in the amount field based on any rounding occurring due to scaling activities.
Counter for All Detailed Values/That are not Zero, Null or Error	This option counts up the number of values in the list/and can ignore the values that are Zero, Null or Errors.
Moving Average/of Detailed Values that are not Zero, Null or Error	This option generates the Average of the values in the list/and can ignore the values that are Zero, Null or Errors.
Normalize According to Next Group Level Result/ to Overall Results/ to Unrestricted Overall Results	This option will calculate a percentage based on the characteristic value combinations. Normalize according to the next group level will generate a % based on the characteristic combinations found directly adjacent to the amounts column. To Overall Results will calculate the % based on the total results row of the query. To Unrestricted Overall Results will calculate the % based on the total amounts discounting any filters in the report.
Rank Number/Olympic Rank Number	This option will generate a ranking number based on the amounts for each characteristic value and display that ranking number in the amount field. Olympic Ranking means that there are no ties.
Hide	This option will hide the values in this column—either for the single values or results.

TABLE 1-9 Options Available from the Calculate Single Values Context Menu (*continued*)

You can also access the properties of key figures through the context menu, under Properties. This opens a Properties dialog box for key figure, which has options to alter the display of a key figure that are very similar to the options you see in the Characteristic dialog box (yet another example of the ability to access the same functionality from separate locations). In the following illustration of the Properties dialog box for a key figure, you can

see that the Calculations tab has the same options that are available in the context menu
under Calculations and Translations.

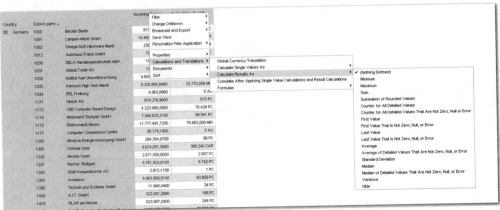

The addition of the ability to create your own formulas (choose Calculations and
Transactions | Formula from the context menu) is very useful. As the following illustration
shows, you have all the same functionality as in the Query Designer to create your CKFs. A
few standard calculation options are not available, but this should not be a significant issue
since about 80 to 90 percent of the functionality is available.

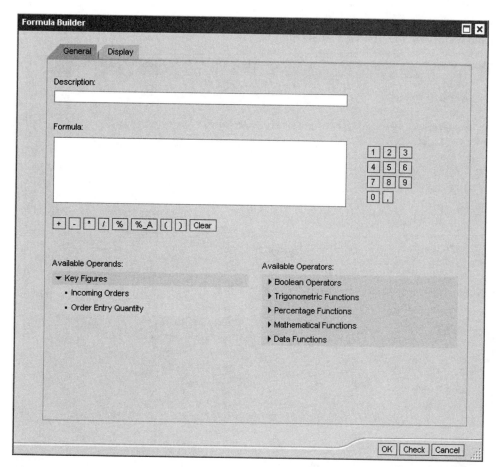

By adding this additional component to the frontend of the query, the business user can generate some very complex calculations. In the following illustration, I simply used the Formula Editor to generate an average value for my incoming orders by using Incoming Orders Value divided by the Order Entry Quantity. You can see that with this capability and the use of the key figure properties to generate calculations such as Rankings, Averages, Standard Deviations and other approaches to manipulate data, the business user can get very creative with their personal views of the queries. This means that each business user needs to be well trained in the areas of performance tuning and data modeling to make sure they are comfortable with the overall processing that the system goes through to deliver the data and results via the BEx Web Analyzer.

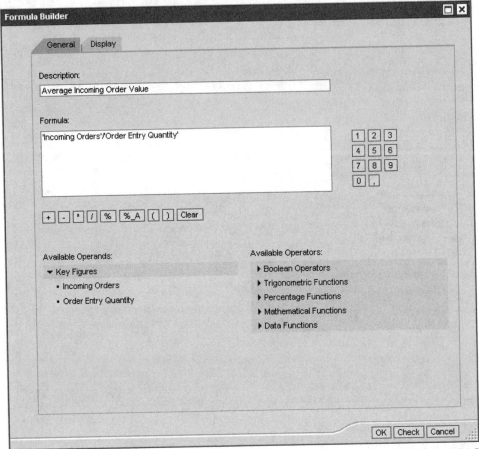

Summary

As you can see, the functionality available via the BEx Web Analyzer is definitely something to take a look at and experience. It has a very user-friendly look and feel to it and can be distributed with little footprint on your current laptops. Don't forget that even though we are not focusing on the BEx Analyzer, you have the option to use either of the frontends of SAP BI on the Web. By "either" in this scenario, I am referring to the BEx Web Analyzer and the BEx Analyzer versus the new reporting components available within SAP BI BusinessObjects. It is critical that you are on the most current Support Package for the BEx Web Analyzer so that all of the functionality explained and demonstrated here is available for you to use. With all the emphasis of reporting, both graphically with dashboards and with actual reports, on the Web, you really need to take a very long look at all the different options for reporting before you choose a reporting toolset. Definitely make the choice based on the business users' needs and requirements. Once you have reviewed and experienced the BEx Web Analyzer I think that you will find that this component can hold its own against any ad hoc reporting toolset.

In this chapter, we worked our way through many different activities on the BEx Web Analyzer, including numerous approaches to saving the queries or query views, which will impact the ability of the business users on the production system; creating on-the-fly calculations to use and then save within your query view; and turning on numerous bells and whistles for the business users and analysts. As with any reporting process, it will take some time before you become proficient with all the functionality. Personally, I still have to refer to documentation to remember how to do different activities that are not normal reporting functions. The important aspect is that you know what functionality is available and what it can do for you and then have the ability to refresh your memory to find, configure, and execute the process. This chapter has taken you through the initial steps that you have to become very familiar with to get to your goal of developing and building dynamic and useful reporting components. This is just the start. There is definitely much more to learn in terms of configuration and the options available within the WAD, all of which you will find in this book. There is so much functionality with the additional Web Items added in the 7.0 version, plus the enhanced formatting and the use of JavaScript and XHTML, that creating any sort of Web report or dashboard is certainly possible.

Getting a Fast Start with BI Patterns in the BEx Web Template

This chapter begins your exploration of the Web Application Designer (WAD) by introducing you to BI patterns. This chapter precedes the full discussion of the WAD coming up in Chapters 3 and 4 because the BI patterns offer an easy way to familiarize yourself with the WAD interface without diving into all the details of its functionality. They also offer a way to deliver Web reports quickly to business users. Frequently, when WAD developers initially review the functionality of the BEx Web templates, they immediately conclude that it is too technically sophisticated for business users to understand and use. This reaction typically is the result of jumping right into the meat of the component by creating a new blank Web template and trying to drag and drop some Web items into it—which can be intimidating, especially upon seeing the degree to which the Web template enhances the Web items that are submitted. The easier, less-intimidating approach is to begin with the Pattern Wizard, an often-overlooked SAP component that can help WAD developers build basic Web templates for both prototyping and complete Web reports and distribute them to customers faster and easier than is otherwise possible. Having worked with many different BI consultants I have found that only about 25 percent of those that work with the frontend components know about the BI Patterns functionality. Using the Pattern Wizard takes a little bit of trial and error but overall is an approach that any developer can master after three to four hours of review. This approach also reduces the concerns about authorizing the business user access to the WAD. If you restrict access to just the BI Patterns templates you can control the activities allowed and also protect the company's standard web templates but still allow the business user the ability to create their own.

Introduction to BI Patterns and the BEx Web Template

Using BI Patterns with the Pattern Wizard

BI patterns are Web applications that are tailored to the requirements of particular user groups and are used to unify the display of BI content and develop Web-based templates. With BI patterns, the user always finds the same function with the same name in the same place for each of the reports. To some degree, the patterns can be configured using some of the same functionality found in the WAD template process itself. The concept of patterns helps to reduce the total cost of ownership because the actual logic for the display and interaction in BI applications for each pattern is stored centrally in only one Web template, so any changes only have to be made there. For example, in the Information Consumer Pattern, a button is configured for exporting the data to Microsoft Excel in the main Web template of the pattern. When you configure the Information Consumer Pattern, you can decide whether you want to see this button.

The BI patterns component of the WAD often is overlooked primarily because the standard template 0ANALYSIS_PATTERN is used by the queries that are generated from the Query Designer. As soon as you create a query using the Query Designer, you can immediately display the results in a Web query, and that query is supported by the 0ANALYSIS_PATTERN template. So, if this procedure works for you, you might not ever have a reason to explore the use of the BI patterns and the BI Pattern Wizard. You should take the time to do so now, because BI patterns enable you to generate Web functionality quickly and are a great gateway into learning about the functionality of the WAD.

To access this component, first open the WAD, shown next.

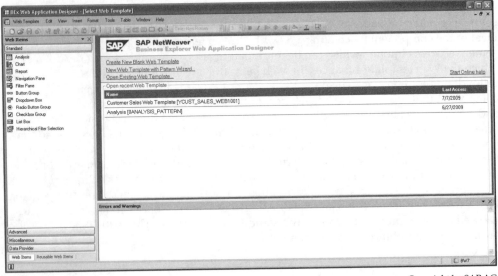

Looking at the three options (hyperlinks) at the top of the screen, you see that you can select

- **Create New Blank Web Template**   This link gives you access to a blank template and allows you to create your own template from scratch.

- **New Web Template with Pattern Wizard**   This link gives you access to the BI patterns via the Pattern Wizard.

- **Open Existing Web Template**   If you already have been working with some Web templates, then you can access them from this link.

In my case, if I see anything that is labeled as a wizard I'm heading for that to see if I can work something out a bit easier than starting from scratch, so this is where we go to access the BI Consumer Patterns and other BI shortcut templates. If you execute this option, a dialog box pops up that gives you access to these patterns. The following illustration shows the results of this process. The initial screen and tab List of Patterns and Web Templates to access all of the standard BI templates for use in developing a BI Pattern Template is shown. This tab just shows you the default option that is chosen from the second tab, All Patterns and Web Templates. So once you start to use each of the individual templates that we will look at shortly and you save and leave this dialog box, it stores the last template in this tab for easy access to what you were working on in the last session. This reduces the amount of time and effort required to restart your work.

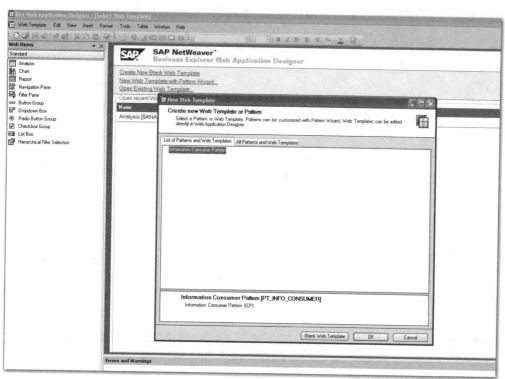

Moving to the right tab, All Patterns and Web Templates, you see two categories: BI Patterns with Pattern Wizard, and Sample Web Template for Direct Editing. The latter option is just another approach to opening a blank template, (shown next), that you can use to start building a template from scratch.

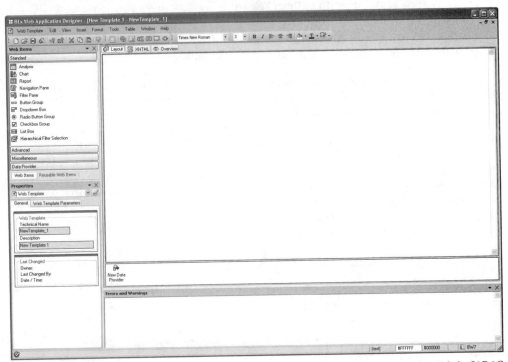

We are interested in the BI Patterns with Pattern Wizard option, commonly known as the Information Consumer Pattern. Using this wizard is the approach within the WAD that will help speed up your implementation of the WAD component and offer a business user the option to work within the WAD without requiring them to have a significant amount of training; to configure something, they would only have to get comfortable using the BI Pattern Wizard. This wizard is very similar to any wizard that you come across in SAP environments. It's a step-by-step process that you can use to build some basic customization into the Web templates without having to work through all the settings. In this section we will look at some examples of using this wizard to demonstrate in what situations we can use this tool to our advantage.

Configuration of the BI Patterns in the Web Application Designer

One of the main points to using this approach to building Web-based reports is that BI patterns are user-friendly BEx Web applications that do not require users to have specific BI knowledge. As mentioned, the BEx Web Analyzer toolset can be as complex or as simple to configure as you would want. The Pattern Wizard is the component that will be on the easy side. The All Patterns and Web Templates tab offers two types of templates. The Information Consumer Pattern is a template for BEx Web applications and can be used in different variations. In general, this pattern includes either a table (Analysis Web item) or a graphic (Chart Web item) in which the data is displayed. The pattern can also include an application toolbar that, depending on the variation of the pattern, includes various pushbuttons and functions. The other option is the Small Web Template, which is a very different component that is driven by the number of data providers (DPs) you will be using, as described in the following sections.

The easiest of the two types to set up is the Small Web Template since it literally steps you through the configuration, providing a very fast and efficient way to set up Web templates. You might not be prepared to configure the Char Web or Analysis Web items, but in either case you can accept the default view and work through the rest of the template. Once you are more comfortable with these web objects you can come back and make any adjustments required. The following sections describe the first three Small Web Template options on the All Patterns and Web Templates tab, after which the Information Consumer Pattern is discussed in more detail.

First, to refresh your memory of what the query looks like, the following illustration shows the display via the Query Designer of the query definition that we will be working with for the most part in this chapter.

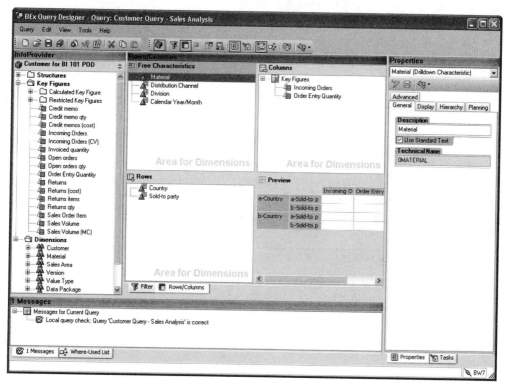

As you can see, the rows are made up of Country and Sold-to Party and the columns are Incoming Orders and Order Entry Quantity. Remember these positions since we will see them quite a bit in this chapter and understanding formatting of each of the queries you are using will help in the development of the different Web items such as the different charts and graphs.

Small Web Template with Analysis Web Item and 1 DP

To begin setting up the Small Web Template with Analysis Web Item and 1 DP (IP_1IT_ ANALYSIS_1DP), select it in the list and then click OK at the bottom of the dialog box. Figure 2-1 shows the list of all of the available templates for the BI Patterns with Pattern Wizard. We will refer to this figure during the rest of the chapter.

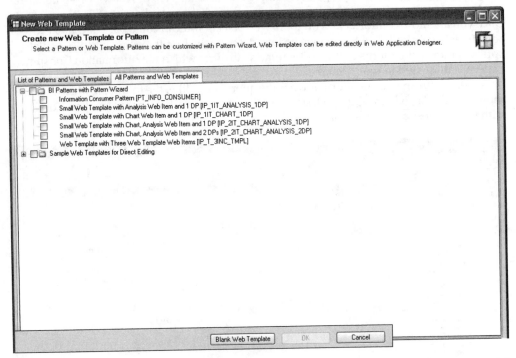

FIGURE 2-1   Options for BI Patterns using the Pattern Wizard

Step 1 of 2 of the wizard is shown in the following illustration. Only a few options are available, as defined in Table 2-1.

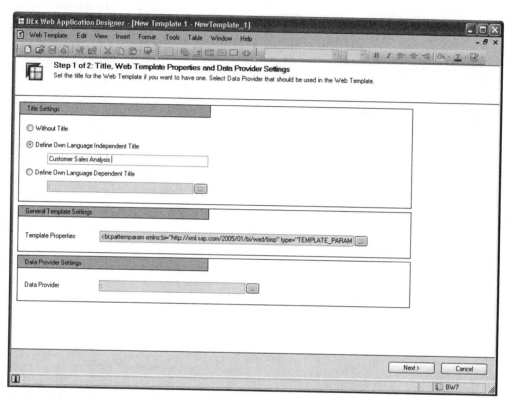

Category	Option(s)	Description
Title Settings	Without Title; Define Own Language Independent Title; Define Own Language Dependent Title	These are options to display a title for the report. If you choose Define Own Language Dependent Title, you are given options to assign a language to your title entry.
General Template Settings	Template Properties	This option enables you to format the template with display options, RRI settings, and other formatting options. We will review these in detail in the next chapter.
Data Provider Settings	Data Provider	Use this option to identify the data provider for the query settings. Click the icon at the end of the field to see the list of queries and InfoProviders that can be used.

TABLE 2-1   Options for Step 1: Title, Web Template Properties, and Data Provider Settings

After you complete Step 1, click Next. Step 2, shown next, enables you to set up the analysis item settings. The options are listed and described in Table 2-2.

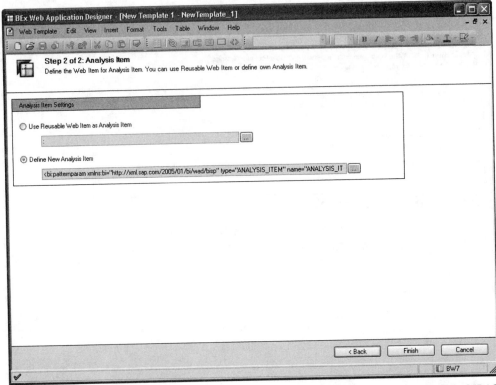

If you decide to create your own analysis template, the second option, then you will have some work to do in terms of setting the appropriate parameters for a good and consistent dashboard. We will cover all of these items in the next chapter.

After you finish this two-step wizard, you can execute this Web Application and see the results, a very basic tabular report, shown next. As you can see, this is not as robust as other

Category	Option	Description
Analysis Item Settings	Use Reusable Web Item as Analysis Item	Enables you to use as an Analysis Web item a Web item that has already been built and is available for reuse.
	Define New Analysis Item	Enables you to use as your analysis a new Web item that you can build from scratch with the help of the analysis parameters.

TABLE 2-2   Options for Step 2: Analysis Items

dashboards or reports, but it was easy to set up and, with a few adjustments, could be a reasonable graphic of the report data.

Customer Sales with Web Template

Country		Sold-to party ≛		Incoming Orders EUR	Order Entry Quantity
DE	Germany	1000	Becker Berlin	913.412,3600	2.097 PC
		1001	Lampen-Markt GmbH	10.469.180,5700	306.043 CAR
		1002	Omega Soft-Hardware Markt	236.664,6900	768,000 MIX
		1012	Autohaus Franzl GmbH	79.577,4800	3 PC
		1030	DELA Handelsgesellschaft mbH	15.494,2400	48 PC
		1031	Global Trade AG	15.036,1600	48 PC
		1032	Institut fuer Umweltforschung	4.655.463,6800	4.305 PC
		1033	Karsson High Tech Markt	6.335.685,8400	23.770,000 MIX
		1034	ERL Freiburg	4.963,0900	0 AU
		1171	Hitech AG	819.276,9600	675 PC
		1172	CBD Computer Based Design	4.223.990,5900	78.428 PC
		1174	Motomarkt Stuttgart GmbH	7.940.820,2100	58.941 PC
		1175	Elektromarkt Bamby	11.777.491,7200	76.863,000 MIX
		1177	Computer Competence Center	90.179,1000	0 AU
		1200	Minerva Energieversorgung GmbH	284.354,9700	98 PC
		1300	Christal Clear	9.674.001,3000	300.240 CAR
		1320	Becker Koeln	2.671.059,9000	2.867 PC
		1321	Becker Stuttgart	5.761.923,0100	6.742 PC
		1350	NSM Pumpentechnik AG	2.812,1100	1 PC
		1360	Amadeus	6.903.959,5100	63.859 PC
		1390	Technik und Systeme GmbH	11.948,4400	24 PC
		1400	A.I.T. GmbH	523.051,5900	186 PC
		1410	PILAR am Neckar	623.907,0400	244 PC
		1460	C.A.S. Computer Application Systems	4.626.367,3900	75.903 PC
		1600	TALPA GmbH	8.600,0000	1 PC
		1900	J & P	6.788.575,5400	56.923 PC
		2000	Carbor GmbH	7.464.387,9500	6.631 PC
		2004	SudaTech GmbH	6.907.076,7700	22.791 PC
		2006	Etelko Textilien	159.054,2800	452 PC
		2007	Software Systeme GmbH	4.794.916,1300	72.195 PC
		2130	COMPU Tech. AG	4.381.592,9300	74.253 PC
		2140	N.I.C. High Tech	10.666.305,1200	22.105 PC
		2141	Jaspers Computers	591.719,8300	780 PC

This Web template could be used for a standard view of the data for Country and Sold-to Party or incorporated into another query or report template. The functionality behind the analysis grid and the chart (discussed in the next section) is very much like that of an Excel component.

Small Web Template with Chart Web Item and 1 DP

This option allows you to create a nice Web query with the use of the Chart Web item rather than the Analysis Web item. As its name states, this BI pattern has only the Chart Web item assigned and one data provider. Start by choosing the correct BI pattern—Small Web Template with Chart Web Item and 1 DP. Please refer to Figure 2-1 for this initial screen.

Like the template presented in the preceding section, this template has only two steps to complete. In fact, the first step has the same options as the previous template, as shown in the following illustration. The Title Settings and General Template Settings work the same in this template as they do in the previous template, as described in Table 2-1.

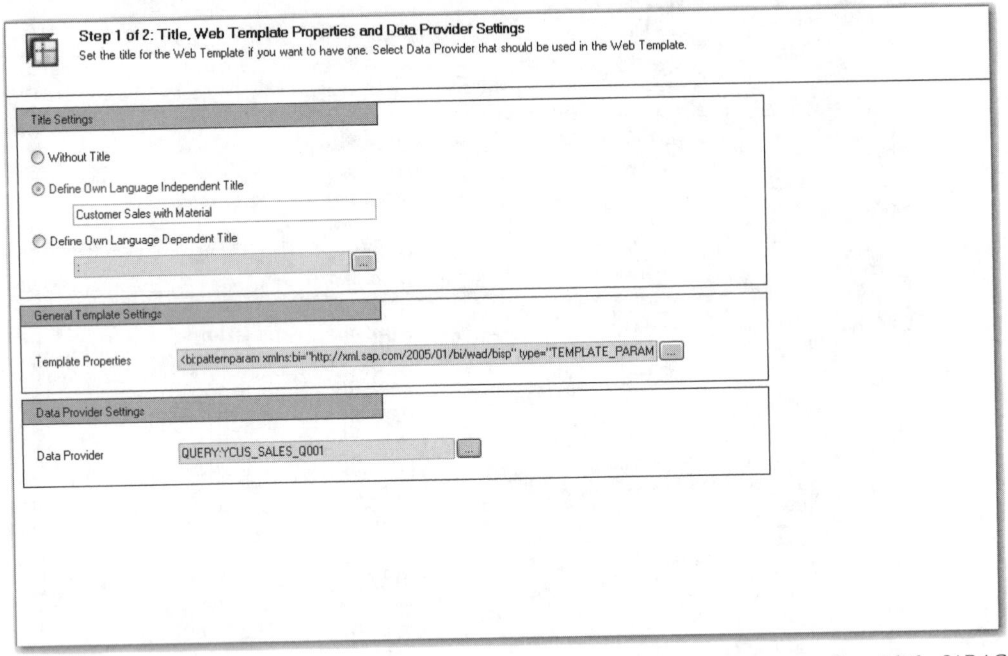

Copyright by SAP AG

The following illustration shows some of the options that are available if we use the General Template Settings functionality. To access this dialog box, click the button to the right of the blank Template Properties field.

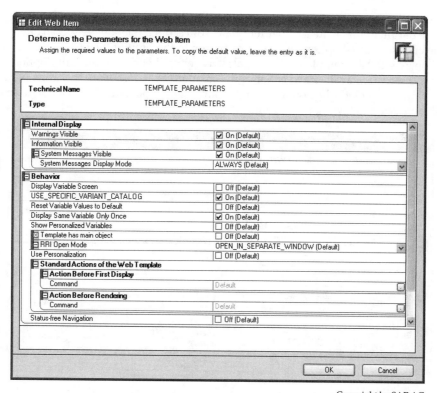

These parameters allow you to set multiple different flags on this template and allow you to configure additional functionality, such as displaying the variables, system messages, and so forth, to be available on this template. So basically, you can choose an easy configuration—just do the basics—or go directly to a more customized display of data by choosing to complete additional parameters. As this illustration shows, the settings available here are no different from those available if you go directly into the Web item for a report and customize using that approach instead of using the BI Patterns component.

Step 2 of this template is shown in the following illustration.

You have only one option: use a template that is already available (Use Reusable Web Item as Chart Item) or create another template from scratch (Define New Chart Item). If we were to choose the first option and click the button to the right of the field, a dialog box would open with Web templates that are already set up. Let's go to the latter option and see what parameters are available to enhance the standard chart. Choose the Define New Chart Item option and click the button to the right of the field to open the Edit Web Item dialog box, shown in the following illustration.

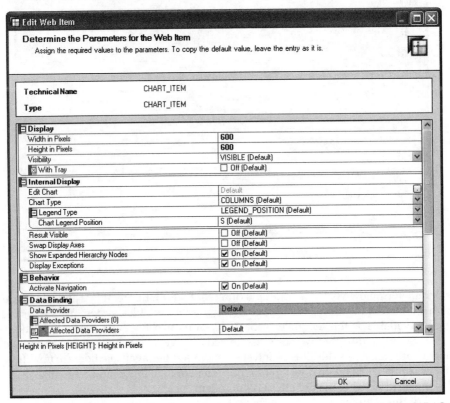

Copyright by SAP AG

All the options are set based on default parameters set by BI for this standard Web template. We can adjust any that we need to for the sake of user flexibility and user-friendly displays. I've changed both the Width and Height in Pixels settings to 600 so that we have a bigger chart. Most of these settings are described in Chapter 3, so for now I'll accept most of the standard settings and move forward. One of the more important settings in this dialog box is the assignment of the data provider, shown at the top of the dialog box in the following illustration. So, we have two locations where we can set the data provider: in the Data Provider field of Step 1 or in Step 2 by accessing the Edit Web Item dialog box via the Define New Chart Item Button. A third option is to go directly into the Web item and set the data provider.

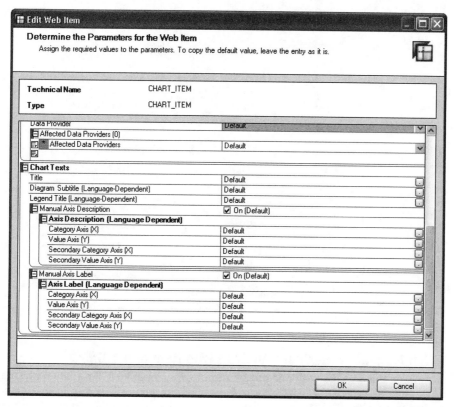

The results of these minor changes and adjustments are shown in the following illustration. So, within about 10 to 15 minutes, your business users can have something to review and base suggestions on. This is a decent-looking chart, though far from the best look and feel that we can achieve. The heading is well displayed, the graphics are direct and easy to read, and the use of different colors enables the business user to identify specific regions quickly and easily.

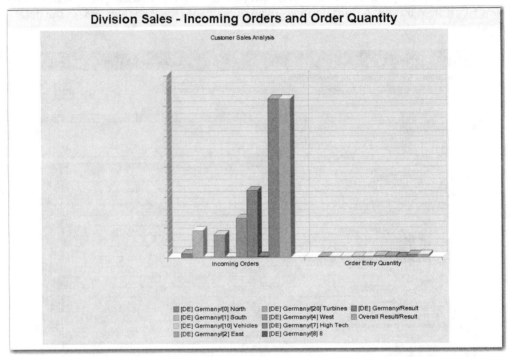

Copyright by SAP AG

Small Web Template with Chart, Analysis Web Item and 1 DP

Let's expand on this process with one more example, the Small Web Template with Chart, Analysis Web Item and 1 DP. Please refer to Figure 2-1 for the initial screen to show the web template for this discussion. This will create, as the title suggests, a Web template with a Chart Web item and an Analysis Web item. This is getting pretty close to approximating the normal formatted Web report, and it could very easily turn into one of the queries that use the standard 0ANALYSIS_PATTERN templates, but the nice thing about this is that you have the choice to either work your way into that format or use this as a basic chart with analysis table for display purposes only.

Click OK to start setting up the configuration of this Small Web Template. As you would expect, the information and settings used for this template are a combination of those used in the two templates previewed in the previous two sections, so our focus here will be the other options in the chart and analysis creation. The one component that is different is Step 1 of this process, shown in the following illustration.

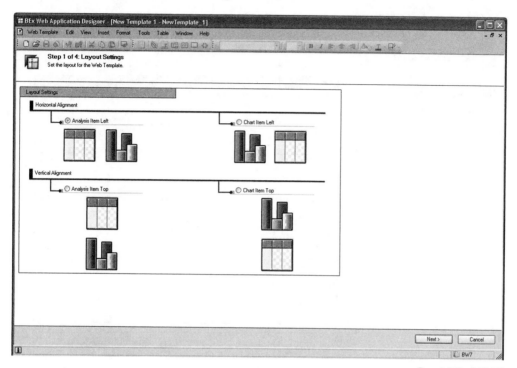

In this step, you decide how to position the chart and analysis table relative to each other on the Web screen. The four different options are clear and very easy to validate once the report is complete. In this case, we will just stay with the default of Analysis Item Left and move on to the next step.

Step 2 offers the same parameters offered in Step 1 in the previous two Small Web Templates: Title Settings, General Template Settings, and Data Provider Settings. Refer to the discussion of Step 1 in the previous sections for details.

Step 3 in this process is the same as Step 2 of the first Small Web Template (IP_1IT_ANALYSIS_1DP) covered in this chapter, in which you choose the Analysis Item Settings. Choosing Define New Analysis Item and clicking the button to the right of the field opens the Edit Web Item dialog box. The following illustration displays the Edit Web Item dialog box options available to format the analysis (table) information. Again, the defaults are fine for purposes of our discussion, and you can tweak the settings at a later time.

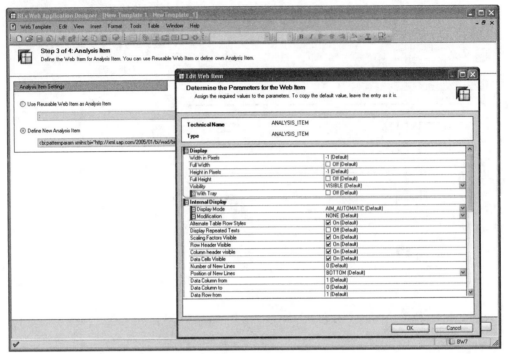

Step 4 in this process is the same as Step 2 of the second Small Web Template (IP_1IT_CHART_1DP) covered in this chapter, in which you choose the Chart Item Settings. By choosing Define New Chart Item and clicking the button to the right of the field, the Edit Web Item dialog box opens. The following illustration displays some of the parameters that you can adjust for this component. Again, leave everything at the default setting—probably not ideal but definitely useable.

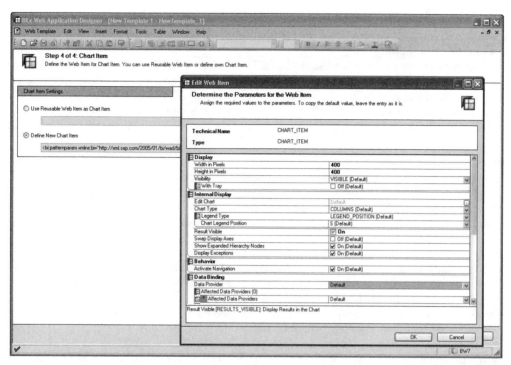

The final process is to review the end result, shown next, and then go back through the different steps and change the default settings. To go back and make any changes to the Web items that you have developed, all you need to do is access them from the main screen and double-click on them. This will open the Web template up and allow access to each of the different Web items. Make any changes you need to from there and you can then re-execute the Web report to review the newer version. This would be the point where you can add additional Web items to your template and expand on the BI Pattern template, if needed.

As you can see, this probably isn't quite what you want to distribute to the business users, but if you are in a hurry and need something as soon as possible, this may do the trick for your situation.

The last two templates in the list, the Small Web Template with Chart, Analysis Web Item and 2 DPs and the Web Template with Three Web Template Web Items are expansions of the Web Templates that we just discussed. Rather than only one DP (data provider) you have two or three that are allowed. The overall configuration and formatting that is available in these last two templates is very similar to what you would see in the others that we have discussed.

Information Consumer Pattern

Now that I've shown you how easy it is to get up and running quickly with the Pattern Wizard, we will look at the Information Consumer Pattern. Although this is the first option under BI Patterns with Pattern Wizard, it should be the last one that you try because it is the most involved. Please refer to Figure 2-1 for the initial screen with the Information Consumer Pattern option.

The Information Consumer Pattern template offers you the choice to increase the functionality and format of each of the Web queries twofold over the Small Web Templates previously discussed. This template is a series of steps that walks you through the entire WAD 0ANALYSIS_PATTERN template, enabling you to turn off or leave on any of the numerous parameters for the query. Step 1, illustrated next, shows immediately that this is very different from the other template wizards.

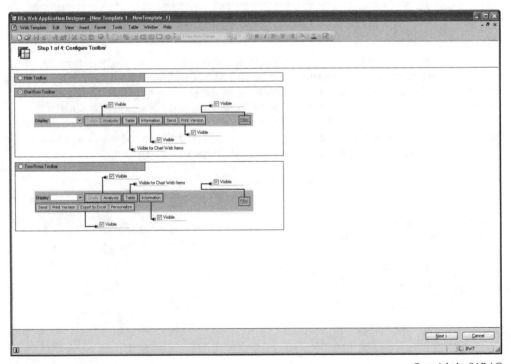

In Step 1, you have several choices:

- **Hide Toolbar**   This requires no explanation.
- **One-Row Toolbar**   If you choose this option, all toolbar buttons will appear in one row on your report. As you can see, in this case as in all of the others, you can hide any of the buttons that have a corresponding Visible check box by clearing the check mark. You will also notice that these Visible boxes are all checked as a default and you will need to manually uncheck them.
- **Two-Rows Toolbar**   As the illustration shows, this will generate a toolbar with two rows rather than one row and offers two additional buttons, Export to Excel and Personalize. You put a check in the corresponding Visible check box for those components that you want to show in the toolbar.

Table 2-3 lists and describes the different items available for the toolbar.

Pushbutton (or Link)	Description
Analysis/Table	This pushbutton switches between the display of data as a table or a graphic. If the data is to be displayed in a table, GRAPHIC appears as the text in the pushbutton. When you switch, the data is displayed in a graphic. Now TABLE appears as the text in the pushbutton.
Information	This pushbutton displays information about the data provider. You can display information about the key date; the current level of the data, which would be the last time the data was uploaded to the infoprovider; the time that the query was last changed; who last changed the query; and the date of the last refresh.
Send	This pushbutton enables you to send the BEx Web application by e-mail. The Broadcasting Wizard appears and helps you to make the necessary entries with step-by-step instructions. For more information, on the process of setting up the Broadcasting Wizard see help.sap.com and access the help for BW, then go to the Information Broadcaster section of the help or see Chapters 11 and 12 of my other book, *SAP Business Information Warehouse Reporting*.
Print Version	This pushbutton enables you to configure the settings for a print version of the BEx Web application. For example, you can set the format for the print version and define whether a header appears on the pages printed. After you make your settings and click OK, a PDF document is generated, which you can then print.
Export to Excel	This pushbutton enables you to export to Excel the report or graphic that you are displaying. If the report is longer than the display—for example, the report is 10 pages long—the export will incorporate all of the pages and not just the page that is being displayed.
Personalize	This pushbutton enables the business user to access and set default values for a variable and use them as "personalized" set values. The next time the same business user accesses this Web report the variable screen will be defaulted with the personalized values.
Filter	This link displays the filter pane, between the application toolbar and the table (or graphic). The filter pane displays characteristics that you can use for filtering. You can select the characteristic values to be used for filtering for each characteristic that is used in the data provider.

TABLE 2-3   Component Buttons on the Consumer Information Pattern Template

Step 2 of the process enables you to choose the settings for the Display dropdown box, as shown next. The options are Show Drop Down Box, which allows the user to see the different data providers that are available to pick from; Sort Alphabetical, which generates a list in alphabetical order; and Keep Filter Values, which allows the data provider (normally a query) to keep any filters that have been defaulted into the definition.

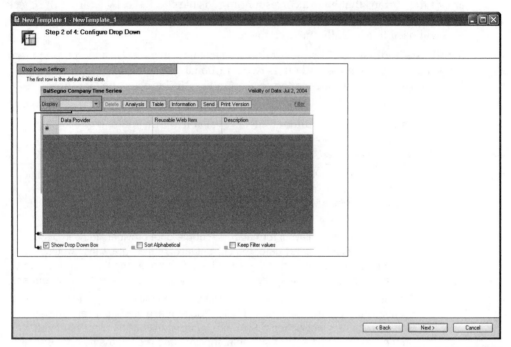

You can also assign the data provider for the dropdown box in Step 2, as shown in the following illustration. The assignment of the information to the next two fields—Resuable Web Items and Description—is a bit tricky. Make sure that you don't leave anything with the filler NULL in the screen or this will generate an error that comments about the fact that there is/are some items that are not compatible. Also in Step 2, you can enhance the analysis by choosing a reusable Web item. Notice that in this template the option to start developing the Analysis item from scratch is not available; you can only use a currently available Web template. Since you have to initially create a Web template that can be used in this field it increases the time it takes to get a completed Web template into the business user's hands.

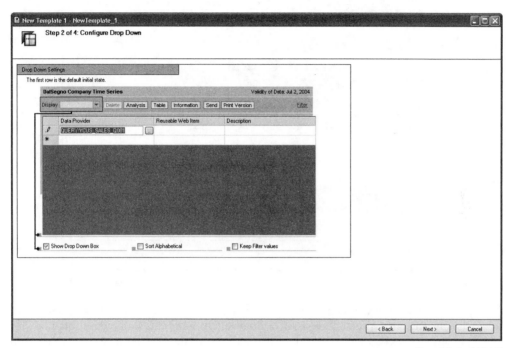

Moving on to Step 3 in this process, shown next, you begin to get into the details of setting up the initial frontend for the business users. In this case, we are assigning characteristics to be available as filter characteristics in report execution. Any characteristics that are identified here will show up under the Filter setting in your Web report. Again, just remember not to allow the filler NULL to appear in any fields.

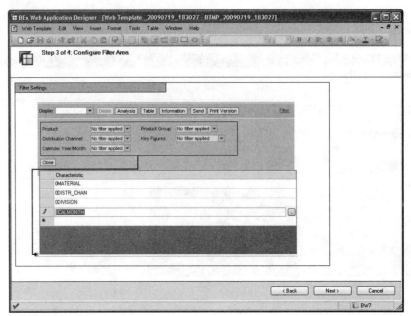

Step 4, shown next, reveals additional parameters for this report, including variable screen display; RRI; title information, which can be either manually entered or obtained from a directory of saved title information; size settings for the Web item; and the other Web templates that you can use for footer or header information.

After this final setting, click Finish, and you are ready to review the results, shown in the following illustration. Remember, we didn't do anything to this query but to step through four screens in the WAD to develop this report. Something very important to observe is the Display dropdown field. This is the InfoProvider (specifically a query) that we set in Step 3 in the Consumer Information Pattern template. The great thing about this report is that we could develop a series of queries and then use this template to line them up in the dropdown list. That way, the user will not have to right-click, go back to the start of the report, or do anything else other than to use the dropdown list to page through all the reports assigned to this Web template.

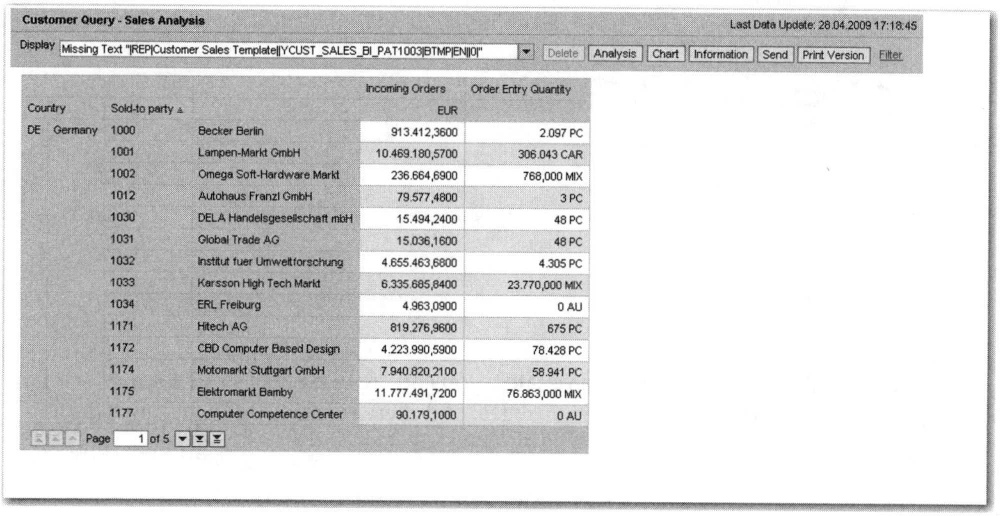

Customer Query - Sales Analysis			Last Data Update: 28.04.2009 17:18:45	
Display	Missing Text "|REP|Customer Sales Template|YCUST_SALES_BI_PAT1003|BTMP|EN|0|"		Delete Analysis Chart Information Send Print Version Filter	
		Incoming Orders	Order Entry Quantity	
Country	Sold-to party ▲	EUR		
DE Germany 1000	Becker Berlin	913.412,3600	2.097 PC	
1001	Lampen-Markt GmbH	10.469.180,5700	306.043 CAR	
1002	Omega Soft-Hardware Markt	236.664,6900	768,000 MIX	
1012	Autohaus Franzl GmbH	79.577,4800	3 PC	
1030	DELA Handelsgesellschaft mbH	15.494,2400	48 PC	
1031	Global Trade AG	15.036,1600	48 PC	
1032	Institut fuer Umweltforschung	4.655.463,6800	4.305 PC	
1033	Karsson High Tech Markt	6.335.685,8400	23.770,000 MIX	
1034	ERL Freiburg	4.963,0900	0 AU	
1171	Hitech AG	819.276,9600	675 PC	
1172	CBD Computer Based Design	4.223.990,5900	78.428 PC	
1174	Motomarkt Stuttgart GmbH	7.940.820,2100	58.941 PC	
1175	Elektromarkt Bamby	11.777.491,7200	76.863,000 MIX	
1177	Computer Competence Center	90.179,1000	0 AU	

Page 1 of 5

We worked though this Web template in about 15 minutes, so some of the text information is a bit rough around the edges. Going back and cleaning this up would be on your project tasks list. Recall that we assigned some characteristics to the report; if you click the Filter hyperlink, you will see that these characteristics are now available in the FILTER portion of the report. The following illustration displays this configuration; here you can see that the Country, Material, and Sold-To Party are available for filtering by clicking on the Filter hyperlink.

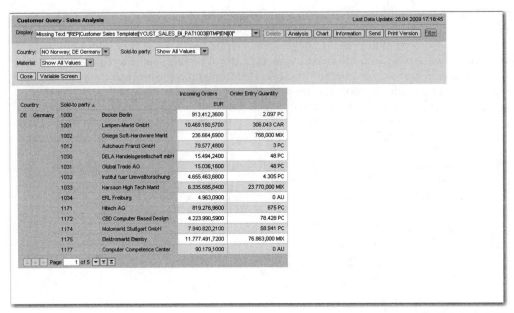

Once you master the use of these templates, you can create sections of a total Web report by using these easy-to-use and -set-up templates, and then incorporate them into a larger Web template for a complete report.

Summary

As you can see there are only a few of these Web templates available in the BI Patterns with Pattern Wizard for you to choose from, and that's okay since we have identified the fact that we can use each of these over again in many different situations. These templates allow a business user to do some configuration of their own Web queries and get up and running very quickly using this component of the WAD. I'm not sure how many of you have looked at these or tried them but if your experience is the same as mine not many people even know that these are available much less how useful they can be to someone that needs some changes to the standard Web template functionality quickly. These Small Web Templates and Pattern templates might also be ideal for the super users to get their hands dirty with some configuration using the WAD component. As a byproduct, any fear that the business user has about attempting to build a Web report should be dispelled, because this will allow them to use much of the components and functionality of the actual WAD toolset.

Another good thing about these Web templates is that once the business user gets comfortable with this functionality they can easily take the functionality that they have developed in the BI Patterns with Pattern Wizard area and expand on it by using other standard Web items to enhance their Web reports. So, any development work in this area doesn't go to waste.

3

Basics of the Web Application Designer

The Web Application Designer is the toolset that's at the top of the BI food chain in terms of the different reporting tools that SAP offers for Web-based reporting. (As a reminder, we are talking about the BI-specific reporting tools and not the current and future reporting components that include integration with the BusinessObject reporting toolset. Those components are discussed in Chapter 9.) The WAD's list of functionality and options will probably make any customer happy with the possibilities available for displaying and enhancing their reports. The WAD offers that finishing touch to all the reports that you are ultimately going to deliver to your customer—the management of your company. The end result is a customized and professional report that can be used for either a static review of results or a more dynamic drilldown of the information. The WAD is well suited for both tasks. To complete this customization process, design principles must be used while constructing the Web template (or templates) that comprises the Web application. Additionally, the developer of the WAD application needs to have a detailed understanding of the sources of the data that will be used. Now, if the customer wants additional functionality beyond what the WAD offers, we can take the Web report that is built using WAD functionality and use the additional enhancements available in the Visual Composer to go above and beyond what has been developed to accommodate other or additional business requirements.

This chapter will get you started on the basics of the WAD, including an introduction to all the component parts and some functionality. This will prepare you for the next chapter, in which you explore each Web item in depth and get your hands dirty using the detailed components. This will take you to the level at which you can build dynamic and effective Web reports and dashboards. We will also review the functionality and components of the WAD standard business content template 0ANALYSIS_PATTERN. This is the cornerstone of all of the standard Web reports and can be used to help support additional templates merely by making a copy of this important template and then adjusting the copied version to accommodate the business user's needs. If you need additional review of the overall WAD process please refer to Chapter 2 for additional information.

Introduction to the Web Application Designer (WAD)

The BEx Web Application Designer is a desktop application for creating Web applications with BI-specific content. If the BI-specific content does not meet your needs, the WAD enables you to create highly individual scenarios with user-defined interface elements by using standard markup languages and the Web Design API. The BI sources that supply data to the Web applications are BI queries, BI query views, and BI InfoProviders—that is, the data available to the Web applications is basically everything in the BI data warehouse environment. We will be using mostly BI queries in our discussion and examples since they are the most widely used for supporting the WAD and the query is the suggested SAP best business practice to be used as the source of data for the Web templates. The BEx query is the most used source of data for support of other components in the BI process, which also includes the new BusinessObject (BOBJ) components.

The WAD allows you to use generic OLAP navigation for your BI data in Web applications as well as in business intelligence cockpits for simple or highly individual scenarios. You can use the WAD to generate HTML pages that contain BI-specific content such as tables, charts, and maps—all of which will be covered in this chapter and the next so that you can develop customized reports and dashboards for your company. Web applications are based on Web templates that you create and edit in the WAD. You can save the Web templates and access them from a Web browser or a portal. Once they have been executed on the Web, Web templates are known as Web applications. The WAD also allows you to create highly individual scenarios with user-defined interface elements by using advanced Web items and the Web Design API. An underutilized component of the WAD is the ability to create reusable Web items, store them in the Web Item Library, and use later. The BEx Web applications that are generated are Web-based applications for data analysis, reporting, and analytical applications on the Web. In addition to the WAD, the BEx Web Analyzer, discussed in Chapter 1, is provided as an independent Web application that can be used to analyze data on an ad hoc basis.

In the WAD, the BI sources are linked into the Web Framework through *data providers*. A data provider provides a logical connection to the data supplied by a BI source. A one-to-one relationship usually exists between the BI source and a data provider, although each data provider is independent, so it is possible to use the same BI source for multiple data providers if necessary. In general, Web items are responsible for formatting the data received from a data provider. For example, a Chart Web item (explained in Chapter 4) would show the data as a chart, whereas the Navigation Pane Web item would list the components of the data provider in the format of the navigation window. Assigning a data provider to a Web item is known as *data binding*. Not every Web item formats data for the user of the Web application. For example, the XML Data Provider Information Web item makes the data and metadata of the Web application available in XML format for use with JavaScript routines. Other Web items, such as Containers and Context Menu, do not supply data but rather are used for formatting. These are just some of the Web items that are available to the analyst. We will be working our way through all of them in Chapter 4.

Web items serve as the building blocks of the Web template because they can represent the data provider data in many different formats. A Web template is the collection of Web

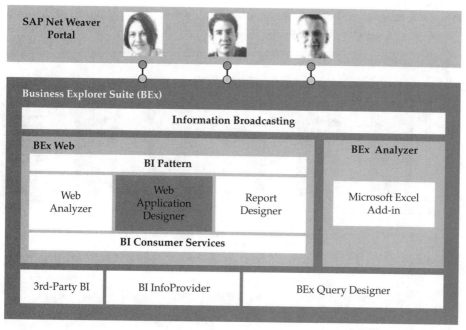

Figure 3-1   Positioning of the Web Application Designer in the BI environment

items, formatting objects, texts, images, and parameters that defines a Web page. Web templates can be either very basic or customized to the customer's needs, depending on their uses in the overall reporting process. Therefore, the WAD user primarily needs to be aware of the applications and uses of each of the Web items in the process of creating and maintaining Web templates. Finally, when the Web templates are executed in the Enterprise Portal, they are referred to as *Web applications*. A Web application can be any combination of Web templates linked together. The Web application design comprises a broad spectrum of Web-based business intelligence scenarios, which you can adjust to meet your individual needs using standard Web technologies. Figure 3-1 shows how the Web Application Designer is integrated into the function landscape and tool landscape of the Business Explorer.

Example WAD Reports

The results that we are looking for might look something like the following illustration, a WAD report that shows the YTD sales trend for the current year. Notice that several options are available for reporting and drilling down in the reports. The detailed analysis of the graphic by material is shown at the bottom of the report, and this detail goes a step further by showing the sales data by material and by sales organization. This seems to be a good combination, because if we were to try to include in the graphic the data on the sales organization level, too much complexity might be added to the screen, thus making the report less effective (as you can see there are multiple sales organizations to each product and this would expand the graph too much).

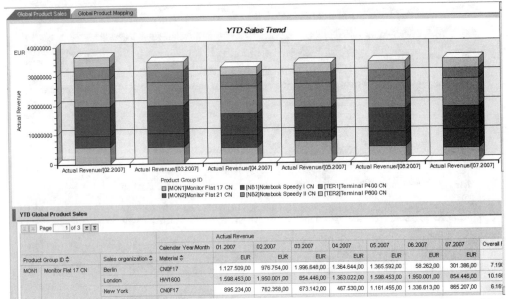

NOTE *The final results from the WAD would probably be delivered to a portal, whether the BI portal or some sort of enterprise portal, but here we will only be working with the results of the WAD.*

The details of the legend are very clear and consistent across the report. The color choices are good, clear, and accurate. As you can see, the final results of WAD reports are not only about the data but also about the presentation. Many projects encounter issues and setbacks due to the customer being uncomfortable with the finished look of the report or being confused by the approach to the display. A dashboard may not be well received due to issues with coloring or the look and feel. Therefore, this is a good example of a finished product. Finally, the additional tabbed page can be used for detailed reports or other activities such as alerts or documentation. Tabbed pages make the display much more user friendly and more manageable to read. There is a tremendous amount of information concerning the formatting and functionality of creating dashboards or any reports required for management. We will discuss this information in Chapter 6.

Another very good example of a finished WAD report is shown in the following illustration. In this case, the customer is looking for a more consistent and static reporting view of the data. As you can see, there are no additional options for drilldown on the screen other than buttons at the top that will execute changes to the current graphic. This is also a very good option since most of the time business users—both casual and executive—want to be able to just click a button rather than doing the analysis process of right-clicking and filtering their information. If required additional buttons can be available after the initial drilldown from the current button grouping. So, what could happen is that after the business user has drilled down to the Customer Level there can be a list of buttons to allow even further drilldown by the customer at that point. Notice that a number of Web items have been used for this display, and the format has been developed around the sizing of the information and the functionality.

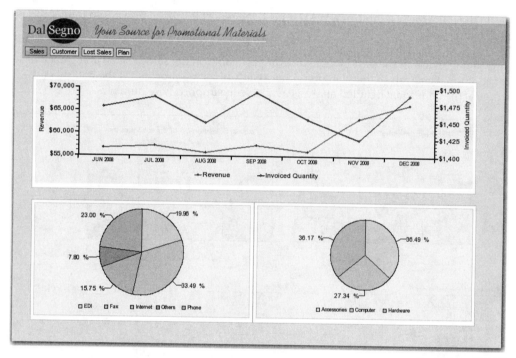

The person reviewing this report, which currently shows total sales, can immediately review sales either by customer or by lost sales by clicking the corresponding button. The bottom of the report shows the information at a more detailed level with graphs by Distribution Channel and Product Line. With the amount of information being presented, the pie charts are an effective way to enable the user to understand the information quickly and effectively. As I will reiterate several times in this book, an executive has about 15 to 20 seconds a day to review the overall information regarding the company's growth and stability. The rest of their day is devoted to trying to drive the company forward by using this information to help support integration with different stakeholders outside of their company.

Another example of a WAD report is the basic Alert Monitor, shown next. In this case, the customer receives these alerts automatically via their personal Company Portal page and can then execute the link to the reports to investigate the detailed information on the alerts. This allows a more focused approach to report analysis rather than getting all of the information no matter whether it's important or not.

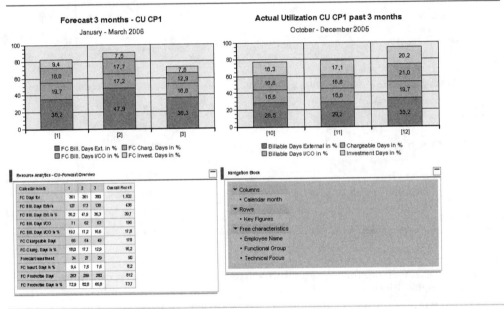

In the following example of a WAD report, the report is broken down into four sections, with navigational capabilities and charts for quick analysis and simulation of the results. The color coding is excellent and spelled out in detail in the legend. A forecast of the billable days and a review of the past billable days are available on the same screen and can be used for additional analysis of the planning process or forecasting process. At the bottom of the screen is the additional detailed analysis available to support these numbers.

In a follow-up report, shown next, we are able to drilldown to the lower-level report to see the breakdown by functional group, but the graphs located above are definitely created at a higher-level characteristic combination.

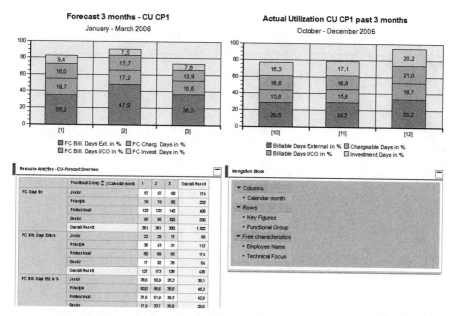

The final example of a WAD report, shown next, is something that is nice to have but not always feasible. Often, by the time a company gets to this level, either the budget doesn't cover these types of reports, the frontend component being used has changed, or something else has happened to redirect the focus of reporting. This type of report incorporates the GIS (geographic information system) or the mapping component of the WAD. This is a very useful frontend display but takes some time and effort to develop and maintain. It is developed using another toolset that is incorporated into the WAD and takes some backend work to get the InfoObjects correctly formatted, but the end result often is well worth the trouble. The format of the maps and content can be adjusted, but this also costs additional funds because these templates have to be obtained from a third-party company that supports this GIS system. As the following illustration shows, the ability to focus on specific information and understand what is going on quickly and easily is supported by the use of these maps and geographic displays. Once this WAD report is set up and functioning, the maintenance is minimal and the uploads of newer versions of maps of countries, regions, or other company-specific locations is not difficult.

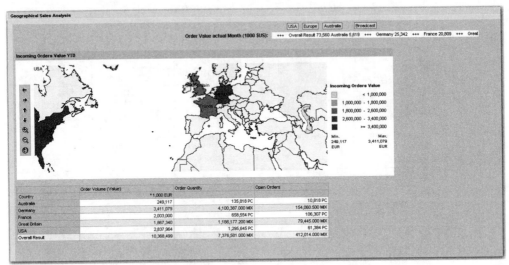

We could go on forever with examples of the functionality of WAD-developed reports, but the preceding examples should give you an idea of the many options and opportunities offered by the use of the WAD in your reporting strategy. The different ways to slice and dice data and the different views in the reports can be tailored to your company's needs. The bottom line in terms of the final presentation of a Web-based report is that you need to use a functional and flexible toolset like the WAD to change basic data into useable information and make it useable for a specific group in an effective manner. Understanding the components of the WAD is important, but you also need to understand design principles and incorporate them into the overall design process. As mentioned, there are specific sources of data, and understanding these objects is also very important.

Overview of the WAD Interface

In this section we will orient you to all of the different components of the WAD interface, including its screen areas, menus, and toolbars. To begin this orientation process, you need to gain access to the WAD so I'll review this activity first to make sure we all know how to do that and discuss our options in this task. To access the WAD, select Start | Programs | Business Explorer | Web Application Designer. With NetWeaver 7.0 BI, you may have access to two versions of the tool, 7.0 and 3.x. Depending on your company's migration process, you may need to use the 3.x version rather than the 7.0 version (as discussed in Chapter 8). The menu path just mentioned accesses the BI version of the WAD. If you want to execute the BW 3.x version of the WAD, you need to select Start | Programs | Business Explorer | Business Explorer (SAP BW 3.x) | Web Application Designer (SAP BW 3.x).

NOTE *The fact that you have two different versions of the WAD tool available may cause some issues. If you are not migrating or making any adjustments to the WAD reports, you may want to either deactivate or remove from the dropdown list whichever version you are not working with. Opening your WAD reports in one version versus the other may cause errors to occur if the correct version is not used. So if you open your WAD report template in the 7.0 version but didn't support the migration of that Web report to 7.0 from 3.5, you may cause errors to occur if you then try to open it again in the 3.5 version.*

The initial WAD screen that is presented to you after logging in for the first time should be similar to the one shown in the following illustration, but with a blank list of recent Web templates.

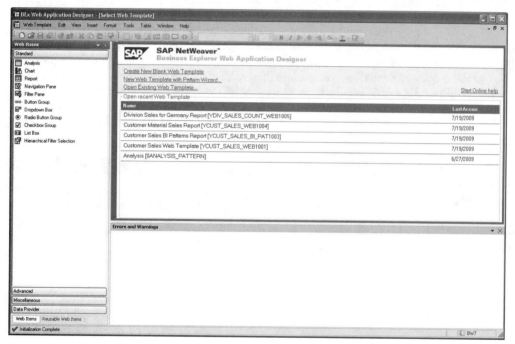

If you have been working in the WAD and have the "historical" view option turned on, you see a list of recent Web templates, as in the preceding illustration (which reflects the Web templates created in the previous chapter).

The WAD Screen Areas

The initial view of the WAD interface has four different screen areas in addition to the menus and toolbars:

- Web Items
- Web Template

- Error and Warnings
- Reusable Web Items

Once you select a Web item to work with, another screen area is identified, which is Properties.

You can adjust the appearance of the WAD to your requirements using the options available in the context menu under View in the toolbar. The Web template is handled differently from the other components such as Tools and Help Windows. In the case of the other components you can show and hide the individual screen areas and toolbars using the View menu options, shown here. The Web Template area is not available in this context menu and therefore can't be adjusted.

Copyright by SAP AG

You can move the three toolbars and the Web Items and Properties screen areas as you require. Depending on where you move an object to, it is anchored or floats freely as a toolbox. The following illustration shows everything in a horizontal position. This is not the greatest format but it does show that you can realign these GUI elements just about any way you want. Because the WAD is a multiple-document interface (MDI) application, you can open and manage different windows with Web templates at the same time. You can use the Window menu to arrange other windows differently: cascading (overlapping), vertically, or horizontally.

Copyright by SAP AG

Web Items Screen Area

The Web Items screen area provides access to all the available Web items and data providers and displays a small help section. The Web items are segmented into three groupings: Standard, Advanced, and Miscellaneous. Clicking the group heading displays the contents of that group. The following illustration shows the result of choosing the Advanced grouping. Because the Web items are the basic building blocks of the Web templates, using this section is not only very common but really almost a requirement to get anything to show up in the WAD. A Web item describes the way in which the data from a data provider is displayed, such as in text (Text Web item), a map (Map Web item), or a graphic (Chart Web item).

Under the Data Provider section, you can create data providers of type Filter or type Query View. You drag and drop the required data provider type into your Web template, and the dialog box for creating data providers opens. Under the selection for Web Items and Data Provider Maintenance, you see the help area, which provides explanations for the Web items and the data providers. To display the texts for the respective Web item, double-click the Web item. To hide the texts, double-click the Web item again. Once you have hidden the display of texts and selected a Web item by single-clicking it, some quick info is displayed for the Web item, as shown here.

NOTE *The Data Provider section in the Web Items area is for creating, assigning, changing, and reviewing the data providers and doesn't offer additional WAD functionality.*

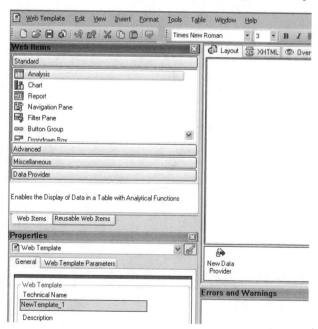

Hidden in the background on this tab is another tab for the Reusable Web Items. This will be covered later in this chapter.

Properties Screen Area

The Properties screen area provides access to all the properties of the selected Web item or the Web template itself. The component you select determines the number of properties associated with the Web item. Also, all the parameters and settings are configured here. The Properties screen area uses two tabs to segment the properties. The General tab, shown next, provides access to the data provider assignment, if required. The Web Item Parameters is, in most cases, the more important portion and shows a listing of the configuration settings of that component. The Properties screen area is very important to developers and is where you will spend most of your time configuring the WAD template.

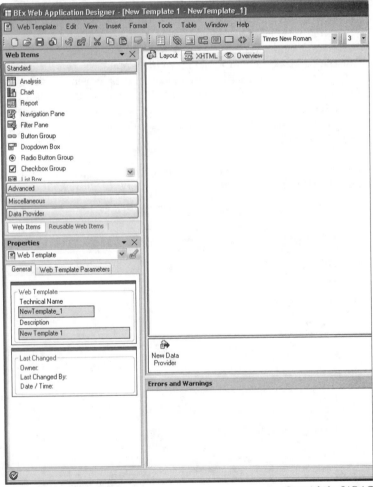

Copyright by SAP AG

In the dropdown box at the top of the Properties screen area, you choose whether you want to define properties for a Web template or for specific Web items. Depending on your choice in the dropdown box, you can then make various settings for a Web template or Web items. If you select a Web template from the dropdown box, you can then set the parameters for the Web template on the Web Template Parameters tab, shown next. It has numerous settings that are important to the overall look and feel of the Web template, including settings for warnings, variable screens, variants, RRI functionality, and document options. Context-sensitive help is available in the lower area of the tab.

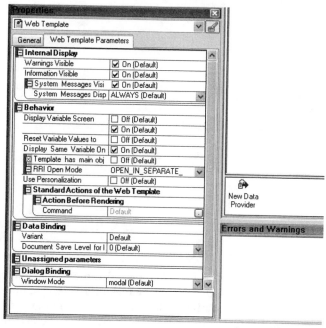

Copyright by SAP AG

If you select a Web item from the dropdown box, you can make the following settings:

- **General tab**   Click the Create New symbol to the right of the dropdown box to create a data provider and assign it to the Web item.

- **Web Item Parameters tab**   Set the parameters for the selected Web item. Context-sensitive help and descriptions of the actual functionality of the parameter is available in the lower area of the tab.

Web Template Screen Area

The Web Template screen area is where you construct the actual Web template. Basically, you drag and drop the Web items into this area and, from there, configure the parameters associated with each Web item. In the following illustration, the Analysis Web item has been dropped onto the Web Template area.

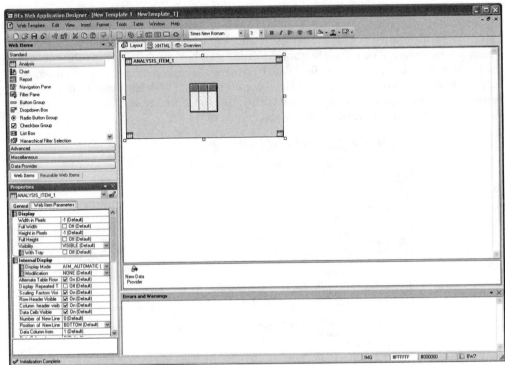

Notice all the parameters available in the Web Item Parameters tab that you can adjust to make the query report more user friendly. We will be looking at these parameters in Chapter 4. The Web Template area contains the Web templates that you edit in the design process and that form the basis of your Web applications. The Web template is the HTML page that you use to specify the structure of the Web application. The HTML page published on the Web is called a Web application. The upper section of the Web Template screen area has three tabs—Layout, XHTML, and Overview—you can use to change the view of the Web template, in the same way you do in an HTML editor.

Layout Tab   The Layout tab (also called layout view) gives you a visual focus and enables you to specify the layout of the Web application (see the previous illustration). To do this, you use drag-and-drop operations to insert Web items from the pool of Web items into your Web template. In the lower section of the Layout tab, you can create data providers by double-clicking New Data Provider, which opens the dialog box for creating data providers. You can also create data providers in the Web Items screen area. The Web Template screen area is not an exact representation of the placement or spacing of the individual Web items when the Web application is executed. The parameters are defined in logical grouping of items that enables you to see the relationship of each Web item within the group to the other.

XHTML Tab The XHTML tab (also called XHTML view) displays the XHTML that corresponds to layout view. Table 3-1 lists the some of the various elements of the XHTML syntax and the different colors associated with them.

In XHTML view, as shown in the next illustration, you can edit the XHTML of a Web template directly or you can edit the XHTML using an external XHTML editor. In the XHTML tab's work area, you can see the code that is automatically generated as Web items are placed in the Web template. Once these Web items are inserted into the template, text is assigned and any of the other items that may apply as standard objects to the Web item are inserted into the XHTML page and are available for the business user to adjust directly in the XHTML language.

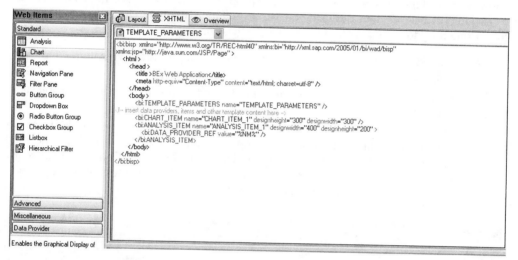

Copyright by SAP AG

After you assign objects to the template via the Layout tab, you can use the XHTML to change the objects by adding additional code directly into this area. It is important to note that although many of the tags used in HTML coding can also be used in the code on the XHTML tab, you must make sure that you are coding in the appropriate area of the tags. As you directly assign code to this area, you will see prompts if there are any issues with the

TABLE 3-1
Syntax Elements
and the Color
Coding

Syntax Element	Color
Comments	Gray
Attributes	Red
Attribute values	Blue
HTML tags	Black
BI-specific content (BI tags) such as Web items, commands, and data providers	Dark red
Texts	Green
Hyperlinks	Violet

appropriate tags or coding. These prompts appear in the Errors and Warnings area. If you are comfortable with XHTML coding, you will find that being able to use and program industry-standard XHTML to enhance the WAD results definitely comes in handy.

Overview Tab   The Overview tab, shown next, lists all Web items, data providers, and commands used in Web templates. By selecting or deselecting check boxes, you specify which of these objects are listed. The objects are listed in the Item Name column. Any data providers and reusable Web items associated with an object are listed in the corresponding columns on the same row as the object. The Overview tab is very helpful to verify that the data binding of the Web items is correct and the parameters/properties are consistent. The logical names of the Web items as well as their properties can be changed in this work area by clicking on the Web item and using the context menu to open the desired screen. Using the Sorting dropdown box, you can specify how these objects are to be listed:

- **Grouped**   The objects used are listed by type: data providers, Web items, and commands.

- **Web Template**   The sequence of the objects used in the Web template is displayed as a flat structure.

- **Web Template (Hierarchical)**   The sequence of the objects used in the Web template is displayed as a hierarchical structure. You see a hierarchical structure if you nest Web items in the Web template (for example, when you use the Container Web item). You can change the parameters of the associated objects using the context menu for each Web item, Web template, and data provider listed.

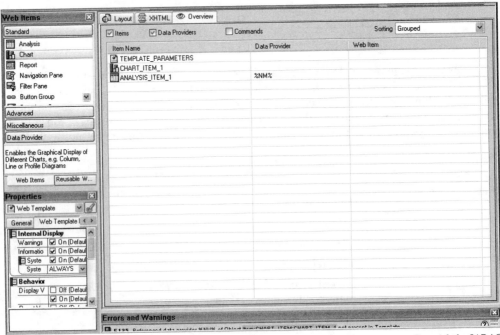

Errors and Warnings Screen Area

The Errors and Warnings screen area, shown next, is used to display errors and warnings when a Web template is being verified. You can use this information and also the actual error or warning to direct you right to the item that is having the issue. Using a right-click on the error or warning, and then using the context menu that appears, you can either go to a help option or in some cases go directly to the error via the link and fix the issue.

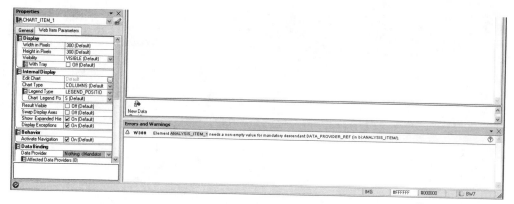

The errors and warnings that are displayed in this screen area refer to the following possible checks of the Web template:

- **Verify**   This check is performed automatically and by default every two seconds. Within the verification, the internal structure of the Web template is checked. You can change the refresh time for the verification in the menu bar under Tools | Settings.

- **Verification on the Server**   With this verification, which you trigger manually, additional conditions for creating a correct Web template are checked on the server side. Here, for example, the system verifies whether a query that is being used as a data provider exists. To trigger the verification, on the WAD menu bar, choose Web Template | Verify on Server.

- **Correct and Format**   During this verification, which you can trigger manually, the internal structure of the HTML is checked. You can trigger this verification only when you are in XHTML view. From the WAD menu bar, choose Edit | Correct and Format.

Reusable Web Items

A final tab that appears on the WAD screen is the Reusable Web Items tab. In most cases, as in the other reporting tools, it may be a good idea to have a "library" of reusable Web items that can be shared by other developers. This reduces development and configuration time and allows for the collection of different Web templates so that everyone can be using the same parameters, when necessary, and also provide the same look and feel to their objects. The use of reusable Web items can help with this process. This option allows the developer to configure Web items and save them in roles or the Favorites folder as reusable Web items. To Save, right-click on the completed Web template and select the context menu item Save as Reusable Web Item. Once this is completed, the Web items can be accessed from this tab in the Web Items screen area. It is important to note that not all properties of the Web items are saved in the reusable Web items. For example, the data binding of a Web item is not retained in the reusable Web item. Data binding must be done on an individual basis for each relevant Web item in the template where it is used. This can be seen in the following illustration.

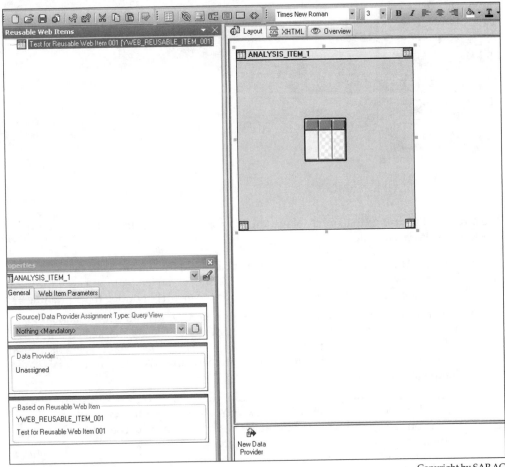

To help increase the efficiency of business users, you should consider to what extent you can reuse a Web application you've created. If one Web application differs from another by only a few objects (for example, a different data provider is displayed, a pushbutton does not appear, or another Web item is used to display the data), you can create a second Web template by just using the Web Template Web item there. Drag and drop the Web Template Web item into the second Web template. You assign the first Web template to this Web item using the Web Template (TEMPLATE_ID) parameter. Save the Web template and open it again. Now you see all the elements that exist in the first Web template. Here, you can overwrite individual Web items or data providers. When you integrate a Web item into your Web template from the Web item groupings in the Web Items screen area and define your settings, you might want to use this Web item again in this form in other Web templates, without having to define the settings over again. The WAD enables you to use your own version of a Web item as the Web template for other items. You store this Web item as a template. You can then access your Web items from the Reusable Web Items tab. Any changes that you make to the settings of the reusable Web item (as previously described) have a *global* effect, meaning the changes are effective in all saved Web templates in which you use that specific Web item.

This does not apply to Web templates in which you changed the parameters of a reusable Web item locally. In this case, the settings that you make locally are effective. If you want to change the settings in a reusable Web item locally (that is, in a specific Web template in which you are using this Web item), proceed as follows:

1. Open the Web template.

2. Select the reusable Web item in the Web template.

3. Change the parameters of this Web item on the Web Item Parameters tab in the Properties screen area.

4. Save the Web template.

The changes that you made to the reusable Web item apply only in this second Web template. The parameter settings of the reusable Web item are not affected by the changes.

NOTE *If you try to overwrite the parameters of a Chart Web item that you have saved as a reusable Web item locally, the Create Local Chart Settings dialog box appears. Here, you are told that you are about to overwrite the settings for a reusable Web item locally. If you choose Yes, the Edit Graphic dialog box appears. To change the parameters for the Chart Web item locally, reset its parameters and close the Edit Graphic dialog box by clicking OK. If you close the Edit Graphic dialog box by clicking Cancel, no local Chart Web items parameter settings are created. The reusable Web item's settings are still effective. If you click No or Cancel, no changes to the saved chart local parameter settings are made.*

The WAD Menu Bar and Toolbar Components

Now that you are familiar with the screen areas within the WAD interface, it's time to focus on the different functions of the WAD menu bar and toolbars. Although you could do most if not all of your configuration using just the Web items from the left navigation pane, you should be mindful that many components are also available via the menu bar embedded at the top of the WAD screen and the three toolbars that you can access via View | Toolbars—Standard, Insert, and Layout. Each of these has multiple functions available for you to use in your configuration process, as described next.

Menu Bar

This seems harmless enough in terms of overall functions and options and that's about right since much of the functionality found on this toolbar is available via the navigation pane and the use of the right-click context menus. It's good to review so if you decide to, you can use this approach to navigation rather than working directly from the Layout area in the

WAD or other options. It's a personal preference as to which approach works best for you but just remember that no matter what format the individual adjusts the other areas of the WAD, the Menu Bar options will always look the same. To explain these items, the best approach is starting from the leftmost menu and working my way across.

Copyright by SAP AG

Web Template Menu   The Web Template menu offers a list of standard functions that you can use throughout the configuration process. Looking at the list, shown here on the right, you can see that it offers options that have more to do with the overall functionality of the WAD than with specific Web items. Table 3-2 lists and briefly describes the Web Template menu options.

You will find that these options are also found on the Standard toolbar that we will come across shortly. At that time we will reference back to this list rather than duplicating the information.

Edit Menu   The Edit menu, shown next, offers tools such as Cut, Copy, and Paste. These tools are also available via the right-click context

Copyright by SAP AG

Menu Option	Description
New	Use this function to create a new Web template that you can use to develop a Web dashboard, then publish as a Web application in a Web browser.
Open	Use this function to open the BEx Open dialog box, from which you can open a Web template in your history, favorites, or roles, or one located by using the search function. This option will give you a display of all existing Web templates available.
Close	Use this function to close a Web template.
Delete	Use this function to delete open Web templates that are already saved.
Save	Use this function to save any changes you make to an existing Web template. When you create a new Web template and choose this option, the BEx Save dialog box appears, enabling you to save your Web template in your favorites or roles. The initial step is to assign a description and technical name to the Web template.
Save As	Use this function to open the BEx Save dialog box, where you can save your Web template in your favorites or roles. If you are authorized to delete Web templates, you are also able to overwrite any existing Web templates saved in your favorites or roles. To overwrite an existing Web template with the new Web template, choose Web Template I Save As. In the Save Web Template dialog box, select the Web template that you want to overwrite from your favorites or roles. Click Save. In the Do You Want to Overwrite <*name of selected Web template*>? dialog box, click OK.

TABLE 3-2   Components of the Web Template Menu

Menu Option	Description
Import from File	Use this function to import back into the WAD a Web template that you edited with an external XHTML editor. This could have occurred if additional XHTML was needed to adjust the XHTML program, then reload it back into BW.
Export to File	Use this function to export to a file system of your choice a Web template that you want to edit with an external XHTML editor.
Validate	Use this function to check that the internal structure of the Web template is correct. By default, the verification is performed automatically every two seconds. You can change the refresh time under Tools I Settings. Any errors found during this check are displayed in the Errors and Warnings screen area. From the Errors and Warnings screen area it would be possible to jump to the object that is having the issue.
Validate on Server	Use this function to trigger an additional check of the Web template. This checks the server conditions for a correct Web template. Any errors found during this check are displayed in the correction assistant, which suggests correction changes for the errors found.
Runtime Format Preview	Use this function to obtain a technical preview of the existing Web application. The runtime format is displayed if you use this functionality. This underutilized tool helps you to do some performance analysis prior to the initial data testing. It also allows you to review the performance statistics for the Web template before you distribute it to your customers.
Execute	Use this function to call your Web application in the portal.
Publish	**To Role** Use this function to publish Web templates to roles. The system saves a link to the current Web template in the selected role. **To Portal** Use this function to publish Web templates as iViews in the Portal Content Directory. This function allows the user to create an iView for the Web query for display in the Portal. **BEx Broadcaster** Use this function to open the BEx Broadcaster, which you can use to precalculate and broadcast the Web template in numerous formats including PDF, Excel, e-mails with links embedded, etc. **Copy URL to Clipboard** Use this function to copy the URL of the Web template to the clipboard so that you can call it in a Web browser or send it as an e-mail, for example.
Recently Used Web Templates	Use this function to display the Web templates that you opened recently, to get quick access to them.
Exit	Use this function to close the WAD. If you want to keep the changes you made to a Web template you created or edited, save the Web template before you close the WAD. If you use this option the system will prompt you to save initially before you exit.

TABLE 3-2   Components of the Web Template Menu (*continued*)

menu, so which approach you use in the configuration process is a matter of personal preference. Table 3-3 lists and briefly describes the Edit menu options.

Copyright by SAP AG

View Menu The View menu, shown next with the Navigate To submenu expanded, makes viewing or hiding different options in either the toolbars or the Web template simple. This menu doesn't offer any additional functionality within the WAD process. It can definitely

Menu Option	Description
Cut	Use this function to cut a highlighted Web item, HTML element, picture, or text. This will cut (or delete) the Web item from the current position but will be available to insert elsewhere.
Copy	Use this function to copy single Web items, pictures, text, and so on, or an HTML table, so that you can paste them, for example, into another Web template. Normally, you copy Web items that have been imported into your WAD components.
Paste	Use this function to paste into a Web template any Web items, texts, pictures, or HTML elements that you have copied.
Delete Web Item	Use this function to delete a highlighted Web item from the Web template.
Edit <head> Element	Use this function, which is only available in layout view, to edit the <HEAD> tag of the Web template. Some parameters available are changing color, font size, and the Style Sheet.
Edit <body> Element	Use this function, which is only available in layout view, to edit the <BODY> tag of the Web template. The same parameters are available here as in the <head> Element
Correct and Format	Use this function, which is only available in XHTML view, to trigger the check of the inner structure of the Web template. The XHTML text is simultaneously structured (formatted). This option can be very useful when reviewing and validating the XHTML text.
Find, Find and Replace	Use these functions, which are only available in XHTML view, to locate specific text or XHTML objects in XHTML view and, with the latter option, replace that text.

TABLE 3-3 Components of the Edit Menu

help you to clean up some of the clutter found on your screen by hiding unused items, but that's about it. Table 3-4 lists and briefly describes the View menu options.

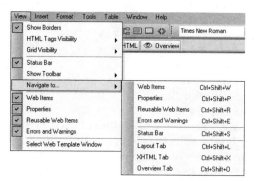

Copyright by SAP AG

Menu Option	Description
Show Borders	Use this function, which is only available in layout view, to display the frames of the inserted HTML tables.
HTML Tags Visibility	Use this function to hide HTML tags, display HTML tags that are not visibly displayed in layout view by default (for example, font tags), or display all HTML tags. You can edit the tags using the context menu of the displayed tags.
Grid Visibility	Use this function, which is only available in layout view, to change the grid and grid pages that the Web template is based on, to suit your needs. You can hide grids, show grids and grid pages, or show the grid or grid pages individually. You can set the size of the grids and grid pages using Grid Visibility I Grid Pages Settings.
Status Bar	Use this function to show and hide the status bar in the lowest screen area of the WAD.
Show Toolbar	Use this function to show and hide the Insert, Format, and Standard toolbars.
Navigate To	Use this function to navigate to different screen areas (such as Web Items, Properties, Reusable Web Items, Errors and Warnings), or the status bar, and the different views in the Web Template area.
Web Items	Use this function to show and hide the Web Items screen area.
Properties	Use this function to show and hide the Properties screen area.
Reusable Web Items	Use this function to show and hide the Reusable Web Items screen area. If you show this screen area, it appears as a tab in the Web Items screen area by default. However, you can move this screen area within the Web application, just as you can with all other screen areas.
Errors and Warnings	Use this function to show and hide the Errors and Warnings screen area.

TABLE 3-4   Components of the View Menu

Insert Menu   You will likely perform most of the functions available on the Insert menu by using either the Web Items screen area and dragging and dropping the Web item into the Layout or one of the toolbars that you can display via View | Toolbar but this is another approach. This way you don't have to keep opening up the different Web item tabs to see what is included in the areas

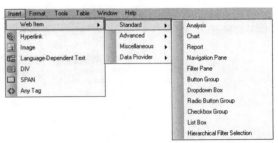

of Standard, Advanced, Miscellaneous or DataProvider. Using this approach wherever you have placed your cursor is where the Web item will be inserted into the Layout screen. As the illustration shows, Insert | Web Item basically is the Web Items screen area in menu form. Table 3-5 lists and briefly describes the Insert menu options.

Format Menu   As you may have noticed, the WAD interface has both a Format menu and a Format toolbar. They offer the same functionality, so we will cover the options here and then simply reference this section when we get to the section covering the Standard, Insert, and Format toolbars. The Format menu functions are very important because, as you build Web reports, you will use them often to help you with the overall look and feel of the Web reports. Options to align text, set the background color, and choose a font size give you tools

to make the display of your information much more focused and personal. You will be using most of these options in the subsequent chapters. Each of the options available here can be applied to specific sections or areas of the Web template or by specific Web items so whatever you choose here doesn't control the entire Web template format but only the items or portion that you define (except for Background Color). The illustration shows the basic list of components and the Background Color palette, and Table 3-6 lists and briefly describes all the Format menu options.

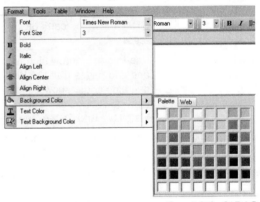

Tools Menu   The Tools menu, shown next, provides an easy way to access the major WAD tools. Table 3-7 lists and briefly describes the different Tools menu options.

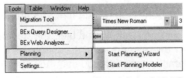

Menu Option	Description
Web Item	Use this function to insert Web items from the various Web item groupings into a Web template. The options found here are exactly the same as those found in the Web Item areas under each of the headings.
Hyperlink	Use this function to insert hyperlinks into your Web templates.
Image	Use this function to insert pictures into your Web templates.
Language-Dependent Text	Use this function to insert language-dependent text into your Web templates.
DIV	Use this function to insert <DIV> tags into your Web templates.
SPAN	Use this function to insert <SPAN> tags into your Web templates.
Any Tag	Use this function to insert favorite tags into your Web templates. The available tags are given in a dropdown box.

TABLE 3-5   Components of the Insert Menu

Table Menu   This menu gives you the basic options to create a table or adjust the formatting of an existing table. We will be using the Table menu quite a bit in latter chapters to help us with positioning of Web items. After you insert a table object into the Web template, you can perform the usual table manipulations from this menu, such as add or delete a column or row.

Menu Option	Description
Font	Use this function to determine the font of the texts that you insert into your Web templates. All normal fonts are available.
Font Size	Use this function to select the font size of the texts that you insert into your Web templates.
Bold	Use this function to format text as bold.
Italic	Use this function to format text as italic.
Align	**Left Align** Use this function to left-align objects. **Center** Use this function to center objects. **Right Align** Use this function to right-align objects.
Background Color	Use this function to specify the background color of the Web template. The Web Tab portion of this context menu offers additional customized colors to use.
Text Color	Use this function to specify the color of the texts that you insert into your Web templates. To use this you will need to highlight the Text that it is to be applied, then the Text Color will change to your choice.
Text Background Color	Use this function to specify the background color of the texts that you insert into your Web templates.

TABLE 3-6   Components of the Format Menu

Menu Option	Description
Migration Tool	Use this function to convert Web templates from SAP BW 3.x to Web templates from SAP NetWeaver 7.0. Chapter 8 reviews this component process in detail.
BEx Query Designer	Use this function to call the BEx Query Designer to define queries.
BEx Web Analyzer	Use this function to call the BEx Web Analyzer to define a new query view.
Planning	Use this function to access BI Integrated Planning functions: **Start Planning Wizard** Use this function to open the Planning Wizard, which supports you when using planning modeling for the first time. **Start Planning Modeler** Use this function to open the Planning Modeler, which you can use to model (configure), administer, and test all the metadata that belongs to a planning scenario.
Settings	Choosing this option will open up a dialog box with the setting of the WAD that have been predefined. You can adjust them from here if needed. Use this function to make the settings for the WAD: **HTML Documentation** Here, you can specify a link to any online or offline HTML documentation that you may need when editing the HTML (such as when inserting HTML tags). **Metadata** In addition to specifying the directory for the metadata, you can update the metadata or refresh the metadata **Errors and Trace Options** Here, you can determine the refresh time for the Errors and Warnings screen area and set the trace level that determines the granularity of the recording.

TABLE 3-7 Components of the Tools Menu

Of course, you can perform the same activities directly in the Web template. Table 3-8 lists and briefly describes the Table menu options.

Copyright by SAP AG

Window Menu This menu at the right provides options to help you organize the overall look and feel of the actual WAD screen. It doesn't have much to do with the functionality and capabilities of the Web-based objects. The functionality is more apparent once you get several screens going in your WAD process. Once additional screens or templates are available you can navigate between them using this option. Table 3-9 lists and briefly describes the features.

Copyright by SAP AG

Help Menu The Help menu enables the business user to get help from the http://help.sap.com Web site at any time. Developers definitely use it from time to time to help solve or validate the processes and configuration they are executing. Table 3-10 describes its two options.

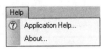

Copyright by SAP AG

Menu Option	Description
Insert Table	Use this function to insert an HTML table into your Web template. Note that to display HTML tables without frames in layout view, the frames display must be switched on. Once you choose this option a dialog box will be displayed and the primary option here is to define the number of rows and columns to the table.
Insert Row	Use this function to insert a row into an inserted HTML table. First click on the row under which the additional row should be inserted.
Insert Column	Use this function to insert a column into an inserted HTML table. First click on the column to the right of which the additional column should be inserted.
Delete Row	Use this function to delete a row from an HTML table. First click on the line to be deleted.
Delete Column	Use this function to delete a column from an HTML table. First click on the column to be deleted.
Merge Cells	Use this function to merge cells in an HTML table. First enter texts in the cells that you want to merge, and then select these cells and choose Merge Cells.
Split Cells	Use this function to split a cell that you created by merging other cells.

TABLE 3-8   Components of the Table Menu

Menu Option	Description
Cascading	Use this function to arrange the various screen areas of the WAD so that they overlap.
Horizontally	Use this function to arrange the various screen areas of the WAD horizontally.
Vertically	Use this function to arrange the various screen areas of the WAD vertically.
Select Web Template	Use this function to open the Select Web Template window. You can create new Web templates or select existing ones from this window. Furthermore, the Web templates that you currently have open in the WAD are executed under the context menu entry.

TABLE 3-9   Components of the Window Menu

Menu Option	Description
Application Help	Use this function to view the SAP NetWeaver online documentation. The Web Application Design: BEx Web Application Designer section in the documentation for the Business Explorer is displayed automatically. This is a standard feature with all SAP components.
About	Use this function to see the release of the Web Application Designer with the number of the patch and the revision.

TABLE 3-10   Components of the Help Menu

Web Application Component Toolbars: Standard, Insert, and Format

The three toolbars available within the WAD environment offer an alternative way to perform many of the same functions available in the menus previously discussed. For example, the Insert toolbar has the same functions and features as the Insert menu. If you decide to use this toolbar rather than the menu, you have to get used to scrolling across the icons to identify via a tooltip what their names are, whereas in the menu, the names of the functions are immediately available alongside the icon.

The Standard toolbar is the only one of the three toolbars that incorporates functions from two different menus. The Standard toolbar combines most of the functions from the Web Template and Edit menus. The Standard toolbar includes all the functions available in the Edit menu and most functions available in the Web Template menu. Again, whether you work with the toolbar or the menus is a personal preference. I've gotten used to using the two menus and turning off the toolbar. This allows me a bit more room on the template screen for display of the actual WAD templates.

Finally, the Format toolbar at the right, has all the same functions as the Format menu, previously discussed.

0ANALYSIS_PATTERN: Standard Web Template

The initial setup of your Web template is critical to what the final structure of the report will be. SAP offers a number of helpful activities and approaches that make the configuration process in the WAD much easier for you. SAP also provides a great standard Web template, 0ANALYSIS_PATTERN, within the WAD. SAP offers quite a few of these standard-delivered Web templates, but 0ANALYSIS_PATTERN is the granddad of them all. It incorporates over 90 percent of all the Web items into its format and offers a number of different approaches to its use. For example, if a customer requests a very unique format, I start by copying the 0ANALYSIS_PATTERN template and then deleting the parts the customer doesn't need. This approach is easier than building from scratch the components that are needed. 0ANALYSIS_ PATTERN also controls about 80 percent of everything that you can do from the BEx Web Analyzer, so getting used to and comfortable with the functions and makeup of this template is very important. Also remember that since it is standard business content in most cases it will be very effective in terms of performance of the report.

Because 0ANALYSIS_PATTERN is the most comprehensive template in the WAD, we will review some of its features to wrap up this chapter. As you will see, many of the other Web templates that are delivered standard in the WAD are incorporated into this template. For example, the Print function available via the 0ANALYSIS_PATTERN template is actually controlled by another template that is embedded into this template; 0ANALYSIS_ PATTERN_EXPORT controls the Print function and the features available for printing.

For the Web application, the placeholder for the data provider is filled during runtime, and Web items, data providers, and commands are generated at runtime based on the data provider chosen. This allows the use of the Web template by multiple data providers. The 0ANALYSIS_PATTERN template, for example, is used by all default BEx Web Analyzer reports, so this requires that the data provider be filled in at runtime by the current query being executed. In the Web template, you determine from which data provider and in what way (based on the inserted Web items) the BI data is displayed. When a request is sent from a Web application to the application server for ABAP, a Template object is generated, from which the structure of the requested XHTML page is derived. The data provider and Web items are the objects generated on this basis.

0ANALYSIS_PATTERN Interface

We will be working our way through all of the different Web items displayed by the 0ANALYSIS_PATTERN template in later chapters, but at this point I want to introduce some of the components of the template and show you what is possible if you get into the details of the WAD. The following illustration shows just one portion of this Web template.

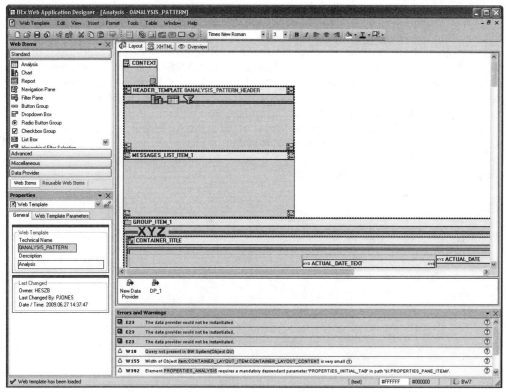

Copyright by SAP AG

First notice that some errors and warnings are already listed in the Errors and Warnings screen area. These refer to the fact that, in this particular Web template, no data providers are assigned. We don't really have to worry to much about this since we're using this Web template for the standard process for all of our BEx Web Analyzer queries.

NOTE   *We will discuss in more detail what a data provider can do for you in terms of chart and graph functionality, but at this point the definition of a data provider has been reviewed in our previous discussion.*

I recommend that, initially, you use this standard Web template until you understand its functionality fully. Then, if necessary, you can tweak this template based on what your company wants to display. If tweaking is required, you might decide to use a Z template rather than change the 0 template. A Z template is a copy of the 0ANALYSIS_PATTERN template with the addition of your company's personalization information. If you decide to go with this approach, you have to make the Z template the default template for all your queries. Again, this is something to review and discuss before configuration, because whatever changes you make will affect all the Web reports for your company. You really want to avoid having multiple Web templates as defaults for different divisions or groups within your corporation. Supporting numerous templates requires too much maintenance and effort. If you can't avoid having multiple Web templates, you can assign the support role for these templates directly to the individual departments, based on the setup of the companies Competency Center for BI.

If you determine that you need to adjust the 0ANALYSIS_PATTERN template for the entire company to meet a critical requirement—such as a disclaimer at the bottom or a corporate logo at the top of all your reports—you need to go into the IMG and insert the required template into the configuration. Normally, the 0ANALYSIS_PATTERN template is the default, but now you want yours to be the default. To do this, go to IMG | SAP Reference IMG | SAP NetWeaver | Business Intelligence | Settings for Reporting and Analysis | BEx Web | Set Standard Web Templates. You will see several options for different templates, but the one you are interested in is the Ad Hoc Analysis field, shown in the following illustration. Inserting your Z template, which is a copy of the 0ANALYSIS_ PATTERN template with the customized changes, into the field will replace the 0 Web template for all BEx Web Analyzer reports.

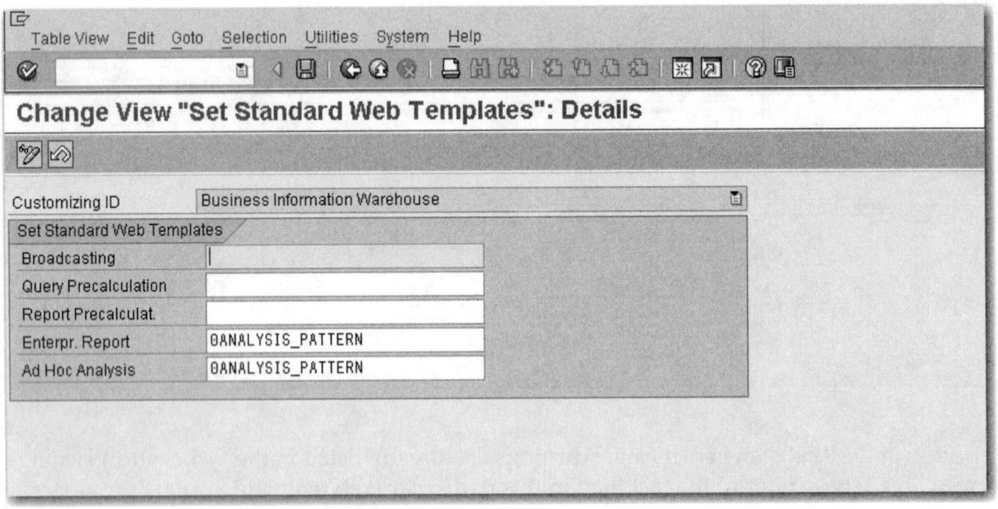

Let's talk for a moment about some of the different components of this standard Web template. The initial screen template that is generated by 0ANALYSIS_PATTERN is shown in the following illustration. This is the Web display of the configuration found in the WAD. This toolbar is what the business user will see based on the standard 0ANALYSIS_PATTERN template we are working with and any changes we might have made. This toolbar offers an impressive amount of functionality that are the standard delivered options built into the Web and available for you from the start of your configuration.

Let's look at just one of the areas of this template to see all the work that goes on behind this toolbar:

1. Scroll down the template configuration about a quarter of the way until you see two containers labeled CONTAINER_LAYOUT_TOOLBAR and TOOLBAR_RIGHT_AREA, as shown next. These two objects control the Web items that you see across the standard template toolbar. Additional Web items are displayed within each of these container areas.

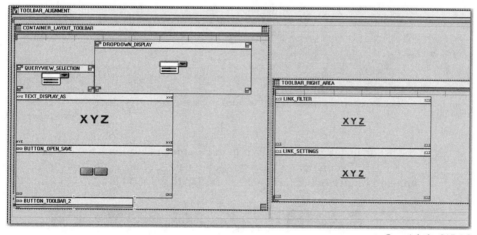

2. Click BUTTON_TOOLBAR_2 in the bottom-left corner and take a look at what is behind the scenes to support this functionality. The Properties screen area changes to show the components of this one item, as shown in the following illustration.

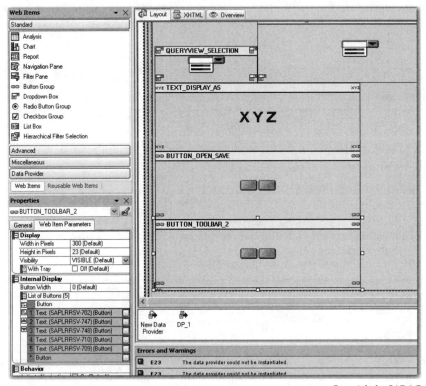

Copyright by SAP AG

3. In the list of Text items on the Web Item Parameters tab, click the third button to open the Edit Parameter dialog box, shown next. In the far right of the row labeled Command (under Action), click the button with a dot on it.

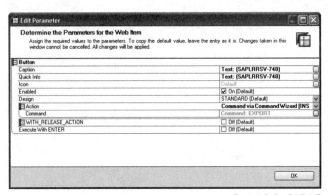

Copyright by SAP AG

4. The Edit Command dialog box opens, shown next. This shows the actual components that make up just that one button on your template toolbar—Print Version. This shows that the Print action will be to a PDF (Default) file and that you need to review another template to see in what format this PDF will be generated. This template is listed at the top of the screen, 0ANALYSIS_PATTERN_EXPORT. As you know, in SAP terminology there are some headings that don't seem to be logical in terms of the English interpretation of the task. In this case we see that the dialog box shows Export Web Application (EXPORT) at the top. Well, this is the SAP-defined term for downloading or exporting the information to a PDF file. You can also see that the PDF is noted on the field for Export Format.

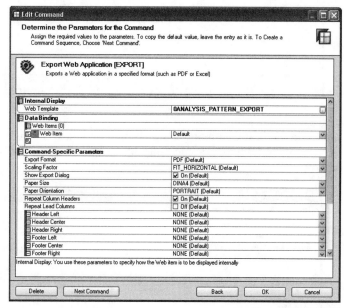

Copyright by SAP AG

0ANALYSIS_PATTERN EXPORT Interface

Now we can continue to drilldown on this portion of the template but needless to say this can be a very complex process. If you drilldown on the template noted above you will see that the format of the PDF will start with some basic information about the variables, then the report name and finally a report of the information. The PDF will not generate a graph or any additional information. If you decide that this is not sufficient for your requirements or that you need to adjust the current format of the PDF, you have two options: tweak the standard content 0ANALYSIS_PATTERN_EXPORT template, or create another template that you have customized and then replace the standard template with your own. This can get a bit tricky, and you may have to go through a few iterations to get this right. Basically, it's just a bit touchy in terms of either changing the standard template or reassigning a new template, but in either case you can alter the look and feel of the Print version of your report.

As a second example, follow the preceding list of steps, but when you get to Step 3, choose the fourth button instead of the third button in the list of Text items. In the Edit

Parameter dialog box that appears, shown next, you can see that this is also an Export action of some sort. Again, click the single-dot button in the far right of the Command row.

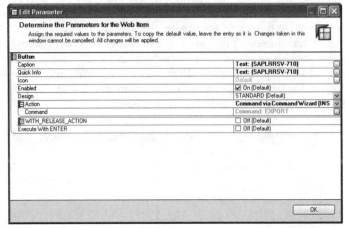

As you can see in the Edit Command dialog box, shown next, this is a bit different from the Print version command but does something similar—export to Excel, as indicated in the Export Format row.

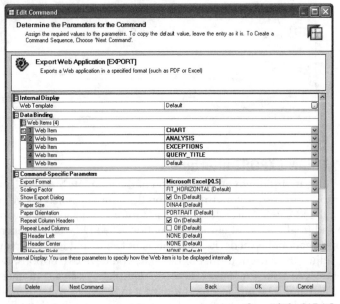

Interestingly, the format of the Excel document is listed in the Data Binding rows above the Export option versus the PDF option. We had to drilldown on another Command to get to the template with these settings. As shown, the Excel document will display a chart, an analysis (report), any exceptions and then the query title. You can easily switch these Web items directly from this dialog box or add to them by using the Web Item Line currently marked Default.

As a final example, go back to Step 2 in the first example, but this time click LINK_SETTINGS (shown in the lower-right corner of the illustration following Step 2). This Web item shows what is behind the functionality of the Settings link on the far right of the toolbar that the business user sees in the Web reports using the standard template. The configuration object for this link is shown in this illustration.

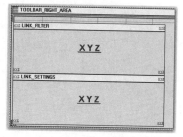

Copyright by SAP AG

Scroll down the screen a bit and you can see that the SETTINGS_TAB lists a series of different Web items, including PROPERTIES_ANALYSIS, PROPERTIES_CHART, EXCEPTIONS, CONDITIONS, and PROPERTIES_DP, as shown in the following illustration.

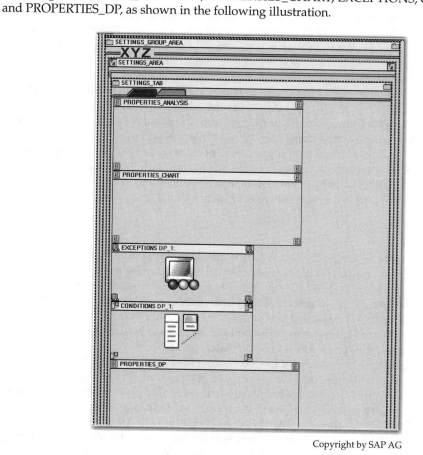

Copyright by SAP AG

If you go to the basic template toolbar and click the Settings link, you will see that each of these Web Items appear as a tab, as shown next.

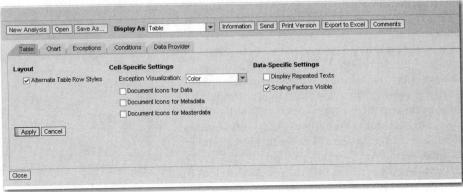

Notice all the different components available for adjusting the settings for just the TABLE object, including the ability to switch the layout and configure both cell- and data-specific settings. This entire configuration is standard delivered by this template. You can now see why using this template and making a copy of it to start any additional formatting is probably not a bad idea.

The preceding examples highlighted just a few of all the items stored within the standard Web template 0ANALYSIS_PATTERN. In the case of this standard Web template, we could go on for quite some time reviewing and digging deeper into the details of each of the Web items. The purpose of these basic examples was to emphasize that you will need to get very familiar with this template to support your configuration. As I mentioned before, if you are going to create a Z template for some reason, a good approach is to start with this standard template, make a copy, and then filter out any of the objects that you don't need. This is better than starting from scratch and trying to build all of this functionality into another template.

Summary

The functionality available via the WAD to enhance your Web reports is very robust and can make your Web reports jump out at the business user instead of putting them to sleep. The functionality included in the BI 7.0 WAD is impressive, and learning how to use it is well worth the time and effort to enhance your reports. This chapter introduced the basic components that you will be using in the WAD. Now that you understand the basics, the advanced functionality and configuration will be much easier to grasp. You will be able to navigate through different configuration approaches and new functions much faster and with more confidence knowing that you are executing the basics correctly. Understanding the basics and actually in time knowing them by heart will improve your final version of a dashboard or report.

The final portion of this chapter dealt with some functionality of Web templates, which is where all the real work will be completed. Specifically, we looked at a small portion of the 0ANALYSIS_PATTERN Web template. We didn't really go into all of the detailed workings of this standard template but if you really want to see the background information just open this template up and switch to the XHTML tab to review the detailed information found behind the scenes that control this template. As you work through the different Web items in the next chapter, you will see just how much detail and functionality has been embedded into this template. You'll find that this toolset is not difficult to work with, and that about 90 percent of all your report requirements will be easily met by the functionality of the WAD.

Advanced Configuration Using the Web Application Designer

Now that you are familiar with the toolbars and overall structure of the WAD, you can start to focus on the actual creation of the WAD template. The first part of this chapter helps you to set up the initial Web template for use in the WAD. It explains the Web template properties and then guides you through the process of creating a custom Web template. The second part of the chapter presents details of all the Web items that you have available to work with in your new Web template, including their parameters. This will take us into a discussion that will include topics on the different Web items themselves. Some of these, such as Text, Information, Input Fields, and Single Documents, are probably familiar to you but others such as Containers, Tab Pages, and others will be somewhat new and we will look at those in more detail. Note that this chapter addresses the use of the WAD strictly from the configuration point of view. It does not cover the details of transferring the finished product, the WAD template, from the WAD into the portal, whether that be a BI portal or some sort of federated portal, so all the processes covered in this chapter take place behind the scenes, out of the sight of business analysts and other users. They see only the end result of the processes, after the Web template has been transferred to the portal.

The coverage of the initial process of using the Web template focuses on what is available once we drag and drop a Web item into the Web Template screen area in the WAD. So, once we move the Web item into the Web Template screen area, what parameter options do we have to influence the formatting and functionality of the Web item such as different pixel sizes, do we want to have a Text line incorporated into the field and what text will show up in that field, and depending on the Web item what characteristics or data provider information will be displayed or influenced? These parameters will be very helpful with the process, especially when you need to position that one Web item in just the right position for the business analyst. Once you get the feel for these options, we can then dig into the actual Web items and see what they offer. As with many different activities in an SAP system, once you understand the initial four or five steps of a configuration process, those steps will be repeated for each of the objects. This is the same approach for the WAD; each one of the many Web items you have to work with will have similar initial steps.

We will start with a basic example of the process of setting up a Web template that has two different Web items. I will refer to this example throughout the chapter. Because this is intended only as an example, we will use two fairly different Web items, the Analysis Web item and the Navigation Pane Web item, to give you a feel for the variety of Web items available. The initial steps to configure any of the different Web items are basically the same; the real differences arise at the very end of the process, when you start the detailed configuration for the specific Web item. So, once we open the new Web template and go through this process, we will be looking more intensely at the ending steps than at the beginning steps.

Another common concept within SAP is the building approach to each of the components. Normally, within all areas of SAP there are several objects that you configure, then collect these objects into one grouping item or format. This approach is used for Web reports as well. The building blocks are the Web templates, which are configured separately, then the Web application is configured with the Web templates being the items to incorporate into the building of the Web application. So as we work with a Web template, you are in fact working within a Web application. I will not dwell on the Web application too much because that starts to move us into the whole area of final display via the portal, which is an entirely different topic, but where necessary I will focus on the configuration side of the Web application component in terms of its connection with the Web template.

My normal approach to defining a chapter is to work through the basic and advanced functionality and finish with several examples. In this book I will not follow my normal approach since we will be looking at complete examples in Chapters 6 and 7. So, within the chapters I will stick to the detailed configuration of each Web item, then offer detailed examples later on in the book.

Setting Up the Initial Web Template for Use in the WAD

We can specify the structure of a Web application with a Web template. Using the WAD rather than something like a Notepad approach makes development of the Web items and Web application much easier. If you have been using SAP since the BI 1.2 or 2.1 version (in those days it was known as the BW1.2 or 2.1 version), you probably remember having to use either another third-party Web tool or Notepad to set up the formatting of the Web page (back then it was a Web page rather than a Web application), then reinsert the finished Web page into BI for use on the Web. This was extremely time consuming and labor intensive in the BI environment because for every change that you made, you had to export and then import your changed objects. Now, in the BI 7.0 version, you can insert placeholders for Web items, data providers, and commands into an XHTML document directly within BI. This approach has been available since version 3.0, but now many more standard objects are available to use during the configuration process, and we have very little dependency upon any third-party components.

The XHTML document with the BI-specific placeholders is called a *Web template* and can be edited in the WAD. The HTML page that is displayed in the Internet browser is called a *Web application*. Depending on which Web items you have inserted into the Web template and the parameter settings within the Web application, you can have a Web application that contains one or more tables, charts, maps, dropdown boxes, and so on.

A Web template is the mainstay of a Web application and contains placeholders for Web items, data providers, commands, and basically any other Web objects that require links to sources of data. For the Web application, the placeholder is filled during run time, and Web items, data providers, and commands are generated. In the Web template, you specify from which data provider and in what way (Web items) the BI data is displayed, which additional operations are possible (commands), and numerous other parameters that you will read about in the "Web Items" section later in the chapter. To process this activity, a request is sent from the Web application to the application server for ABAP, this in turn generates a Template object from which the structure of the requested XHTML page is derived. So, you create a Web template on the application server for ABAP. Once this is executed, the Web applications are started and displayed in the portal, which in turn runs in a Web browser sourced from the Java server.

Web Template Properties

The Web template properties are the parameters that control activities for the Web application for the entire object. So, these settings are critical to the overall mechanics of the Web application; they aren't focused on a specific Web item, but rather are "global" settings for the Web template. You can specify the properties for your Web application in each Web template. This is where you start to get into all the parameter settings assigned to each of the Web applications. You'll discover in this chapter just how many different parameters you have to work with. You'll also see that if one of these parameters is not set correctly, functions available from the Web application will not work correctly. A good example of this is the functionality of the variables screen, which is part of the Web application parameters (see Table 4-1). If your data provider has variables, you will want them to work a certain way, and this is where you can set the parameters to control the format and functionality. Another component that you can control from this properties panel at right is whether or not messages are displayed in the Web application. The properties are set, as with all Web items, using the associated parameters.

The Web template properties are defined in Table 4-1, presented in the order in which they appear on the Web Template Parameters tab, shown in this illustration at right. The comment in upper case shows what, in most cases, will appear in the description text if you click on the parameter in the properties box.

Grouping	Parameter	Description
Internal Display	Warnings Visible (WARNINGS_VISIBLE)	You use this parameter to specify whether messages based on warnings are to be displayed in the Web application.
	Information Visible (INFORMATION_VISIBLE)	You use this parameter to specify whether messages based on information are to be displayed in the Web application.
	System Messages Visible (SYSTEM_MESSAGES_VISIBLE)	You use this parameter to specify whether messages based on system messages are to be displayed in the Web application. You can also select a value for Display Mode for System Messages (SYSTEM_MESSAGES_DISPLAY_MODE): • Always Display Messages (ALWAYS) and (DEFAULT) • Display Messages Once a Day (ONCE_A_DAY)
Behavior	Display Variable Screen (DISPLAY_VARIABLE_SCREEN)	This allows input-ready variables to be called and visible in the Web template. You use this parameter to force display of the variable screen. If this parameter is not set, the variable screen is suppressed when possible; however, it is displayed if input-ready mandatory variables have not been filled.
	Use Specific Variant Catalog (USE_SPECIFIC_VARIANT_CATALOG)	Relevant when calling a Web template that contains one or more query views with input-ready variables that have variants. Using this parameter, you can use the variant catalog for the queries used. If the Web application contains just one query, you can use the variants for this query.
	Reset Variable Values to Default (CLEAR_VARIABLES)	Relevant when calling a Web template that contains one or more query views with input-ready variables. This resets the values within the variable to the default values from the variable definition.
	Display Same Variable Only Once (MELT_VARIABLES)	Relevant when calling a Web template that contains multiple query views with input-ready variables. You use this parameter to specify for the variable screen whether variables that are used in all the query views and in the same context (same compounding and initial value) are to be displayed for input just once. Realize that these variables must have the same parameters and same technical name. If the variables are based on different InfoProviders, the input help is read from the master data table.
	Show Personalized Variables (SHOW_PERSONALIZED_VARIABLES)	You use this parameter to specify whether the personalized variable values are already displayed as initial in the General Variables screen area and saved in the Personalization Data Store Object.

TABLE 4-1   Parameters Available for the Web Template Properties

Grouping	Parameter	Description
	Web Template Has Main Object (TEMPLATE_HAS_MAIN_OBJECT)	You use this parameter to define a main object for a Web template and use it for personalization (for example, for generic Web templates) or the Text Web item. You can use reports (report default template), or query views (query view template) as main objects. If you activate this parameter, you specify the Web template MAIN_TEMPLATE_OBJECT) as the main object: • Data Provider—The main object is a data provider. Specify the relevant data provider. • Web Item—The main object is a Web item. It is particularly useful to use the Report Web item.
	RRI Open Mode (RRI_OPEN_MODE)	You use this parameter to specify how the jump target for the report-report interface (RRI) is to be opened. • Open in Separate Window (OPEN_IN_SEPARATE_WINDOW) • Replace Current Web Application (REPLACE_WEB_APPLICATION) • Replace the Parent Frame of the Current Web Application (REPLACE_PARENT_FRAME) • Replace the Top Frame of the Frameset (REPLACE_TOP_FRAME) • Open in Named Window (OPEN_IN_NAMED_WINDOW) You specify the name of the window in the parameter WINDOW_NAME. • Replace Named Frame (REPLACE_NAMED_FRAME) You specify the name of the frame in the parameter FRAME_NAME.
	Use Personalization (USE_PERSONALIZATION)	You use this parameter to specify whether a personalized or non-personalized Web template is to be used. This will allow the option for Personalization to show up on the Web template.
	Standard Actions of the Web Template (WEB_TEMPLATE_ACTIONS)	You use this parameter to specify a command sequence that is to be executed at specific times on the server. The following times are currently supported: • Action Before Rendering (ACTION_BEFORE_RENDERING) The command sequence is always executed before a Web application is rendered. This allows you, for example, to set UI elements as active or visible depending on the status of Web items.

TABLE 4-1   Parameters Available for the Web Template Properties (*continued*)

Grouping	Parameter	Description
	Standard Actions of the Web Template (WEB_TEMPLATE_ACTIONS) (*continued*)	• Action Before First Display (ACTION_BEFORE_ FIRST_RENDERING) The command sequence is always executed once before a Web application is first rendered. By executing this command sequence once, you can use this command sequence to adjust the initial state of data providers.
	Status-free Navigation (STATELESS)	The status is removed on the server after each navigation step. Using this parameter is only recommended with pages that are rarely navigated to. Between two navigation steps, the status of the Web application on J2EE and ABAP is not retained in the main memory. During a navigation step, however, additional computing effort arises in order to restore the status at the beginning of the navigation step and to remove the status at the end of the navigation step. This makes navigation slower for the user due to the additional computing effort. As users generally pause between two navigation steps.
Data Binding	Variant (VARIANT)	You use this parameter to specify the variant with which the Web application is to be executed.
	Document Save Level for InfoProvider Data (DOCUMENT_SAVE_LEVEL)	You use this parameter to specify for which area of the InfoProvider data the documents are to be created: • Query Level (0) New documents are assigned to the current InfoProvider and the current query (that is, the query on which the data provider is based). The documents are not displayed in other Web applications based on other queries, even if the selections are otherwise identical. • InfoProvider Level (1) New documents are assigned only to the current InfoProvider. The documents are displayed in other Web applications based on other queries, but only if the additional selections match and the queries are based on the same InfoProvider. ***Note*** For BI-IP—Planning applications are typically created for the InfoProvider level: plan data is generally recorded with other data and later evaluated. If you create comments that are also to be visible for the analysis, you have to choose InfoProvider level for the planning application.

TABLE 4-1 Parameters Available for the Web Template Properties (*continued*)

From a technical standpoint, Web template parameters that we talked about in Table 4-1 are Web items. The Web item is not included in the list of Web items in the WAD, but is available in the Properties screen area in the WAD. From the dropdown box in the header of the Properties screen area, choose the Web template for which you want to make the settings.

Web Template Formatting Components

Before you start using the Web items, there are additional activities that you can perform to help with the formatting process within the Web template. One approach that you can use is to arrange Web items on the page. You can perform numerous activities, such as:

- Change the size of the placeholders. You can see what effect resizing a Web item in a Web application has by looking at the values, shown in the XHTML view by the parameters Height and Width for the corresponding Web item.
- Align the Web items horizontally by setting up the Web template in WAD, as follows:
  - Choose Format | Align Left to left-justify the Web item.
  - Choose Format | Align Right to right-justify the Web item.
  - Choose Format | Align Center to center the Web item.
- Change the position of a Web item in the Web template by dragging and dropping it into the required position.
- Place several Web items next to each other. To do so, you have to take the width of the Web template into account. If the Web template is wide enough for a second Web item, this is positioned to the right of the first Web item because the Web browser breaks up pages according to standard HTML.

One of my favorite approaches to formatting before I start to use the Web items is to create an HTML table and arrange the Web items using this component. You can use an HTML table to arrange Web items optimally next to and below one another. You can apply this grid as required. To accomplish this in the WAD:

1. Choose Table | Insert Table.
2. Set up the table according to your settings and requirements.
3. Click OK. The table is inserted into the Web template.
4. You can drag different Web items into the individual table cells, depending on whether you want to arrange your Web items horizontally or vertically.

You would also adjust the number of rows and columns that you need to use, as shown in the next illustration.

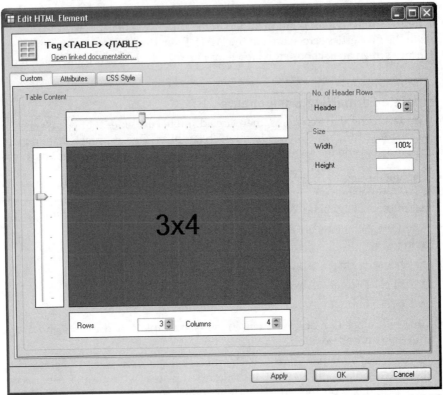

Click OK, and you will see the table format within the Web template, as the following illustration shows.

Don't be concerned with the sizing of the table cells. They will expand as needed to accommodate the different Web items.

Along with the ability to adjust and rearrange the Web items, you also have options to enhance the Web templates with simple text that you can insert. This is one of the great enhancements about the WAD from the 3.5 version onward. You can type in information and/or titles, and the WAD will take that information and insert it into the appropriate coding with background color, font changes, and other tweaks to the lettering, and present this in your Web report. Just position the cursor in the Web template where you want to enter the text, and type in the information. Initially, you will need to work with this feature to get comfortable with the outcome, but it's well worth the time and effort. If you use this approach, you don't really have to worry about the use of any Web items for this purpose. This does not mean that the Web items for Text can be replaced with basic text that you type in, but it does offer you a quick and easy approach to entering in some static text for your report headings. The options to adjust the look and feel of the information might include changing Font, Font Size, Bold, Italic, Align Left, Right, and Center, Text Color, and Background Color of the text.

In addition to inserting and arranging Web items and texts, you can insert images, such as corporate logos, into your Web templates. These images are stored in the MIME Repository of the BI server. The system supports GIF, JPG, and BMP formats. To execute this option:

1. Position the cursor where you want to insert an image into the Web template.

2. Right-click and choose Insert | Image, as shown in Figure 4-1.

3. In the Edit HTML Element dialog box for the IMG tag, shown next, click the button with the ellipses, located to the right of the Source field, to access the images in the MIME Repository.

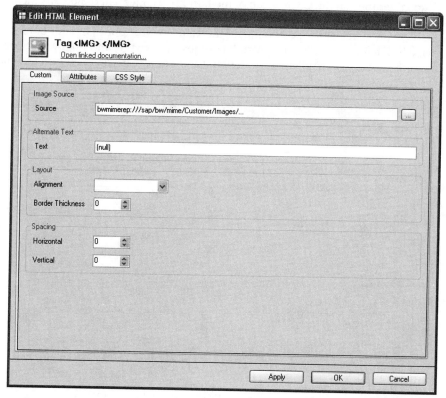

Copyright by SAP AG

4. In the BEx MIME Browser, shown in Figure 4-2, pick the image that you want to show in the Web report and click Insert. (Of course, the image you want to use must already be stored in the BW SAP MIME Repository.)

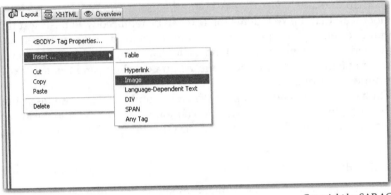

FIGURE 4-1   The right-click context menu of the Web template

Additional settings on the Custom tab of the Edit HTML Element dialog box include Alternate Text, which enables you to enter additional text for titles; Layout Alignment, which enables you to adjust the positioning of the image on the report; Layout Border Thickness, which helps you adjust the overall outline of the image; and finally the Spacing settings, which enable you to adjust the horizontal and vertical spacing between the image and other objects.

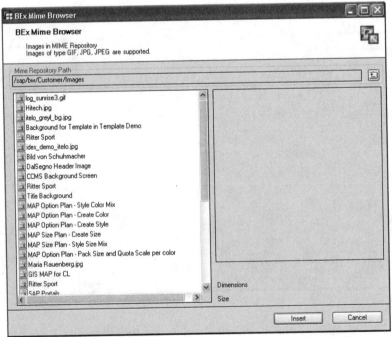

FIGURE 4-2   The BEx Mime Browser

As we mentioned the image insert is found on the context menu from a right-click anywhere in the Web template work area. The different options can help with the overall look and feel of the Web items and as we discussed before, the look and feel of the reports is all important to the business user. Web items and HTML elements (for example, tables, texts, and images) that you insert into a Web template, as well as the Web template itself, all have a context menu. Each context menu has context-sensitive menu entries that you can use to call various WAD functions. You can, for example, use the context menu to save a Web item (for which you have specified properties by using the parameters) as a reusable Web item, call the Properties dialog box for this Web item, copy the Web item and paste it into another Web template, or delete the Web item from the Web template. The options available on the standard context menu, found in most sections of the Web template and shown in Figure 4-1, are listed in Table 4-2.

Insert | Any Tag warrants further comment. This option offers some very useful tags that you can insert into your report. There are over 40 different tags that you can insert, from a simple button to additional components such as an applet. There is some documentation available on each of the tags but I would look to find detailed information about each of the options and what they do from a more Web-based documentation site such as a professional Web design site. For example, the ability to use some applets is still available in the BI 7.0 version, but you need to be careful with the coding required to make them work with XHTML versus HTML. There can be differences in the different object tags being used between the two languages.

Other options that are available from the context menu of the Web item you have previously inserted into your Web template. We will discuss and review the Edit option

Item	Description
<BODY> Tag Properties	If you choose this function, you can edit the <BODY> tag of the Web template.
Insert Table	If you choose this function, you can insert an HTML table into your Web template.
Insert Hyperlink	If you choose this function, you can insert hyperlinks into your Web template.
Insert Image	If you choose this function, you can insert images into your Web template.
Insert Language-Dependent Text	If you choose this function, you can insert language-dependent texts into your Web template.
Insert DIV	If you choose this function, you can insert the <DIV> tag. This allows you to adjust the distance between two objects.
Insert SPAN	If you choose this function, you can insert the <SPAN> tag. This allows you to adjust the sizing of the object.
Insert Any Tag	If you choose this function, you can insert any tag from the list.
Cut, Copy, Paste, Delete	These options work the same as the corresponding options on the Edit menu.

TABLE 4-2   Options Available in the Context Menu for Web Items

later in this chapter since this is actually the Properties dialog box for each of the Web items.

- **Properties** You use this function to call the Properties dialog box for the Web item in the Properties screen area.
- **Save as Reusable Web Item** You use this function to save the Web item as a reusable Web item.
- **Cut, Copy, Paste or Delete** You use this function to cut, copy, paste, or delete all the elements that you have inserted into your Web template (such as Web items, hyperlinks, texts, images, and HTML tables).

You can also merge cells in a table to help arrange Web items horizontally and vertically in the optimum way, without line breaks, using an HTML table. You can apply this grid as required. You can also merge cells that are situated next to each other in the table. To do this you have included an HTML table to your Web template, and then add some text to both cells in the table.

NOTE *SAP recommends that you merge cells in tables only if you have not already inserted Web items.*

Then select the text from both cells and select Table | Merge Cells (the *Merge Cells* menu entry is now active); you now see one cell instead of two.

If you are good at coding using XHTML, you can then go into the XHTML tab on the WAD and edit the source code directly from this location. You can edit the XHTML source code of a Web template directly in the WAD or with an external XHTML editor (as done in the BI 3.0 version and earlier). You can also make changes to the XHTML source in the Layout view of the WAD. Once you have made your adjustments, the system will validate the XHTML against the server when you choose Web Template | Validate on Server in the WAD menu bar. The system checks, where possible, whether the XHTML is syntactically correct. Changes in the XHTML are not added to the Web template during the validation. If errors are found, the correction assistant is displayed. The correction assistant suggests corrections for the errors found. The system *automatically* starts validating the Web template if:

- You switch from the XHTML view in which you edited the XHTML to another view of the WAD.
- You save the Web template.

If you are a really hard-core XHTML expert, you can export the XHTML from the WAD editor into another third-party toolset and adjust it there. Once you finish, you can import it back into the WAD for use and validation. To process a Web template further using an external XHTML editor, choose Web Template | Export to File in the WAD menu bar. Your Web template—that is, the XHTML file—is stored on a file system of your choice. You can call it from there with your XHTML editor. To call a Web template that you have edited in the XHTML editor (that is, the edited XHTML file) in the WAD again and edit it further, store the file on your file system again. In the WAD, choose Web Template | Import from File and specify the name and location of the saved file.

If you are more comfortable with ABAP programs than with getting into the XHTML process, another great option is that you can use an ABAP program that is available in the BI system. To use this ABAP program to make changes to the Web template, proceed as follows:

1. In the menu bar of the SAP Easy Access screen in the BI system, choose System | Services | Reporting (transaction SA38).
2. In the Program field, enter report RS_TEMPLATE_MAINTAIN_70.
3. Enter the name of the Web template that you want to edit.
4. Edit the Web template.

Now that you have reviewed all of these possible functions available in the WAD, you are ready to focus on the actual creation of a Web application. We start with the Web template, which is the key item in the development of the Web application.

Creating a Web Template

As stated previously, the Web template is the starting point for creating a Web application. The Web template is an XHTML document that is used to define the structure of a Web application. It contains placeholders for Web items, data providers, and commands. As we have seen during the design process, you change the Web template by embedding placeholders for Web items and data providers. You can keep track of these changes in the XHTML view. To create a new Web template, you have the following options:

- In the WAD menu, choose Web Template | New. A dialog box appears. Choose Blank Web Template.

- Choose Create New Blank Web Template in the upper area to the right in the initial WAD view.

- In the WAD toolbar, click the New icon (or press CTRL-N) as you can see in the following illustration.

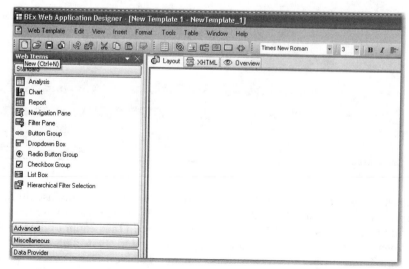

Your next step could be to set the data binding or select the data providers that you will be using. The data for your Web items is provided by data providers that you create in the WAD. You can assign a data provider to multiple Web items. The data provider concept makes it possible to change the data source of a Web item easily. If a particular data provider is assigned to more than one Web item, any changes made affect all the assigned Web items. By means of navigation (by changing the drilldown), the Web item always displays the current drilldown data. Another very important concept to remember here is that if you change the data provider—change the query or InfoProvider—these changes are displayed via the Web items that you've attached this data provider to. So, any changes made will be reflected in the Web template.

There are several ways to create data providers:

- **Use the Data Provider button in the Web Items screen area**   Select whether you want to create a data provider of type Filter or type Query View, and drag the corresponding line into the lower data provider section of the Web Template screen area. The New Data Provider dialog box appears. Assign a name to the data provider and make the remaining settings. Alternatively, you can use the New Data Provider icon in the lower data provider section of the Web Template screen area to assign a data provider to this object. If you need to create additional data providers, double-click the New Data Provider icon to open the New Data Provider dialog box, shown in the following illustration. The small icon with "??" under it that appears in the lower data provider section is a result of dragging and dropping the Data Provider Type from the Web items to the Web template layout screen.

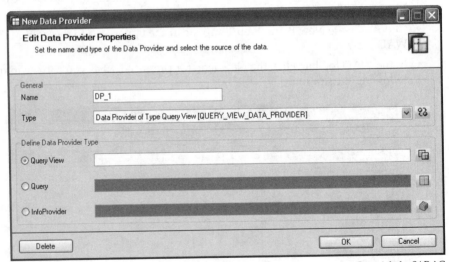

- **Use the General tab in the Properties screen area**   You can only use this option if you have already inserted a Web item into your Web template. To use this option, you first need to select a Web item from the list, so in the header of the Properties screen area, select the Web item for which you want to create a data provider. Then, on the General tab, choose New Data Provider. The New Data Provider dialog box appears. Assign a name to the data provider and make the remaining settings. The standard name that is assigned is DP-X (X = 1, 2, 3, etc) and this is normally accepted as the technical naming convention. The data provider is assigned to the selected Web item. You can also create more than one data provider, as described in the previous bullet. The data providers are listed in the dropdown box under Assigning Data Providers. This enables you to assign a different data provider to the selected Web item. The New Data Provider dialog box appears under data provider <name of assigned data provider>. You can modify or change the settings for the data provider here.

When you have created a data provider, it is assigned to the inserted Web item. Assigning depends on the order of the data providers in the inner structure of the Web template. This can be seen in the following illustration. For this example, I used the Chart Web item. Clicking the New icon to the right of the DP_1 field opens the New Data Provider dialog box, and from there we can assign the data provider.

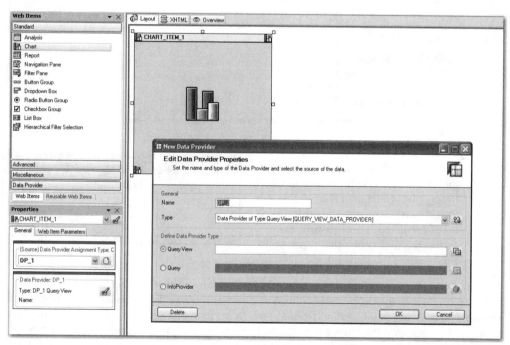

If you want to rename the inserted Web item, proceed as follows:

1. In the Properties screen area, click the Rename Web Item button to the right of the dropdown box in which the added Web items are listed.

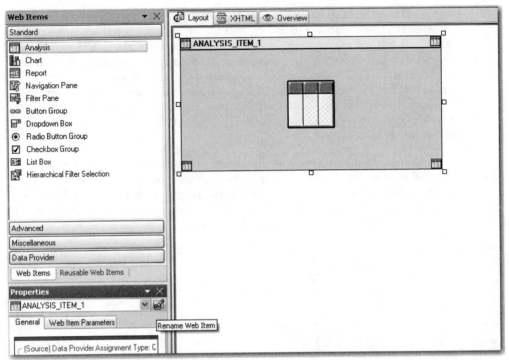

2. Name the Web item by overwriting the predefined text for Name in the Properties screen area next to the dropdown box where the added Web items are listed. This illustration shows the dialog box that pops up to change the Web item's name.

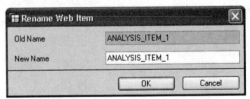

Once you have added the appropriate Web items and formatted them as needed, you then can move into the properties of the Web items and make the necessary adjustments in this area also. When you insert additional Web items using Insert | Web Item, pay attention to where you position the cursor in your Web template. The cursor position determines where the new Web item is inserted. When you insert Web items using drag and drop, the position of the cursor is irrelevant. Make sure that you set the data binding and any Web-item-specific parameter settings for the correct Web item. To make settings for a Web item, select the Web item in the Layout view. In the header of the Properties window, the system displays the Web item for which you can change the settings. As an alternative to selecting the individual Web items, you can use the dropdown box to toggle between the attributes of individual Web items. Once you've completed these activities, you can save your Web application.

In this situation, the Web template becomes a Web application, which means the template is saved on the application server for ABAP and a URL is generated for this Web application. At run time (triggered by calling the URL), the BI tags are replaced by corresponding HTML with the information determined by the Web item and data provider settings. When this is done, the Web template on the application server for ABAP is accessed. Therefore, you must save your Web template before you execute it. Your Web application is started and displayed in the portal, which in turn runs in a Web browser. This information is some additional technical background of what really happens once you start the process of executing this Web template via a Web browser or portal.

Some of the detailed configuration of the parameters that we've talked about in terms of images and formatting could be assigned to you for development. With this in mind it is important that we get more background detail of what we need to do to use these images or formatting components.

Storing and Accessing Images

You've already seen how you can assign an image or picture to your Web template. This section explains how you store those images and pictures and then access them to use in your Web template.

You store all of these objects in the BEx MIME Repository. MIME objects are stored in the MIME Repository on the Web Application Server. On the SAP Easy Access screen in the BI system, choose SAP Menu | Business Explorer | MIME Repository (transaction SE80). MIME objects are stored only in the Web browser cache (client cache). The retention period for MIME objects in the Web browser cache is specified using the back-end profile parameter icm/HTTP/server_cache_0/expiration; the retention period is specified in seconds. The default value for this parameter is 86400, though you can change this value as required. If you want the changes to the MIME objects to take effect before the end of the retention period, you can manually delete the original MIME objects from the Web browser cache. To do this, in your Web browser, choose Tools | Internet Options | General tab | Delete Files.

To include your own images and icons in your Web application, you first have to store them in the MIME Repository. The procedure is fairly straightforward. You can store your MIME objects anywhere in the MIME Repository under SAP | BW. To store MIME objects, right-click a folder and choose Import MIME Objects from the context menu. If you want to set up your own folder, you can just choose Create | Folder and provide the information for the new folder such as name, technical name, etc. You can then add images and icons to that folder and they will be available in the BEx MIME browser, shown earlier in Figure 4-2.

To include your images and icons in Web templates, you use the BEx MIME Browser. There are two ways in which you can include images and icons in your Web templates:

- **Use the Insert menu** In the WAD, choose Insert | Image in the context menu in the Layout view or in the menu bar. The Edit HTML Element dialog box appears. Under Image Source, click the button to the far right with the ellipses (the path to the MIME Repository is entered under Source). The BEx MIME Browser appears. Select one of the images listed and choose Insert. The Edit HTML Element dialog box appears again. Click OK. The selected image is inserted into the Web template.

- **Use Web items**   Some Web items also allow you to use the BEx MIME Browser to include images and icons. For example, for the Tab Pages Web item, click the Tab Panel parameter icon to open the Edit Parameter dialog box, shown here.

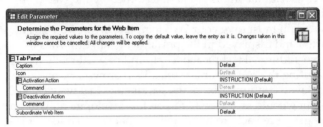

Then choose the Icon (ICON) parameter for the Tab Panel List (TABPANEL_LIST) parameter. The dialog box for selecting the URI (Uniform Resource Identifier) appears as shown here.

Select the Mime Repository Resource radio button. You can either enter the path to the MIME Repository or click the ellipses button. The BEx MIME Browser appears, as shown in Figure 4-2. Select one of the images listed and click Insert. The URI Selector dialog box appears again. Click OK. The selected image is inserted into the tab page.

Use of Themes in the WAD Reports

The process of using themes in WAD reports has changed dramatically in the latest BI version, 7.0. In BI 3.5 and previous versions, the use of themes was controlled by BI itself using cascading style sheets (CSS), but in BI 7.0, this process is managed by the portal rather than BI. In the 3.5 version of BI formatted reports, the Web applications were formatted using CSS. Each of the HTML elements in the Web application has a specific BW style class, which is defined in the style sheet. Style classes contain information about background color, font, font size, font color, borders, spacing, and so on.

In 7.0, the Theme Editor of the portal is used to adjust the formatting of Web applications within the Unified Rendering Framework. The Theme Editor enables you to create themes. These themes determine the visual appearance of the user interface elements of a portal desktop with respect to control elements, font sizes, colors, and contrasts. Style sheets are also created within the Unified Rendering Framework; however, they are generated by the Theme Editor and cannot be changed manually. In the Unified Rendering Framework, it is therefore not possible to use style sheets to adjust the formatting for Web applications. However, you can use the Theme Editor to change style classes. Formatting information for background color, font type, and so on is stored in separate style classes; these style classes can each be changed individually in different areas of the Theme Editor.

In BI 7.0, the appearance of an HTML element is no longer defined using just one style class, but using multiple style classes, such as:

```
<td class="urText, urBackground, urBorder">
```

In this example, multiple style classes define the appearance of a table cell in a Web application. Text, background, and border are distributed across different classes and merged in one tag. You cannot change the style classes directly; you change them using the Theme Editor.

In versions of BI prior to 7.0, the HTML elements use only one style class, such as:

```
<td class="SAPBExStdItem">
```

The style class SAPBExStdItem defines the appearance of a table cell in a Web application. The semantic information is therefore merged in one style class.

Because this process is controlled primarily by the portal team, I will outline the process here. At a high level, using the Theme Editor, you can easily create and introduce a corporate design across various applications. The Theme Editor is a cross-application tool that can be used for all portal applications, and you are no longer required to use external tools or text editors. The Theme Editor contains a preview function that allows you to display the effects of changes instantly. If you move the cursor over the format names, the corresponding area in the preview is highlighted. The Theme Editor generates style sheets automatically. Style sheets cannot be changed because manual changes that are made can potentially be overwritten by the next change in the Theme Editor. Using the Theme Editor, you can define individual formats such as font, color, or background color, but you cannot directly define individual style classes. The Theme Editor uses one or more of these formats to generate a style class. One or more style classes are then used to specify the appearance of an HTML element.

At a more specific, BEx WAD level, themes determine the colors and appearance of the portal desktop. In the portal, content from BI and BEx Web applications is always displayed with the current user's theme. Web applications are created using Web items that use elements from the Unified Rendering Framework. The formatting for these elements, which are also used in the portal, is specified using the Theme Editor. This enables you to format the Button Group, Link, and Analysis Web items by selecting the relevant Button, Link, or Table elements in the left area of the Theme Editor. To change the portal themes, you go to iView System Administration | Portal Display | Portal Theme. Then, using the Theme Editor, you change the formats for the elements. Before you can use a modified portal theme, you must first assign it to the user. Once the portal theme has been assigned, all BEx Web applications for this user are displayed with this changed portal theme.

Configuration of Web Items

Now that we have reviewed the basic initial steps in the use of the Web template and other activities around the Web template process, we can focus on the Web items. Web items will be the mainstay of your Web templates, so you really need to become very familiar with the functionality of the basic Web items and other Web items that you will use frequently. Based on my experience, those typically include the Chart, Analysis, Navigation Pane, Text, and Filters Pane Web items. Over 30 different Web items are available to use during the configuration process, each of which will be discussed in this chapter, but for the initial steps involved we will use only a couple of Web items so that you can get used to the process.

Configuration of a Web Template with Two Web Items

As I mentioned, my favorite initial step when working with Analysis, Navigation Pane, or other Web items that need to be managed in terms of space is to insert a table to help me position the objects, so that's where we'll begin.

1. Choose Table | Insert Table from the menu bar (or use the toolbar) to insert a table.

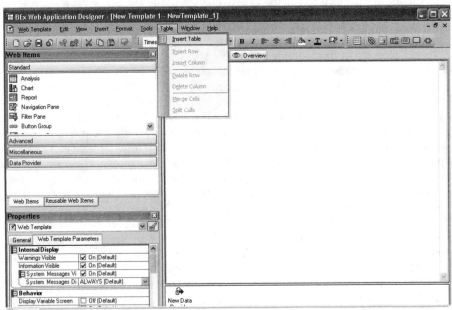

2. In the Edit HTML Element dialog box for the TABLE tag, shown next with the Custom tab displayed, set the table to have two columns and two rows (2×2). (Also notice that this dialog box includes two additional tabs to configure the attributes and CSS style). Click Apply and then OK to go back to the original WAD screen.

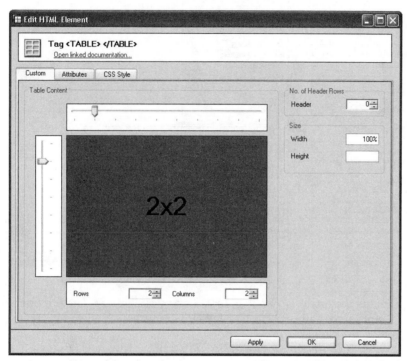

Copyright by SAP AG

NOTE *We just talked about the use of themes in the WAD to manage the entire Web template. This CSS is referencing the specific Web object in this case and if you use this approach you will be formatting each Web item, which will cause quite a bit of additional maintenance per Web item.*

The following shows the results in the Web application template. The table is available for positioning your Web items.

3. Drag and drop the Navigation Pane and Analysis Web items into the appropriate cells in the table, as shown next.

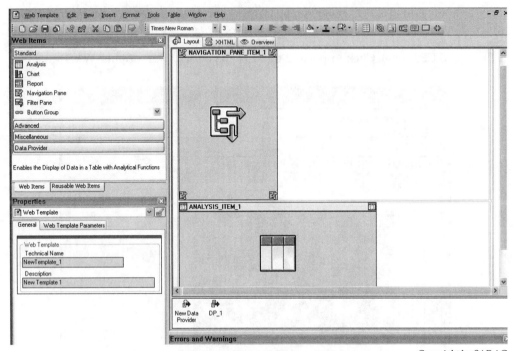

4. Configure the Analysis Web item first. Start by assigning a data provider in the Properties screen area, on the General tab, shown here.

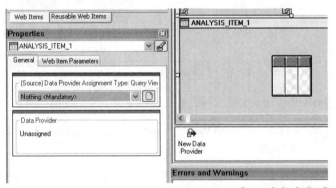

5. Click the New Data Provider icon on the General tab to access the New Data Provider dialog box. Alternatively, you could double-click New Data Provider in the Web Template screen area to open the dialog box.

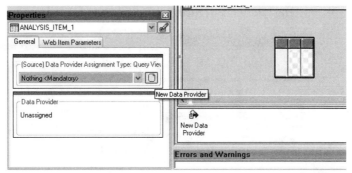

6. The New Data Provider dialog box offers three different options to fill the required data provider: Query View, Query, and InfoProvider. Choose the Query radio button and fill in the field with BWUSER_CUST_Q001, as shown next.

7. Click OK, and the query is assigned, as shown next.

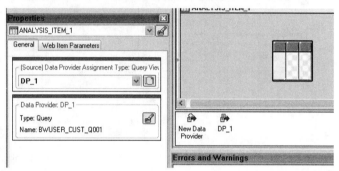

Copyright by SAP AG

8. In the Properties screen area of the ANALYSIS_ITEM, click the Web Item Parameters tab, shown next. Six different areas can be affected from this tab: Display, Internal Display, Behavior, Data Binding, Paging, and Cell Content (scroll down to see the last two). All the different settings are described later in this chapter. Suffice it to say for now that you can alter most of the attributes of the Analysis Web item on this tab. For example, you can change the total pixel size, change the color line by line, adjust navigation, and alter the data provider if required.

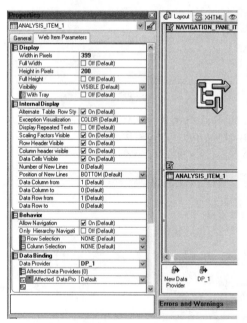

Copyright by SAP AG

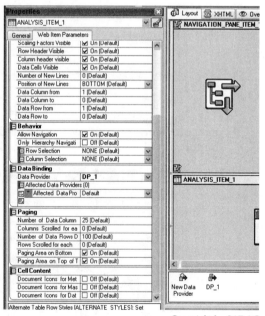

Copyright by SAP AG

9. Now it is time to configure the Navigation Pane Web item. Because you are going to use this navigation pane to help with the query, first assign the DP_1 data provider, as shown next.

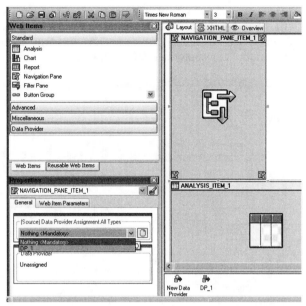

10. Click the Web Item Parameters tab, shown next. You can adjust a series of attributes for the Navigation Pane Web item, including the Display, Internal Display, Behavior, and Data Binding. Generally, this is all you need to do to complete the basic WAD template, but you are going to add a few items to the WAD template.

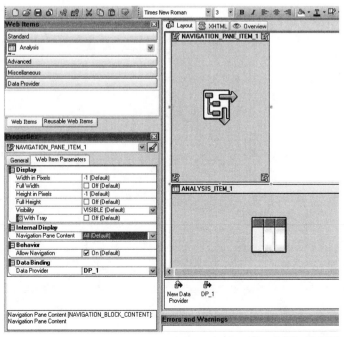

To improve the look and add additional information, you can easily use the Tray function of the Navigation Pane Web item and add a caption. As shown next, under the Display category, check the On indicators for With Tray and under Tray Settings. This opens additional parameters under the Tray Settings field for adding text.

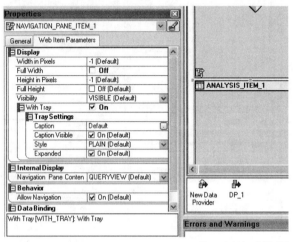

11. Alternatively, you could use a manual approach to adding text. If you use an empty table cell in the Web Template screen area and go to the context menu to Insert | Language-Dependent Text, another dialog box appears. Fill in the additional information BWUSER Customer Query.

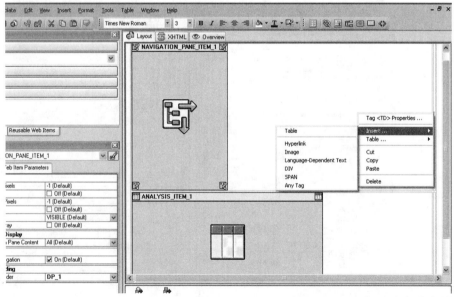

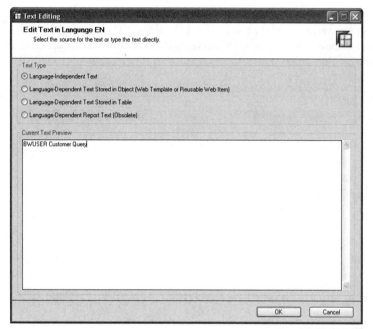

The final result of the preceding configuration steps is shown here in the Layout view.

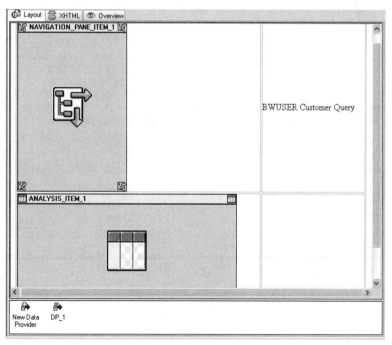

Now we can review the XHTML that was generated in this WAD template by clicking the XHTML tab, shown next. Notice in the middle of the XHTML screen that the two different captions are available. One is "Navigational Pane for Customer Query" and the other is "BWUSER Customer Query."

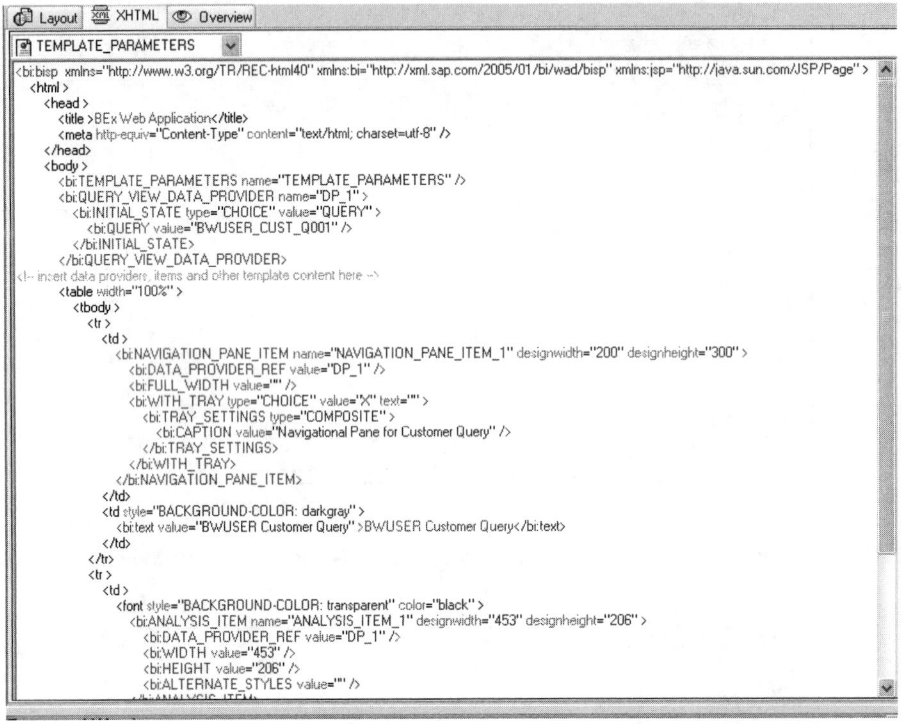

Copyright by SAP AG

Finally, you can execute this example and review the results, shown next. To execute the final view of this Web application, simply use the Execute icon found in the Web template toolbar or in the context menu from Web Template Based | Execute. Based on what you've done to this WAD template so far, it is not ready for prime time yet, but at least you have completed the steps necessary to produce a basic WAD template in short order.

Navigational Pane for Customer Query

- ▼ Columns
  - • Key Figures
- ▼ Rows
  - • Division
  - • Distribution Channel
- ▼ Free characteristics
  - • Sold-to party

BWUSER Customer Query

Division ⇕		Distribution Channel ⇕		Incoming Orders ⇕	Order Entry Quantity ⇕
				EUR	
00	Cross-division	10	Final customer sales	9.000,00	15 PC
		12	Sold for resale	25.500,00	30 PC
		14	Service	8.155,10	0 AU
		Result		42.655,10	45 PC
01	Pumps	10	Final customer sales	45.102.784,12	14.897 PC
		Result		45.102.784,12	14.897 PC
02	Motorcycles	12	Sold for resale	57.846.845,32	195.279 PC
		Result		57.846.845,32	195.279 PC
04	Lighting	12	Sold for resale	67.656.161,73	168.239 CAR
		Result		67.656.161,73	168.239 CAR
07	High Tech	10	Final customer sales	52.428.399,72	231.477 PC
		12	Sold for resale	56.095.407,88	62.028 PC
		14	Service	17.532,20	27 PC
		16	Factory sales	0,00	0 PC
		Result		108.541.339,80	293.532 PC
08	Service	14	Service	2.351.003,56	0 AU
		Result		2.351.003,56	0 AU
10	Vehicles	12	Sold for resale	79.577,48	3 PC

As you saw in this example, many different parameters are configurable for each of the Web items and, depending on how complex the data provider is, the impact of these settings will be more critical to the final display of the WAD template. The data provider is something that we will be running into most of the time with the creation of these Web templates and as mentioned, almost every Web template will have at least one data provider, and most of the Web items may have their own data provider. Data providers can be either a Filter or a Query View type. Data providers of the Filter type usually provide data for Web items that are related to restricting data, such as the dropdown box or the radio button groups. They cannot be used with Web items that display the results of a query or query view, such as the Analysis and Chart Web items. The more common data provider is the Query View type, which can reference queries, query views, and InfoProviders.

The process of assigning a data provider is called *data binding*. You did this for both the Analysis and Navigation Pane Web items in the example. In the previous example we showed the two locations for data binding. For some Web items such as the Commands, the data binding can be done directly in the command wizard. We will review the parameters of the command wizard later in this chapter.

As you will see, the majority of the time spent in the process of setting up a Web template is not in the identification of the Web items you need. Instead, after the items are assigned to the Web template, the process of confirming all the settings and parameters for each Web item can be quite time-consuming. These parameters can change the overall look of the object if not correctly formatted. For example, if the pixels for different screens are not consistent, you will be viewing reports that only fill a portion of the screen rather than sharing the screen equally and filling the entire screen. So, bear that in mind while reviewing each of the objects. Some are straightforward in their setup, but others have numerous parameters. Understanding what each does is very important.

Groups of Web Items

This section reviews all the Web items and the major parameters for each. This information is extensive, but you will find that having a reference guide can be invaluable to the setup process.

Web items are objects that either display data in a Web application or are used to design Web applications. These objects are represented by generated HTML at runtime. Web items that display data must be connected to a data provider. All Web items have parameters such as header, width, and height that can be used to define the appearance of the Web items, as well as their behavior in the Web application. Each of the Web items, once positioned in the Web template, have a default setting for each parameter. There are a number of instances where you can adjust these parameters such as at design time, in the WAD using the parameter settings or at run time, in Web applications using the property dialog boxes for the Web item, or using commands from the Web Design API. If the data, the navigational state, or the parameters change, the HTML for the Web item is regenerated.

NOTE *There will be a number of references in each of the Web item descriptions and configuration to the use of the Command Options in the list of Web items. The Command Option will be discussed in a separate section, "Command Wizard," and it will be applicable to all sections.*

There are several ways that we could approach the discussion of these Web items. One approach would be to address the different objects based on responsibilities or functionality. For example, we could group together the Web items used to format the Web template, such as Tab Pages, Groups, Containers, and Container Layout, and then group together the Web items used for generating text or information, such as Data Provider, Text, Information Field, and System Messages. But we will use the most direct approach, which is to go through these items based on how they are grouped within the WAD in the Web Items screen area. The Web items are broken down into the following groupings:

- **Standard**   Analysis, Chart, Report, Navigation Pane, Filter Pane, Button Group, Dropdown Box, Radio Button Group, Checkbox Group, List Box, and Hierarchical Filter Selection

- **Advanced**   Web Template, Container Layout, Container, Tab Pages, Group, Single Document, List of Documents, Map, System Messages, Info Field, Input Field

- **Miscellaneous**   List of Conditions, Data Provider – Information, List of Exceptions, Text, Link, Menu Bar, Properties Pane, Ticker, Context Menu, Script, Custom Extension

---

NOTE *Two of the Web items are not discussed together with the other Web items in their respective category.*
First, the Map Web item in the Advanced category includes a large amount of configuration that is non-Web application functionality (configuration using GIS), making its coverage beyond the scope of the book. For more information, check out my book SAP Business Information Warehouse Reporting *(McGraw-Hill/Professional, 2008).*
Second, the Chart Web item (configuration using Excel Chart objects) in the Standard group will be discussed in the following chapter.

The preceding Web items are also available as master Web items in the Web Items window in the BEx WAD. You choose a master Web item from the list, assign a data provider to the Web item, if necessary, and set the parameters. You then have created your own Web item, which you can add to your Web template or save for later use.

Standard Web Items

If we look at this group we see the Web items that are consistently used the most in the process of setting up either Web templates or dashboards or just simple groups of reports. These Web items have also been around the longest of all of the options that are available in the WAD. If you were to mention any of the different Web items to someone who has been around Business Intelligence for a time they would be able to very quickly understand what functionality these Web items bring to the table. On the other hand many of the Web items in the Advanced and Miscellaneous are new to the 3.x or 7.0 version of BI or are a bit more involved in their responsibilities. Let's take a closer look at each of the Web items in the Standard Web Items group.

Analysis   The Analysis Web item displays the values of a data provider in the Web application in a table or report format. A similar list of functionalities used in the BEx Analyzer is supported. You may find some minor differences but the overall functionality and process is the same. The characteristics and structures can be displayed in both rows and columns. The ability to drilldown in a similar manner as the BEx Analyzer is also supported. This is one of the most commonly used Web items. Table 4-3 lists and describes the parameters for the Analysis Web item, arranged according to the various parameter groupings. The list of parameters in the system is shown in the following illustrations.

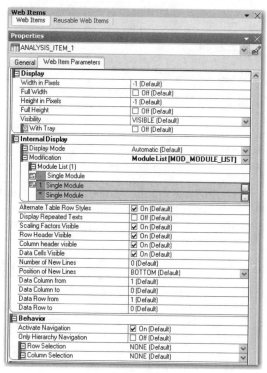

Copyright by SAP AG

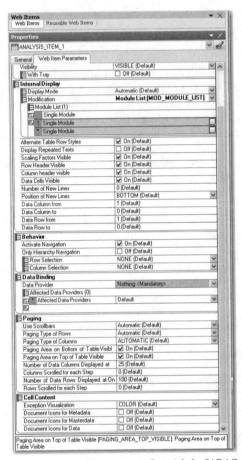

Copyright by SAP AG

Parameter	Description
DISPLAY	
Width in Pixels (WIDTH)	You use this parameter to specify the width of the Web item.
Full Width (FULL_WIDTH)	You use this parameter to specify that the value in the Width in Pixels (WIDTH) parameter is to be ignored and that the width is to be set to 100% instead.
Height in Pixels (HEIGHT)	You use this parameter to specify the height of the Web item.
Full Height (FULL_HEIGHT)	You use this parameter to specify that the value in the Height in Pixels (HEIGHT) parameter is to be ignored and that the height is to be set to 100% instead.
Visibility (VISIBILITY)	You use this parameter to specify whether the Web item is to be visible in the Web application.
With Tray (WITH_TRAY)	You use this parameter to specify whether the Analysis Web item is to have an icon that allows the Web item to be expanded and collapsed.

TABLE 4-3   Parameters for the Analysis Web Item (*continued*)

Parameter	Description
INTERNAL DISPLAY	**Description**
Display Mode (ANALYSIS_ITEM_MODE)	You use this parameter to specify in which mode the Analysis Web item is to be displayed: The following options are available: <ul><li>Automatic (AIM_AUTOMATIC)—The system automatically selects the most suitable mode for the Analysis Web item.</li><li>Standard Analysis Grid (AIM_STANDARD_GRID)—The default display is used to display the Analysis Web item.</li><li>Plain HTML (AIM_PLAIN_HTML)—The Analysis Web item is displayed as plain HTML. This mode is particularly suitable for displaying large amounts of data quickly or for accessing data using JavaScript. For example, you can hide the Analysis Web item in an application and access the data by using JavaScript.</li></ul>
Modification (MODIFICATION)	This parameter provides a generic interface for changing the Analysis Web item. This enables you to use similar options to those available in earlier releases with the Web Design API for Tables.
Alternate Table Row Styles (ALTERNATE_STYLES)	You use this parameter to specify whether the styles for the odd and even table rows are to alternate and be displayed in a striped list.
Display Repeated Texts (REPEATED_TEXTS_DISPLAYED)	You use this parameter to specify whether repeated texts or keys are to be displayed more then once or whether the repetitions are to be suppressed and the cells merged.
Scaling Factors Visible (SCALING_FACTORS_VISIBLE)	You use this parameter to specify whether the scaling factors are to be displayed, if supported.
Row Header Visible (ROW_HEADER_VISIBLE)	You use this parameter to specify whether the row header area is to be displayed. The row header area displays the labels to the left of the data.
Column Header Visible (COLUMN_HEADER_VISIBLE)	You use this parameter to specify whether the column header area is to be displayed. The column headers display the labels above the data.
Data Cells Visible (DATA_CELLS_VISIBLE)	You use this parameter to specify whether the data cells are to be displayed.
Number of New Lines (NEW_LINES_COUNT)	You use this parameter to insert any required number of empty rows into the table. The parameter is set to 0 by default.
Position of New Lines (NEW_LINES_POSITION)	You use this parameter to specify the position at which the additional empty rows are to be inserted. You can select from TOP or BOTTOM.
Data Column From (DATA_COLUMN_FROM)	You use this parameter to specify the data column from which the data is to be displayed. The parameter is set to 1 by default. The setting for this parameter is independent of the setting for the Data Column To (DATA_COLUMN_TO) parameter.

TABLE 4-3 Parameters for the Analysis Web Item (*continued*)

Parameter	Description
INTERNAL DISPLAY	**Description**
Data Column To (DATA_COLUMN_TO)	You use this parameter to specify the data column up to which the data is to be displayed. The parameter is set to 0 by default. If the value is 0, the system tries to display all columns. If there are too many, a scrolling area is inserted. If the value is not 0, data is displayed up to the specified column only. No scrolling area is provided. The setting for this parameter is independent of the setting for the Data Column From (DATA_COLUMN_FROM) parameter.
Data Row From (DATA_ROW_FROM)	You use this parameter to specify the data row from which the data is to be displayed. The parameter is set to 1 by default.
Data Row To (DATA_ROW_TO)	You use this parameter to specify the data row up to which the data is to be displayed. The parameter is set to 0 by default. If the value is 0, the system tries to display all rows. If there are too many, a scrolling area is inserted. If the value is not 0, data is displayed up to the specified row only. No scrolling area is provided.
BEHAVIOR	**Description**
Allow Navigation (INTERACTION_ALLOWED)	You use this parameter to specify whether navigation and other interactions are to be possible in the Web application.
Only Hierarchy Navigation (ONLY_HIERARCHY_NAVIGATION)	You use this parameter to specify whether the context menu is to be hidden and whether expand and collapse options only are to be provided for the list.
Row Selection (SELECT_ROWS)	You use this parameter to specify whether and how many rows the user can select at runtime. You can also use this row selection in commands so that a command can also be executed when rows are selected at runtime. You can choose from the following options: • None (NONE) (default value)—Rows cannot be selected at runtime. • Single (SINGLE)—Users can select one row at runtime. • Single with Commands (SINGLE_WITH_COMMAND)—Users can select one row at runtime. When a row is selected, an activation or deactivation action is executed with a corresponding command. You can either Activate or Deactivate this action. Using the command wizard, you can choose a command that is to be executed when the selected row is activated or deactivated. • Multiple (MULTIPLE)—At runtime, users can select multiple rows.
Column Selection (SELECT_COLUMNS)	You use this parameter to specify whether and how many columns the user can select at runtime. You can also use this column selection in commands so that a command can also be executed when columns are selected at runtime. The options available are the same as those available for the Row Selection parameter (see above).

TABLE 4-3 Parameters for the Analysis Web Item (*continued*)

Parameter	Description
DATA BINDING	**Description**
Data Provider (DATA_PROVIDER_REF)	You use this parameter to assign a data provider to the Web item. The Web item obtains the data and metadata that it needs to generate the output and commands from this data provider. We recommend that you keep to the conventions supported by the Web Application Designer when specifying names: Names can be a maximum of 30 characters and consist of characters A-Z, 0-9 and _, but cannot start or end with _.
Affected Data Providers (LINKED_DATA_PROVIDER_ REF_LIST)	You use this parameter to create a list of data providers to which all commands are sent. For each entry in the data provider list, you select a data provider in the Affected Data Provider parameter (LINKED_DATA_PROVIDER_REF).
PAGING	**Description**
Use Scroll Bars (USE_SCROLLBARS)	You use this parameter to specify whether the Analysis Web item is to contain a scroll bar for page navigation. The following options are available: • Automatic (AUTOMATIC)—The system automatically adds a scroll bar as soon as the table becomes too large for the display area. • Enabled (ENABLED)—The scroll bar is added. • Disabled (DISABLED)—The Analysis Web item is displayed without scroll bars.
Paging Type for Rows (PAGING_TYPE_ROWS)	You use this parameter to specify the scrolling logic in the rows. The following options are available: • Automatic (AUTOMATIC)—The system automatically uses the most suitable scrolling logic, either by page or by row. • By Page (BY_PAGE)—You can scroll through the rows page by page. • By Row (BY_ITEM)—You can scroll through the rows row by row.
Paging Type for Columns (PAGING_TYPE_COLUMNS)	You use this parameter to specify the scrolling logic in the columns. The following options are available: • Automatic (AUTOMATIC)—The system automatically uses the most suitable scrolling logic, either by page or by column. • By Page (BY_PAGE)—You can scroll through the columns page by page. • By Column (BY_ITEM)—You can scroll through the columns column by column.
Paging Area on Bottom of Table Visible (PAGING_AREA_ BOTTOM_VISIBLE)	You use this parameter to specify whether the area for scrolling is to be displayed at the bottom of the table.

TABLE 4-3 Parameters for the Analysis Web Item (*continued*)

Parameter	Description
PAGING	**Description**
Paging Area on Top of Table Visible (PAGING_AREA_TOP_ VISIBLE)	You use this parameter to specify whether the area for scrolling is displayed at the top of the table.
Number of Data Columns Displayed at Once (BLOCK_COLUMNS_SIZE)	You use this parameter to specify the number of data columns to be displayed simultaneously. Once this number is exceeded, a scrolling area is inserted.
Columns Scrolled for Each Step (BLOCK_COLUMNS_ STEP_SIZE)	You use this parameter to specify the scrolling logic you want. For example you can specify the number of data columns to be scrolled for each step. The default setting "0" corresponds to 2/3 of the display columns. The value entered corresponds to the number of columns scrolled through. If you want to scroll through all displayed data columns, enter the same value that you entered for the Number of Data Columns Displayed at Once parameter (BLOCK_ COLUMNS_SIZE).
Number of Data Rows Displayed at Once (BLOCK_ ROWS_SIZE)	You use this parameter to specify the number of data rows to be displayed simultaneously. Once this number is exceeded, a scrolling area is inserted.
Rows Scrolled for Each Step (BLOCK_ROWS_STEP_SIZE)	You use this parameter to specify the scrolling logic you want. For example you can specify the number of data rows scrolled for each step. The default setting "0" corresponds to 2/3 of the display rows. The value entered corresponds to the number of rows scrolled through.
CALL CONTENT	**Description**
Exception Visualization (EXCEPTION_RENDERING)	You use this parameter to specify the display type for exceptions. The following options are available: • Color (COLOR) (default value) • Symbol (SYMBOL) • Symbol and Text (SYMBOL_TEXT) • Text and Symbol (TEXT_SYMBOL)
Document Icons for Metadata (DOCUMENT_ICONS_ METADATA)	You use this parameter to specify whether links to metadata documents are to be displayed.
Document Icons for Master Data (DOCUMENT_ICONS_ MASTERDATA)	You use this parameter to specify whether links to master data documents are to be displayed.
Document Icons for Data (DOCUMENT_ICONS_DATA)	You use this parameter to specify whether links to InfoProvider data documents are to be displayed.

TABLE 4-3   Parameters for the Analysis Web Item (*continued*)

Report   Using the Report Web item, you can insert formatted reports (BEx Web Report Designer reports) into a Web application. This is very useful when it comes to fixed formatted reports such as Profit & Loss Statements and Balance Sheet Statements. In the properties of the Report Web item, the Internal Display – Report Design property is used to specify which BEx reporting object will be displayed. In the case of the BEx Report Designer, the Planning Modeler, and the BEx Query Designer, you can call the component from the WAD and either select an existing object or create another query or report. Table 4-4 lists and describes the parameters for the Report Web item, arranged according to the various parameter groupings. The following illustration shows these parameters in the Properties screen area.

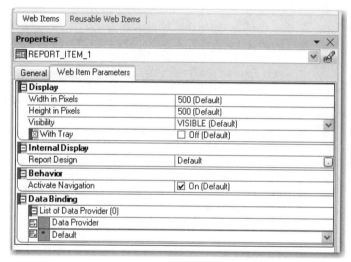

Copyright by SAP AG

Navigation Pane   The Navigation Pane Web item shows the navigation status of a data provider. This is a default Web item in the standard Web template 0ANALYSIS_PATTERN and is used quite heavily. All the characteristics and structures of the data provider are listed. You can alter the navigation status by using drag and drop to drag characteristics or structures to an axis (rows or columns) of the table, or to remove them from the axis. You can swap axes in the navigation pane using drag and drop, and the table changes accordingly. You can also drag characteristics into the filter pane using drag and drop. In the properties of the Navigation Pane Web item, the Navigation Pane Content property (under Internal

Parameter	Description
Display	
Width in Pixels (WIDTH)	You use this parameter to specify the width of the Web item.
Height in Pixels (HEIGHT)	You use this parameter to specify the height of the Web item.
Visibility (VISIBILITY	You use this parameter to specify whether the Web item is to be visible in the Web application.
With Tray (WITH_TRAY)	You use this parameter to specify whether the Web item is to have a symbol that allows the Web item to be expanded and collapsed.
Internal Display	
Report Design (REPORT)	You use this parameter to specify the design of the report. To do this, you select a report. You have the following options: You can enter the name of an existing report beside Report Design. You can call the Report Designer by choosing the pushbutton beside Report Design. In the Report Designer, you can create and save a new report or open an existing report. When you have completed your selection, you close the Report Designer. The name of the report you selected is copied automatically to the field beside Report Design. When you have selected a report, the data provider on which the report is based is listed automatically in the List of Data Providers parameter (REPORT_DATA_BINDING_LIST) (see below) and at the bottom of the Web Template screen area in the layout view of the Web Application Designer.
Behavior	
Allow Navigation (INTERACTION_ALLOWED)	You use this parameter to specify whether navigation or other interaction is to be possible in the Web application.
Data Binding	
List of Data Providers (REPORT_DATA_BINDING_LIST)	You use this parameter to create a list of data providers for the Web item by setting the parameter DATA_PROVIDER_REF for each entry in the list.

TABLE 4-4 Parameters for the Report Web Item

Display) allows you to choose which elements of the assigned data provider will be shown in the Web application.

Table 4-5 lists and describes the parameters for the Navigation Pane Web item, arranged according to the various parameter groupings. The following illustration shows the Navigation Pane Web item parameters in the Properties screen area.

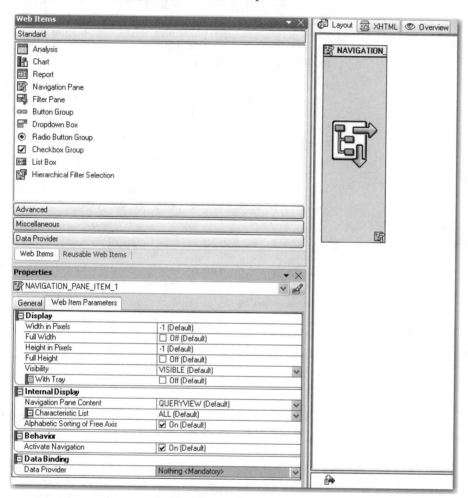

Filter Pane   Using the Filter Pane Web item, you can set filters for individual characteristics. The characteristic values are provided for each characteristic in dropdown boxes. In addition, you can drag characteristics from the navigation pane or the table to the filter pane using

Parameter	Description
Display	
Width in Pixels (WIDTH)	You use this parameter to determine the width of the Web item.
Full Width (FULL_WIDTH)	You use this parameter to determine that the specification in the Width in Pixels (WIDTH) parameter be ignored and that the width be set to 100% instead. The full width depends on the width of the environment in which the Web item is embedded.
Height in Pixels (HEIGHT)	You use this parameter to determine the height of the Web item.
Full Height (FULL_HEIGHT)	You use this parameter to determine that the specification in the Height in Pixels (HEIGHT) parameter be ignored and that the height be set to 100% instead. The full height depends on the height of the environment in which the Web item is embedded.
Visibility (VISIBILITY)	You use this parameter to determine whether the Web item is visible in the Web application.
With Tray (WITH_TRAY)	You use this parameter to determine whether the Navigation Pane Web item has a symbol that allows the Web item to be expanded and collapsed.
Internal Display	
Navigation Pane Content (NAVIGATION_BLOCK_CONTENT)	You use this parameter to determine the characteristics that are displayed in the navigation pane. You have the following selection options: • All: All characteristics are displayed. • Columns: Only the characteristics in the columns are displayed. • Rows: Only the characteristics in the rows are displayed. • Free characteristics: Only the free characteristics are displayed.
Characteristics List (NAV_CHARACTERISTIC_SEL)	You use this parameter to specify which characteristics are displayed in the Free Characteristics part of the navigation pane. You have the following selection options: • All: All characteristics contained in the free characteristics in the query start view are displayed. • List of characteristics: You can select certain characteristics, so that only these characteristics are displayed in the free characteristics.
Alphabetic Sorting of the Free Axis (NAV_FREE_CHAR_SORTING)	You use this parameter to specify that characteristics in the Free Characteristics part of the navigation pane are sorted alphabetically. Otherwise, the characteristics are displayed in the order defined in the query start view in Query Designer. Any characteristics that you move from rows to the free characteristics during navigation in the Web application will be inserted in alphabetical order if you have activated this option. Otherwise, they will be placed at the end of the list.

TABLE 4-5 Parameters for the Navigation Pane Web Item

Parameter	Description
Behavior	
Activate Navigation (INTERACTION_ALLOWED)	You use this parameter to determine whether navigation and other interactions are possible in the Web application.
Data Binding	
Data Provider (DATA_PROVIDER_REF)	See previous discussion in Table 4-3 on Data Provider.

TABLE 4-5   Parameters for the Navigation Pane Web Item (*continued*)

drag and drop. Table 4-6 lists and describes the parameters for the Filter Pane Web item, arranged according to the various parameter groupings. The following illustration shows this Web item in the system.

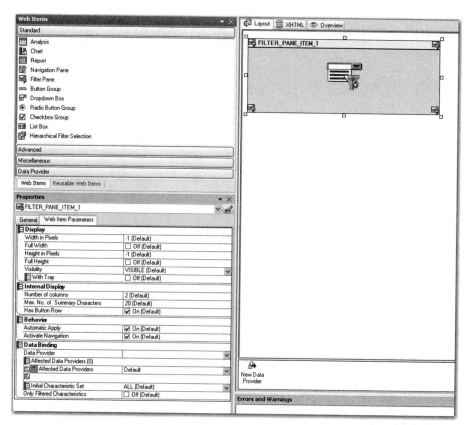

Parameter	Description
Display	
Width in Pixels (WIDTH), Full Width (FULL_WIDTH), Height in Pixels (HEIGHT), Full Height (FULL_HEIGHT), Visibility (VISIBILITY), With Tray (WITH_TRAY)	See Table 4-5; these Display parameter definitions are the same as those for the Navigation Pane Web item.
Internal Display	
Number of Columns (COLUMNS)	You use this parameter to specify the number of entries displayed adjacent to one other.
Max. No. of Summary Characters (MAX_SUMMARY_CHARACTERS)	You use this parameter to specify the maximum number of characteristics for the filter summary field.
Has Button Row (HAS_BUTTON_ROW)	You use this parameter to specify whether the filter pane is to have a pushbutton row.
Behavior	
Allow Navigation (INTERACTION_ALLOWED)	You use this parameter to specify whether navigation and other interaction are to be possible in the Web application.
Automatic Apply (AUTOMATIC_APPLY)	You use this parameter to specify whether the system is to make changes to the data provider automatically.
Data Binding	
Data Provider (DATA_PROVIDER_REF)	See Table 4-3 for the detailed information.
Affected Data Providers (LINKED_DATA_PROVIDER_REF_LIST)	You use this parameter to create a list of data providers to which all commands are sent. For each entry in the data provider list, you select a data provider in the Affected Data Providers parameter (LINKED_DATA_PROVIDER_REF).
Initial Characteristic Set (CHARACTERISTIC_SET)	You use this parameter to specify the initial set of characteristics to be displayed on the Filter Pane. The options are None, All, List of Characteristics, and Axes Selection.
Only Filtered Characteristics	You can define that the only Characteristics that show on this parameter would be the Filtered Characteristic.

TABLE 4-6   Parameters for the Filter Pane Web Item

Button Group   The Button Group is a Web item that can execute one or more commands from the Web Design API, as selected. Using the Button Group Web item, you can add commands from the Web Design API to your Web application. To do this, you define a command or sequence of commands for each button. You can insert any text (language-dependent and language-independent) for the button labels, assign a quick link to them, and specify their design. This Web item is used quite frequently in the Integrated Planning Process within BW. Table 4-7 lists and describes the parameters for the Button Group Web item, arranged according to the various parameter groupings. The following illustration shows the options within the system for this Web item.

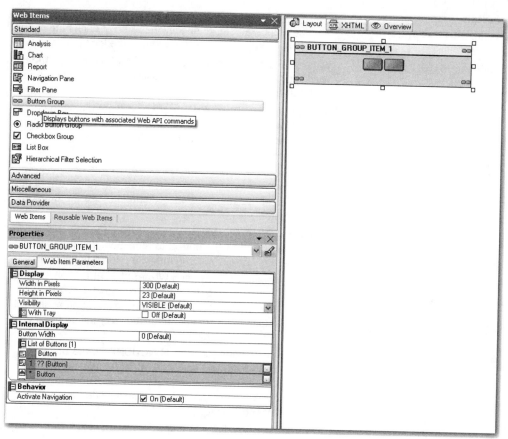

Dropdown Box   The Dropdown Box Web item is used for displaying a list of values for filtering purposes. This is very useful when there are multiple values to be displayed and to use either a Button Group or a Radio Button would be too cumbersome and the ability to pick from a list is a better option. There are a number of different options for the content of the dropdown box. You can specify the content as follows:

- **Characteristic values for filtering**   Using the Dropdown Box Web item, you can easily filter one or more connected data providers by a characteristic value. When you select an entry from the dropdown box, the connected data provider is filtered according to this value. If a different method is used to select a filter value for the characteristic in the dropdown box, the current filter value appears in the dropdown box.

Parameter	Description
Display	
Width in Pixels (WIDTH); Height in Pixels (HEIGHT); Visibility (VISIBILITY); With Tray (WITH_TRAY)	See the detailed description of these parameters in Table 4-5.
Internal Display	
Button Width (BUTTON_WIDTH) Default value: "0"	You use this parameter to specify the width of each button. The default value adjusts the button width to the length of the text.

List of Buttons (BUTTON_LIST)	You use this parameter to create the list of buttons for the Web application. You specify the following parameters for each button:
	
	• Caption (CAPTION) You use the text input dialog to enter the text to appear on the button. You can select whether the texts are to be language-dependent or language-independent.
	
	• Quick Info (TOOLTIP) You enter a quick info text here. The text for the quick info can be created according to various criteria, in the same way as the caption. See the Caption parameter.
	
	• Action (Command Triggered) (ACTION) You use this parameter to link the button to an action. You first specify the type of action. You can insert the following actions:
	
	  • Command via Command Wizard (INSTRUCTION) Using the pushbutton to the right of Command (INSTRUCTION), you can call the command wizard to insert an additional command. (The command functionality will be discussed in detail later in this chapter.)
	
	  • Script Function (SCRIPT_FUNCTION) In the Script Function field, you specify a script function to be executed. You generate the script function using the Script Web item that you previously added and set in the Web template.
	
	• Enabled (ENABLED) You specify whether the button is to be enabled in the Web application.
	
	• Design (BUTTON_DESIGN) You select the design for the button:
	Standard (STANDARD)
	Emphasized (EMPHASIZED)
	Previous (PREVIOUS)
	Next (NEXT)

Behavior	
Allow Navigation (INTERACTION_ALLOWED)	You use this parameter to specify whether navigation or other interaction is to be possible in the Web application.

TABLE 4-7 Parameters for the Button Group Web Item

- **Selection of query views**   By selecting an entry from the dropdown box, you can switch, in one step, from a data provider and its display (in a table, for example) to another data provider that may be displayed in a different way (in a chart, for example). This has been one option that has moved position from the 3.x version to the 7.0 version and many people have lost track of where to find this capability.

- **Fixed options list**   When you select an entry from the dropdown box, an associated command from the Web Design API is executed.

- **Fixed option list with manual update**   When you select an entry from the dropdown box, an associated command from the Web Design API is executed. It is also possible to trigger a manual update (of data).

- **Variable Selection**   When you select an entry from the dropdown box, the data displayed depends on the variable selection.

This Web item is shown in the system here.

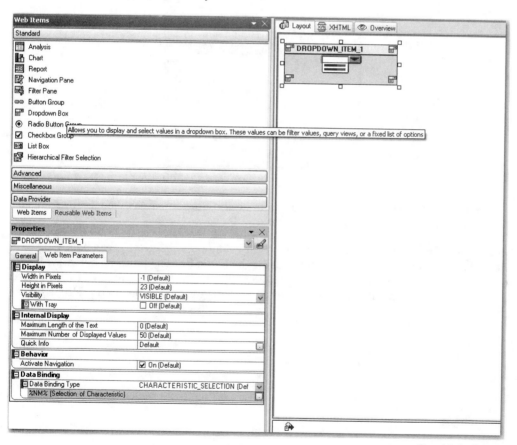

Depending on the specific selection, there may be additional parameters to set for the characteristics or InfoProviders. Also, the command offers options of the timing of the execution of the value from the dropdown box. The following shows the menu that appears when you click on the button to the right of %NM% (Selection of Characteristics).

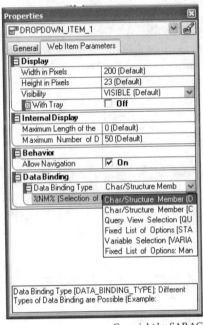

Copyright by SAP AG

Table 4-8 lists and describes the parameters for the Dropdown Box Web item, arranged according to the various parameter groupings.

Radio Button Group   The Radio Button Group Web item puts characteristic values to be filtered into a group of selection buttons. Using the Radio Button Group Web item, you can easily filter one or more connected data providers by a characteristic value. When you select a value, the connected data provider is filtered according to this value. If you select a filter

Parameter	Description
Display	
Width in Pixels (WIDTH); Height in Pixels (HEIGHT); Visibility (VISIBILITY); With Tray (WITH_TRAY)	See Table 4-5 for the detailed definition of these parameters.
Internal Display	
Maximum Length of the Text (TEXT_MAXLENGTH)	You use this parameter to specify the maximum text length for the values.
Maximum Number of Displayed Values (ENTRIES_MAXCOUNT)	You use this parameter to specify the maximum number of values to be displayed in the dropdown box.
Behavior	
Allow Navigation (INTERACTION_ALLOWED)	You use this parameter to specify whether navigation and other interactions, such as in the Web application, are to be possible.
Data Binding	
The default value is: "CHARACTERISTIC_SELECTION" Char/Structure Member: CHARACTERISTIC_SELECTION Query View Selection: QUERY_VIEW_SELECTION Fixed List of Options: STATIC_OPTION_LIST Variable Selection: VARIABLE_SELECTION Fixed List of Options: Manual Update: STATIC_OPTION_LIST_MANUAL	These parameters have been described earlier.

TABLE 4-8   Parameters for the Dropdown Box Web Item

value in another way for the characteristic of the radio button group, the current filter value is selected. The following illustration shows this Web item in the system.

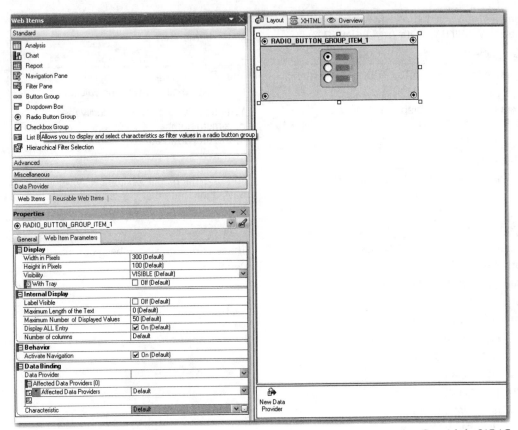

Table 4-9 lists and describes the parameters for the Radio Button Group Web item, arranged according to the various parameter groupings.

Checkbox Group   The Checkbox Group Web item allows free characteristics to be displayed and selected as filter values in a group of check boxes. Using the Checkbox Group Web item, you can easily filter one or more connected data providers according to one or more characteristic values. You can set or remove filter values in the Web application by setting one or more indicators. The significant difference between the Radio Button Group and the Checkbox Group is that the Radio Button Group Web item allows the selection of only one

Parameter	Description
Display	
Width in Pixels (WIDTH); Height in Pixels (HEIGHT); Visibility (VISIBILITY); With Tray (WITH_TRAY)	See Table 4-5 for the detailed definition of these parameters.
Internal Display	
Label (LABEL_VISIBLE)	You use this parameter to determine whether the long text of the characteristic is written as a label in front of the radio button group.
Maximum Text Length (TEXT_MAXLENGTH)	You use this parameter to determine the maximum text length for the values. Specify the number of characters for this.
Maximum Number of Displayed Values (ENTRIES_MAXCOUNT)	You use this parameter to determine the maximum number of values that are to be displayed in the radio button group.
Entry Display ALL (ALL_VALUE_ENTRIES_INCLUDED)	You use this parameter to determine whether the All entry is displayed as a selection option in the radio button group.
Number of Columns (COLUMNS)	You use this parameter to determine the number of entries displayed adjacent to one other.
Behavior	
Activate Navigation (INTERACTION_ALLOWED)	You use this parameter to determine whether navigation and other interactions are possible, like in the Web application.
Data Binding	
Data Provider (DATA_PROVIDER_REF); Affected Data Providers (LINKED_DATA_PROVIDER_REF_LIST);	See Table 4-6 for the detailed definition of these parameters.
Characteristic (CHARACTERISTIC)	You use this parameter to select the characteristic according to its technical name. Also note that you also control what characteristics you can select. Select the button to the right of the field for Characteristic and you will be able to identify the selection process for the characteristic. The options available are:
	(M): All values from the master data table. In some circumstances, values that do not appear in the data provider under the current filter conditions and that, upon filtering, produce the result "No Suitable Data Found" are also displayed. However, under certain conditions this process is the fastest.

TABLE 4-9   Parameters for the Radio Button Group Web Item (*continued*)

Parameter	Description
Characteristic (CHARACTERISTIC) (*continued*)	(D): Values that are basically posted, whereby the current drilldown status is not fully taken into consideration.
	(Q): Only values that are also posted in the data provider under the currently valid filter conditions are displayed. Under certain circumstances it can take a long time.
	The "master data" read mode may lead to many "unposted" values being displayed; the "posted values" read mode may be slow.

TABLE 4-9   Parameters for the Radio Button Group Web Item (*continued*)

value at a time, the Checkbox Group Web item allows for multiple values to be selected. The following illustration shows this Web item in the system.

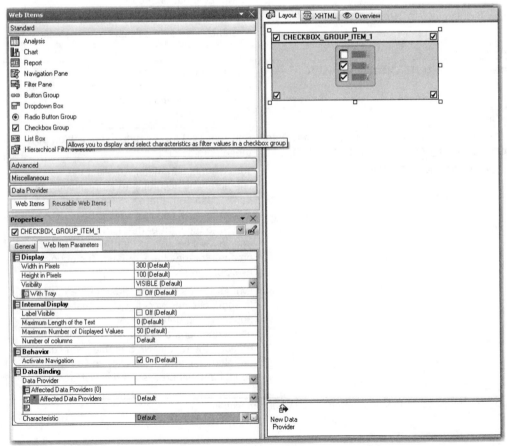

Table 4-10 lists and describes the parameters for the Checkbox Group Web item, arranged according to the various parameter groupings.

List Box   The List Box Web item allows you to make multiple selections on characteristic values of one or more data providers. All of the parameters are consistent with the Radio Button Group Web item. Refer to Table 4-9 for a list and description of the parameters.

Parameter	Description
Display	
Width in Pixels (WIDTH); Height in Pixels (HEIGHT); Visibility (VISIBILITY); With Tray (WITH_TRAY)	See Table 4-5 for the detailed definition of these parameters.
Internal Display	
Label (LABEL_VISIBLE)	You use this parameter to determine whether the long text of the characteristic is written as a label in front of the checkbox group.
Maximum Text Length (TEXT_MAXLENGTH)	You use this parameter to determine the maximum text length for the characteristic values.
Maximum Number of Displayed Values (ENTRIES_MAXCOUNT)	You use this parameter to determine the maximum number of values that are displayed in the checkbox group.
Number of Columns (COLUMNS)	You use this parameter to determine the number of entries displayed adjacent to one other.
Behavior	
Activate Navigation (INTERACTION_ALLOWED)	You use this parameter to determine whether navigation and other interaction is possible, like in the Web application.
Data Binding	
Data Provider (DATA_PROVIDER_REF); Affected Data Provider (LINKED_DATA_PROVIDER_REF_LIST); Characteristic (CHARACTERISTIC)	See Table 4-9 for the detailed information.

TABLE 4-10   Parameters for the Checkbox Group Web Item

This includes all parameter groupings—Display, Internal Display, Behavior, and Data Binding. The following shows this Web item in the system.

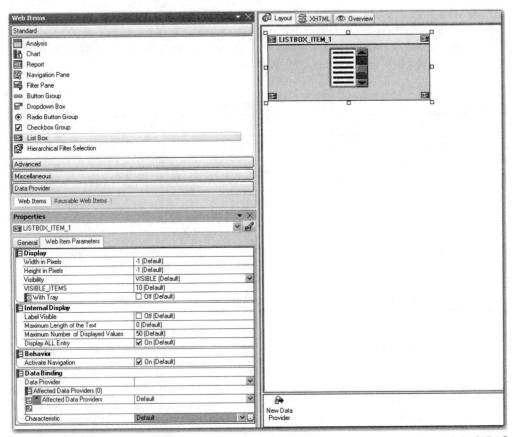

There is an additional parameter that the List Box has and that is the Number of Visible Items in the Display Parameters. This allows the configuration as to how many items will be visible in the list box and also affects the height of the Web item.

Hierarchical Filter Selection   The Hierarchical Filter Selection Web item generates a hierarchical filter selection from the hierarchy of a characteristic or a structure, where the hierarchy nodes are displayed in a tree that can be expanded and collapsed. This is another function that has been changed from the 3.x version to the 7.0 version. This hierarchy filter selection was normally for the hierarchy of the user role in 3.x versions whereas in this version it is for the display of the actual hierarchy of a characteristic. The hierarchy nodes (including leaves of the hierarchy) can be set as a filter. Using the hierarchical filter selection, you can filter a data provider by hierarchy nodes. This Web item configuration in the system is shown next.

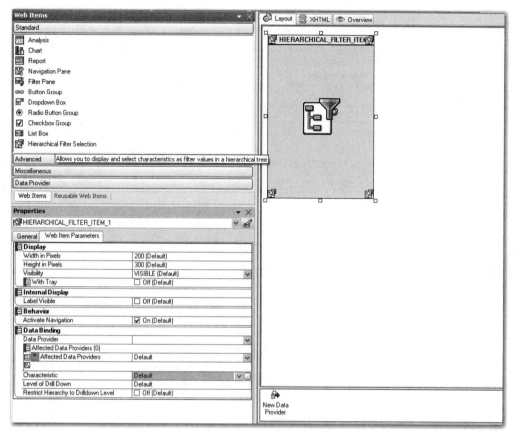

Table 4-11 lists and describes the parameters for the Hierarchical Filter Selection Web item, arranged according to the various parameter groupings.

Advanced Web Items

The Advanced Web items are comprised of a number of objects that are fairly new to the WAD. Other than the Map and Document Web items the remaining ones are from the Business Planning and Consolidations component of SEM (Strategic Enterprise Management). Since BI-IP has taken over the planning functionality, the WAD needed to accommodate the portal requirements for the posting of data into the InfoCubes. These Web items are part of that migration from SEM-BPS to BI-IP. So, they are advanced in functionality and in many cases specific to BI-IP rather than reporting. As mentioned the Map and Document Web items are definitely reporting components.

Web Template   The Web Template Web item allows you to insert other Web templates into a Web template. With the Web Template Web item, you can easily manage consistent sections in your Web applications centrally in a Web template and can integrate them into any Web template as required. For example, you can define a header or footer section with the

Parameter	Description
Display	
Width in Pixels (WIDTH); Height in Pixels (HEIGHT); Visibility (VISIBILITY); With Tray (WITH_TRAY)	See Table 4-5 for the detailed definition of these parameters.
Internal Display	
Label Visible (LABEL_VISIBLE)	You use this parameter to determine whether the description of the characteristic is written in front of the hierarchy.
Behavior	
Activate Navigation (INTERACTION_ALLOWED)	You use this parameter to determine whether navigation or other interactions are possible in the Web application.
Data Binding	
Data Provider (DATA_PROVIDER_REF); Affected Data Provider (LINKED_DATA_PROVIDER_REF_LIST); Characteristic (CHARACTERISTIC)	See Table 4-9 for a discussion on data binding.
Level of Drilldown (HIERARCHY_EXPAND_TO_LEVEL)	You use this parameter to specify the expansion level of the filter selection. By default, the initial expansion depth specified for the query definition is used.
Restrict Hierarchy to Drilldown Level (HIERARCHY_RESTRICT_TO_LEVEL)	You use this parameter to restrict the filter selection. You can only set filter values up to the drilldown level.

TABLE 4-11   Parameters for the Hierarchical Filter Selection Web Item

corporate logo and heading as a Web template and then integrate this Web template into your Web applications as a Web Template Web item. This Web template is then inserted during run time. In contrast to HTML frame technology, the system does not generate a new page during this process. The context of the main template remains the same. This is another reason to use the reusable Web items more frequently and store them in the Library. The following illustration shows this Web item in the system.

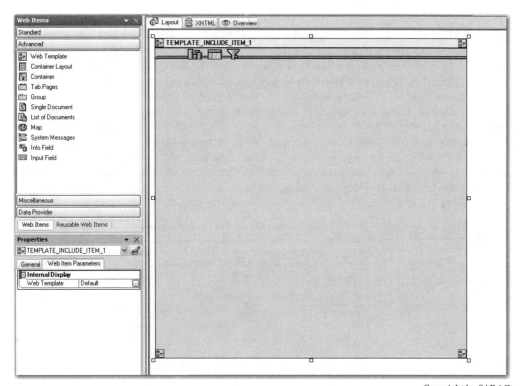

Table 4-12 lists and describes the single parameter of the Web Template Web item. After you set the Web Template (TEMPLATE_ID) parameter, you then save the Web template. When you reopen this Web template, the contents of the inserted Web template are displayed with all Web items and data providers. This allows you to overwrite the Web item and data provider parameters of the inserted Web template directly in the Layout view of the WAD. As I mentioned above, this is another approach to working with reusable Web items and objects. This really helps with configuration of Web items that are very similar in design or are being used multiple times in different Web applications.

NOTE   *The next several Web items were developed to accommodate the loss of the Web Interface Builder used in SEM-BPS, or at least to assimilate that functionality into the WAD for use in the BI-IP component. These Web components were very useful objects in SEM-BPS and allowed quite a bit of formatting to occur without requiring much coding.*

Parameter	Description
Web Template (TEMPLATE_ID)	In this parameter you enter the technical name of the Web template to be inserted.

TABLE 4-12   Parameter for the Web Template Web Item

Container Layout   The Container Layout Web item allows Web items to be arranged systematically into rows and columns. The Container Layout Web item helps you to arrange visually the content in a Web application. You can specify for each cell in the layout grid which Web item is to be displayed; only one item can be displayed for each cell. In this way, you can systematically arrange Web items over, under, or adjacent to one another.

You can also use an HTML table to arrange the content in a Web application systematically but if you use the HTML table you have to re-create another Web template rather than just using a Web item. Another reason to use the Container Layout versus the HTML table is that additional technical components such as accessibility are automatically applied with the Container Layout Web item. This is the difference between the Container Layout Web item and the Container Web item. The Container Web item does not offer the ability to align and structure objects within it; it only allows the inclusion of those items.

The following illustration shows this Web item in the system.

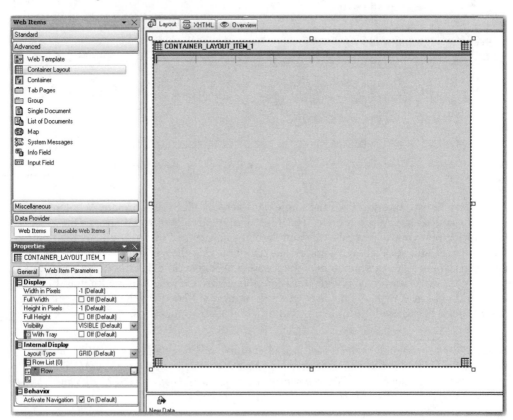

Copyright by SAP AG

Table 4-13 lists and describes the parameters for the Container Layout Web item, arranged according to the various parameter groupings.

Parameter	Description
Display	
Width in Pixels (WIDTH); Full Width (FULL_WIDTH); Height in Pixels (HEIGHT); Full Height (FULL_HEIGHT); Visibility (VISIBILITY); With tray (WITH_TRAY)	See Table 4-5 for the detailed definition of these parameters.
Internal Display	
Layout Type	Set to the appropriate format to be used during configuration. Either FIXED GRID, Rows Cells Floating, or Column Cells Floating.
Row List (ROW_LIST)	You use this parameter to determine how the Web items are to be arranged in your Web applications. You determine in which cell a specific Web item is to be placed. Make sure that the Web item has been inserted into the Container Layout Web item beforehand. First find the row into which the Web item is to be placed using the Row List parameter. Then choose the column into which the Web item is to be placed under List. Set the following parameters under Definition for the respective column: • Subordinate Web Item (CHILD_ITEM_REF) Here you select the Web item that is to be displayed in the cell and that you have previously inserted into the Container Layout Web item. • Width in Pixels (WIDTH) Here you set the width of the cell. • Height in Pixels (HEIGHT) Here you set the height of the cell. • Rowspan (ROWSPAN) Here you merge rows into one cell. For example, when you enter the number 2, it means that the cells span over two rows. • Colspan (COLSPAN) Here you merge columns. For example, when you enter the number 2, it means that the cells span over two columns.
Row List (ROW_LIST)	• Vertical Alignment (VALIGN) You specify the vertical alignment of the Web item—Beginning (BEGIN), Center (CENTER), End (END) • Horizontal Alignment (HALIGN) You specify the horizontal alignment of the Web item—Beginning (BEGIN), Center (CENTER), End (END)
Behavior	
Activate navigation (INTERACTION_ ALLOWED)	You use this parameter to determine whether navigation or other interactions are possible in the Web application.

TABLE 4-13   Parameters for the Container Layout Web Item

Container   The Container Web item allows the combining of any content, whether to be displayed or hidden. With the Container Web item, you can combine any content and nest Web items. You can use this Web item to insert free HTML into other Web items, such as tab pages. To do this, first insert free HTML into the Container Web item and include it in the Tab Page Web item. The Container Web item is simply an object that includes other Web items, text, graphics, or HTML code. No method of aligning the items is provided. Another use for this item is to place multiple Web items on one tab page. We will discuss the Tab Page Web item next. You can only assign one Web item to a tab page. Using the Container to include multiple Web items, then including the Container into one tab page will produce multiple Web items on one tab of the tab page. The following illustration shows this Web item in the system. Both the Container Web and the Container Layout Web items are excellent options to help with the formatting and controlling of the items within a Web template.

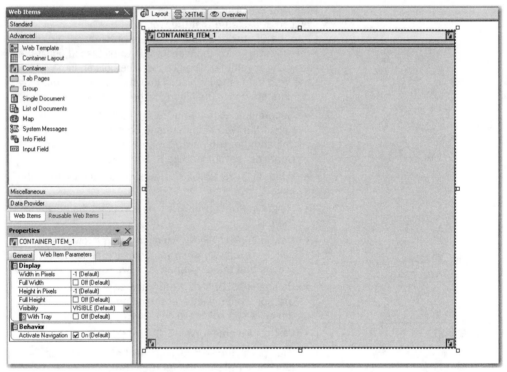

Table 4-14 lists and describes the parameters for the Container Web item, arranged according to the various parameter groupings.

Tab Pages   The Tab Pages Web item is very useful. It not only enables you to apply a very professional format to the report, but also helps with the performance of the report. The Tab Pages Web item allows you to arrange and display Web items on one or more tab pages in your Web application. The sequence in which items are added to the Tab Page Web item determines the sequence of the tab pages. This technique might be a bit elusive initially, but once you work with this object, it will become second nature. Only one Web item can be assigned to each tab, but a workaround exists to assign multiple objects to a tab as mentioned in the paragraph above. In terms of performance, if you have multiple tab pages you can set up the execution of the Web item to generate the results set for the initial Tab page only. When you move to the next Tab page by clicking on the tab, that report or Web item gets filled with the required information. So the initial execution of the Web template doesn't take as long to pull the data for all of the tab pages.

Tab pages definitely provide a professional-looking arrangement of items in a Web application. This arrangement enables users to navigate from tab to tab instead of having to scroll up and down one page to see all the objects, and is definitely an object to use for managing space in a Web application. To add Tab Panels, click the button at the right end of

Parameter	Description
Display	
Width in Pixels (WIDTH); Full Width (FULL_ WIDTH); Height in Pixels (HEIGHT); Full Height (FULL_HEIGHT); Visibility (VISIBILITY); With Tray (WITH_TRAY)	See Table 4-5 for the detailed definition of these parameters.
Behavior	
Activate Navigation (INTERACTION_ALLOWED)	You use this parameter to determine whether navigation or other interactions are possible in the Web application.

TABLE 4-14   Parameters for the Container Web Item

the Tab Panel line, and another tab will be created automatically for you to use. This is another very useful display object. The following shows this Web item in the system.

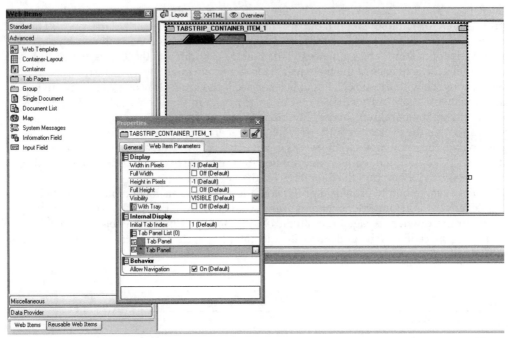

Table 4-15 lists and describes the parameters for the Tab Pages Web item, arranged according to the various parameter groupings.

Parameter	Description
Display	
Width in Pixels (WIDTH); Full Width (FULL_WIDTH); Height in Pixels (HEIGHT); Full Height (FULL_HEIGHT); Visibility (VISIBILITY); With Tray (WITH_TRAY)	See Table 4-5 for the detailed definition of these parameters.
Internal Display	
Initial Tab Index (INITIAL_TAB) Default value: "1"	You use this parameter to specify the tab page that is to be initially displayed as active. For example, when the default value 1 is used, the first tab page is initially displayed as active.

TABLE 4-15   Parameters for the Tab Page Web Item

Parameter	Description
Internal Display	

Tab Panel List (TABPANEL_LIST)	You use this parameter to specify the list of tab pages for the Web application. You must set the following additional parameters for each tab page:
	
	• Caption (CAPTION) You enter the label for the tab page using the text dialog.
	• Icon (SYMBOL) You use this parameter to incorporate icons.
	• Activation Action (ACTIVATION_ACTION) You can specify an action to be triggered when the tab pages are switched. The action is executed when you choose a tab page. To do this, call the command wizard under Command via Command Wizard.
	• Deactivation Action (DEACTIVATION_ ACTION) You can specify an action to be triggered when the tab pages are switched. The action is executed when you switch from one tab page to another tab page. To do this, call the command wizard under Command via Command Wizard. Note the following points in relation to activation and deactivation actions:
	  1. The activation action is not executed when the Web template is initially loaded.
	  2. When the user switches tab pages, the deactivation action of the last active tab page is followed by the activation action for the new tab page.
	• Subordinate Web Item (CHILD_ITEM_REF) You use this parameter to select the Web item that you previously inserted into the tab page Web item and that is to be displayed on this specific tab page.

Behavior	
Allow Navigation (INTERACTION_ALLOWED)	You use this parameter to specify whether navigation or other interaction is to be possible in the Web application.
Update	This will allow you to manage how the different tab pages get updated. Either using a Roundtrip at the time you activate the Web application or Passive and only based on the access to the particular page.

TABLE 4-15   Parameters for the Tab Page Web Item (*continued*)

Group   The Group Web item enables visual grouping of contents in a Web application. You use this Web item if you want to display certain areas together in a Web application. To use this Web item, simply drag and drop the other Web items that you want to group together in a particular section. You will see once we start to develop the dashboards that there are sometimes issues with spacing between Web items and if you collect them into the Group Web item they will all be positioned directly next to each other. This Web item is shown in the system here.

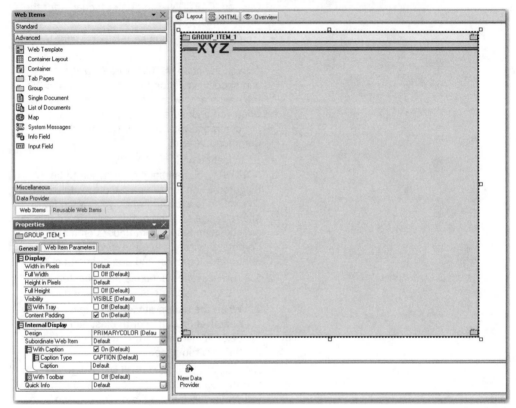

Table 4-16 lists and describes the parameters for the Group Web item, arranged according to the various parameter groupings.

Single Document   The Single Document Web item allows you to display single (non-migrated) documents that you created in the Data Warehousing Workbench or in master data maintenance, in the Web application. You can use the Single Document Web item to embed single documents of all formats in place, without needing frames or IFrames in the Web application.

As an example of using this Web item, suppose that you have a Web application that displays cost center data for the cost center manager. Every cost center manager requires this data for his or her cost center, so the data is filtered according to cost center. The Web application always displays the data for the current month. If you stored a master data document for each cost center (for example, a short description of all people belonging to

Parameter	Description
Display	
Width in Pixels (WIDTH); Full Width (FULL_WIDTH); Height in Pixels (HEIGHT); Full Height (FULL_HEIGHT); Visibility (VISIBILITY); With Tray (WITH_TRAY)	Please see the detailed definition for these parameters from Table 4-5.
Content Padding (PADDING)	You use this parameter to specify whether a uniform distance between the content of the Group Web item (such as Web items) and its boundaries are to be displayed.
Internal Display	
Design (GROUP_DESIGN) Values: Primary Color (PRIMARYCOLOR) SAP Color (SAPCOLOR) Secondary Box (SECONDARYBOX) Color of Secondary Box (SECONDARYBOXCOLOR) Secondary Color (SECONDARYCOLOR)	You use this parameter to specify the format and design of the Web item.
Subordinate Web Item (CHILD_ITEM_REF)	You use this parameter to specify the Web item that is to be displayed in the Group Web item.
With Caption (WITH_CAPTION)	You use this parameter to specify whether the Group Web item has a caption. If a caption is to be displayed, depending on the type of caption, you need to set the following other parameters: Caption Type (CAPTION_TYPE) You use this parameter to specify whether the caption is a simple text or a subordinate Web item: • Text (CAPTION) If you choose a text as caption, enter it using the text input dialog under Caption. • Web Item (CHILD_ITEM_REF) If you choose a Web item as a caption, select the associated Web item in the dropdown box. Make sure that you have inserted the Web item into the Group Web item.
With Toolbar (WITH_TOOLBAR)	You use this parameter to specify whether the Group Web item has a toolbar. If a toolbar is to be displayed, the following additional parameters must be set: Subordinate Web Item (CHILD_ITEM_REF) Under this parameter, select the Web item that is to function as the toolbar. Make sure that you have inserted the Web item into the Group Web item. In a typical example scenario, the Button Group Web item is used in the toolbar.

TABLE 4-16   Parameters for the Group Web Item

the cost center), you can configure the Web item so that this document is always displayed next to the table with the figures. The context-sensitive selection of the table ensures that each manager can only see the document for their cost center. Assuming that each cost center manager must comment on the cost center expenses, you can additionally display this document for InfoProviders in a second Web item. The context-sensitive selection of the documents for InfoProvider data ensures that the appropriate document for the cost center/ month combination is always displayed. This Web item is incorporated into the standard Web template 0ANALYSIS_PATTERN to support the documentation capabilities. Once the option to access the document is turned on, the use of the Single Document Web item helps support the display of those items.

The following illustration shows this Web item in the system.

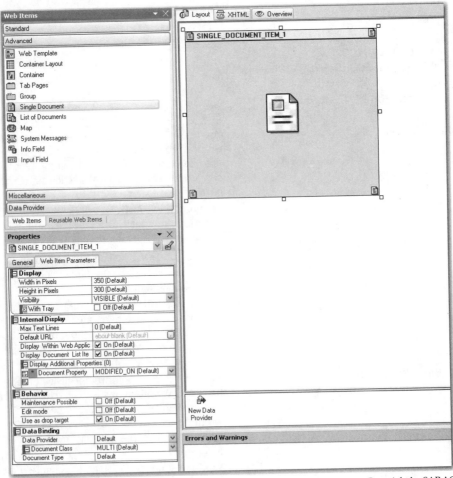

Table 4-17 lists and describes the parameters for the Single Document Web item, arranged according to the various parameter groupings.

Parameter	Description
Display	
Width in Pixels (WIDTH); Height in Pixels (HEIGHT); Visibility (VISIBILITY); With Tray (WITH_TRAY)	See Table 4-5 for the detailed definition of these parameters.
Internal Display	
Maximum Text Lines (MAX_TEXT_LINES)	You use this parameter to determine the maximum number of text lines for text documents that can be displayed.
Default Picture URL (DEFAULT_PICTURE_URL)	You use this parameter to determine the default URL that is displayed when no document is found. You set the link to the document in Knowledge Management.
Document Positioned (IS_INPLACE)	You use this parameter to determine whether the document is embedded in the Web application (On) or if only a link to the document is displayed (Off).
Display List (DISPLAY_LIST)	You use this parameter to determine whether the List of Documents Web item should be displayed if more than one document qualifies for the Web item context.
Property List (PROPERTY_LIST)	You use this parameter to determine the properties of the document to be displayed under the document. You have the following selection options: • Modified On (MODIFIED_ON) • Modified By (MODIFIED_BY) • Created On (CREATED_ON) • Created By (CREATED_BY) The Modified On (MODIFIED_ON) option is the default value.
Behavior	
Maintenance Possible (MAINTENANCE_POSSIBLE)	You use this parameter to decide whether it is possible to maintain the Single Document Web item. The default value is Off.
Edit Mode	You can use this parameter to allow documents to be opened immediately in Edit mode.
Drop Targets	The drag and drop functionality is available if this is turned on. It allows the use of icons and the ability to move them around the screen using the drag and drop process.

TABLE 4-17   Parameters for the Single Document Web Item

Parameter	Description
Data Binding	
Data Provider (DATA_PROVIDER_REF)	See Table 4-9 for a discussion on data binding.
Document Class (DOCUMENT CLASS)	You use this parameter to set the document class. You have the following selection options: • Meta (BW_OBJECT) • Reference (CHARACTERISTIC) • InfoProvider (MULTI) Once you have identified the class, then an additional field appears that requires the technical name of the actual object, whether it is a query, query view, or InfoObject. For example, for master data you must also enter the characteristic whose documents are to be displayed. For metadata you must also enter the meta object whose documents are to be displayed.
Document Type (WWW_DOC_TYPE)	You use this parameter to classify documents by assigning a freely selectable document type to them. If you have set the parameter to Web item, only the corresponding document types are displayed. For example, if you assign two documents to a cost center, one document with pictures of employees and another with a description of the cost center. You can then classify all pictures as "PICTURE" and all descriptions as "DESCRIPTION." To do this, you assign the value "PICTURE" or "DESCRIPTION" to the Document Type property of the document. Set this Web item property accordingly in the Web application. This allows you, for example, to include two Web items in the Web application, one of which displays the pictures and the other the description.

TABLE 4-17   Parameters for the Single Document Web Item (*continued*)

List of Documents   The List of Documents Web item displays a list of documents in the Web application. This Web item allows you to call or create context-sensitive information for data (master data, InfoProvider data, or metadata) used in the Web application. If you navigate in the Web application and, for example, restrict a characteristic to a certain characteristic value, the document list is automatically adjusted. This means that only those documents relevant for the restricted navigation status are displayed.

NOTE *Only those characteristics that are set as a document property in the Data Warehousing Workbench are taken into account when the documents for the InfoProvider data displayed for the most recent navigational state are determined.*

For example, suppose you have a Web application that displays cost center data for the cost center manager. Every cost center manager performs this for his or her cost center, so the data is filtered according to cost center. The Web application always displays the data for the current month. Assuming you have stored a master data document for each cost center, you can configure the Web item so that this document is always displayed in addition to the table with the figures. The context-sensitive selection of the table ensures that managers can only see the document for their own cost center. Assuming each cost center manager has to comment on the cost center expenses, you can additionally display this document for InfoProviders in a second Web item. The context-sensitive selection of the documents for InfoProvider data ensures that the appropriate document for the cost center/ month combination is always displayed.

The following shows this Web item in the system.

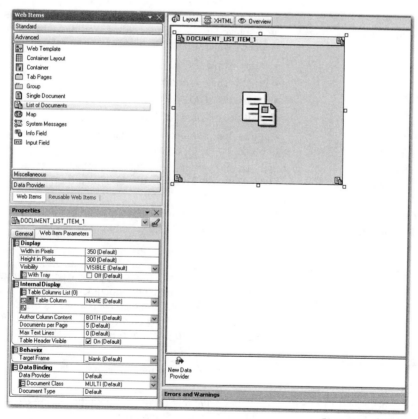

Table 4-18 lists and describes the parameters for the List of Documents Web item, arranged according to the various parameter groupings.

Parameter	Description
Display	
Width in Pixels (WIDTH); Height in Pixels (HEIGHT); Visibility (VISIBILITY); With Tray (WITH_TRAY)	See Table 4-5 for the detailed definition for these parameters.
Internal Display	
Maximum Text Lines (MAX_TEXT_LINES)	You use this parameter to specify the maximum number of text lines for text documents.
Table Columns List (DOC_ITEM_TABLE_COLUMN)	You use this parameter to specify the table columns. You can select from the following options for the columns: • Name (Default) • Name (NAME) • Content (CONTENT) • Assignment (ASSIGNMENT) • Author (Author)
Author Column Content (COLUMN_AUTHOR_CONTENT)	You use this parameter to specify which information is to be displayed in the author column. You have the following selection options: • Author Only (Default) • Author Only (Author) • Date Only (DATE) • Author and Date (BOTH)
Documents per Page (DOCUMENTS_PER_PAGE)	You use this parameter to specify how many documents are to be displayed on a page.
Table Frame Visible (TABLE_FRAME_VISIBLE)	You use this parameter to specify whether the table frame is to be displayed. The selection options are On and Off. The default value is Off.
Table Header Visible (TABLE_HEADER_VISIBLE)	You use this parameter to specify whether the table header is to be displayed. The selection options are On and Off. The default value is Off.
Behavior	
Target Frame	This function allows the use of specific types of formatting and display to be used by the document. Once the document is executed and displayed it allows the document to be displayed as a New page, within the current page, Same Frame, entire page, or a Higher Level Frame.
Data Binding	
Data Provider (DATA_PROVIDER_REF)	See Table 4-9 for a discussion on data binding.
Document Class (DOCUMENT CLASS); Document Type (WWW_DOC_TYPE)	See Table 4-17; this parameter definition is the same as for the Single Document Web item.

TABLE 4-18   Parameters for the List of Documents Web Item

System Messages   The System Messages Web item displays system messages, information, warnings, and error messages. Using the System Messages Web item, you can make the decision as to what different types of messages are to be displayed in a Web application. You use the Web template parameter to determine the type of messages that are displayed. These parameters are shown here.

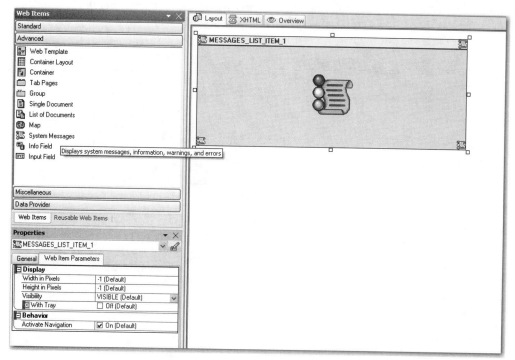

Table 4-19 lists and describes the parameters for the System Messages Web item, arranged according to the various parameter groupings.

Parameter	Description
Display	
Width in Pixels (WIDTH); Height in Pixels (HEIGHT); Visibility (VISIBILITY); With Tray (WITH_TRAY)	See Table 4-5 for the detailed definition of these parameters.
Behavior	
Activate Navigation (INTERACTION_ALLOWED)	You use this parameter to determine whether navigation or other interactions are possible in the Web application.

TABLE 4-19   Parameters for the System Messages Web Item

Info Field The Info Field Web item displays information about the data provider, the user, and the filter values, as well as information about the Web application. With the Info Field Web item, you can display additional information about the data provider in the Web application. Unlike the System Message Web item, which only offers the ability to show the system messages, errors, and warnings, this Web item allows additional detailed information to be displayed about the InfoProvider users, and other information about the Web template. This allows you to display any or all of the text elements associated with the data provider. These parameters are shown in the next illustration.

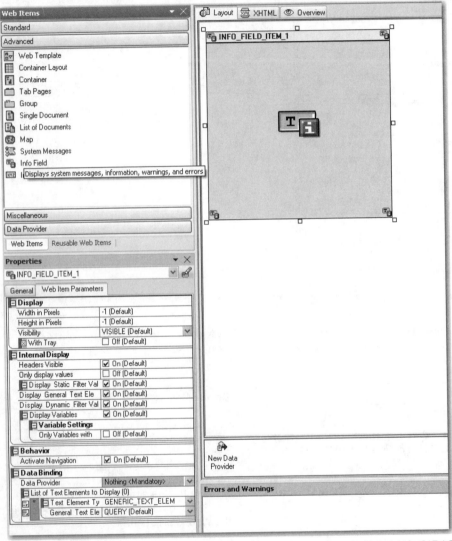

Copyright by SAP AG

Table 4-20 lists and describes the parameters for the Info Field Web item, arranged according to the various parameter groupings.

Parameter	Description
Display	
Width in Pixels (WIDTH); Height in Pixels (HEIGHT); Visibility (VISIBILITY); With Tray (WITH_TRAY)	See Table 4-5 for the detailed definition of these parameters.
Internal Display	
Headers Visible (HEADERS_VISIBLE)	You use this parameter to determine whether headers are displayed in the Web application.
Display Static Filter Values (STATIC_FILTERS_VISIBLE)	You use this parameter to specify whether static filter values for the data provider are to be displayed in the Web application by using the Web item. Static filter values (or restrictions) are set in the Query Designer.
Display General Text Elements (GENERAL_INFORMATION_VISIBLE)	You use this parameter to specify whether general text elements such as InfoCube and current user, are to be displayed in the Web application.
Display Dynamic Filter Values (DYNAMIC_FILTERS_VISIBLE)	You use this parameter to specify whether the dynamic filter values are to be displayed in the Web application.
Display Variables (VARIABLES_VISIBLE)	You use this parameter to specify whether variables are to be displayed in the Web application.
Behavior	
Allow Navigation (INTERACTION_ALLOWED)	You use this parameter to specify whether navigation or other interaction is to be possible in the Web application.
Data Binding	
Data Provider (DATA_PROVIDER_REF)	See Table 4-9 for a discussion on data binding.
List of Text Elements to Display (INFORMATION_ELEMENT_LIST)	You use this parameter to create a list of all text elements that are to be displayed in the Web application. Different parameters are to be set for each element in the list depending on the text element type. The following text element types are possible: • General Text Elements (GENERIC_TEXT_ELEMENT) • Dynamic Filter (CHARACTERISTIC_LIST) • Static Filter (STATIC_CHARACTERISTIC_LIST) • Variable Value (VARIABLE) If you do not specify this list, all text elements are displayed.

TABLE 4-20 Parameters for the Info Field Web Item (*continued*)

Parameter	Description
Data Binding	
If you selected the text element type General Text Elements (GENERIC_TEXT_ELEMENT), you will need to set the following parameter(s):	
General Text Elements for a Data Provider (GENERIC_TEXT_ELEMENT)	You use this parameter to choose the generic text element that is to be displayed: Query Name (QUERY) Query Description (QUERY_DESCRIPTION) InfoProvider Name (INFOPROVIDER) InfoProvider Description (INFOPROVIDER_DESCRIPTION) Key Date (QUERY_KEYDATE) Last Data Update (ROLLUPTIME) Author (AUTHOR) Changed At (CHANGED_AT) Changed By (LAST_CHANGED_BY) Current User (CURRENT_USER) Last Refresh (LAST_REFRESHED) Web Template (TEMPLATE) System (SYSTEM)
If you selected the text element type Dynamic Filter (CHARACTERISTIC_LIST), you need to set the following parameter(s):	
List of Characteristics (CHARACTERISTIC_LIST)	You use this parameter to specify for each row the characteristic that is displayed as a dynamic filter.
If you selected the text element type Static Filter (STATIC_CHARACTERISTIC_LIST), you need to set the following parameter(s):	
List of Characteristics for Static Filter (STATIC_CHARACTERISTIC_LIST)	You use this parameter to specify for each row the characteristic that is displayed as a static filter.

TABLE 4-20   Parameters for the Info Field Web Item (*continued*)

Input Field   The Input Field Web item is used for either text or numeric data entry. This information can be assigned to another object for additional comments. The Input Field Web item is a 60-character field for information entries. The following illustration shows this Web item in the system during configuration. This Web item can also be used in the BI-IP planning process by allowing the input of values to restrict different activities. For example by entering the detailed values you can use the Input Field to allow a copy process from a specific company code to another company code for all data or let us say that you are using the actual data to copy over to your plan information (2008 actuals for the start of planning for 2009). Then you can use this Web item to help support that process.

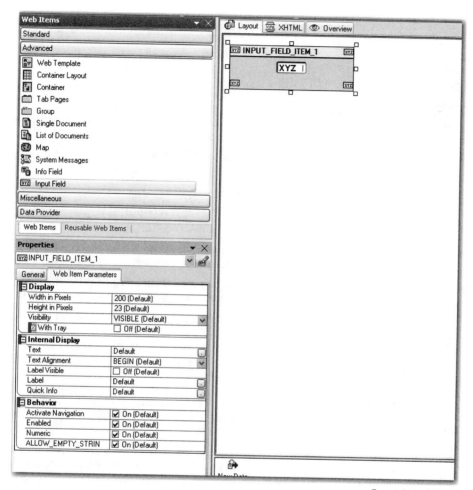

Table 4-21 lists and describes the parameters for the Input Field Web item, arranged according to the various parameter groupings.

Miscellaneous Web Items

With the Miscellaneous group of Web items, we really start to head into more advanced configuration. Some of the Web items, such as List of Exceptions and List of Conditions, should not be an issue in terms of configuration, but the Script and Custom Extension Web items definitely require you to have additional experience in the use of script logic and ABAP coding. We will take these a bit out of order so that we can cover them from the more obvious Web items to the more complex ones. In this case, some of the more complex Web items may require additional support from other resources to help with the ABAP programming or the Script Logic language that would be required. None of the other groups required additional resources nor are the Web items explained in those two groups unusual or require additional configuration outside of adjusting their parameters.

Parameter	Description
Display	
Width in Pixels (WIDTH); Height in Pixels (HEIGHT); Visibility (VISIBILITY); With Tray (WITH_TRAY)	See Table 4-5 for the detailed definition of these parameters.
Internal Display	
Text (TEXT_CONTENT)	You use this parameter and the text input dialog to specify the initial content in the input field.
Text Alignment (TEXT_ALIGNMENT)	You use this parameter to specify the alignment for the content or text in the input field. • Left-Aligned (BEGIN) • Centered (CENTER) • Right-Aligned (END)
Label Visible (LABEL_VISIBLE)	You use this parameter to specify whether a label is to be displayed for the input field.
Label (LABEL)	You use this parameter and the text input dialog to specify the label for the input field.
Quick Info (TOOLTIP)	You use this parameter and the text input dialog to specify a quick info text, which could be additional information or details about a field in the report or other critical information.
Behavior	
Activate Navigation (INTERACTION_ALLOWED)	You use this parameter to specify whether navigation or other interaction is to be possible in the Web application.
Enabled (ENABLED)	You use this parameter to specify whether the input field is to be set as active or inactive and then displayed accordingly in the Web application (for example, grayed out if set as Inactive). This will enable the ability to post information into the cells or fields in the report.
Numeric (NUMERIC)	You use this parameter to specify whether numeric input only is to be permitted in the input field.
Allow Empty String (ALLOW_EMPTY_STRING)	You use this parameter to specify whether the empty string ("") is to be regarded as a valid value when the input is checked.

TABLE 4-21   Parameters for the Input Field Web Item

Data Provider – Information   You can use the Data Provider – Information Web item for XML generation of query results data or of the navigation state of a query. The Web item is not visualized in the Web application, but you can see the generated XML in the source text for the Web application. This would help with debugging activities or some sort of investigation of what exactly the Web item is doing. Including an XML program here would analyze the process being executed for online or background planning functions. This can be very helpful in terms of planning activities where you would be able to analyze the XML program within the Web application. The following illustration shows the configuration screen for the Data Provider - Information.

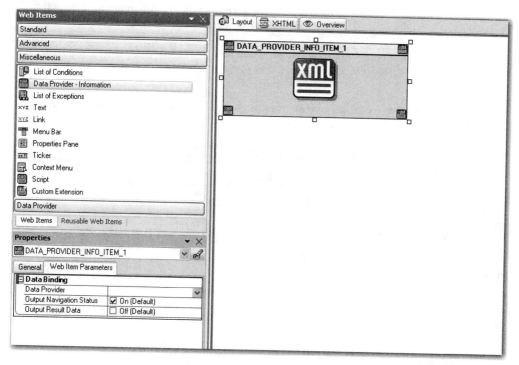

Copyright by SAP AG

Table 4-22 lists and describes the parameters for the Data Provider – Information Web item, arranged according to the various parameter groupings.

List of Conditions   The List of Conditions Web item displays for a data provider of type query view all the available conditions including their corresponding statuses (active/not active/can be used/cannot be used) in the Web application. The Web item displays the status of conditions in the form of a table in the Web application. All the conditions that can be applied to the current navigational state and the data provider of type query view are listed. You can activate or deactivate the conditions using the Toggle State button. The following illustration shows this Web item in the system. So, rather than having to find the

Parameter	Description
Data Connection	
Data Providers (DATA_PROVIDER_REF)	See Table 4-9 for a discussion on data binding.
Output Navigational State (NAVIGATIONAL_STATE)	You use this parameter to determine whether the navigational state of the data provider is generated as XML in the source text of the Web application.
Output Result Data (RESULT_SET)	You use this parameter to determine whether the query results are generated as XML in the source text of the Web application.

TABLE 4-22   Parameters for the Data Provider – Information Web Item

conditions or exceptions by using context menus or right-clicking, you see a pushbutton onscreen that you can click to execute these items.

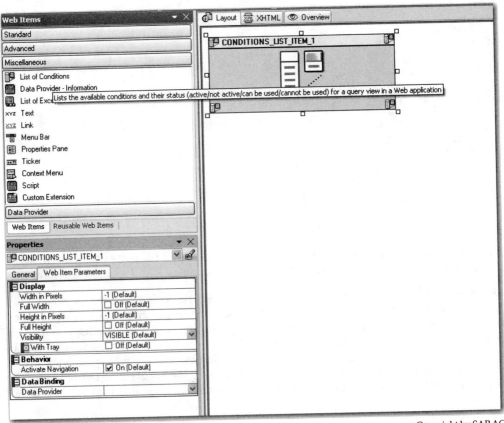

Table 4-23 lists and describes the parameters for the List of Conditions Web item, arranged according to the various parameter groupings.

List of Exceptions   As discussed in the previous section about List of Conditions, the List of Exceptions Web item has very similar functionality. These are two very useful Web items and can help with the formatting of a dashboard by allowing multiple views of a report to be available with one toggle process. The List of Exceptions Web item displays for a data provider of type query view the existing exceptions and their status (active/not active) in the Web application. The Web item displays the status of exceptions in the form of a table in the Web application. For each exception, the status of the exception (active/not active) is also displayed. You can activate or deactivate the exceptions using the Toggle State button. As shown next, the parameters for the List of Exceptions Web item is very similar to those of the List of Conditions Web item.

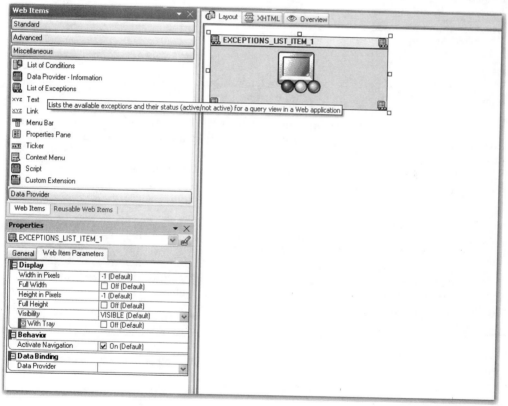

Parameter	Description
Display	
Width in Pixels (WIDTH); Full Width (FULL_WIDTH); Height in Pixels (HEIGHT); Full Height (FULL_HEIGHT); Visibility (VISIBILITY); With Tray (WITH_TRAY)	See Table 4-5 for the detailed definition of these parameters.
Behavior	
Activate Navigation (INTERACTION_ALLOWED)	You use this parameter to determine whether navigation and other interaction is possible in the Web application.
Data Connection	
Data Provider (DATA_PROVIDER_REF)	See Table 4-9 for a discussion on data binding.

TABLE 4-23   Parameters for the List of Conditions Web Item

Table 4-24 lists and describes the parameters for the List of Exceptions Web item, arranged according to the various parameter groupings.

Text   The Text Web item allows simple texts, characteristic names, and generic text elements (for example, last changed by, key date of the query, query name, and so on) to be displayed in Web applications. Since the texts are language dependent, the text is automatically displayed in the logon language. Language dependency is the key item in this case. You can always insert text just about anywhere you want on the Web report, but with this Web item

Parameter	Description
Display	
Width in Pixels (WIDTH); Full Width (FULL_WIDTH); Height in Pixels (HEIGHT); Full Height (FULL_HEIGHT); Visibility (VISIBILITY); With Tray (WITH_TRAY)	See Table 4-5 for the detailed definition of these parameters.
Behavior	
Activate Navigation (INTERACTION_ALLOWED)	You use this parameter to determine whether navigation and other interaction is possible in the Web application.
Data Connection	
Data Provider (DATA_PROVIDER_REF)	See Table 4-9 for a discussion on data binding.

TABLE 4-24   Parameters for the List of Exceptions Web Item

you can both set up the text to be language dependent and reference a repository for standardized text. This Web item is shown in the system here.

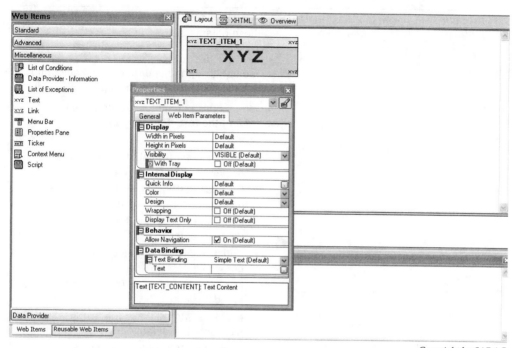

Table 4-25 lists and describes the parameters for the Text Web item, arranged according to the various parameter groupings.

Link   The Link Web item allows you to display and execute a command in the form of a link. This is the same functionality that is available with the 0ANALYSIS_PATTERN template for the Filter and Settings. With the Link Web item, you can easily add commands from the Web Design API to your Web application. To do this, you define a command for a link. You can design the link, add any text (language dependent and language independent) and assign a quick link to it. The next illustration shows this Web item in the system. This is just another approach to using the commands available in the WAD. As you read earlier,

Parameter	Description
Display	
Width in Pixels (WIDTH); Height in Pixels (HEIGHT); Visibility (VISIBILITY); With Tray (WITH_TRAY)	See Table 4-5 for the detailed definition of these parameters.
Internal Display	
Quick Info (TOOLTIP)	You use this parameter to define a quick-info text using the text input dialog.
Color (TEXT_COLOR)	You use this parameter to determine the color of the text. The text can be displayed as follows: • Default Value (DEFAULT) The text is displayed in black by default. • Diminished (DIMINISHED) The text is displayed in gray by default. • Positive (POSITIVE) The text is displayed in green by default. • Critical (CRITICAL) The text is displayed in orange by default. • Negative (NEGATIVE) The text is displayed in red by default. • Marked1 (MARKED1) The text is highlighted by default. • Marked2 (MARKED2) The text is highlighted by default. The display of colors is tied to the respective BEx theme.
Design (TEXT_DESIGN)	You use this parameter to determine the design of the text in the Web application. The text can be displayed as follows: • Standard (STANDARD) • Emphasized (EMPHASIZED) • Small Label (LABEL_SMALL) • Label (LABEL) • Header1 (HEADER1) • Header2 (HEADER2) • Header3 (HEADER3) • Header4 (HEADER4) • Legend (LEGEND) • Reference (REFERENCE) • Non-proportional (MONOSPACE)

TABLE 4-25   Parameters for the Text Web Item

Parameter	Description
Internal Display	
Line Break (TEXT_WRAPPING)	You use this parameter to determine whether a line break is to be applied to a text length that is longer than the width of the Web item.
Behavior	
Activate Navigation (INTERACTION_ALLOWED)	You use this parameter to determine whether navigation or other interactions are possible in the Web application.
Data Binding	
Text Binding (TEXT_BINDING)	You use this parameter to determine the content of the Web item text. • Simple Text (TEXT_CONTENT) You use a text input dialog to define a simple text as the content of the Web item. • Characteristic (CHARACTERISTIC_TEXT_ BINDING) You define a characteristic whose text is to be displayed as the content of the Web item. Choose a Data Provider (DATA_PROVIDER_REF) and a characteristic (CHARACTERISTIC) by technical name. • Generic Text Elements (GENERIC_TEXT_ BINDING) You define which generic text elements of a data provider are to be displayed. To do this, first select a data provider and then the required text elements: Query Name (QUERY) Query Description (QUERY_DESCRIPTION) Name of an InfoProvider (INFOPROVIDER) InfoProvider Description (INFOPROVIDER_DESCRIPTION) Last Data Update (ROLLUPTIME) Key Date (QUERY_KEYDATE) Changed On (CHANGED_AT) Changed By (LAST_CHANGED_BY) Last Refreshed (LAST_REFRESHED) Template (TEMPLATE) System (SYSTEM)

TABLE 4-25   Parameters for the Text Web Item (*continued*)

you can also access the commands using the Button Group Web item. We take into account all of the commands later in this chapter since this topic is very involved.

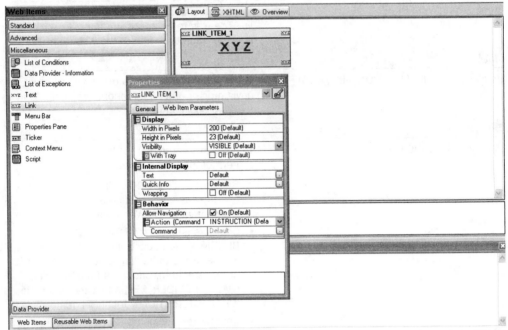

Table 4-26 lists and describes the parameters for the Link Web item, arranged according to the various parameter groupings.

Menu Bar   The Menu Bar Web item allows the display of a menu. It generates a menu similar to the one used in desktop applications on the Web, into which you can add commands from the Web Design API. You can specify whether the menus or menu entries are to trigger an action that is based on a command (as in the use of the commands in the Link Web item) from the Web Design API, or whether the menus are to group menu entries and thus display a nested menu. Nesting is restricted to a maximum of three levels. You can also specify whether a menu or menu entry is to be displayed in the menu bar or menu only, in the toolbar only, or in the menu bar and toolbar. You can also design the menu bar and toolbar by specifying, for example, that a menu is to be displayed with apostrophes, or is to contain a separator. As with a number of these Web items, this is another display option for the different commands and a good formatting component of the WAD.

Parameter	Description
Display	
Width in Pixels (WIDTH); Height in Pixels (HEIGHT); Visibility (VISIBILITY); With Tray (WITH_TRAY)	See Table 4-5 for the detailed definition of these parameters.
Internal Display	
Text (TEXT_CONTENT)	You use this parameter to specify a link text using the text input dialog.
Quick Info (TOOLTIP)	You use this parameter to specify a quick info text for the link in the Web application using the text dialog.
Wrapping (TEXT_WRAPPING)	You use this parameter to specify whether a line break is to be inserted when a text exceeds the width of the Web item (see WIDTH parameter).
Behavior	
Allow Navigation (INTERACTION_ALLOWED)	You use this parameter to specify whether navigation or other interaction is to be possible in the Web application.
Action (Command Triggered) (ACTION)	You use this parameter to connect the link to an action. You first specify the type of action. Actions are available via: • Command via Command Wizard (INSTRUCTION) Using the pushbutton to the right of Command (INSTRUCTION), you can call the command wizard to insert an additional command. • Script Function (SCRIPT_FUNCTION) In the Script Function field, specify a script function to be executed. You generate the script function using the Script Web item that you previously added and set in the Web template.
Command	Multiple different commands can be accessed from this location. These include commands for planning (BI-IP), data providers, Web items, and Web templates. All of these are duplicate processes that you can access via either a context menu or some other option. The planning functions are unique but are still available as a pushbutton rather than a link.

TABLE 4-26   Parameters for the Link Web Item

This Menu Bar Web item offers additional enhanced configuration for customizing the Menu Bars based on the user groups. The following shows this Web item in the system.

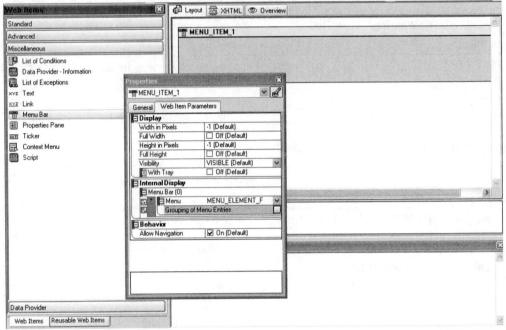

Table 4-27 lists and describes the parameters for the Menu Bar Web item, arranged according to the various parameter groupings. In the configuration process for the Menu Bar Web item there are a series of activities that build on each other. In the table, the tasks involved are identified up to the point of actually assigning a Command or Script Logic. Again, since there are numerous commands, we will work with those individually later in this chapter. As for Script Logic, after selecting to add script logic, a dialog box appears for you to enter the actual script logic. Other items to be included are captions, quick info, and icons (if required).

Properties Pane   The Properties Pane Web item allows you to display and change the properties of a Web item. This can be very useful if the different business users are interested in changing the properties of the Web items on a more personal basis. This will allow them to change the properties of the different Web items directly from the business user screen after execution of the report. Therefore, as a developer you can set the properties

Parameter	Description
Display	
Width in Pixels (WIDTH); Full Width (FULL_WIDTH); Height in Pixels (HEIGHT); Full Height (FULL_HEIGHT); Visibility (VISIBILITY); With Tray (WITH_TRAY)	See Table 4-5 for the detailed definition of these parameters.
Internal Display	
Menu Bar (MENU_CONTAINER_L1)	You use this parameter to design the menu bar. To do this, you create the individual menus and menu entries.
Menu (MENU_ELEMENT_L1)	You use this parameter to specify the individual menus of the menu bar; you also specify the type of menu.
	Grouping of Menu Entries (MENU_ELEMENT_FOLDER_L1)
	If the menu is to group menu entries, you need to set the following additional parameters:
	Caption (CAPTION)
	Using the text input dialog, you enter the name you want to give the menu. You can select whether the texts are to be language-dependent or language-independent.
	Quick Info (TOOLTIP)
	Use the text input dialog to enter a quick info text for the menu.
	Icon (ICON)
	Use this parameter to incorporate icons.
	Display Separator Above
	(MENU_HAS_SEPARATOR_ABOVE)
	You use this parameter to specify whether the top part of the menu is to have a separator.
	You need to set additional parameters for the other list of menu entries that follow.
Menu (MENU_ELEMENT_L1)	**Trigger an Action** (MENU_ELEMENT_ACTION)
	If the menu is to trigger an action, you need to set the following additional parameters:
	Caption (CAPTION)
	Quick Info (TOOLTIP)
	Icon (ICON)
	Action (Command Triggered) (ACTION)
	You can select which action is to be executed and how this is to be done.
	Command via Command Wizard (INSTRUCTION)
	Using the pushbutton to the right of Command (INSTRUCTION), you can call the command wizard to insert a command.
	Script Function (SCRIPT_FUNCTION)

TABLE 4-27   Parameters for the Menu Bar Web Item

Parameter	Description
Internal Display	
Menu (MENU_ELEMENT_L1) (*continued*)	In the Script Function field, you specify a script function to be executed. You generate the script function using the Script Web item that you previously added and set in the Web template.
	Display Ellipsis (MENU_HAS_ELLIPSIS)
	You use the Menu Entry Display (MENU_ELEMENT_DISPLAY) parameter to specify the type of display you want for the menu entry in the Web application.
	Only Menu (VISIBLE_ONLY_IN_MENU)
	You use this parameter to specify that the menu entry is to be displayed in the menu only. If you select this parameter, you need to make the following additional settings:
	Display Separator Above (DISPLAY_SEPARATOR_ABOVE)
	Only Toolbar (VISIBLE_ONLY_IN_TOOLBAR) You use this parameter to specify that the menu entry is to be displayed in the toolbar only. If you select this parameter, you need to make the following additional settings:
	Position in Toolbar (TOOLBAR_ITEM_POSITION)
	Display Separator in Toolbar (TOOLBAR_ITEM_HAS_SEPARATOR)
If you chose the Grouping of Menu Entries (MENU_ELEMENT_FOLDER_L1) type of menu under menu (MENU_ELEMENT_L1), you create a list of menu entries and set the following parameters for each menu entry.	
Menu Entry (MENU_ELEMENT_L2)	You use this parameter to specify a menu entry and the type this menu entry is to be:
	Grouping of Menu Entries (MENU_ELEMENT_FOLDER_L1) If the menu entry is to group additional menu entries, you need to set the following additional parameters:
	• Caption (CAPTION)
	• Quick Info (TOOLTIP)
	• Display Separator Above(MENU_HAS_SEPARATOR_ABOVE)
	If the menu entry itself displays a menu and groups additional menu entries, specify the command that is to be stored for each of these submenu entries:
	• Trigger an Action (MENU_ELEMENT_ACTION)
	You also need to set the following parameters:
	• Caption (CAPTION)
	• Quick Info (TOOLTIP)
	• Display Ellipsis (MENU_HAS_ELLIPSIS)
	• Action (Command Triggered) (ACTION) You can select which action is to be executed and how this is to be done.
	• Command via Command Wizard (INSTRUCTION) Using the pushbutton to the right of Command (INSTRUCTION), you can call the command wizard to insert an additional menu item command.
	• Script Function (SCRIPT_FUNCTION) In the Script Function field, specify a script function to be executed. You generate the script function using the Script Web item that you previously added and set in the Web template.

TABLE 4-27   Parameters for the Menu Bar Web Item (*continued*)

Parameter	Description
Internal Display	
Menu Entry (MENU_ELEMENT_L2) (*continued*)	You also specify how the menu entry is to be displayed: <ul><li>Only Menu (VISIBLE_ONLY_IN_MENU) If you select this parameter, you need to make the following additional setting: Display Separator Above (MENU_HAS_SEPARATOR_ABOVE)</li><li>Only Toolbar (VISIBLE_ONLY_IN_TOOLBAR) If you select this parameter, you need to make the following additional settings: Position in Toolbar (TOOLBAR_ITEM_POSITION) Display Separator in Toolbar (TOOLBAR_ITEM_HAS_SEPARATOR)</li><li>Menu and Toolbar (VISIBLE_IN_MENU_AND_TOOLBAR) If you select this parameter, you need to make the following additional settings: Display Separator Above (MENU_HAS_SEPARATOR_ABOVE) Position in Toolbar (TOOLBAR_ITEM_POSITION) Display Separator in Toolbar (TOOLBAR_ITEM_HAS_SEPARATOR)</li></ul>**Trigger an Action (MENU_ELEMENT_ACTION)** If the menu entry is to trigger an action, you need to set the following additional parameters:<ul><li>Caption (CAPTION)</li><li>Quick Info (TOOLTIP)</li><li>Action (Command Triggered) (ACTION) You can select which action is to be executed and how this is to be done.</li><li>Command via Command Wizard (INSTRUCTION) Using the pushbutton to the right of Command (INSTRUCTION), you can call the command wizard to insert an additional command.</li><li>Script Function (SCRIPT_FUNCTION) In the Script Function field, specify a script function to be executed. You generate the script function using the Script Web item that you previously added and set in the Web template.</li><li>Display Ellipsis (MENU_HAS_ELLIPSIS) You use the Menu Entry Display (MENU_ELEMENT_DISPLAY) parameter to specify the type of display you want for the menu entry in the Web application.</li><li>Menu Only (VISIBLE_ONLY_IN_MENU) If you select this parameter, you need to make the following additional setting: Display Separator Above (DISPLAY_SEPARATOR_ABOVE)</li><li>Only Toolbar (VISIBLE_ONLY_IN_TOOLBAR) If you select this parameter, you need to make the following additional settings: Position in Toolbar (TOOLBAR_ITEM_POSITION) Display Separator in Toolbar (TOOLBAR_ITEM_HAS_SEPARATOR)</li><li>Menu and Toolbar (VISIBLE_IN_MENU_AND_TOOLBAR) If you select this parameter, you need to make the following additional settings: Display Separator Above (DISPLAY_SEPARATOR_ABOVE) Position in Toolbar (TOOLBAR_ITEM_POSITION) Display Separator in Toolbar (TOOLBAR_ITEM_HAS_SEPARATOR)</li></ul>
Behavior	
Allow Navigation (INTERACTION_ALLOWED)	You use this parameter to specify whether navigation or other interaction is to be possible in the Web application.

TABLE 4-27   Parameters for the Menu Bar Web Item (*continued*)

as defaults and allow the business users to adjust accordingly. The following illustration shows this Web item in the system.

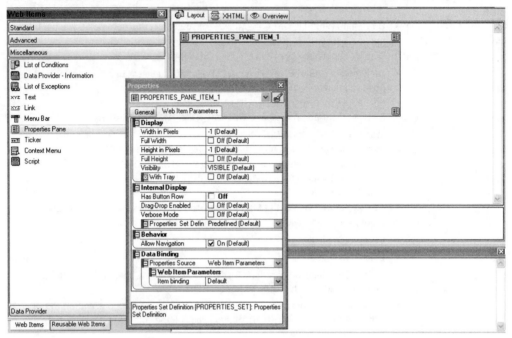

Table 4-28 lists and describes the parameters for the Properties Pane Web item, arranged according to the various parameter groupings.

Ticker   The Ticker Web item allows you to display table content as a ticker. This creates a scrolling list of information from the assigned data provider and is very handy when you want to draw attention to a specific statistic. This is an excellent approach to generating an

Parameter	Description
Display	
Width in Pixels (WIDTH); Full Width (FULL_WIDTH); Height in Pixels (HEIGHT); Full Height (FULL_HEIGHT); Visibility (VISIBILITY); With Tray (WITH_TRAY)	See Table 4-5 for the detailed definition of these parameters.
Internal Display	
Has Button Row (HAS_BUTTON_ROW)	You use this parameter to specify whether the Web item with the pushbutton row is to be displayed.
Allow Drag and Drop (DRAGDROP_ENABLED)	You use this parameter to specify whether the drag and drop function is to be enabled for the Web item.
Verbose Mode (VERBOSE_MODE)	You use this parameter to display the technical name of all properties.

Properties Set Definition (PROPERTIES_SET)	You use this parameters to specify the properties that can be displayed and changed using the Web item in the Web application. The various options are listed below.
	• Predefined (PROP_SET_PREDEFINED) When you select this value, the properties that are predefined by SAP are displayed.
	• All (PROP_SET_ALL) When you select this value, all properties for the object are displayed.
	• Single Value (PROP_SET_SINGLE_VALUE) When you select this value, you can specify a property to be displayed. To do this, specify the technical name of the property (PROPERTY_NAME) and assign a useful description to it (PROPERTY_CAPTION).
	• Matrix Layout (PROP_SET_MATRIX) When you select this value, you can display the properties you specified in table form. To do this, you create groups of properties:
	  • You assign a description for each group (GROUP_DESC).
	  • You specify the number of columns (COLUMN_INDEX).
	  • For each group, you specify the list of properties. For each property in the list, you make the following settings:
	    • You specify a property by entering the technical name of this property (PROPERTY_NAME).
	    • You give the property a meaningful description (PROPERTY_CAPTION).
	    • You specify the property parent (PROPERTY_PARENT).

TABLE **4-28**   Parameters for the Properties Pane Web Item

Parameter	Description
Internal Display	
Properties Group Display (PROPERTIES_GROUP_DISPLAY)	You use this parameter to group the properties. The various options are listed below. • Default (DEFAULT)—When you select this value, the properties that are predefined by SAP are displayed with the group display. • Tab Pages (TABS)—If you select this, the properties are aligned on tab pages. • Headline (HEADLINE)—If you select this, the properties are aligned under the group name.
Name of First Tab Page (PROPERTIES_INITIAL_TAB)	You use this parameter to specify which tab page to display.
Behavior	
Allow Navigation (INTERACTION_ALLOWED)	You use this parameter to specify whether navigation or other interaction is to be possible in the Web application.
Data Binding	
Properties Source (PROPERTIES_SOURCE)	You use this parameter to specify the element of the Web application for which the properties can be displayed and changed. You can choose from the following properties: • Web Item Parameters (ITEM_PROPERTIES) • Data Provider Properties (QUERYVIEW_PROPERTIES) • Conditions (CONDITIONS_PROPERTIES) • Exceptions (EXCEPTIONS_PROPERTIES) • Axis Properties (AXIS_PROPERTIES) • Characteristic Properties (CHARACTERISTIC_PROPERTIES) • Characteristic Properties – Input Help (MEMBER_ACCESS_PROPERTIES) • Characteristic Properties – Filter Values (FILTER_PRESENTATION_PROPERTIES) • Properties of Structure Element (STRUCTURE_MEMBER_PROPERTIES) • Data Cell Properties (DATA_CELL_PROPERTIES) • Properties of All Data Cells (ALL_DATA_CELL_PROPERTIES)
Depending on the properties selected for the Properties Source parameter (PROPERTIES_SOURCE), there are additional parameters that you need to set.	
Web Item Parameters	
Web Item (ITEM_REF)	You use this parameter to select the Web item for which the properties can be displayed and changed in the Web application. Ensure that you insert the Web item, for which the properties are to be displayed.

TABLE 4-28 Parameters for the Properties Pane Web Item (*continued*)

Parameter	Description
Properties of the Data Provider, Conditions, Exceptions	
Data Provider (DATA_PROVIDER_REF)	You use this parameter to select the data provider for which the properties can be displayed and changed in the Web application. Ensure that you define the data provider, for which the properties are to be displayed.
Characteristic Properties, Input Help, and Filter Values	
Data Provider (DATA_PROVIDER_REF)	You use this parameter to select the data provider for which the properties can be displayed and changed in the Web application. Ensure that you define the data provider, for which the properties are to be displayed.
Characteristic (CHARACTERISTIC)	You use this parameter to select a characteristic of the data providers selected under Data Provider (DATA_PROVIDER_REF).
Axes Properties	
Data Provider (DATA_PROVIDER_REF)	You use this parameter to select the data provider for which the properties can be displayed and changed in the Web application. Ensure that you define the data provider, for which the properties are to be displayed.
Axis (AXIS)	You use this parameter to specify where to position the characteristic: • Rows (ROWS) • Columns (COLUMNS) • Free Characteristics (FREE)
Data Cell Properties	
Data Provider (DATA_PROVIDER_REF)	You use this parameter to select the data provider for which the properties can be displayed and changed in the Web application. Ensure that you define the data provider, for which the properties are to be displayed.
First Structure Element (FIRST_STRUC_MEMBER)	You use this parameter to specify a structure element of the first structure.
Second Structure Element (SECOND_STRUC_MEMBER)	You use this parameter to specify a structure element of the second structure.
Structure Element Properties	
Data Provider (DATA_PROVIDER_REF)	You use this parameter to select the data provider for which the properties can be displayed and changed in the Web application. Make sure you define the data provider, for which the properties are to be displayed.
Structure Element Properties (STRUCTURE_MEMBER)	You use this parameter to specify the properties of the key figure.

TABLE 4-28   Parameters for the Properties Pane Web Item (*continued*)

up-to-date display of information around your critical key indicators, especially if you have set up a multiple data loading process per day. This information is shown here.

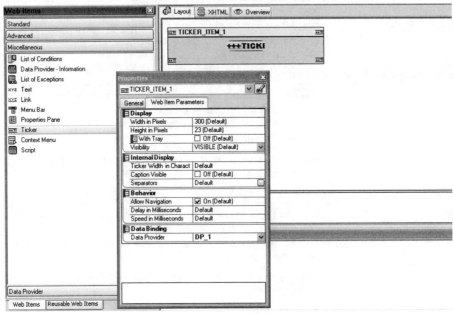

Table 4-29 lists and describes the parameters for the Ticker Web item, arranged according to the various parameter groupings.

Context Menu   The Context Menu Web item enables you to display a context menu in a Web application and to specify which context menu choices are available to the user of the Web application. If you do not drag the Web item onto the Web template and make your settings, the standard context menu is displayed in the Web application. The following illustration shows this Web item in the system. This has replaced the option in the older version for the Basic Context Menu items versus the Advanced Context Menu list. This only has the option to turn the item on or off, not to have enhanced and basic context menus. The alternative to having an Enhanced and Basic Menu would be to use some functionality via the Menu Bar Web item.

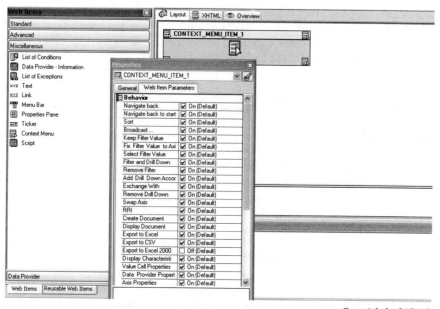

Copyright by SAP AG

Parameter	Description
Display	
Width in Pixels (WIDTH); Height in Pixels (HEIGHT); Visibility (VISIBILITY); With Tray (WITH_TRAY)	See Table 4-5 for the detailed definition of these parameters.
Internal Display	
Width of the Ticker Text in Characters (TICKER_SIZE)	You use this parameter to set the width of the ticker text in characters.
Label Visible (CAPTION_VISIBLE)	You use this parameter to determine whether the label (name of the query) is displayed for the ticker.
Separator (SEPARATOR)	You use this parameter to set the separator between two ticker rows. Separators are added when the data for a new data row is displayed.
Behavior	
Activate Navigation (INTERACTION_ALLOWED)	You use this parameter to determine whether navigation or other interactions are possible in the Web application.
Delay in Milliseconds (DELAY) Default Value: 3000	You use this parameter to determine the delay in milliseconds until the ticker starts.
Speed in Milliseconds (SPEED) Default Value: 200	You use this parameter to determine the time after which the ticker moves one character. You can only specify the time in milliseconds.
Data Binding	
Data Provider (DATA_PROVIDER_REF)	See Table 4-9 for discussion on data binding.

TABLE 4-29   Parameters for the Ticker Web Item

Table 4-30 lists and describes the parameters for the Context Menu Web item. Note that in all cases, if this indicator is turned on, the item will appear in the context menu. These parameters are the same items that you would see in the standard context menu used on the standard template 0ANALYSIS_PATTERN.

Parameter	Description
BEHAVIOR	
Back One Navigation Step (MENU_BACK)	This displays the Back One Navigation Step option in the context menu of the Web template. You can use this option to navigate back one navigation step for a data provider.
Back to Start (MENU_BACK_TO_START)	This displays the Back to Start option in the context menu of the Web template. You can use this option to navigate back all navigation steps for a data provider.
Sort (MENU_SORT)	This displays the Sort option in the context menu of the Web template. You use this option to sort the underlying data providers.
Broadcast (MENU_BROADCASTER)	This displays the Broadcast option in the context menu of the Web template. You use this option to call broadcaster applications to distribute the result.
Keep Filter Value (MENU_FILTER)	This displays the Keep Filter Value option in the context menu of the Web template.
Keep Filter Value on Axis (MENU_FILTER_ON_AXIS)	This displays the Keep Filter Value on Axis option in the context menu of the Web template.
Select Filter Value (MENU_SELECT_FILTER)	This displays the Select Filter Value option in the context menu of the Web template.
Filter and Drill Down By (MENU_FILTER_DRILL_DOWN)	This displays the Filter and Drill Down option in the context menu of the Web template.
Remove Filter (MENU_REMOVE_FILTER)	This displays the Remove Filter option in the context menu of the Web template.
Add Drilldown According To (MENU_DRILL_DOWN)	This displays the Add Drilldown According To option in the context menu of the Web template.
Swap With (MENU_EXCHANGE_OBJECTS)	This displays the Swap With option in the context menu of the Web template.
Remove Drilldown (MENU_REMOVE_DRILL_DOWN)	This displays the Remove Drilldown option in the context menu of the Web template.
Swap Axes (MENU_SWITCH_AXIS)	This displays the Switch Axes option in the context menu of the Web template.
Goto (MENU_RRI)	This displays the Goto option in the context menu of the Web template.
Create Document (MENU_DOCUMENT_CREATE)	This displays the Create Document option in the context menu of the Web template.
Display Documents (MENU_DISPLAY_DOCUMENTS)	This displays the Display Documents option in the context menu of the Web template.

TABLE 4-30   Parameters for the Context Menu Web Item

Parameter	Description
BEHAVIOR	
Export to Excel (MENU_EXPORT_TO_XLS)	This displays the Export to Excel option in the context menu of the Web template.
Export to CSV (MENU_EXPORT_TO_CSV)	This displays the Export to CSV option in the context menu of the Web template.
Export to Excel 2000 (MENU_EXPORT_TO_XLS2000)	This displays the Export to Excel 2000 option in the context menu of the Web template.
Properties - Characteristic (MENU_CHARACTERISTIC_ PROPERTIES)	This displays the Properties - Characteristic option in the context menu of the Web template.
Properties - Data Cell (MENU_VALUE_PROPERTIES)	This displays the Properties - Data Cell option in the context menu of the Web template.
Properties - Data Provider (MENU_ DATAPROVIDER_PROPERTIES)	This displays the Properties - Data Provider option in the context menu of the Web template.
Properties - Axis (MENU_AXIS_PROPERTIES)	This displays the Properties - Axis option in the context menu of the Web template.
Properties - All Data Cells (MENU_ALL_DATA_CELL_PROPERTIES)	This displays the Properties - All Data Cells option in the context menu of the Web template.
Conditions (MENU_CONDITIONS)	This displays the Conditions option in the context menu of the Web template.
Global Currency Translation (MENU_CONVERSION)	This displays the Global Currency Translation option in the context menu of the Web template.
Hierarchy Active (MENU_HIERARCHY_STATE)	This displays the Hierarchy Active option in the context menu of the Web template.
Expand Hierarchy (MENU_HIERARCHY_DRILL)	This displays the Expand Hierarchy option in the context menu of the Web template.
Hierarchy Node Expanded (MENU_HIERARCHY_NODE_DRILL)	This displays the Hierarchy Node Expanded option in the context menu of the Web template.
Calculate Results As (MENU_CALCULATE_RESULT)	This displays the Calculate Results As option in the context menu of the Web template.
Calculate Single Values As (MENU_CALCULATE_VALUE)	This displays the Calculate Single Values As option in the context menu of the Web template.
Variable Screen (MENU_VARIABLE_SCREEN)	This displays the Variable Screen option in the context menu of the Web template.
Print Version (MENU_PRINT)	This displays the Print Version option in the context menu of the Web template.
Properties - Web Item (MENU_ITEM_PROPERTIES)	This displays the Properties - Web Item option in the context menu of the Web template.
Exceptions (MENU_EXCEPTIONS)	This displays the Exceptions option in the context menu of the Web template.

TABLE 4-30   Parameters for the Context Menu Web Item (*continued*)

Parameter	Description
BEHAVIOR	
Save View (MENU_VIEW_SAVE)	This displays the Save View option in the context menu of the Web template.
Local Formulas (MENU_LOCAL_FORMULAS)	This displays the Local Formulas option in the context menu of the Web template.
Personalize (MENU_PERSONALIZE)	This displays the Personalize option in the context menu of the Web template.
Bookmark (MENU_BOOKMARK)	This displays the Bookmark option in the context menu of the Web template.

TABLE 4-30 Parameters for the Context Menu Web Item (*continued*)

Script   The Script Web item makes it possible to integrate JavaScript in Web templates. Use this Web item if you will be affecting another Web item with some additional enhancements that need to be applied via JavaScript. For example, the use of an alternative Print function would need to be applied via a JavaScript Web item. If you create the JavaScript with additional ABAP programs embedded to help with calls to the ABAP programming, this will allow you to use other, non-WAD-related objects in the WAD report. The following illustration shows this Web item in the system.

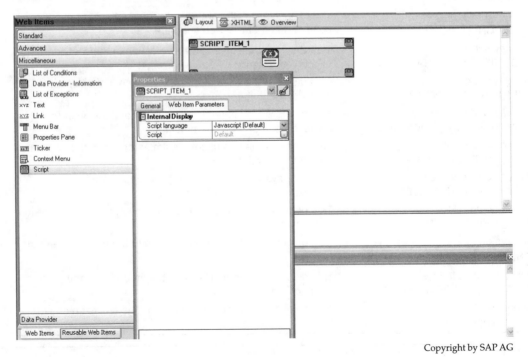

Copyright by SAP AG

Table 4-31 lists and describes the parameters for the Script Web item.

Parameter	Description
Internal Display	
Script Language (SCRIPT_CONTENT_TYPE_LIST)	You use this parameter to specify the script language. JavaScript (JAVASCRIPT)
Script (SCRIPT)	You use this parameter to create a script function to integrate it into the Web template.

TABLE 4-31   Parameters for the Script Web Item

Custom Extension   The Custom Extension Web item is for the additional availability to include some Custom Exit programming for use with variables. Using this Web item based on the class name, you can take your coding, whether in ABAP or Java, and assign it to a variable or other executable command (this is also possible) in your Web template. The following illustration shows this Web item in the system.

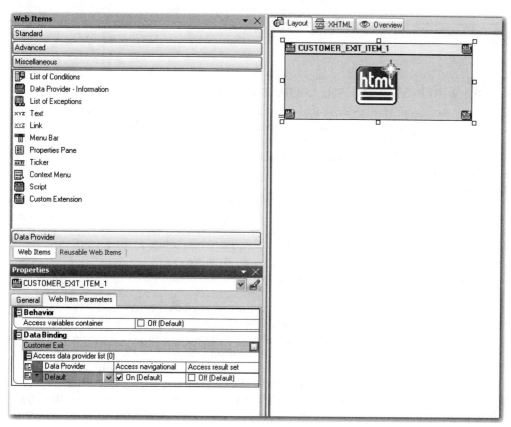

Table 4-32 lists and describes the parameters for the Custom Extension Web item.

Parameter	Description
Behavior	
Access Variables Container (VARIABLES_CONTAINER_ACCESS)	You use this parameter to turn on the access to variable containers and affect the variables with the coding included in this Web item.
Data Binding	
Customer Exit (CUSTOMER_EXIT)	This option allows you to enter your program coding. ABAP or Java class name is required. You will need to identify the Exit Type (CUSTOMER_EXIT_TYPE) and the Properties List (NAMED_PROPERTY_LIST). Additional use of a Text option is available also.
Access data provider list (DATA_PROVIDER_ACCESS_LIST)	You use this parameter to enter a list of data providers that you want to access. For each data provider, you can specify whether to pass the navigational state or the result set to the ABAP class.

TABLE 4-32   Parameters for the Custom Extension Web Item

Formatting with Web Template Layouts Format

One of the most important things that you will need to do with your Web reports is to format them correctly so that you offer business users a view of the data that is consistent and easy to read. You should review the formatting on an ongoing basis during the development of the dashboards and Web reports. Take the time and have a group review of the different phases of the report development. This will help to ensure that you obtain signoff at the end of the project.

Business users must be able to read, understand, and assimilate the results of their queries. The normal rule of thumb when configuring a report is to make sure that the results can be understood in less than seven seconds. In other words, after a business user executes the report and the information is available, the user should be able to walk away from the report in less than seven seconds with a good understanding of the analysis and what was being communicated through the report. This means you must make sure that the display of the data has as few issues as possible.

Failing to format a report properly and make sure that all the objects are aligned correctly for display purposes renders the report ineffective. Creating Web applications in which the content is arranged incorrectly onscreen leads to user complaints, time-consuming analyses, and, ultimately, a lack of trust in the data and therefore a decision not to use the reporting tools. The WAD offers numerous objects and options that we can use to help us with the formatting process. Some of them were identified in the previous section, such as the Container, Container Layout, and Groups Web items. Investigating and understanding the functionality of these Web items is definitely worth your time. In this section, I'll provide a few examples of working with the formatting functionality in certain areas of a Web template, then we will get into full examples in Chapters 6 and 7. Let's start with my favorite option for fast, consistent formatting—inserting a table.

The HTML table serves as a grid into which you can place Web items. This provides an effective method for placing Web items side by side or in a vertical arrangement on the Web page. It's very easy to get started, and for testing purposes, a table helps you to format the data so that basic testing results are easier to read. Open the Web Template page and use the Table icon or Table | Insert Table to access the table option. Identify the number of rows and columns that you need in your table and then click Apply to insert the table into the Web template.

The table will be inserted into your Web template at the current cursor location. At any time, you can use the context menu in the table to make changes, as shown next.

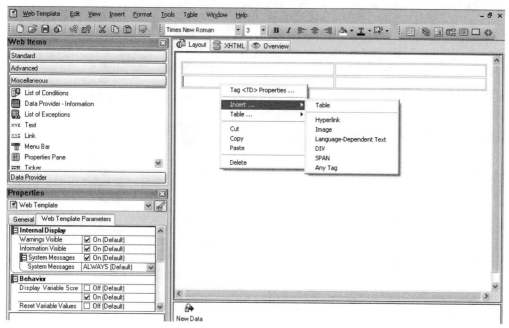

Copyright by SAP AG

From the context menu of the table, you can

- Insert or delete rows or columns or delete the table itself
- Edit the table properties
- Split and merge cells
- Add a URL link to the information, add images, and add objects (DIV, SPAN) to help with the sizing of the spaces between objects

In some cases, the formatting provided by the Web items won't quite suit your needs, so you may need to do some of the formatting manually. In such cases, options available on the WAD menu and toolbars can be useful to you. For example, you will often need to provide some basic text information to help the user put the data into context, or to provide additional direction regarding the Web application or the results being displayed. For these purposes, you can easily insert text directly into the Web template by just using the context menu off of the cell and choosing Insert | Language Dependent Text or you can just start to type in what you want in one of the table cells. For example, suppose you need to add some text to make sure that specific directions are followed after the user reads the report. Simply type them in and the XHTML will be automatically generated to support the text. The results are shown here.

DDIC: SAP Training System Powered by .NET Microsoft Technology

After Reading this Report please contact Mr. Miller with any questions at X3550

Division ⇕		Distribution Channel ⇕		Incoming Orders ⇕ EUR	Order Entry Quantity ⇕
00	Cross-division	10	Final customer sales	9.000,00	15 PC
		12	Sold for resale	25.500,00	30 PC
		14	Service	8.155,10	0 AU
		Result		42.655,10	45 PC
01	Pumps	10	Final customer sales	45.102.784,12	14.897 PC
		Result		45.102.784,12	14.897 PC
02	Motorcycles	12	Sold for resale	57.846.845,32	195.279 PC
		Result		57.846.845,32	195.279 PC
04	Lighting	12	Sold for resale	67.656.161,73	168.239 CAR
		Result		67.656.161,73	168.239 CAR
07	High Tech	10	Final customer sales	52.428.399,72	231.477 PC
		12	Sold for resale	56.095.407,88	62.028 PC
		14	Service	17.532,20	27 PC
		16	Factory sales	0,00	0 PC
		Result		108.541.339,80	293.532 PC
08	Service	14	Service	2.351.003,56	0 AU
		Result		2.351.003,56	0 AU
10	Vehicles	12	Sold for resale	79.577,48	3 PC
		Result		79.577,48	3 PC
20	Turbines	10	Final customer sales	1.660.000,00	2 PC
		Result		1.660.000,00	2 PC
Overall Result				283.280.367,11	671.996,600 MIX

Copyright by SAP AG

By using some of the functionality in the Format toolbar, you can adjust quite a few items with very little effort. The next illustration shows the basic formatting that was done in the preceding example, with some background color added using the Format toolbar and going to Format | Text Background Color and choosing a color for the background of the text.

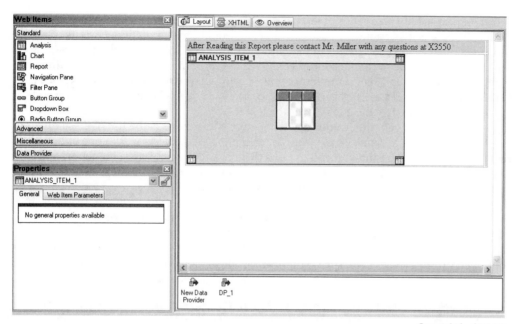

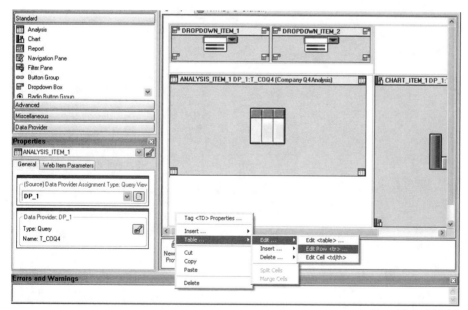

The Format toolbar lets you modify the font and font size; apply bold and italic; adjust the alignment of the selected text; and change the background color of the Web template, the text color, and the text background color. You can also use the <DIV> and <SPAN>

HTML tags to specify properties of textual information. For example, you can use the <DIV> tag to specify a container within which you can put text and apply various properties such as font, color size, and alignment of the text. This is useful for formatting the different properties of the header of your Web application. The <SPAN> tag defines an inline text container and is often used to apply specific CSS styles to parts of a text block. For example, you could use the <SPAN> tag to insert a style to change the color and style of the text if the user hovers the cursor over the text.

An example of a very quick and easy fix to your Web reports is the use of these different functions. For example, suppose we want to realign the Web objects within one of our Web reports. We can use the context menu options to help, and we can access the report and tweak the results as we go. To do this, we access an existing Web template, right-click to open the context menu, and choose Table | Edit | Edit Row.

When this command is executed, the dialog box appears for the format of the table. In this dialog box, shown next, we can adjust the format of the report by rows and columns, adjust the sizing, alter the attributes, and add another CSS style sheet. (Remember, the CSS can only be used via some manual text that is included; the overall style of the Web report is controlled by the Themes style sheet.) In this case, all we do is change the setting for the vertical alignment to Top. This will move all the Web objects to the top level of the cells.

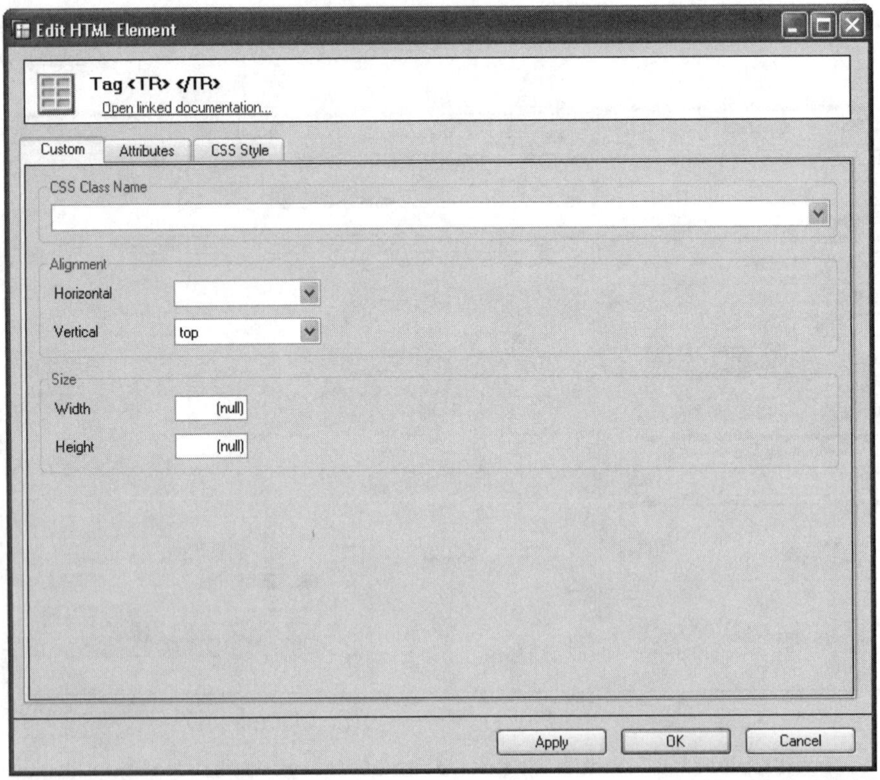

Finally, execute the WAD report and see the results, shown next. Notice how much more consistent this looks versus the basic WAD query that you would have by just including individual Web items in a Web application. This improves the overall format and appeal of the report with just one minor change in a setting. Therefore, work with all the options available and see what they can do for your WAD reports.

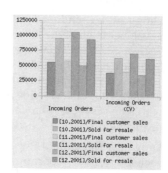

Copyright by SAP AG

If a Web application needs to accommodate multiple languages, you can use language-dependent text in your Web application. Since the Web application is executed in the NetWeaver portal, it is the logon language of the NetWeaver portal user ID that determines which text language is displayed.

To use language-dependent text, right-click anywhere in the Web template and choose Insert | Language-Dependent Text. This opens the Text Edition dialog box, shown here, which offers the choices for text input described next.

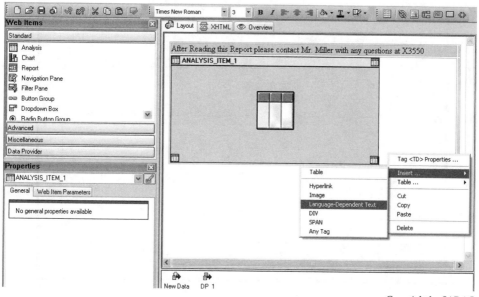

Copyright by SAP AG

- **Language-Independent Text**   This text will always show in the Web application regardless of the logon language of the user.
- **Language-Dependent Text Stored in Object (Web Template or Reusable Web Item)**   The text can only be entered in the current logon language of the Web template developer. Therefore, if the text was required in two languages, the developer would have to log on twice, once in each language, and enter the text in each language.
- **Language-Dependent Text Stored in Table**   This option allows the Web template developer to enter the text in as many languages as needed in the same session. Each text has a language key to identify it. The text is stored in separate tables (technical name of the table that stores the multiple Text languages is RSBEXTEXTS) and needs to be transported separately from the Web template. This option supports the ability for all text that is to be used to be managed centrally via one screen. This would be very helpful if your project has many developers and you want all of the text being used to be consistent.
- **Language-Dependent Report Text (Obsolete)**   If you need to access another object, such as an ABAP report program, you would use this option.

By choosing the option Language-Dependent Text Stored in Table, we can use text that has been stored in different languages, as shown in the following illustration.

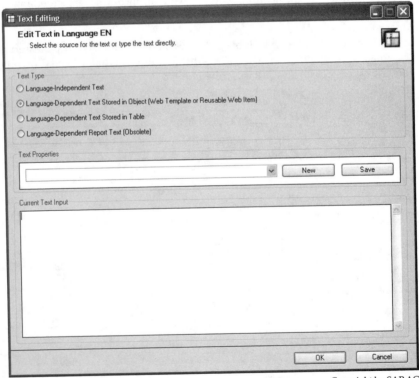

Copyright by SAP AG

Another easy option to use from this context menu is the ability to insert images into the Web template. If you need to add a company logo or divisional logos or even just some background color that is specific to the customer, you can accomplish this using the option Insert | Image. Graphic files with the extensions .BMP, .JPG, and .GIF can be used. The initial step is to access the MIME Repository (transaction code SE80) and go to the location in which to store customer images—SAP | BW | Customer | Images. Here, you can insert or upload your images. After you do so, you can use the context menu again to access the Insert | Image option. You will then be able to insert your image in the appropriate location in the WAD template via the Edit HTML Element dialog box, shown here.

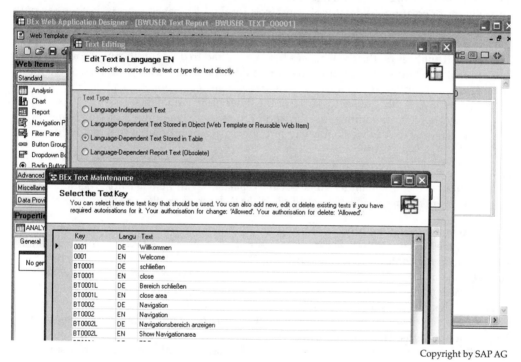

Copyright by SAP AG

The use of themes is another option that will make a big impact on your WAD templates with little effort. Because all BI Web applications are displayed in the NetWeaver portal, the portal themes are used to apply HTML-like styles to the objects in the Web application. Prior to NetWeaver 7.0 (2004S) BI, a cascading style sheet was assigned to each Web template. Therefore, the portal themes are replacing the cascading style sheets. These portal themes serve the same purpose, but are created and maintained with the Theme Editor in the NetWeaver portal. These themes are, in turn, assigned to a *portal desktop*, a collection of parameters that defines the look and feel of the specific portal environment.

All of the configuration functionality covered in this section is directly available from the context menu. The ability to adjust the look and feel of the report can be accomplished quickly and easily from these parameters. Definitely keep the context menu in mind when you are configuring and implementing a WAD component.

Command Wizard

As you reviewed the parameters for the Button Group, Link, Menu Bar, and Tab Pages Web items, you likely noticed that you can assign commands to some of these parameters by using the command wizard to create Web-based activities for users. This gives you more flexibility when using the different functions within the WAD, enabling you not only to develop and display some existing components in a different manner, but also to develop new functionality. This capability is especially useful now that BI enables you to create planning activities in addition to reporting activities, because the commands available include quite a few planning processes. The command wizard functionality offers so many possibilities for creating different looks and feels for the Web-based reports that we can only touch the surface in this book.

The command wizard enables you to set up reports that offer business users the ability to do what-if analysis on the fly. Whereas before you had to do a significant amount of work to set up a dashboard with a sliding indicator to do what-if scenarios, with the command wizard, you can configure and make available this type of component in about the same amount of time as it takes to set up some of the other basic Web items.

Now, we've seen the command setup and process used in a number of Web items up to this point and now we can work our way through an example of what this can do for us.

NOTE *We can use a similar approach to this in the development of the functionality within the BEx Analyzer and the BEx Analyzer Workbook and commands. This functionality is not unique to the Web but there are more options available in the Web versus the BEx Analyzer.*

As you go through the process of using the command wizard, notice some of the overlap of the Web items that we can create commands for and the fact that the commands already are in the context menu of a particular Web API or available in the BEx Web Analyzer. Because some of the functionality overlaps, the choice comes down to what the business user is more comfortable using—the context menu or a button on the screen. The additional flexibility of the command process allows developers to extend the navigational and processing power of the Web items without having to go immediately to developing JavaScript programs. This offers much more flexibility for the developers and the business users. The combination of the Web Design API functionality and embedding the command option into it offers the ability to enhance Web templates, Web items, data providers, and planning application commands. These commands extend the interaction and capabilities of objects to enhance the integration of Web-based analysis objects.

The command wizard is the main tool for creating commands from the Web Design API. You can use it to create commands easily by following a step-by-step procedure and include them in your Web template, enabling you to create highly individual Web applications with

BI content. In the command wizard, all of the parameters available for each command are listed so that they can also be set directly there. You also see a description for each command and each parameter directly in the command wizard. The command wizard is part of the WAD and does not require any additional installation. You usually call the command wizard in the WAD from the Web item parameter Action (Command Triggered) (ACTION). If you insert a hyperlink into the Web template, you can also call the command wizard in the dialog box that follows by clicking the button next to the text-entry field.

This functionality is embedded into numerous Web items, including Button Group, Dropdown Box, Menu Bar, and Group, to name a few. One of the most popular areas for this functionality is the Button Group, which offers individual buttons for each command assigned. The Web Design API enables you to create commands for any data providers, planning applications, Web items, and Web templates. Any context menu navigation can be replaced with a command that offers the ability to develop a step-by-step view of querying on different reports. So, rather than having the business user work through a context menu–driven drilldown, you can enable them to use a series of buttons from the Button Group, with commands executing in the system.

Commands can also help with the parameterization of different Web items. The Web Design API tool, which is accessible from anywhere that a command is relevant, guides the user through the necessary parameters without the need to master HTML syntax or XHTML syntax.

NOTE *Although you will be introduced to many of the commands in this chapter, we will not go into details of all the different commands available, such as those for Integrated Planning (BI-IP) activities.*

This is definitely one area in which we cannot possibly cover all the bells and whistles in detail. As you read through this section, you'll understand why. Each command has a list of additional parameters that can be used to enhance the functionality of the command. In some cases, the list is extremely long, and it would be impractical to attempt to define each parameter. Therefore, I will show you through an example the basic procedural steps to set up a command. As you read through the list of commands, follow these steps to try out some of the other commands, to get comfortable with their functionality.

If you use one of the Web items the command wizard is called from the Properties tab option of that particular Web item. When you access the initial screen, you see two tabs: Favorite Commands and All Commands. If you select the Button Group Web item and then access the command wizard, the initial screen is the Favorite Commands tab, shown next. You can assign any number of commands to this Favorite Commands tab by choosing them in the list.

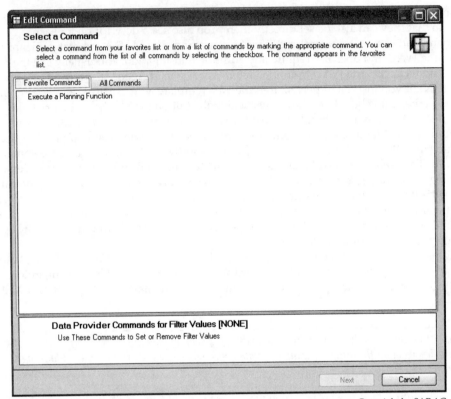

The All Commands tab provides full access to all the available commands. It includes a series of folders, listed next, that hold all of the commands:

- Commands for Data Provider
- Commands for Planning Applications
- Commands for Web Items
- Commands for Web Templates

The Commands for Data Provider folder supports all functionality that is available within the standard 0ANALYSIS_PATTERN Web template. These will be the primary commands that you will want to assign to your reports or dashboards. The Commands for Planning Applications are very good and you might use some of them for a report but 95 percent of the time these will be used for the purpose of planning and consolidation using BI-IP. As for the Commands for Web Items and Web Templates, we have worked with these in the earlier portions of this chapter. These incorporate all of the functionality of the context menus for both of the areas and are very similar. So we will focus on an example from the Data Provider and the Web Template Commands in this section.

In the Commands for Data Provider folder, you can find a summary of all commands you can use to change the status of a data provider. You can use these commands to set filter values, for example, or to change the navigational state of a data provider. When you select a command, the parameters for that specific command are displayed. You choose parameters either by direct entry or by selecting them from dropdown lists. Many command parameters have additional subscreens for entering additional parameters. With the help of the command wizard, you can step through each of these items and confirm the values of the parameters without having to program JavaScript as you go.

Taking an example and working through this process will give you a good idea of the steps involved and some of the functionality that is available. You will work with a series of Web items, so set up a Web template with Navigation Pane, Button Group, Dropdown Box, and Analysis Web items. Looking at the Button Group, you can see in the Properties screen area of the following illustration that it has two buttons assigned to it—Save View and Print to PDF. As you can see, the Button Group has direct access to the command process; by clicking on the icon directly to the right of the field, you are able to directly access the Commands screen.

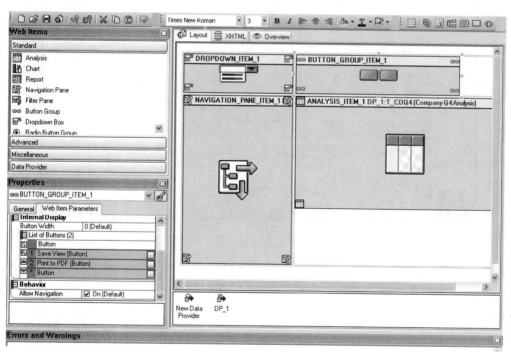

Stepping into the Edit Parameter screen that supports the Commands, we can start to review the configuration of each of the Command buttons. The following illustration shows the initial view of the configuration for the Save View command button. These configuration settings are standard for most command options. You start by confirming the Caption, confirming whether or not you would like to have Quick Info, enabling the command, and selecting what the format would be—in this case we will accept the Standard format.

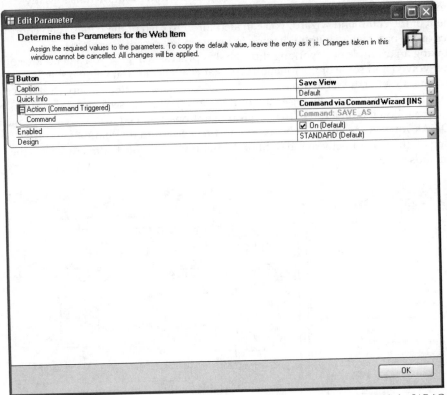

Clicking the box next to the line with Command: SAVE_AS (right side), we get to the configuration screen. The following illustration shows this result. This view of the command wizard is the result once the Web API has been chosen.

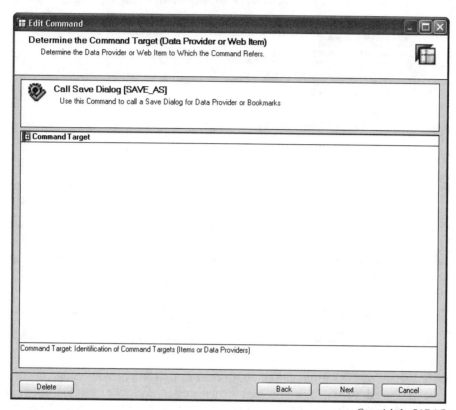

If we look at the details of the configuration, we see the complete set of parameters available to work with, and this is where the Save option was assigned. Notice that because the commands are already configured, the only activity completed by the developer was to check off the box for Save Query View (SAVE_VIEW). These results are shown next.

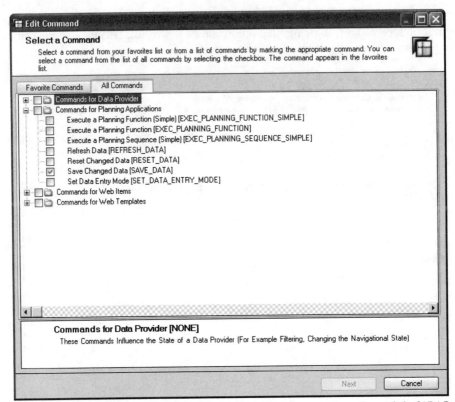

Finally, reviewing the additional setting for the Printing and drilldown into the details screen, we see the additional indicators that were necessary to accomplish the assignment of the Print option. Notice that on the dropdown there are a series of options to choose from including Print to Excel 2000. The next illustration shows the results of this process.

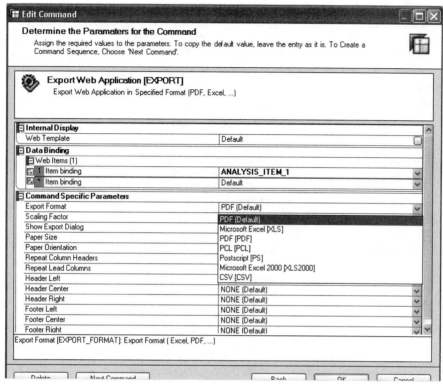

As shown in the following illustration, the final result of this process is that instead of having to drilldown by using the context menu to save the view or print to PDF, the user now can simply click one of the two buttons at the top of the WAD report, Save View and Print To PDF, to execute the respective option.

DDIC: SAP Training System Powered by .NET Microsoft Technology

T_COQ4 (default)

| Save View | Print to PDF |

		Incoming Orders ⇕	Incoming Orders (CV) ⇕
Calendar Year/Month ⇕	Distribution Channel ⇕	EUR	EUR
10.2001	Final customer sales	550.962	380.003
	Sold for resale	944.337	625.999
	Result	1.495.299	1.006.002
11.2001	Final customer sales	576.969	397.584
	Sold for resale	1.053.835	702.639
	Result	1.630.804	1.100.222
12.2001	Final customer sales	493.215	340.163
	Sold for resale	934.783	617.860
	Result	1.427.999	958.022
Overall Result		4.554.102	3.064.247

▼ Columns
  • Key Figures
▼ Rows
  • Calendar Year/Month
  • Distribution Channel
▼ Free characteristics
  • Division
  • Material
  • Material group
  • Sales Organization

Table 4-33 lists all the current commands for data providers.

Grouping	Commands
Basic Data Provider Commands	Set Data Provider Parameters Set Zero Value Display Set Sign Display Back to the Initial Settings Back to the Previous State Translate Currency Report to Report Interface Export Data Provider as XML
Data Provider Commands for Axes	Drill Down a Characteristic Exchange Characteristics/Structures Set Hierarchical Display of Axis Set Position of Result Row Swap Axes Remove Drilldown
Data Provider Commands for Characteristics	Set Display Attributes Set Presentation Set Display of Result Row Set Sorting
Data Provider Commands for Conditions/ Exceptions	Set Condition Set Status of a Condition Set Exception Set Status of an Exception Calling the Conditions Dialog Calling the Exceptions Dialog
Data Provider Commands for Data Cells	Set Data Cell Properties Set Local Calculations
Data Provider Commands for Filter Values	Remove All Filter Values Calling Input Help Dialog Set Filter Value for a Characteristic Set Filter Values Remove Filter Values for a Characteristic Remove Filter Values for a List of Characteristics Set Filter Values by Different Sources Set Filter Values by Filter
Data Provider Commands for Hierarchies	Expand/Collapse Hierarchy Nodes Set Hierarchy Set Node Alignment
Data Provider Commands for Open/Save Functionality	Calling the Open Dialog Calling the Save Dialog Save View
Data Provider Commands for Documents	Open Document Browser Open Dialog for New Document

TABLE 4-33   List of Current Commands for Data Providers

The commands found in the Commands for Web Items folder and Commands for Web Templates folder of the command wizard are basically all the commands found using a right-click and accessing the context menu on a standard report. Additional detailed documentation and descriptions for each of these commands can be found within the Web template by clicking on the command and viewing the help field at the bottom of the dialog box. Again, we will run into these commands in the process of configuring some of our dashboards and reports in subsequent chapters.

XHTML Features

In some cases, you may find that the WAD functionality is not quite sufficient for what you require in your Web application. In such cases, if you are comfortable enough with XHTML, you may decide to manually configure some coding in the XHTML tab. In the WAD, the tab formerly known as the HTML tab has been replaced by the XHTML tab. This new view to the components of the Web template provides many new enhancements for those designers who want to extend the functionality of the Web template beyond the standard functions provided by the Web items. SAP has incorporated into this XHTML tab the functionality of an XHTML Editor and therefore you will be able to insert, create, and change the XHTML directly in the WAD environment. This capability was available in 3.x and early versions but in the 7.0 this is a fully functional Web editor just as you would find if you used a third-party component from Microsoft or other companies supporting Web-based development.

HTML code that is entered into the template can be locally verified to catch syntax or tab usage mistakes. As you enter HTML code, the Auto Complete function assists you by suggesting available and appropriate tags based on the context of the entry. This can speed up the configuration of complex HTML code strings and help ensure accuracy. For example, if you enter a URL in HTML, the Editor will correct the URL and add the necessary tags to have it conform with the XHTML that is already included. As you enter code for a Web template, the Editor dynamically checks the syntax of the code, displays the appropriate error messages in the window below the code, and, in many cases, makes suggestions as to the correct formatting of the code. Highlighting the icon at the end of the message will provide a longer explanation of the error, and clicking the link within the error message will position the cursor at that location within the code. The following illustration shows an example of the errors and the prompts that are offered as a person is coding. A full list of BI tags is available in each section that you are coding, whether it be the Body, Header, or actual BI portion of the Editor.

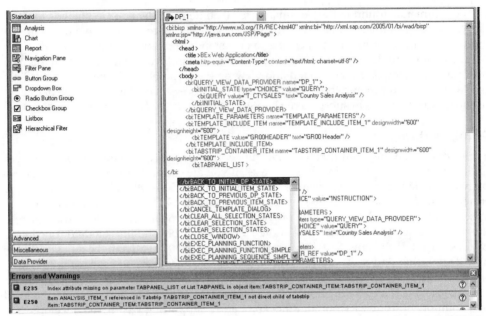

Additionally, you can identify exactly where a particular object's coding starts. Click the dropdown arrow at the top of the XHTML tab and you will see a listing of all the Web objects that are used in the Web template, as shown next. Select the one that you are interested in and you will be directed to the initial tag for that Web object.

As you know, all the different objects within the WAD and some outside the WAD generate XHTML; therefore, for example, selecting Insert | Table generates XHTML, as does including any text or inserting other objects. With all the different approaches to assign CSSs and overwrite formatting, a hierarchical depiction of what works at what level is useful. Figure 4-3 identifies the prioritization of each of the Web objects and what formatting will be used; therefore, if you set up the parameters to be confirmed via a URL parameterization, this will be the overriding control.

As Figure 4-3 confirms, URL parameterization has the highest priority when changing Web template parameters and Web item settings. To use this functionality to embed commands and parameters, follow this process:

1. Insert a Web item into your Web application that can be used to execute a command (for example, a Button Group Web item).

2. Use the command wizard to create the required command. This enables you to identify the required parameters.

3. In the XHTML view of the WAD, find the command that was just created.

4. Use the parameters of this command for your URL parameterization.

There are a number of different activities that you can do with these options, such as dynamically parameterize a command at run time of the query. An example of this would be to fill in the appropriate values of a variable at run time based on the user. This would be similar to having an authorization variable but without the security and authorization set up and to have this identified using a table search. Another option would be to use objects that identify system activities to parameterize a command at run time (for example, using the system date object to fill a date field, and so forth).

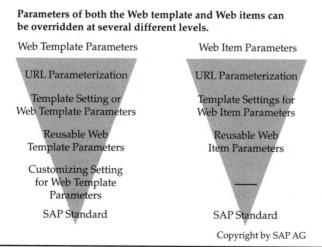

Parameters of both the Web template and Web items can be overridden at several different levels.

Web Template Parameters / Web Item Parameters

URL Parameterization / URL Parameterization

Template Setting or Web Template Parameters / Template Settings for Web Item Parameters

Reusable Web Template Parameters / Reusable Web Item Parameters

Customizing Setting for Web Template Parameters / ——

SAP Standard / SAP Standard

Copyright by SAP AG

FIGURE 4-3   Priority of Web template and Web item parameters

JavaScript Features

Another approach to getting additional functionality into the Web application is to use JavaScript to integrate objects directly into the WAD template. To enhance Web applications, a JavaScript API is now available, with which you can also execute commands within JavaScript functions to achieve a more flexible design for your Web application.

JavaScript can be incorporated into Web applications in two ways:

- Using a JavaScript include file from the MIME Repository
- By incorporating JavaScript in a Web template using the Script Web item

---

NOTE *Due to the XHTML format, writing JavaScript directly in the Web template is not supported.*

Using a JavaScript Include File from the MIME Repository

As we have seen there are a number of different approaches to help the Web templates and objects we will generate from these present the information. An approach that you can use is to reference JavaScript from the MIME Repository and use this in the Web templates. To do so, first load the JavaScript include file to the MIME Repository of the BI system. On the SAP Easy Access screen, choose Business Explorer | MIME Repository. You can store customer-specific scripts in the MIME Repository under SAP | BW | Customer | JavaScripts. You can reference the JavaScript include file as follows in the XHTML view for the Web template:

```
<script src="bwmimerep:///sap/bw/mime/Customer/Javascripts/myscript.js"
type="text/javascript"></script>
```

Incorporating JavaScript Using the Script Web Item

Now that you have inserted your JavaScript into the MIME Repository, you can use it in the Script Web item. In the WAD, drag the Script Web item from the Miscellaneous Web item grouping to your Web template and choose the Web Item Parameters tab page in the Properties screen area. Then from the Properties tab choose the icon to the right of the Script field; this will open up the editing dialog box for the parameter Script. You can insert your JavaScript in this dialog box. The command wizard helps you to generate the JavaScript code for executing the command.

In addition to the direct use of commands using the command wizard, some Web items also provide the option of using JavaScript functions. This can be useful, for example, if you want to assemble commands dynamically, or if you use portal eventing and want to link this action to a Web item. JavaScript functions linked to a Web item always have the same signature:

```
function functionname(currentState, defaultCommandSequence)
```

The parameters currentState and defaultCommandSequence are used for Web items that already execute standard commands themselves. This applies, for example, to the data binding type CHARACTERISTIC_SELECTION for the Web item Dropdown Box. The command for setting the filter values is generally run here. You can insert this standard command sequence before or after your command, or you can choose to ignore it and not execute the standard command. You can also execute commands or command sequences using JavaScript. To execute a command, you must first generate the command and its parameters. The command object sapbi_Command and the parameter object sapbi_Parameter are available for this purpose. In the Script Web item, the command wizard provides help generating the JavaScript. Once you select the command and set the parameters, the JavaScript code is generated.

As a final note to this section of the WAD, I suggest that before you decide to create XHTML manually or use the Script Web item, you make sure that no other option is available in all the different Web items and formatting activities that will satisfy the business requirements. Only after you have exhausted all other alternatives should you manually create XHTML or use the Script Web item. When we discuss the development of dashboards and Web reports in subsequent chapters, we will try to stick to standard processes and objects to accomplish our desired display of the information, but if necessary we will access ABAP, JavaScript, and other supported objects.

Summary

This chapter covered a ton of material that incorporates almost all of the Web items and their respective parameters. The one that I didn't cover and will be of great help to us is the Chart Web item. The reason is that we will focus on this one Web item in the process of setting up some of our dynamic Web templates. In the context of this chapter we would have defined the Chart Type in detail but would not have much context to a real life example and as mentioned this is the one Web item that will be used more frequently than any other Web item when creating dashboards. The other is the May Web Item, coverage of which is beyond the scope of this book. Other than that one has there been enough material included in this chapter on the WAD and its functionality to keep you busy for quite some time. The WAD has gone through an incredible leap in functionality and configuration from the 3.x version to the 7.0 version. The new Web Items have been an exceptional addition to the components in the WAD and all of the basic enhancements have increased the usability of the WAD. With the addition of the functionality directly from the context menus to help with formatting the WAD is definitely a strong component to use in developing an executive level dashboard for your Web-based reports. You will be using most, if not all, of these items in the next two chapters during the development of professional reports and dashboards for the business users and analysts.

I realize that there is much more configuration and detailed information, in terms of advanced use of XHTML functionality if you are an XHTML programmer, that we couldn't possibly cover in this book, but by using this basic information you will definitely get going in the right direction using the WAD. If you decide to develop your own XHTML programs and insert them into the WAD XHTML layout, then just about all of the limitations of the Web items are eliminated and you can develop dashboards and Web items that would be able to do more complex functions with both the formatting and the capabilities of the WAD application. If you are looking to use the XHTML Editor more frequently, a retooling around the new language is in order and depending on the complexity of the business user requirements it may be sooner than later.

I have found using the new version of the WAD to be more comfortable than the 3.x version. With all of the new functionality and toolsets included in the context menus and having addressed the formatting issues from 3.x, there was a geometric leap in this component. It will take some time to assimilate all of the different scenarios available for the business user in the WAD, but I find that getting to understand the pros and cons of the WAD really makes the development of Web reports pretty understandable, quick, and consistent.

Advanced Functionality of the Report Designer

Although this chapter reviews some of the basic functionality of the Report Designer, it primarily looks at some of the advanced Report Designer functionality that makes setting up and formatting reports required by corporate management quicker and easier. Fortunately, many of the formatting options and settings are the same as or very similar to those for the Web Application Designer, so we do not need to cover them again here. This chapter also assumes that you are already very familiar with the Report Designer activities and processes or have used something similar, such as Crystal Reports, to format and structure reports such as annual statements and corporate financial reports. Thus, this chapter does not cover basic reporting activities that should be familiar to a seasoned report designer.

One of the options that was needed in the toolset for BI reporting was the ability to create these formatted types of reports and the Report Designer fills that gap. The Report Designer is the component that the BI 7.0 version is using for all types of formatted reports in BI and will not be seeing any enhancements in the future roadmap of BI reporting components. As you know by now, SAP has acquired Business Objects, and with that acquisition comes Crystal Reports. If you used the early versions of BW, you probably recall that Crystal Reports was the preferred third-party toolset for creating formatted reports. I even created a workshop for SAP Education in the 2002/2003 time frame to help others work through the process of integrating Crystal Reports to BW and using some of the functionality Crystal Reports offered for BW reports. So, I feel a bit of déjà vu as Crystal Reports returns as a prospective frontend for BI reports. That being said, SAP is not going to turn off or cease to support the Report Designer functionality for the foreseeable future, though SAP likely won't make additional enhancements to the Report Designer. So, if you have some gaps in your reporting standards and you need the Report Designer to fill those gaps, basically what you see is what is available.

In this chapter, we start to get more involved in real-world examples of formatting reports. To determine which types of examples would be most useful to you, I reviewed several SAP-related Web sites to find out what questions users are asking about the Report Designer. Thus, I'll address some of the most significant issues here and offer you some guidance as to what approach might be the best to take care of those issues.

Functionality of the Report Designer

In this chapter the discussion about the Report Designer will include comments in terms of dealing with certain issues and limitations. These comments and configuration suggestions are not necessarily final solutions to each of these issues but very good starting points in your analysis. As you know, with all possible solutions additional review and testing are necessary to make sure that they work properly in your environment. In addition we will be looking at functionality that is standard delivered with the Report Designer and that discussion is more consistent with the statement that this configuration will definitely work within your BI environment. To start, the positioning of the Report Designer in the current BI architecture is shown in the following illustration. In this position the Report Designer is normally a component that is used by the BI Power User or Super User but, depending on the delegation of responsibilities in the reporting area, could be used by the technically oriented business user.

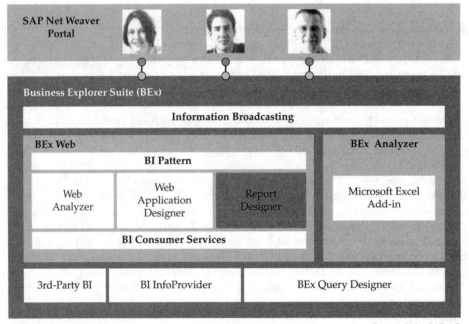

Copyright by SAP AG

The purpose of the Report Designer is to make information that is available more user friendly and easier to review and understand. This includes getting the critical information to the decision maker in a timely manner and in an efficient format, such as with a dashboard. (Chapter 7 discusses developing dashboards.) The following illustration shows an example of what a minor change to the information, using the Report Designer, would do to the look and feel of information and what this can mean to the business user. Changing the format from a list of information to a true report can be very important to ensuring the business user interprets the information correctly.

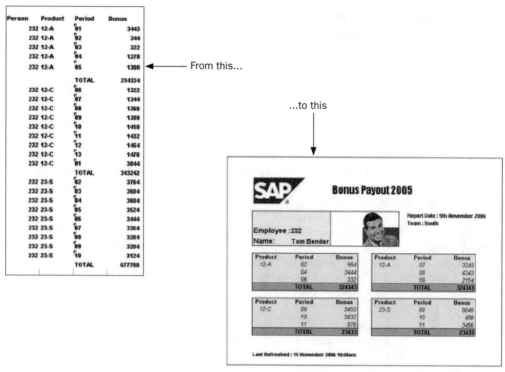

From this...

...to this

This chapter does not cover the details of all the components used in the Report Designer, such as the Information Broadcaster and printing processes, unless the details are relevant to the discussion of those issues I've identified from the different questions posted on Web sites about the Report Designer. Suffice it to say that you should be aware of these components and their use with the Report Designer toolset.

It is also important to be aware of exactly what types of reports you can create with the Report Designer. If you have a query whose report requirements don't allow for a static format—for example, the query involves variables, and the format of the report must expand or adjust when the variables are entered—you may not be able to use the Report Designer to accomplish the desired results. I've seen this happen many times, and it can cause quite a bit of frustration before the designer realizes that either the report requirements can't be met with the Report Designer or the query that they want to use will not format correctly in the Report Designer. An example of this would be if you have a report that allows a variable to be used for the total number of columns in your formatted report, this is not a suitable query structure for the Report Designer. You would need to alter your report to have a set number of columns so that you can fix the format within the Report Designer. Prior to starting your configuration and formatting process, you should review your requirements and the functionality available in the Report Designer and validate that the final results are possible.

In the overall process of using the Report Designer, we have really two specific approaches for formatting reports. First is the Static and Dynamic sections of the Report Designer report and once the type of sections of the Report Designer is identified the second is the development of the Row Patterns.

Static and Dynamic Sections in a Report Designer Report

A report can include both static and dynamic sections. The distinctive feature of static sections is that query fields can be positioned freely. You do not specify the type of section in the Report Designer; rather, the section type is automatically set depending on the type of data provider you are using. In the case of a static section of a query (or a query view), the architecture of the query contains two structures—one structure in the rows and one in the columns. A static section is unique because you can freely position all the fields within the section. This is possible because each field is unique in a static section and each cell of the result is uniquely defined, so the formatting and positioning of information is related directly to an individual cell. In this case, the type of query we are identifying is unique in that there are structures in both the rows and columns and this format for a query or query view is not common but when using the Report Designer it's not just about the data but also about the formatting of the data so that the Report Designer can use it appropriately. If the query being used as a source of information to the Report Designer is not consistent with the functionality available, then the resulting formatted report will not work for either you or your business user. Therefore, the initial view in the Report Designer corresponds to the executed query (query view). Each row in the executed query has one row pattern. The following illustration shows an example of this structure.

[Struct.] Text	Incoming Orders	Sales Volume
01.2005	[Incoming Orders/01.20051.Val	Sales Volume EUR/01.20051.Val
02.2005	[Incoming Orders/02.20051.Val	Sales Volume EUR/02.20051.Val
03.2005	[Incoming Orders/03.20051.Val	Sales Volume EUR/03.20051.Val
04.2005	[Incoming Orders/04.20051.Val	Sales Volume EUR/04.20051.Val
05.2005	[Incoming Orders/05.20051.Val	Sales Volume EUR/05.20051.Val
06.2005	[Incoming Orders/06.20051.Val	Sales Volume EUR/06.20051.Val
07.2005	[Incoming Orders/07.20051.Val	Sales Volume EUR/07.20051.Val
08.2005	[Incoming Orders/08.20051.Val	Sales Volume EUR/08.20051.Val
09.2005	[Incoming Orders/09.20051.Val	Sales Volume EUR/09.20051.Val
10.2005	[Incoming Orders/10.20051.Val	Sales Volume EUR/10.20051.Val
11.2005	[Incoming Orders/11.20051.Val	Sales Volume EUR/11.20051.Val
12.2005	[Incoming Orders/12.20051.Val	Sales Volume EUR/12.20051.Val

Copyright by SAP AG

A static section can also be a report section without a data provider. Such sections include the page header and page footer, as well as the report section (for example, for inserting gaps or your own text and comments), which you can integrate into your report using the Insert menu in the Report Designer. We will use this technique a bit later to help us solve one of the questions about the functionality of the Report Designer.

A query (or query view) forms the basis of a dynamic section that has one or more characteristics in the drilldown. This means that one or more group levels are designed for the initial view in the Report Designer. There is one group level for each characteristic. Within a dynamic section, query fields can only be taken from external group levels into internal ones. For example, you can move a cell from group level 1 to group level 2, but you cannot move it the other way. The cell repositioning options are limited with a dynamic section because the cells are not all uniquely defined. Therefore, in dynamic sections, the number of rows varies at run time, whereas the number of columns is fixed. For example, in the following illustration, there are three levels and a dynamic section view. Group level 1 and group level 2 are related to the two characteristics: level 1 is related to Country and level 2 is related to Sold-to Party. Group level 0 relates to the header and footer information, and in all Report Designer configuration there will be a group level 0.

Copyright by SAP AG

If a query (or query view) contains two structures and also one or more characteristics, a dynamic section will be used. The dynamic section generates individual cells for each intersection of the two structures, which means you will be able to reposition these cells freely. You cannot use a query or query view that contains more than one structure in the columns (this is a unique format for a query so we will not run into this issue many times). So, this format is actually a hybrid of the two types and has formatting capabilities that drive it to a dynamic format rather than a static format, but this structure is a bit trickier to work with and can be a bit more complex to align correctly. This discussion leads us directly into the details of row patterns.

Row Patterns

A central component of the Enterprise Report Design concept is the concept of the row pattern and is essential to the development of the dynamic sections of a Report Designer report. With reports of this type, the number of characteristic values in the drilldown is not set at the time of report creation. It becomes visible during run time. To understand the row pattern concept, you need to look at the structure of a report with dynamic sections. Figure 5-1 shows an example of this structure.

In Figure 5-1, you can see that a number of row types can be identified in a report. This means that there is a specifically formatted row that is applied to column headers or a specifically formatted row for results values. Each group level has three row types: header, details, and footer. For each row type, there is a template, called a *row pattern*, that describes the color, font, height, and width of the rows, and so on.

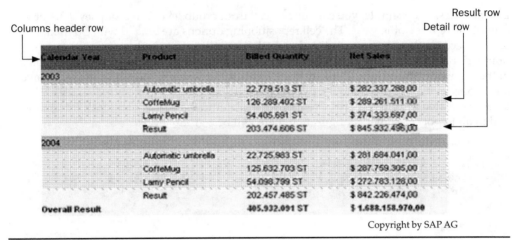

Columns header row

Result row

Detail row

Copyright by SAP AG

FIGURE 5-1 Groups and row types for Row Patterns

The layout of a query is defined in the drilldown of the structure elements in the columns and rows of the query. Every structure element in the rows of the query corresponds to a group level in the row pattern concept. Thus, the number of possible group levels in a report depends on the drilldown status of the query. Additionally, the detail area itself can also represent a group level (with header and footer and a detail area). This is how group levels can be nested in each other. The innermost group level of a report has detail rows that contain key figures. The Report Designer generates a row pattern for each area of a group level. Row patterns are the smallest units of a BEx report that are not divided by page boundaries. Row patterns comprise cell grids whose cells can have specific properties.

The Report Web item uses the row pattern and data to generate the header, detail, and footer areas of a report. Using the properties of the row pattern, you specify the format of cells and the entire cell grid. These properties are applied when the report is executed. The row pattern concept and its properties enable you to design reports in the Business Explorer. The Report Web item found in the WAD uses these row patterns to display reports. SAP delivers numerous standard row patterns and you can change these according to your needs in the Report Designer. You can also create new row patterns by setting the properties of the cells for a cell grid. The cell grid, and therefore every cell in a row pattern, has the properties detailed in Table 5-1.

In the Report Designer, you can specify or change these properties for each cell in either the Properties window, Format dialog box, or cell itself. A cell can have a corresponding, associated format that has the properties described in Table 5-1. The format set can be applied to multiple cells and does not have to be set for each individual cell separately. In the Report Designer, you make these settings in the Properties window. At run time, the row pattern is applied to the relevant rows of the report.

Property	Description
Background Color (Background Color)	This property sets the background color of the cell.
Padding Lead (PaddingLead)	This property sets the gap between the cell boundary used as the start direction for the cell content, and the cell content.
Padding Trail (PaddingTrail)	This property sets the gap between the cell boundary used as the end direction for the cell content, and the cell content.
Padding Top (PaddingTop)	This property sets the gap between the upper cell boundary and the cell contents.
Padding Bottom (PaddingBottom)	This property sets the gap between the lower cell boundary and the cell contents.
Left Border (BorderStyleLead)	This property sets the border type for the cell boundary used as the start direction for the cell contents.
Right Border (BorderStyleTrail)	This property sets the border type for the cell boundary used as the end direction for the cell contents.
Top Border (BorderStyleTop)	This property sets the border type for the upper boundary of the cell.
Bottom Border (BorderStyleBottom)	This property sets the border type for the lower boundary of the cell.
Left Border Color (BorderColorLead)	This property sets the border color for the cell boundary used as the start direction for the cell contents.
Right Border Color (BorderColorTrail)	This property sets the border color for the cell boundary used as the end direction for the cell contents.
Top Border Color (BorderColorTop)	This property sets the border color for the upper boundary of the cell.
Bottom Border Color (BorderColorBottom)	This property sets the border color for the lower boundary of the cell.
Left Border Width (BorderWidthLead)	This property sets the border width for the cell boundary used as the start direction for the cell contents.
Right Border Width (BorderWidthTrail)	This property sets the border width for the cell boundary used as the end direction for the cell contents.
Top Border Width (BorderWidthTop)	This property sets the border width of the upper cell boundary.
Bottom Border Width (BorderWidthBottom)	This property sets the border width of the lower cell boundary.

TABLE 5-1   Properties of the Cell in a Row Pattern (*continued*)

Property	Description
Text Wrapping (Wrapping)	You use this property to insert text wrapping at the end of the cell. Word wrapping is applied to a line break within a field; field wrapping is applied to a break between the fields of a cell.
Width (Width)	This property specifies the width of the cell.
Height (Height)	This property specifies the height of the cell.
Vertical Alignment (VerticalAlignment)	This property specifies the vertical orientation of the contents of a cell (align top, vertically centered, align bottom).
Horizontal Alignment (HorizontalAlignment)	This property specifies the horizontal orientation of the contents of a cell (start of line, end of line, align top, left align, centered, right align).
Horizontal Merging of Cells (Colspan)	You use this property to merge two cells that are next to each other.
Vertical Merging of Cells (Rowspan)	You use this property to merge two cells located above one another.

TABLE 5-1   Properties of the Cell in a Row Pattern (*continued*)

In addition to the cell properties listed in Table 5-1, you can also use text properties to format the contents of a cell. You also use them to set or change the cell properties in the Report Designer. Table 5-2 lists and describes these text properties.

You need to be aware of some other basic components for navigation and use of the Report Designer. You can use the drag-and-drop functionality to move report elements from the Field Catalog, Report Structure, and Format Catalog screen areas to the design area of the report. You can also use drag and drop to move cells and fields within the design area. Finally, you can use the context-sensitive menu in the design area, Report Structure, and Format Catalog to access various functions for creating reports.

Property	Description
Text Color (TextColor)	This property specifies the color of the text.
Background Color (BackgroundColor)	This property specifies the background color of the text.
Font (FontFamily)	This property specifies the font (for example, Times New Roman or Black Arial).
Bold (FontWeight)	This property specifies the font weight.
Font Size (FontSize)	This property specifies the size of the font.
Italic (FontStyle)	This property specifies the font style (italic or normal).

TABLE 5-2   Text Properties in the Report Designer Patterns

Tips and Tricks for Using the Report Designer

Based on the information I've reviewed at a number of Web sites and group discussion boards, several Report Designer issues in particular are prompting users to ask questions and request additional development in certain areas of this component. I will discuss those issues in this section and suggest approaches that you can take within the Report Designer to resolve them. The topics we will discuss here seem to be the functionality that is the most popular and required and the highest visibility in terms of the number of companies that are looking to use or are using the Report Designer.

One common question for which very little help seems to be available online is how to incorporate a change to the underlying query used in a Report Designer report. Unfortunately, once a query is used within the Report Designer, any changes made to that query definition are difficult to incorporate within the Report Designer report. This does not mean that if you change the query definition by adding a characteristic or key figure, your Report Designer report will not work; rather, it means that any changes made regarding the data provider to the Report Designer report will not be available for use in the report, in which case there's a chance that the report itself will not work.

The Report Designer concept is to have a fixed format for the report so that we can offer displays of information that are usable by both internal and external management.

An adjustment to the data provider format or definition will require that we review the configuration of the Report Designer report and make sure that we still have all the necessary components and that all the query definition changes abide by the rules and requirements of the Report Designer. Unlike the situation in which an adjustment is made to the query definition and the report using that ad hoc query immediately picks up that change and can accommodate it, the Report Designer uses specific cells of the query definition to format the final results, and thus the report has to be in a specific structure. So, again, any changes to the query definition of the Report Designer more than likely will not be available in the Report Designer report. That being said, the only true solution for this situation is to create another Report Designer report for the changed query. Of course, there are exceptions to any rule, an example of which would be using some text from the new characteristic on a row or column heading—a change that is cosmetic in nature and not core to the report format or report information.

Using Hierarchies in Your Reports

Using hierarchies in the Report Designer process is a concept that seems to prompt many questions on the Web. The issues being raised address the overall use of hierarchies within the configuration of a report using Report Designer. The Report Designer is not limited to the use of "flat views" of the data within a query. The use of a hierarchy in the query does not preclude the query from additional formatting in the Report Designer. The hierarchy is presented in the normal fashion, as it would be in a query or on the Web, but additional formatting can be applied for each of the individual levels of the hierarchy. Each of these levels shows up in the Report Designer as a unique node, and you can use all the normal formatting options against each level. The Report Designer can accommodate any of the different versions of the hierarchies whether they are text type hierarchies, hierarchies with only one text node and all of the others are postable nodes, or even if there are several characteristics within one hierarchy. So the use of hierarchies has no limitations (unlike some of the other BI components). It is important to note that if you want the hierarchy to be displayed immediately at a specific level, you need to adjust the display level in the properties of the characteristic in the Query Designer. After you make the adjustment there, the hierarchy will be displayed at that level with the initial display of the Report Designer report in the WAD.

At each level, settings for text colors, text size, font type, bold, italic, cell colors, cell height, and borders are available. To demonstrate this functionality, we will use a basic Material hierarchy off of the InfoObject 0MATERIAL. The following illustration shows the Query Designer with the query we will use. Notice that the characteristic 0MATERIAL has a hierarchy assigned to it. This is a standard hierarchy for the material levels from an ECC system.

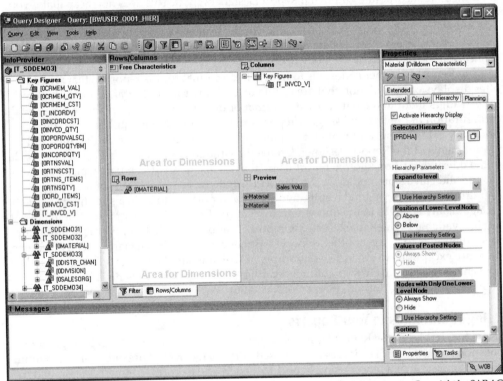

The next illustration shows the actual hierarchy from the Data Warehousing Workbench. Notice that this hierarchy has uneven levels (0MATERIAL and 0PRODH3) that occupy the same level, has text levels, and has more than one InfoObject.

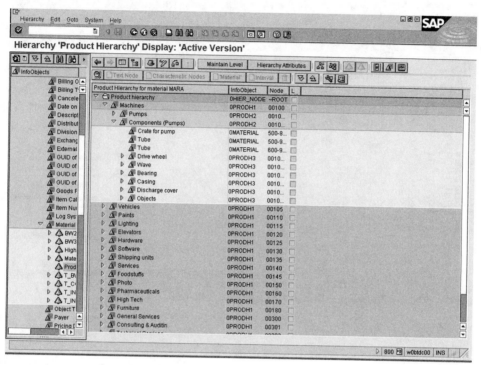

Also note that a variable for the hierarchy node is included in this query. The following illustration shows this scenario.

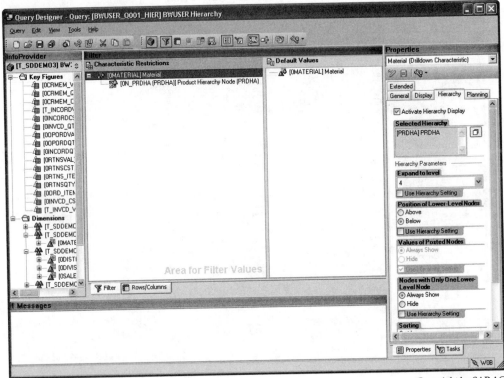

The query is initially inserted into the Report Designer, as shown in the following illustration. Here, the hierarchy and all levels can be seen in the Report Designer and specifically in the Report Designer work area. This is where you can set up unique views of each of the different levels of the hierarchy.

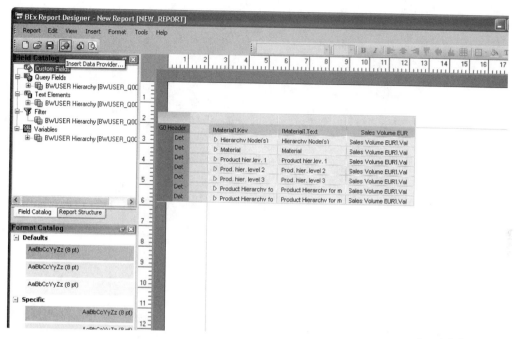

In the following illustration, we begin the process of realigning the format by using the Edit Format option on the context menu of the cell. This option opens an Edit Format dialog box with a number of different options, as shown in the second illustration.

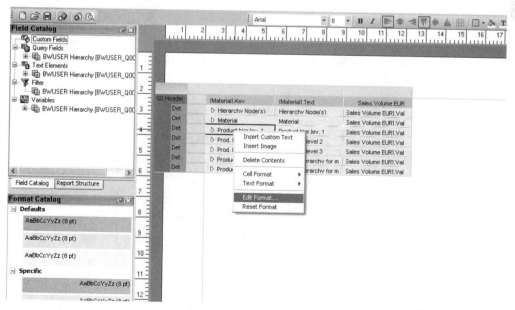

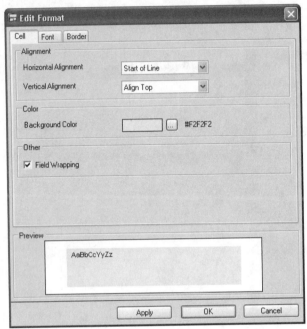

Copyright by SAP AG

As you can see, the dialog box has three tabs, Cell, Font, and Border. Each of these tabs has the same options as those you can access via the dropdown menus in the Report Designer toolbar or the context menu's Cell Format and Text Format options. This dialog box allows you to make the adjustments all in one place. As an example, use the options on the Cell tab to adjust the background color. Click the small button (with three dots) to the right of the Background Color field to open the color pallet, shown next, which offers the different colors available as well as the ability to create a customized color for your use. Choose any of the different colors to use, and then click OK to go back to the Edit Format dialog box. The second illustration shows the end result.

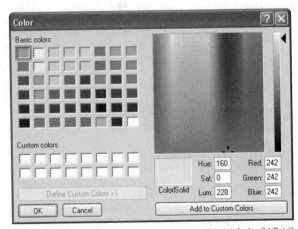

Copyright by SAP AG

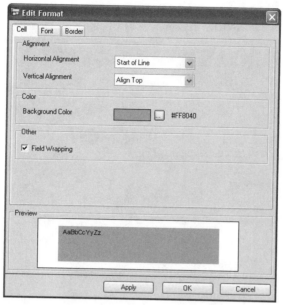

Copyright by SAP AG

The following illustration shows the second tab, Font, which is used to change the font of the text. The options are straightforward, so experiment with them on your own to find the look and feel that you want for your reports. You'll likely find yourself using only the options that are consistent with your corporate colors and formats.

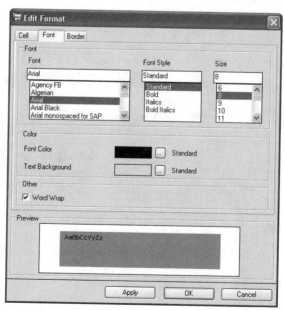

Copyright by SAP AG

The Border tab, shown next, enables you to create borders around any set of cells you need to emphasize, such as cells for certain text or titles.

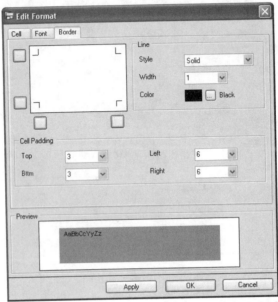

To adjust the font of the other levels of the hierarchy, we will choose Format | Font and select a font from the dropdown list, as shown in the following illustration.

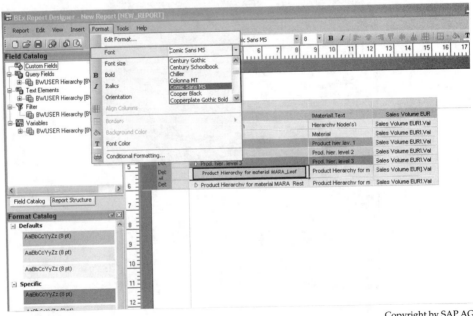

Finally, upon executing the report, the initial screen that appears offers a field to enter the variable hierarchy node, as shown in the next illustration. The second illustration shows the results of assigning the variable. Notice that during the process of formatting, we included both the text and the technical naming convention with the appropriate background color and font format. We also could have changed the background color for key figures and made other adjustments.

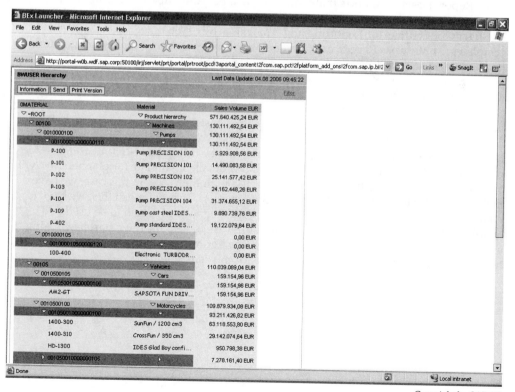

Copyright by SAP AG

Copyright by SAP AG

Therefore, when it comes to hierarchies in the Report Designer configuration, all of the functionality and flexibility standard within the hierarchies delivered in BI are available and the additional enhancement using the Report Designer is that additional configuration can easily be done with the levels to differentiate between hierarchy text nodes and hierarchy postable nodes as we accomplished in this example. If I were to try and do this exact same configuration within the BEx Analyzer I would have to develop a completely new workbook template with all of the formatting embedded into the workbook template for the different levels of the hierarchy nodes. This would be quite difficult and time consuming.

Using Templates in the Report Designer

Another question or topic commonly asked in Report Designer–related online discussion forums is whether templates designed in the Report Designer can be used with other queries. This basically goes back to the whole idea of having queries that change and the data provider needs to be able to pick up that change. In this case, we are looking for a template to be used that will have the appropriate header, footer, or other information that is required for a specific set of reports and not incorporate any core changes within the query or report itself. So, creating a template to manage the "soft" content such as text is possible.

There are a couple of approaches to this issue and the easiest one would be to go into the Implementation Guide - IMG (transaction code SPRO) and review the template 0REPORT_DEFAULT_TEMPLATE to make the necessary adjustments so that every one of the Report Designer reports that you create will be using this changed template. To do this, go to the SAP Customizing Implementation Guide under SAP NetWeaver | Business Intelligence | Settings for Reporting and Analysis | BEx Web | Set Standard Web Templates | Enterprise Report. You can copy this Web template to make changes and set it as your new standard Web template for reports in the IMG. This approach is preferable if you want only one default template for the Report Designer reports to be used by all of the corporate departments.

On the other hand, if you want to have a specific template for each of the different departments in your corporation, you need to use a custom template and continue to reuse it as you develop your reports. This is similar to what you might do to create unique templates for each of the different groups that would be using the BI-IP (integrated planning) frontend, which included more than one detailed template for planners. We will also look at a similar situation in Chapter 4 for use with the WAD. In this case, we have multiple formats for each of the Report Designer reports. To accomplish this, we have to build our customized template within the Report Designer and save it to be used as a template. We can use the header and footer in this case to help us. If we start by creating a header and footer, as shown in the following illustrations, and using these as part of the template, we can develop the required outline for this template.

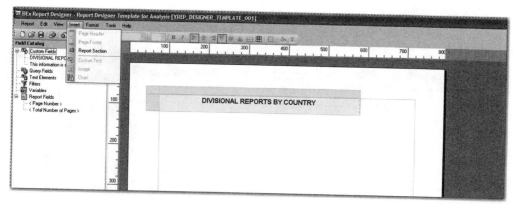

Copyright by SAP AG

Copyright by SAP AG

Now we step into the WAD and confirm that this template will display the results the way we would like to see them. We access the Report Web item and insert the Report Designer template we just developed. The following illustration shows this information.

Notice the Report Design parameter under Internal Display on the Web Item parameters tab; it indicates that the custom Report Designer report is being used.

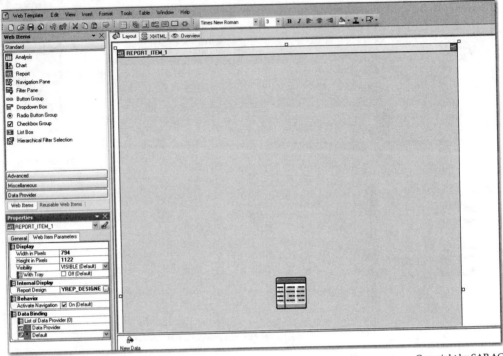

The results of this custom Report Designer template and what the business user would see via a Portal are displayed in the following illustrations.

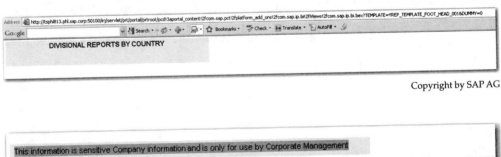

Now that we have reviewed the results of the template without data, we can go back into the Report Designer and make a copy of this template and insert a data provider into the template. The following illustration shows the process of Save As to make a copy of the template for your use.

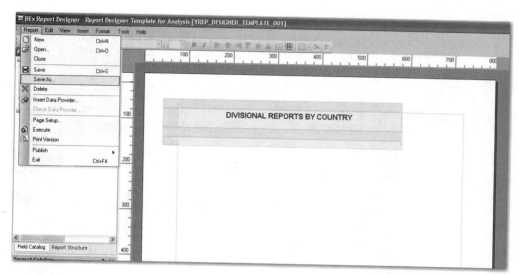

Choose the appropriate query to be a data provider, as shown in the following illustration, and once this is complete insert a data section into the copied template.

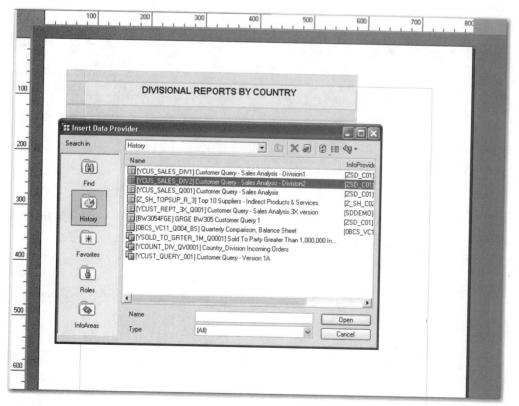

You have now created a copy of the template, inserted a query into the template and inserted a data section so that the query could be displayed in the Report Designer format. The final result of the configuration is shown in the following illustration. Save these changes by saving with a different technical name. This can be seen in the second illustration.

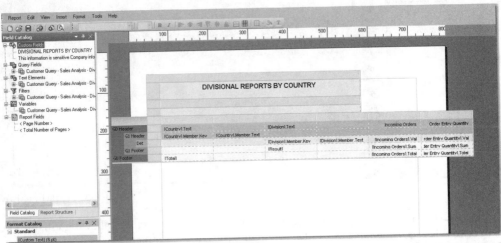

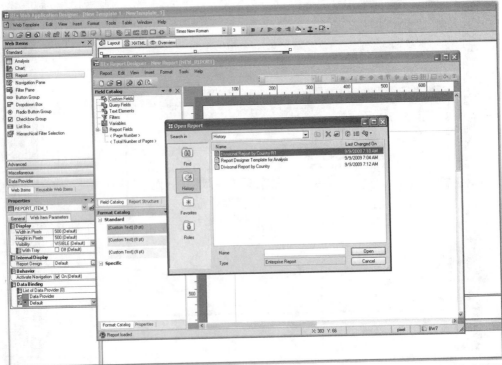

Now, stepping back into the WAD and using the Report Designer report in conjunction with the Report Web item as a support, we can complete this process. The following illustration shows the process of inserting the Report Designer report into the WAD.

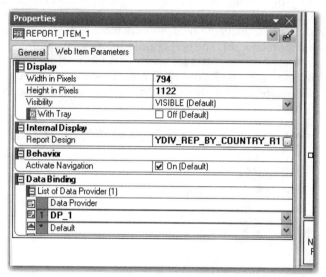

The following illustration shows the final results, verifying that the header, footer (not shown in this illustration), and information are all available for reporting out of the WAD.

Country	Division		Incoming Orders	Order Entry Quantity
DIVISIONAL REPORTS BY COUNTRY				
DE	Germany			
	7	High Tech	54.649.643,1400 EUR	382.541 PC
FR	France			
	7	High Tech	0,0000 EUR	0 PC
US	USA			
	7	High Tech	1.648,2600 EUR	45 PC
#	Not assigned			
	7	High Tech	74.326,0000 EUR	4.451 PC
Overall Result			54.725.617,4000 EUR	387.037 PC

Header and Footers

The option to use headers and footers in a report offers additional approaches to increase the professional look and feel of the report itself. In addition to inserting a header and footer, you can also insert an additional "section." This allows you to add an additional data provider with other functionality, such as adding another query to the Report Designer format, or simply add additional text and fields.

When you use the header and footer options, the Field Catalog comes into play. The Field Catalog stores all the elements that you can drag and drop into the header and footer.

In most cases, a report has some type of vital information that needs to be available to business users to enable them to understand what they are looking at and what types of data are available. All these different elements are available in the Field Catalog, including information such as the date of the data refresh, a reminder of the current filter values and variable values, the name of the data provider, and other fields. Although you can insert these elements into any of the available cells, they are more appropriately positioned either in the header or footer of the report. The best approach is to insert additional fields into the header and footer so that you can control the spacing and formatting on an individual basis for these cells and information. The following illustration shows the different sections available in the Field Catalog and the different elements available for use in the header and footer sections.

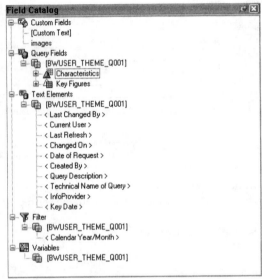

Copyright by SAP AG

Query Fields

Another section of the Field Catalog is the query fields. The query fields represent all the different characteristics and key figures available in the data provider. This means the query fields provide access to every characteristic text, member id, and description as a field that can be used in a Report Designer report header or footer. In addition, the query fields provide access to every key figure for each member and also the totals of each key figure cumulated to every characteristic.

Taking this a step further, you can present the total sales revenue amount in the header of the report before the results have even appeared. It is important to note that restrictions apply to the placement of the individual characteristic members. They can only be placed in a group level of the characteristic. For example, if your report contains Month and Region, you can only place the query fields for Region in the group level for the region. You could not place this in the group level for the month and definitely not in the header and footer sections. The technical reason for this is that the characteristic member and its related key figures are only known at the time of row generation for the group level. All other query fields, such as the final result of the query, can be placed anywhere in the report, including within any group level.

Text Elements

Another component that is very important in the Field Catalog is the text element. Text elements represent a comprehensive range of informational parameters that can be used to provide the user with useful supporting information about the report. These include items such as date of data refresh, query name, author, and so on. If you review this list and there are other text elements that you would like to assign to the Report Designer report, you can add them to the report by using another Text Field insert but within this section of the Report Designer component these are the only standard text elements that are available. In terms of location on the report, there are no restrictions for the placement of the text elements.

Filter Fields

The filter fields, which can be any of the available characteristics, are used to remind the user of the current filter values applied to the report. This is especially useful if the filters are not obvious—they may be background filters. These are no restrictions for the placement of these filters fields in the report.

Variable Fields

Variable fields are just like filter fields except they are used to remind the user of the specific variable values chosen. There are no restrictions for the placement of these variable fields in the report.

Custom Fields

Custom fields are automatically generated whenever you create custom text in the report. Each unique custom text that is defined in the report's cells is automatically added to the custom text fields list. These can be reused in any of the other cells in the report with a simple drag-and-drop process.

Sample Use of Parameters in the Field Catalog

As an example of some of the use of some of these functions, we will use the hierarchy report introduced earlier in the chapter and enhance it with these different options. The following illustration shows the hierarchy report in the Report Designer with the Page Header and Page Footer options. Choose the Page Header option and we will customize a field.

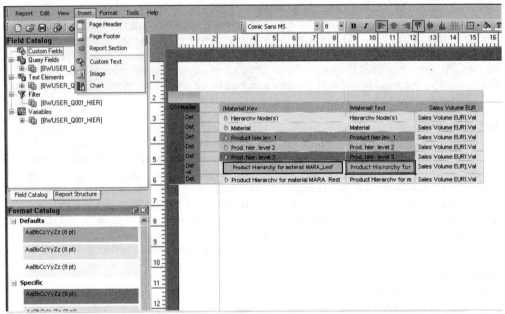

Next, right-click the report and choose Insert Image on the context menu, as shown in the following illustration. Once the image item is assigned to the header field, double-click it, and the text "Image" appears. In the Properties tab of this item, all the different options for inserting the image are available.

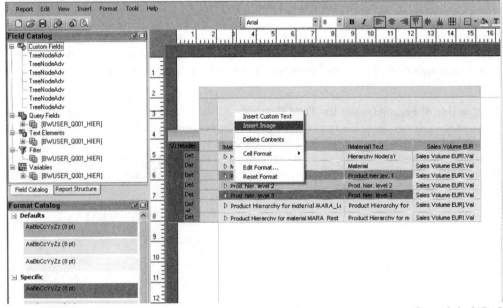

Using the file path for the MIME Repository to review the location of the images and what is available (sap/bw/customer/images/...) shows where the images are stored. You can use this menu path to find the appropriate folder in which to save the images for use in the Report Designer. The following illustration shows the menu path to the folder holding the images for the Report Designer as well as for the WAD. Using the image's technical name, available in the MIME Repository (sap_logo.gif), type that information into the filename so that the system can identify the appropriate image to use.

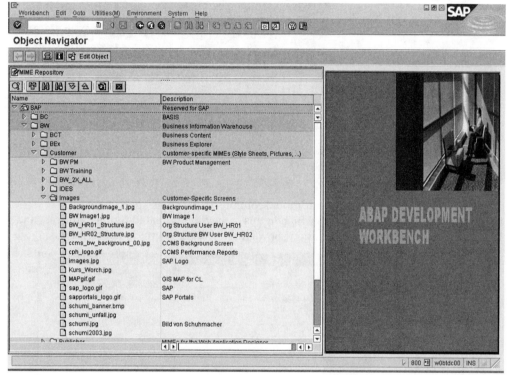

Copyright by SAP AG

Once you have inserted the image into your Report Designer field you will notice that the ability to adjust the size of the image is just below the field. You can choose the Keep Ratio check box to have the width and height stay in the same proportion throughout the process, or you can clear the check box and adjust the size of the image manually.

Next, we can turn our attention to the footer information in the report. Again, we can use the Insert menu to insert the footer into the report, as shown in the following illustration.

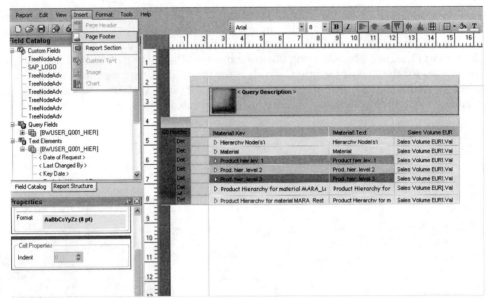

The footer will be divided by additional columns to get some space between the information displayed in the field, which in this case will be Created By, Last Refresh, and InfoProvider. The following illustration shows these objects inserted into the footer.

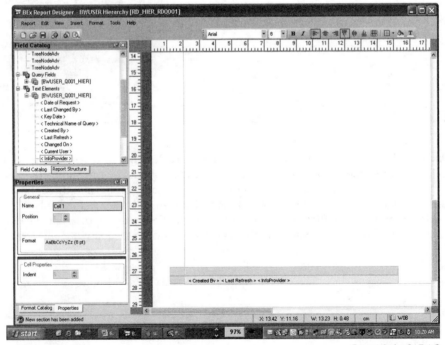

Finally, after all these changes, we can execute the report, the result of which is shown in the following illustration. Notice the image for the logo of SAP and also the enhanced text for the title of the report.

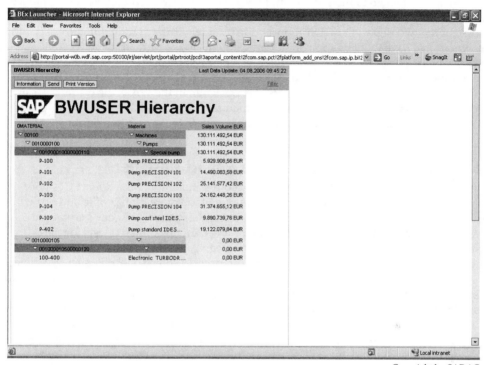

In addition, the footer has been inserted, as shown in the following illustration. Notice the use of additional columns to separate the information.

Positioning Queries in the Report Designer

Multiple queries can be positioned in one Report Designer screen, but the standard view for multiple reports (data providers) is to display one under the other, with some formatting to make the overall picture consistent with the report requirements. It is possible to position two queries one next to the other, but the queries must be built with this specific requirement in mind. If you were to try to place two queries side by side within a Report Designer component, you would have a very difficult time. The two queries would need to be sized accordingly so that they can "fit" the Report Designer work area. If you switch the display of the Report Designer from regular to landscape view, you will have a better chance to accomplish this.

In my opinion, it's easier to just create two Report Designer reports with the two query definitions and then go to the WAD component and use the Report Web item in conjunction with a Table Web item (a table set up with two columns and one row). This allows the display of the two Report Designer reports side by side with very little difficulty. After this, you would just have to make some minor adjustments to the formatting and the separation between the two displays to accommodate the report requirements. So, regrettably, in this case, the easiest approach to be able to place these reports in a particular position requires working in the WAD rather than in the Report Designer. In the WAD, the result is easier to accomplish, faster to configure, and easier to maintain. Since we have all these different tools at our disposal, we may as well use the appropriate tool to get this right.

Example Using the Functionality of the Report Designer

Now that you have studied some of the advanced functionality of the Report Designer, including tips and tricks for working through some of the more high profile and difficult issues, we will look at a real-world example of using the Report Designer's advanced functionality. During a number of projects I have been involved in, requests for these formatted types of reports came from the finance team, and in some cases a "report book" needed to be generated for the corporate headquarters. In some countries, such as China and Japan, the government requires a specific set of reports in a specific series in a book to be submitted for review. This was very difficult to do with BW before, but with the Report Designer this task can be set up just once and then generated on a monthly basis. The Information Broadcaster can be used for distribution over the Web, and the Adobe printing functionality can be used to create the actual "accounting book" for period-end analysis. With this scenario in mind, we will develop a full example by setting up a Balance Sheet report for a corporation using a basic query from BI and the Report Designer.

The first of the following two illustrations shows the basic query that we will use for this example. As you can see, the Balance Sheet accounts are listed as a long line of GL accounts and are not in the format that we are used to seeing them in, which would be side by side. The second illustration shows the remaining accounts at the bottom of the list for reporting purposes using the basic BEx Analyzer process.

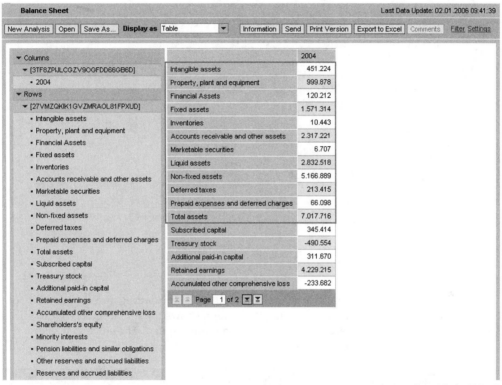

Copyright by SAP AG

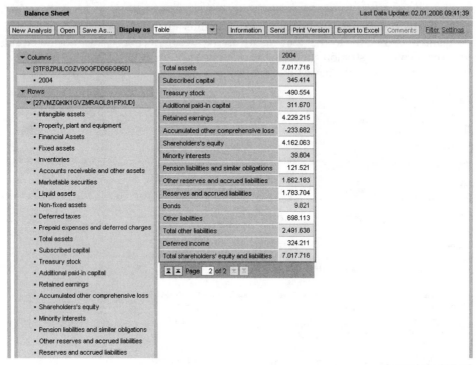

Now, we'll move to the Report Designer to enhance the formatting and functionality of this Balance Sheet statement. The following illustration shows the initial screen of the Report Designer with the Insert Data Provider button highlighted. The steps that follow take you through the rest of the example.

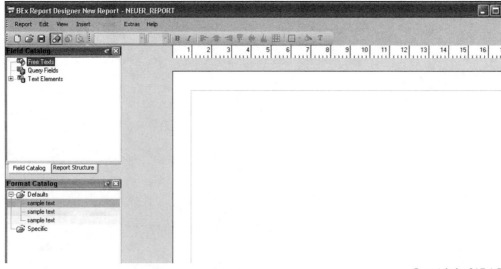

1. Click the Insert Data Provider button to open the Open dialog box, shown next, in which you choose the query or query view.

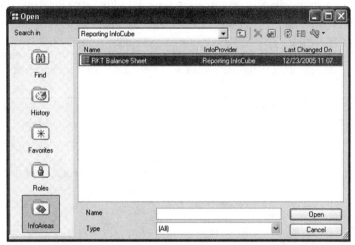

2. Choose the Balance Sheet report and click Open. Once this query is inserted into the Report Designer, the GL accounts and information such as the text and the actual key figure values are available in the Report Designer's design area.

3. Add two columns to the right of the last column, as shown in the following illustration, to accommodate the display of two portions of the Balance Sheet statement side by side—Assets, and Stockholders' Equity and Liabilities.

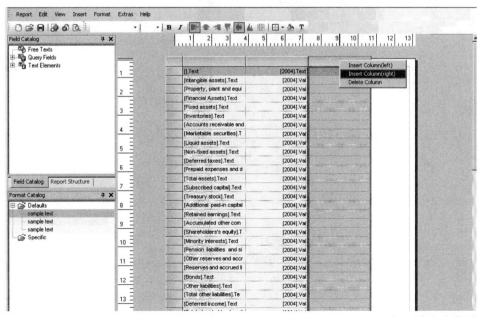

4. Drag and drop the GL accounts from the left side of the query to the right side of the Report Designer design area so that you can start to format the GL accounts in the appropriate display, as shown in the following three illustrations.

This is a manual process, and if there are a number of GL accounts to move around on the screen, it may take some time to complete. However, this is a one-time setup for the Balance Sheet display. Once this is complete, the query is refreshed with the new data and the formatted report will reflect the amounts appropriately.

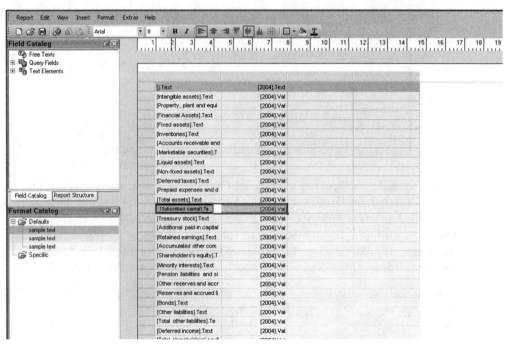

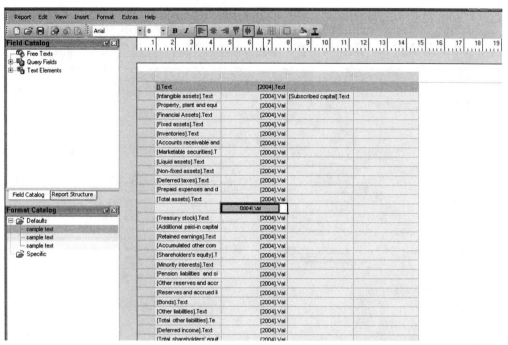

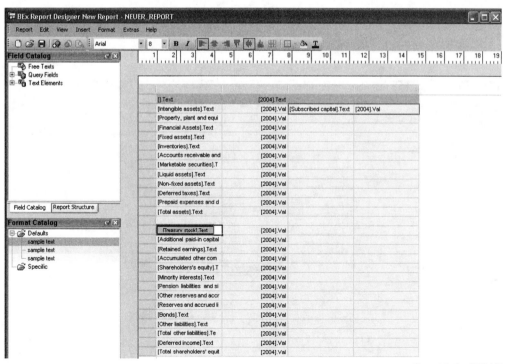

5. Move the Total lines to set up the alignment of the totals for the assets and liabilities. The following two illustrations show the movement of the cells, which are lined up directly across from each other.

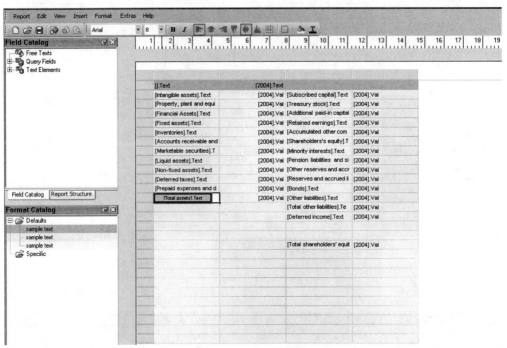

Copyright by SAP AG

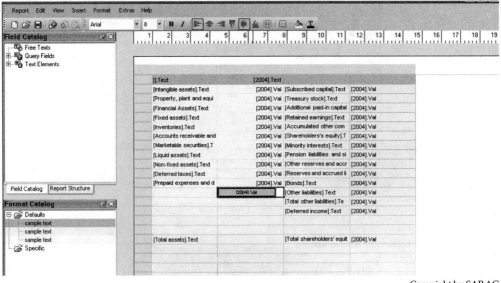

Copyright by SAP AG

The actual report is coming along nicely, and in the following illustration you can see how this report is beginning to resemble a normal Balance Sheet report that would be submitted to shareholders and stakeholders for review. Although a number of options still need to be completed, the initial format is visible.

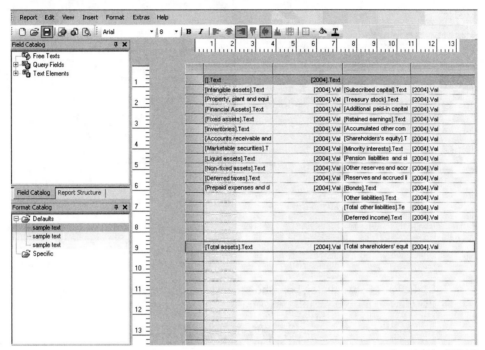

6. Because in many cases this final report will be printed, you need to format the print settings. Choose Report | Page Setup, as shown next.

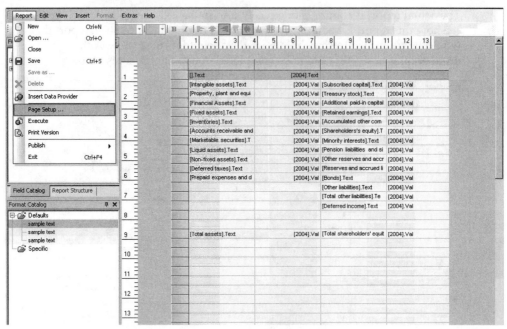

7. In the Page Setup dialog box, shown next, configure the margins, height, width, and the view of the report and click OK.

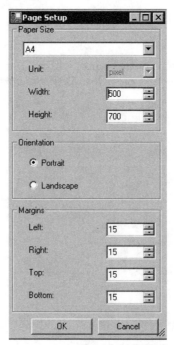

NOTE *Be sure to save your work frequently if you are new to this tool, because there may be a time when a particular indicator or option is executed but doesn't work like you expected and all your work will be lost. As a rule of thumb, save often when you feel that the work you've completed is consistent with the expected outcome.*

8. Now begin the process of setting up the headers and titles for the columns. As shown in the following two illustrations, delete the current text in the top-left cell (right-click and choose Delete Field) and change it to "Assets."

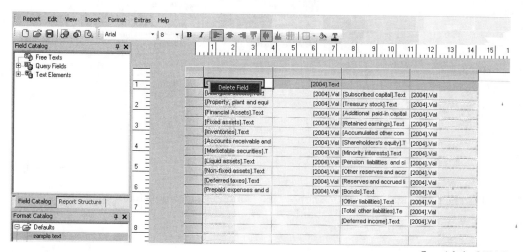

Copyright by SAP AG

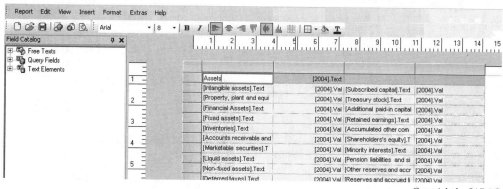

Copyright by SAP AG

9. Use the same approach to designate the "Stockholders' Equity and Liabilities" column.

The following illustration shows the final result of the adjustments made with the formatting options for the font, background color, and size of the headings of the columns. As you can see, the report is starting to take shape and looks like something that can be published to all the appropriate stakeholders of the corporation.

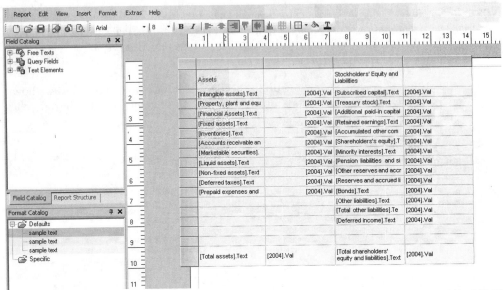

10. The following illustration shows the addition of highlights to the total lines for the subtotals of Assets and Liabilities.

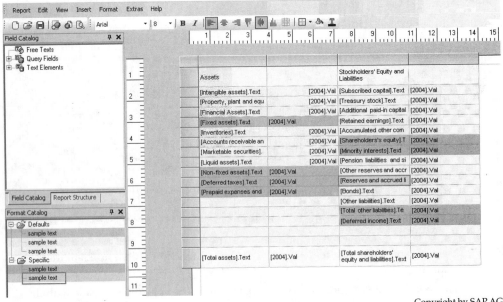

11. Realign the columns and add a separator column between Assets and Stockholders' Equity and Liabilities. The following illustration shows the result.

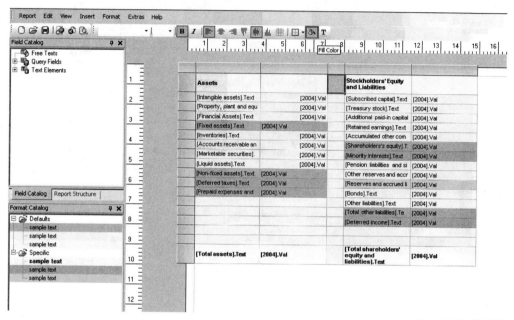

NOTE *To some, this process may not seem that exciting, but for anyone who has been working in BW for the past several years, this one example sums up many different formatting requests from a typical corporate headquarters.*

12. You can do additional work on the borders of the headings and also of the report itself. The following two illustrations show the use of the Borders option on the report toolbar. To accomplish this, highlight the cells that are to have borders and use the options either from the toolbar or from the Format | Borders menu.

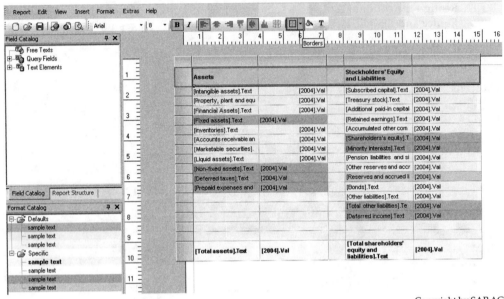

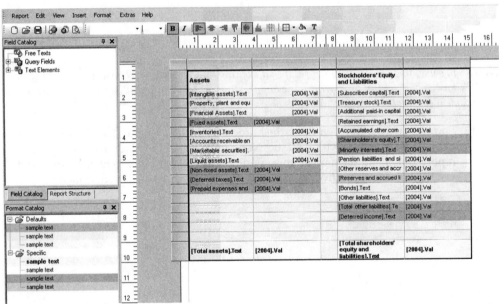

13. Double-click the column separator, and the columns will automatically "fit" the information in the column. The following illustration shows the results of this activity. The actual report is very close to being completed.

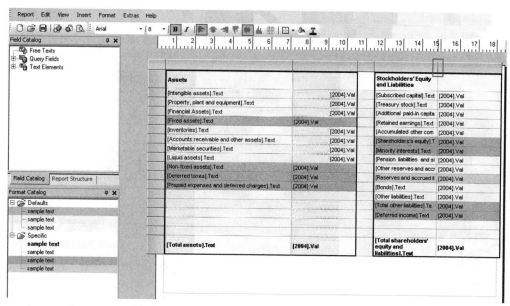

14. Insert an additional section for the header, as shown in the following two illustrations.

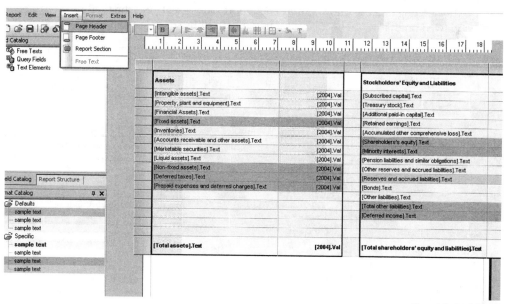

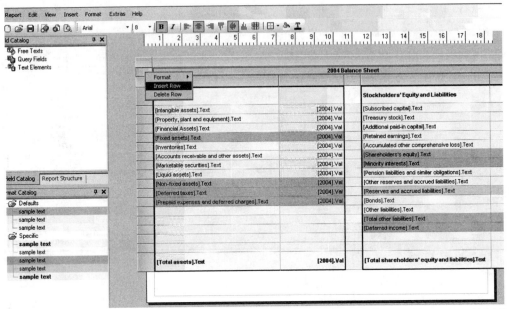

15. Finally, add a title for the report and also another line to provide some space between the heading and the information. The report looks great, and the final result can be viewed on the Web. The following two illustrations show the end results.

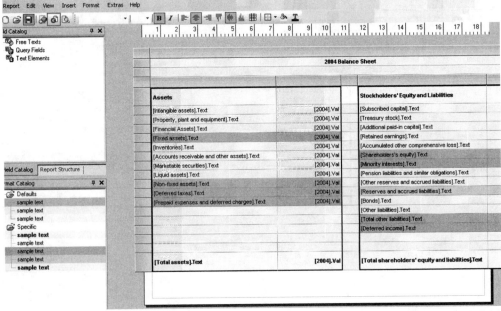

Balance Sheet			Last Data Update: 02.01.2006 09:41:39
Information	Send	Print Version	Filter

2004 Balance Sheet

Assets		Stockholders' Equity and Liabilities	
Intangible assets	451.224	Subscribed capital	345.414
Property, plant and equipment	999.878	Treasury stock	-490.554
Financial Assets	120.212	Additional paid-in capital	311.670
Fixed assets	1.571.314	Retained earnings	4.229.215
Inventories	10.443	Accumulated other comprehensive loss	-233.682
Accounts receivable and other assets	2.317.221	Shareholders's equity	4.162.063
Marketable securities	6.707	Minority interests	39.804
Liquid assets	2.832.518	Pension liabilities and similar obligations	121.521
Non-fixed assets	5.166.889	Other reserves and accrued liabilities	1.662.183
Deferred taxes	213.415	Reserves and accrued liabilities	1.783.704
Prepaid expenses and deferred charges	66.098	Bonds	9.821
		Other liabilities	698.113
		Total other liabilities	2.491.638
		Deferred income	324.211
Total assets	**7.017.716**	**Total shareholders' equity and liabilities**	**7.017.716**

The end result is an excellent formatted report that we were not able to accomplish in the older versions of BI. This report can now be printed or viewed either in the BEx Web Analyzer or in the enterprise portal.

Summary

This chapter began with a review of some of the basic concepts used in the Report Designer and then moved into addressing some of the issues that are encountered within projects using the Report Designer. The chapter finished with a good example of how the Report Designer can really make a difference in the reporting strategy. The Report Designer is an invaluable tool in the process of achieving the correct format and view of report data for business users. Projects often fail due to reports and queries being formatted incorrectly. Therefore, another toolset may be required to get the formatting correct for each level of management. It's very important to make sure that the requirements fit the functionality of the Report Designer and that there is a very high probability that we can achieve the desired results for the specific management level. The Report Designer solves many formatting issues but is not a solution for all formatting concerns. Make sure you have investigated the required result and functionality thoroughly before committing to a proposed solution that incorporates the Report Designer component. Also, keep in mind that this is the final version of the Report Designer. If you encounter any gaps between what the Report Designer can do and what you need to accomplish, you may have to rely on a third-party formatting component or look to the BOBJ component, Crystal Report Designer, for the added enhancements needed.

The Report Designer is a very consistent component of the reporting toolset within BI, and with a little work can be quite easy to format and configure. To see what additional enhancements can be accomplished with the Report Designer, you can take the basic queries you use and add small changes to them, and add some bells and whistles for your reports. See what you can accomplish and then offer these enhancements to your business users to get their feedback.

Developing Effective
Web Reports

In this chapter we will build on what we developed in Chapters 4 and 5 and take all of the parts that we have worked with and pull them together into the development of good Web reports or templates. We will review the basics as well as the advanced configuration of the Chart Web item and the Command Web feature. These are the last two items that we didn't cover in Chapter 4. Now I know you are also thinking about the Map Web Item and as mentioned, that Web item requires much more configuration to the actual characteristic than we can incorporate into this book, so we will not delve into that configuration or a conversation about the third-party tool that is required to set up the Map Web item. The Chart Web item is one of the more important and widely used Web items for setting up the dashboard, and the Command Web feature, is excellent because it enables us to set up all the commands found in the context menu within the BEx Web Report directly on the business user's screen and make everything available via a button. Although this chapter covers many of the different commands, it does not cover all 70+, because the focus of the chapter is to develop actual Web reports. Only the more common and widely used commands will be covered.

The Commands items are also important because one of the really cool aspects of certain types of Web reports is the ability to execute a what-if analysis. If we were to take the combination of some commands and the functionality of SAP NetWeaver Visual Composer (VC, which is not covered in this book), we could have a really nice report that includes scroll bars for what-if analyses, dynamically changing graphs, and interactive screens for documentation and analysis. If we just use the WAD functionality, we can deliver this type of report, but only to the point of having a field for entering a value and then executing the function to move the values in the report. With the ability of the VC and the SAP Business Add-Ins (BAdIs), we can add additional functionality, such as a scroll bar, to enhance the look and feel (although we probably do not want to overuse the scroll bar component in the development of a dashboard, the reasons for which are covered in the next chapter).

This chapter also looks at how to make your reports and charts more robust and really stand out to the business users, with several examples of what you can do with the Chart functionality and the use of some Excel components. The goal here is to lay the foundation for the next chapter, in which you will develop the entire dashboard and be able to pull everything together into a set of dynamic dashboards for your company.

Overview of Web Report Development

The process of working with different charts and diagrams to develop a dynamic and successful Web report has more to do with understanding the report requirements and audience than with the actual configuration. As you know, numerous reporting systems exist in addition to the SAP BI reporting options. Even within SAP, another set of tools is available to help with the reporting process—Business Objects (BOBJ). These BOBJ components are going to be fully integrated into the BI/BW landscape in the near future. The ability to use the BOBJ components is already available and fully integrated into the BI landscape, but soon the complete integration of the two different toolsets, BI and BOBJ, will occur. After that integration is completed, instead of having two reporting toolsets, you will have one that is the combination of the best of both. This does not mean that you won't be able to use the current versions of BI reporting components, but after the toolsets are combined, you will be able to use either immediately under the same license of BI.

Many of the other reporting systems that are available, such as Brio and Cognos, can be bolted onto the BI system and, based on the appropriate linkage, can read the data from either the queries or the InfoCubes. So, again, the ability to create dynamic Web reports is more an art than a science. You need to understand the approaches to building a good Web report that is useful, consistent, and easy to understand. The normal business users in the "C" management suite (CEO, CIO, and so forth) have about five minutes a day to spend reviewing the current company information before they must tend to the business of managing the health and growth of the company. These responsibilities are more important in the current economy than ever before. So, we need to understand the use of colors, spacing, diagrams, alignment, and any other aspects of the Web reports that will make the information highly accessible. I will give you some helpful hints and tools to support your use of these attributes. I will discuss more of the dashboard-related concepts in the next chapter.

Introducing the Chart Web Item

One of the last two Web items that we have yet to cover is the Chart Web item. This is a very powerful component of the overall structure of a good, dynamic Web report that can be either used as a standalone or within a dashboard. Chart Web items are definitely part of the basic architecture, and once you work with them, you will be able to develop the core objects of a corporate Web report or dashboard. If you've worked with the Excel Chart functions in the past, you'll find that you can transfer that knowledge directly to this Chart process within the BEx Web items. So, you may find that the configuration of the Chart Web item is easy to pick up and use immediately. As we go through the functions and configuration of the Chart Web item, keep in mind that no matter whether you choose the WAD or the BOBJ toolsets for BI reporting, you more than likely will work with these same functions, because several of the reporting frontends that BOBJ offers also use this functionality—maybe not exactly as it works with the Excel functions, but very close.

Charts

The Chart Web item is the cornerstone of about 99 percent of all Web reports and dashboards. Just based on the underlying concepts of a dashboard, we need to have good charts to make that information available and apparent. The Chart Web item allows data to be displayed graphically in various charts, such as column, profile, waterfall, and line charts. Using the

Chart Web item, you can display data graphically in your Web application. You'll encounter numerous parameters as we go through the configuration of the Chart Web item and based on the specific type of chart that we pick, these parameters will change, but some are standard settings. Table 6-1 lists and describes the standard parameters that we can set within the Chart Web item itself, arranged according to the various parameter groupings. These parameters are shown in the following illustration.

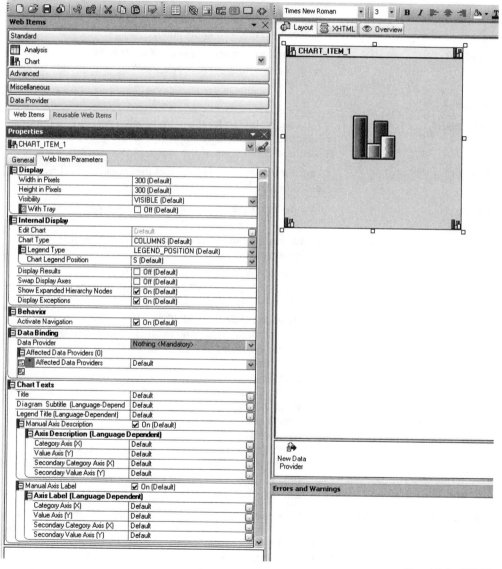

Parameter	Description
Display	
Width in Pixels (WIDTH)	This parameter is used to specify the width of the Web item. Default is 300.
Height in Pixels (HEIGHT)	This parameter is used to specify the height of the Web item. Default is 300.
Visibility (VISIBILITY)	This parameter is used to specify whether the Web item is to be visible in the Web application.
With Tray (WITH_TRAY)	This parameter is used to specify whether the Chart Web item is to have a symbol that allows the Web item to be expanded and collapsed.
Internal Display	
Edit Chart (CHART_CUSTOMIZING)	You use the button for this parameter to navigate to the Chart Designer. In the Chart Designer, is where you adjust the standard parameters of the chart.
Chart Type (CHART_TYPE)	This parameter is used to select the required chart type. The default value is Column Chart.
Legend Type (LEGEND_TYPE)	This parameter is used to make the following settings for the legend: • **Legend (default setting)** In the default setting, the legend is displayed with position South. • **None (NONE)** The legend is hidden. • **Data Table (DATATABLE)** Specifies that the system is to display the data in a table below the chart. • **Legend (LEGEND_POSITION)** The legend is displayed. The option Chart Legend Position is also displayed. You can choose from the following options: North (N) East (E) South (S) (default value) West (W) North-East (NE) North-West (NW) South-East (SE) South-West (SW) • **Only Legend (LEGEND_ONLY)** The legend is displayed without a chart.
Display Results (RESULTS_VISIBLE)	This parameter is used to specify whether the results are to be displayed in the chart or hidden. This parameter is deactivated by default and the totals rows and columns for the underlying data provider are not displayed in the chart. This means that you can suppress totals that may affect the chart display adversely without having to change the data provider.

TABLE 6-1 Web Item Parameters for the Chart Web Item

Parameter	Description
Swap Display Axes (AXES_SWAPPED)	This parameter is used to swap the chart axes in the display without changing the navigational state of the query view. The same effect is achieved if you swap two free characteristics with one another in the underlying query view.
Show Expanded Hierarchy Nodes (OPEN_HIERARCHY_NODES_VISIBLE)	This parameter is used to specify whether expanded hierarchy nodes are to be displayed or hidden in the chart. If you deactivate this parameter, it is possible to remove the expanded nodes from the chart generation when the display hierarchy is active. This ensures that the total of the values displayed is the overall result.
Display Exceptions (EXCEPTIONS_VISIBLE)	This parameter is used to specify whether exceptions are to be displayed in the chart or are hidden. This parameter is deactivated by default and no exceptions are displayed in the chart, even though the data provider on which it is based has exceptions.
Behavior	
Activate Navigation (INTERACTION_ALLOWED)	This parameter is used to specify whether navigation and other interactions are to be possible in the Web application.
Data Binding	
Data Provider (DATA_PROVIDER_REF)	This parameter is used to assign a data provider to the Web item. The Web item gets the data and metadata that it needs to generate the output and commands from this data provider. SAP recommends that you keep to the conventions supported by the Web Application Designer when specifying names: Names can be a maximum of 30 characters and consist of characters A–Z, 0–9, and _, but cannot start or end with _.
Affected Data Providers (LINKED_DATA_PROVIDER_REF_LIST)	This parameter is used to specify the list of data providers to which all chart commands are sent.
Chart Texts	
Title (TITLE)	This parameter is used to specify the language-dependent text for the title of the chart.
Diagram Subtitle (Language-Dependent) (SUBTITLE)	This parameter is used to specify the language-dependent text for the subtitle of the chart.
Legend Title (Language-Dependent) (TITLE_LEGEND)	This parameter is used to specify the language-dependent text for the title of the legend.

TABLE 6-1   Web Item Parameters for the Chart Web Item (*continued*)

Parameter	Description
Manual Axis Description (OVERRIDE_AXIS_DESC)	This parameter is used to specify whether you want to override automatic axis labeling. If you do not select this parameter, the system creates labeling for the chart axes of simple charts such as column, bar, line, and profile charts. If you select this parameter, you can choose from the following options for overriding automatic labeling of the axes: • Category Axis (X): Title (Language-Dependent) (TITLE_ CATEGORY_AXIS) This parameter is used to specify the language-dependent text for the title of the category axis (X). • Value Axis (Y): Title (Language-Dependent) (TITLE_VALUE_ AXIS) This parameter is used to specify the language-dependent text for the title of the value axis (Y). • Secondary Category Axis (X): Title (Language-Dependent) (TITLE_SEC_CATEGORY_AXIS) This parameter is used to specify the language-dependent text for the title of the secondary category axis (X). This parameter is only needed for specific chart types such as histograms or scatter charts. • Secondary Value Axis (Y): Title (Language-Dependent) (TITLE_SEC_VALUE_AXIS) This parameter is used to specify the language-dependent text for the title of the secondary value axis (Y).
Manual Axis Label (OVERRIDE_AXIS_LABEL)	This parameter is used to specify whether you want to override the automatic display for the axis label (for example, units or currencies). If the units and currencies in the query and other settings for the axis are the same and you do not select this parameter, these units, currencies, and settings are displayed automatically in the chart. Selecting this parameter, you can choose from the following options for overriding the automatic display: • Category Axis (X): Unit (Language-Dependent) (UNIT_ CATEGORY_AXIS) This parameter is used to specify the language-dependent text for the unit of the category axis (X). • Value Axis (Y): Unit (Language-Dependent) (UNIT_VALUE_ AXIS) This parameter is used to specify the language-dependent text for the unit of the value axis (Y). • Secondary Category Axis (X): Unit (Language-Dependent) (UNIT_SEC_CATEGORY_AXIS) This parameter is used to specify the language-dependent text for the unit of the secondary category axis (X). This parameter is only needed for specific chart types such as histograms or scatter charts. • Secondary Value Axis (Y): Unit (Language-Dependent) (UNIT_SEC_VALUE_AXIS) You use this parameter to specify the language-dependent text for the unit of the secondary value axis (Y).

TABLE 6-1   Web Item Parameters for the Chart Web Item (*continued*)

The texts, such as chart titles and chart subtitles, as well as the titles and units of the axes, are all language-dependent. You can enter the texts in the Chart Designer or in the Web Application Designer using the text input dialog box for the relevant parameters.

Automatic Axis Labeling

For basic charts, you can choose to label the chart axes automatically by activating the attribute Automatic Axis Labeling for Simple Charts (AUTOMATIC_DESCRIPTION) in the WAD. For this to work consistently, three prerequisites must be met: 1) you have selected a chart type (under Edit Chart) of Column, Bar, Line, or Profile; 2) the data provider on which the chart is based contains *only one key figure* used in a structure; and 3) there are no additional structures. Using the Automatic Axis Labeling for Simple Charts function has the following effect:

- The name of the (only) key figure is displayed on the Y axis of the chart.
- The name of the key figure, which is generally displayed on the X axis, in order to enable interaction in the chart, is hidden.
- The names of the characteristics (or the name of the characteristic if only one is used) are displayed on the X axis.

If the key figures are mixed with characteristics on an axis, the labels are not displayed automatically on the X axis. The preceding descriptions are valid for the bar and profile chart types with swapped X and Y axes.

Editing Charts

Displaying a series of numbers or data graphically as a chart instead of as a list enables users to interpret business data much more quickly and easily. That is the primary purpose of using charts in your Web reports, of course. However, the initial chart that you produce typically isn't in the best possible format to help business users interpret the data, so you often will need to edit the chart to meet your requirements.

NOTE *If a migration process is required to convert charts from the BW 2.x or 3.x version to the BI 7.0, you will need to upgrade your IGS from the 6.40 version to the 7.0 version. In the previous version of BW, the required Internet Graphics Server to support Web-based graphs was the 6.4 IGS and as we mentioned along with all of the application upgrades for the 7.0 version also comes platform upgrades and this is a significant enhancement. IGS 7.0 is the required environment to use the WAD for BI 7.0.*

In the case of the 7.0 BI you can edit a chart via the Web Application Designer or the Report Designer but in either case you have to access the WAD to actually configure the chart type. The following illustration identifies the various elements of a chart. You will encounter these terms as you read about the process of configuring a chart. The information shown on a chart is broken out into four different areas: data information, axis information, chart titles, and the formatted area behind the chart. The data information is referenced by the Data Point and Data Series, the axis information is referenced by the Value Axis (Y), Category Axis (X), and Axis Title, the chart titles are referenced by Chart Title, Legend Text, and Legend Icon, and the formatted area behind the chart is referenced by Drawing Area, Background, and Gridlines. In this section, you will learn how to configure and adjust each of these areas to produce a robust chart for the business user.

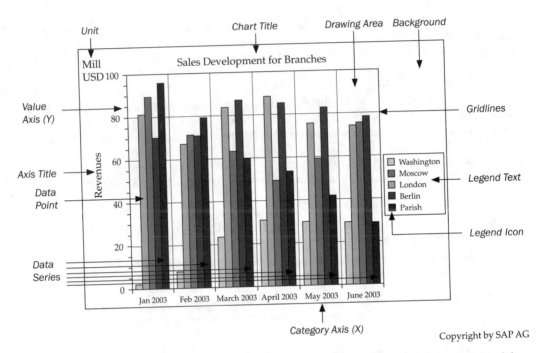

To start the process of editing the chart in the WAD, either create a new Web item of the type Chart or select an existing Web item of the type Chart. Then, on the Web Item Parameters tab of the Properties screen area, under Internal Display, click the button for the Edit Chart property to access the Edit Chart dialog box (or *Chart Designer*), shown in the following illustration.

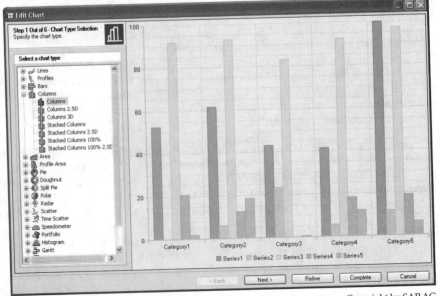

Alternatively, you can open the Chart Designer by right-clicking the Chart Web item and choosing Edit. This is shown in the following illustration.

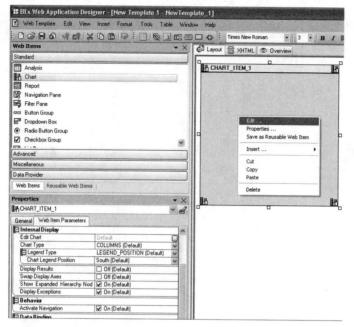

The nice thing about the Chart Designer is that it is set up similarly to other wizards in the SAP system. It offers you a step-by-step process of moving through the configuration of the chart from start to finish. You can also go back, after previewing your chart, and change information and settings until you are happy with the results.

The first step in the process of publishing a chart is to specify which chart type you want to display. You can determine how the data provider is to be built by using the class of the chart type. Now a task that we didn't really talk about for this process and it's something that should already be completed and that is creating a query or selecting an existing query that you can use to generate a suitable view of the data. Once this has been identified in the Data Provider section, then you can move through the wizard steps one at a time and validate or change any parameters you need to.

NOTE *You probably have noticed that this is very similar to the Chart Designer in Excel. If you are comfortable with all the functionality of the Chart Designer in Excel, you will have very few issues with this process, perhaps with the exception of figuring out where a particular parameter is located.*

As you can see we have exactly six steps to work through to develop a chart with a display of data. If at any time you feel that the setup that you have completed is good enough, then all you need is to skip to the finish. At this point you can choose to refine the format. Once in this particular view of the graph the only other option you have is to finish the chart or, if you require, use the Wizard button to go back to the actual six steps. The following illustration shows these options.

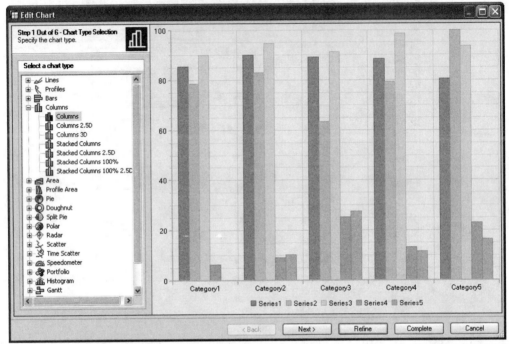

If you choose the Refine button, you move to detailed display level. Here you can configure all of the parameters by clicking on the header in the overview or clicking a particular portion of the chart. We will be working through all of these options later in this chapter. At this point just realizing that you can use this approach to configure rather than the wizard is all we want to reinforce. This information is found in the illustration.

After you click the Refine button, as the preceding illustration shows, your only option to move from this screen is Wizard or Complete. The option to use the refine approach is nice to have and much of the configuration can be accomplished from this but in most cases you have to return to the full Chart Designer to finish your work. One of the lesser-used parameters is the SWAP DISPLAY AXES, which enables you to swap the data providers in the chart. So, if you want to swap automatically the data providers used for the rows and columns, you can use this setting to accomplish the task.

When you edit the chart, the Web Application Designer or Web Application Wizard first shows the default setting, that is, a column chart. Initially, format the chart using the wizard so that the most important settings and the number of displayed data series and data points correspond to your data provider. Then assign the required chart type to the chart and format the chart as required. All chart elements that you can format are displayed in the list of properties on the right of the screen. You can modify the properties as required here based on the list supplied in Table 6-1.

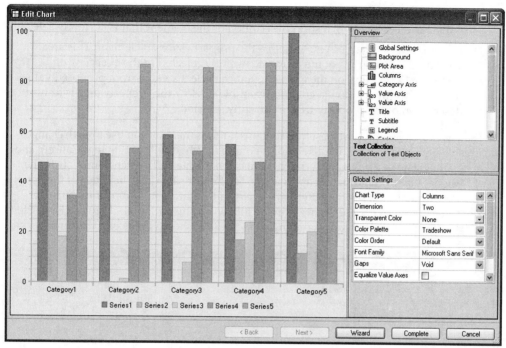

FIGURE 6-1   Structure of the Chart Designer

Working with the Chart Designer

When you edit a chart, you use the Chart Designer to view and edit the preview of the chart. The structure of the Chart Designer window has three areas: chart preview (left side of the screen), list of elements (top-right side of the screen), and property area (bottom-left side of screen), as identified in the Figure 6-1.

Depending on the Chart Designer feature you are using, these sections can switch sides of the window. If you are going through the wizard process, the chart preview appears on the right side of the window; if you are using the Refine mode, the chart preview appears on the left. The following list describes the three areas:

- **Chart preview**   Shows an example chart that displays the values and properties that you set. New charts have five data series and six categories by default, regardless of how the data provider is structured. The important thing to remember is that the preview does not correspond to the results after publishing. The data series and data categories are only sample data used to show you what the effects of formatting are. You see the actual data only after it has been published. So, focus on the format rather than the actual data and information.

- **List of elements**   Contains all elements of a chart. These elements are partially ordered in logical groups. You can expand these groups by clicking the plus sign in front of the group name. You click the minus sign to collapse the group again. This is a list of elements with a short description of the element that is currently selected.

- **Property area** Enables you to define the properties for an element. This area displays the properties of the element currently selected in the overview of elements. Depending on the element, you can select a value from proposed values or enter your own value (a color for example). Below the property area is a short description of the property that is currently selected.

The lower area of the Chart Designer contains buttons that you can use to save changes and finish editing the chart (Complete), finish editing the chart without saving (Cancel), and call up and navigate in the wizard (Wizard). You can navigate and switch your view in the Chart Designer via several different approaches. My favorite is to just click each of the options in the list of elements and see the different, more-detailed parameters appear in the lower property area of the screen. For example, in the following illustration, Background is selected in the list of elements and its corresponding properties are shown in the property area.

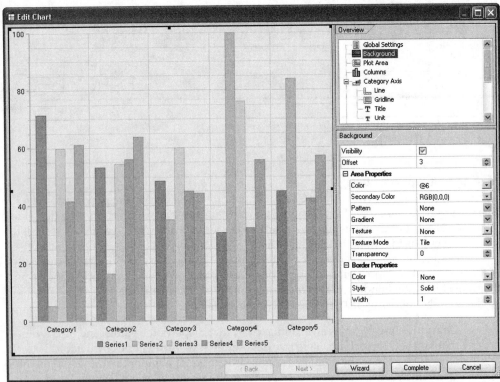

As you can see, the properties include filters and parameters for Color, Texture, Style, and other background elements that can be configured. Also notice that as you choose each of the different elements and its properties are displayed, the affected area is also highlighted in the Chart Designer chart preview. An example of selecting the Columns element is shown in the following illustration.

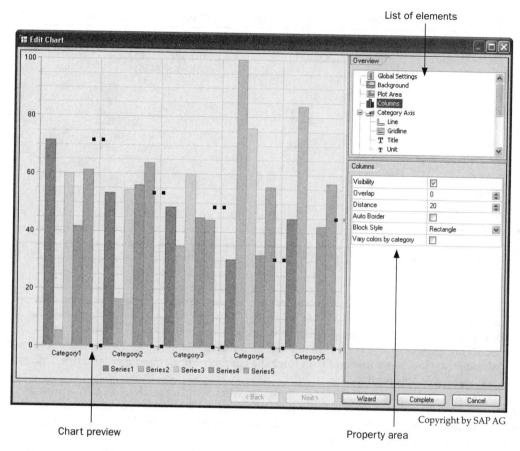

List of elements

Chart preview

Property area

Copyright by SAP AG

You can modify the size of areas in the Chart Designer according to your requirements. For example, you may want to increase the size of the property area so that you can display all properties at once. To do so, position the cursor at the intersection of two areas until the cursor changes into two parallel lines. Click and pull the area to the required size. When you have finished editing a chart, or want to terminate editing, close the Chart Designer and return to the WAD. Before you close the Chart Designer, make sure you save your work before exiting, if you want to save it.

Chart Types

Before we start to work our way through the six different steps to develop a chart, let's look at the chart types so that you are familiar with your choices. The chart type defines how your data is displayed graphically. The chart types can be divided into five classes with respect to processing and complexity. With chart types of the same class, the rows and columns of the underlying table (that is, of the data provider) are processed immediately.

The class to which each chart type belongs is listed in Table 6-2. Before you configure or publish a chart, you need to specify which chart type you want to display. You can determine how the data provider is to be built by using the class of the chart type. You can then select

Class 1	Class 2	Class 3	Class 4	Class 5
Line chart	Scatter chart	Portfolio	Gantt chart	Delta chart
Profile chart	Time scatter chart		Milestone trend	(waterfall chart)
Column chart	Histogram		analysis (MTA)	
Bar chart	Heatmap			
Doughnut chart				
Radar chart				
Area chart				
Profile area chart				
Pie chart				
Polar chart				
Speedometer				
Split pie chart				

TABLE 6-2   Chart Types and Corresponding Classes

an existing query or formulate a new query with which the appropriate view of the data can be created. I learned the hard way that failing to follow this procedure—that is, specifying the chart type to display before publishing the chart—wastes a lot of time. Instead of identifying the format of the chart first and then building the query to the appropriate view, I would create the query first and then force the chart type to fit my query structure. I do not recommend this approach.

As you can see, the charts that you normally work with are in classes 1 and 2 primarily (but I have run into the waterfall chart type in a number of projects). As long as you are comfortable working with class 1 and 2 chart types, you should be able to support over 85 percent of your customers' needs.

Most of the charts listed in Table 6-2 can be displayed with various dimensions, such as 2 dimensions, 2.5 dimensions (limited three-dimensionality), and 3D (regular three-dimensionality). Bar and column charts can be converted into pyramid, cone, or cylinder diagrams in 2.5D and 3D mode. The dimensional look and feel of the charts is a good "nice to have" but, depending on the amount of information and data points on the chart, the 3D format may be more distracting than useful. I recommend using the 3D format only if the customer requests it.

Another variant that exists for line, column, bar, profile, and radar charts is a "stacked" variant. These values of the data series are added and displayed on top of one another in a category and normally are differentiated by colors. Stacked charts display the relationship between individual elements and the total of all values.

You can also set 100% variants for line, profile, column, bar, area, and profile charts. The sum of all data series in a category is 100 percent. The values of individual data series are converted into percentage values and displayed accordingly.

Class 1 Chart Types
As listed in Table 6-2, class 1 includes the following chart types: line, profile, column, bar, doughnut, radar, area, profile area, pie, polar, speedometers, and split pie.

You build the underlying table of the chart types of class 1 (with the exception of pie charts and speedometers) as follows:

- The data columns correspond to the categories.
- The rows contain the values for each category. Each row is converted into a data series in the chart.

The difference when using a pie chart is that the underlying table has only one row. The values in the columns form the pie segments. If the table contains more than one row, the additional rows are ignored when the table is converted into a chart. However, you can define which row is to be used. When using a speedometer, the difference is that the underlying table has only one data column. Each value in the data column is displayed in the chart as a pointer. The speedometer will be readable if the data column does not contain too many values. If the table contains more than one data column, the additional columns are ignored when the table is converted into a chart. You can define which data column is to be used for the speedometer.

After reviewing these nuisances to building the queries to use for the specific chart types, you should start to get a good idea of what the formatting process for your queries needs to be for each of the different chart types. The following illustration shows the data table that is the basis for line, profile, column, bar, doughnut, and radar charts.

▼ Columns		Fiscal year	2007	2008	Overall Result
• Fiscal year			Sales Volume (MC)	Sales Volume (MC)	Sales Volume (MC) ⇕
• Key Figures	Material group ⇕		$	$	$
▼ Rows	90001	Accessories	894.500,00	1.023.454,00	1.917.954,00
• Material group	90002	Bags and Outdoors	1.289.870,00	1.565.600,00	2.855.470,00
• Free characteristics	90003	Clothing	980.989,00	1.176.787,00	2.157.776,00
	Overall Result		3.165.359,00	3.765.841,00	6.931.200,00

NOTE *You could also generate a split pie chart from this data source, but we will work with another example in order to clarify the possibilities for this chart type.*

Most of the examples mentioned here were created using the chart attribute Switch Axes to Display (SWITCHMATRIX='X').

Line Chart   Data trends are shown in a *line chart*. The data is entered at regular intervals. Categories such as items groups are groups of similar characteristic values such as material types, product types, customer attributes, etc. and are normally entered on the X axis and values such as revenue on the Y axis. This can be seen in the illustration shown here.

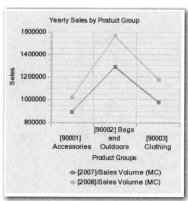

Completing this initial basic line chart simply required adding some minor text to the chart. Most of the time was spent creating the query to support this chart. With the appropriate data available, a reasonable chart can be created almost immediately. To create this chart, I adjusted the default chart type from column to line by right-clicking on the Chart Web item and choosing Edit from the context menu and I then chose basic lines rather than the dimensional options, as shown in the following illustration.

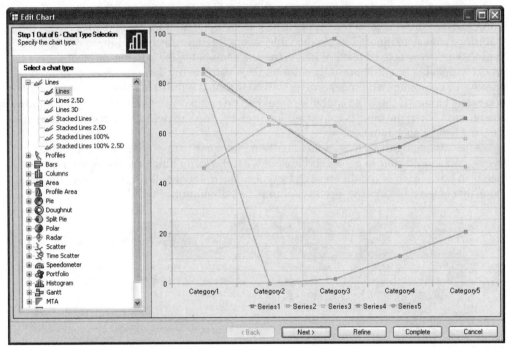

In step 2 of the Chart Designer, I added text for the titles of the chart and the axes, as shown next. As you can see, when you enter text in the fields on the left, it appears in the chart by default. At this point, if you click the Complete button, you have just built a line chart.

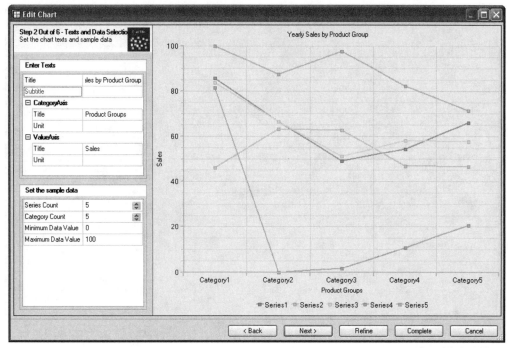

Copyright by SAP AG

For line charts, you can set the manner in which the lines pass between data points: direct, as in the preceding example; as curved lines; or in varying increments. To do so, go to the next step in the Chart Wizard, choose Data Series Format | *<name of series>* | Line Type. In all the other examples in this section, we will only add some text to the formatting process, so they all can be developed in a matter of seconds.

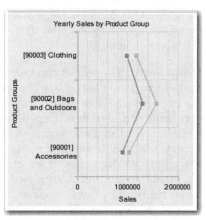

Profile Chart   In a *profile chart*, the lines are arranged vertically, as shown here, and not horizontally as in a line chart. Otherwise, the profile chart corresponds to the line chart. Basically, the axes are switched for a different view of the data. Notice that the text also automatically adjusts to the appropriate axis.

Profile charts have the same options as line charts for setting the manner in which the lines pass between data points. Rather than a direct line that passes between the data points, as shown in the previous

Copyright by SAP AG

example, you can also have the lines curve by different levels. Again, you choose Data Series Format | *<name of series>* | Line Type from the next step in the Chart Wizard. Another option to allow this same formatting option is that you can find these parameters if you go to the Refine screen and choose the Data Series Format. This can be seen in the following illustration.

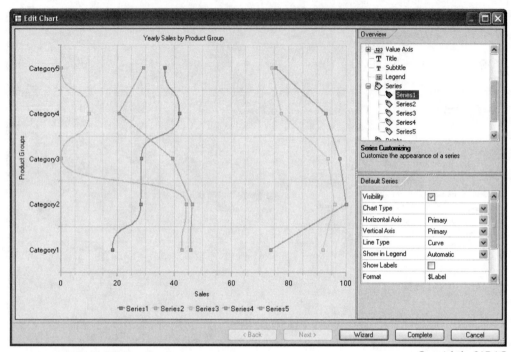

Copyright by SAP AG

And the results of this are in this illustration. As in this situation, not the best display but there are many other options within that area. Before you attempt zigzag lines, I recommend experimenting with the dimensional profiles and lines first to see if this helps produce a dynamic chart.

Column Chart The *column chart* seems to be one of the most popular chart types, probably because it can be easily understood and assimilated within a very short period of time. Depending on your audience, you can make a column chart very robust or very basic. As its name suggests, in a column chart, the comparisons between individual elements are shown in a column. Categories are arranged

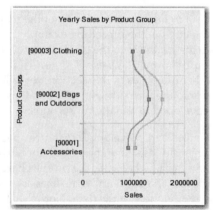

Copyright by SAP AG

horizontally and values are arranged vertically. To show changes within a certain time interval, you can use either column charts or XY scatter charts (described in the "Class 2 Chart Types" section). The following illustration shows the numerous different column options that are available.

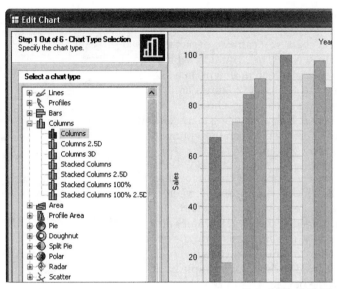

An example of the look and feel of the Stacked Columns option is shown in the following illustration. You can see that this would also be a very direct chart to offer for analysis.

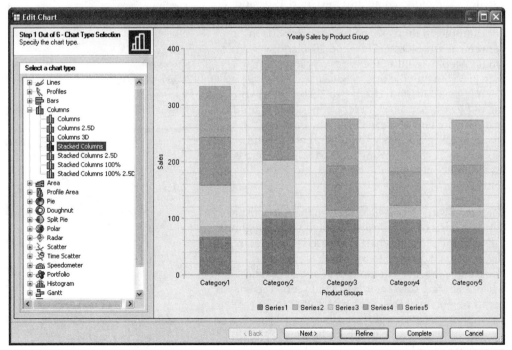

The result of choosing the basic Columns option is shown here.

In a 3D column chart, you can also depict the columns as cylinders, cones, or pyramids, which can really be a great visual enhancement. In a 2D column chart, you can depict the columns as triangles (2D pyramids). To do this, choose Columns | BlockStyle. If you are using a 2D column chart, there is no difference between the setting Pyramid and the setting Cone.

Bar Chart   The next most popular chart type might be the *bar chart*, in which comparisons between individual elements are shown in a bar chart. Categories are arranged vertically and values are arranged horizontally. The emphasis is on the comparison of values and not on displaying a change during a period of time. An example bar chart is shown in the next illustration.

In cases such as this example, you will need to make some additional changes to the chart. Here, the data points for Sales are probably not sufficiently detailed. Therefore, going into the Chart Type and identifying the types of values would be required. For example, in this case we have a comparison between Yearly Sales of 2007 and 2008 and we would need to identify the types of values rather than just showing the title of Sales.

As in a 3D column chart, in a 3D bar chart you can depict the bars as cylinders, cones, or pyramids. In a 2D bar chart, you can depict the bars as triangles (2D pyramids). To do this, choose Bars | BlockStyle. If you are using a 2D bar chart, there is no difference between the Pyramid and Cone settings.

Doughnut Chart   In a *doughnut chart*, the relationship between parts of a whole are displayed in a doughnut. This is similar to a pie chart, discussed a bit later in this section. In contrast to the pie chart, however, the doughnut can represent more than one data series, where each ring corresponds to a data series, as shown here. I do not favor this chart type, but in the correct situation it can work well.

You can change the width of the rings by setting the size of the hole. To do so, choose Doughnut | Hole Size | *<value as percentage of ring size>*.

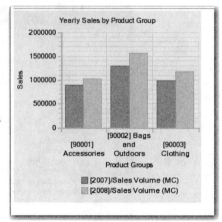

Copyright by SAP AG

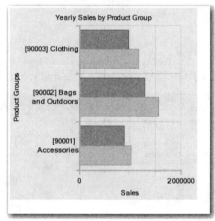

Copyright by SAP AG

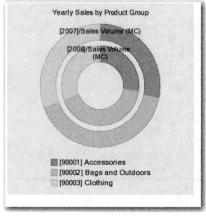

Copyright by SAP AG

Radar Chart   Another chart that is a bit conceptual in nature is the *radar chart*, shown next. In this case, each category has its own value axis emanating from the middle. The values of a data series are linked with lines. Radar charts can be used to compare data series: The data series with the highest values occupies the most space. The radar chart is a bit more direct than the doughnut chart, but still I can't think of many situations in which to use it. There are definitely more types of charts that are easier to explain and understand.

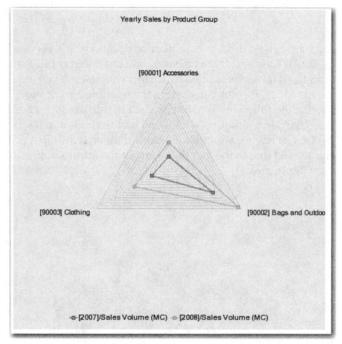

Copyright by SAP AG

You can also depict the chart areas filled in. Choose Radar | Filled to do so. Depending on the size of the individual data series, the areas may overlap.

For the following series of chart types, understanding what types of data show up in specific chart types becomes very important. For this series of chart types, we will be using a different data set. The following illustration is the basis for these charts. As you can see, the data provider has been changed to only one key figure for Material Group (note that in the initial query this is listed as the Product Group information and we have adjusted for reporting purposes to show as Material Group).

- Area charts
- Profile area charts
- Pie charts
- Polar charts
- Speedometers

		Fiscal year	2008	Overall Result
▼ Columns			Sales Volume (MC)	Sales Volume (MC) ⇕
• Fiscal year				
• Key Figures	Material group ⇕		$	$
▼ Rows	90001	Accessories	1.023.454,00	1.023.454,00
• Material group	90002	Bags and Outdoors	1.565.600,00	1.565.600,00
• Free characteristics	90003	Clothing	1.176.787,00	1.176.787,00
	Overall Result		3.765.841,00	3.765.841,00

Area Chart   The *area chart* can be used in a number of situations. It's very easy to read and interpret and has a similar look and feel as a bar or line chart that is filled in. The area between the axes and the data series is filled in an area chart. A stacked area chart depicts the sum of the applied values, thereby illustrating the relationships of parts to each other. An example is shown in the following illustration. Just to mix things up a bit, I used the 2.5D view of the area chart. In a situation where you had two sets of data (two key figures), you would see this chart as having another area behind the first area in a different color. This can get difficult to read due to the fact that some of the information may be hidden behind the initial key figure area.

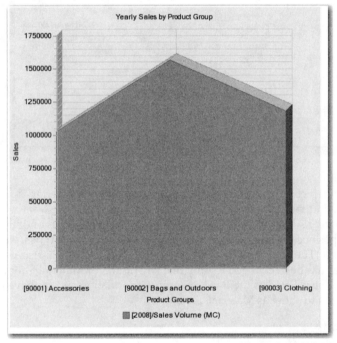

You can determine the line type in an area chart in the same way as for a line chart. The only difference is that the line type Curve is not supported for an area chart. I would definitely not highlight that as a big deal since the direct line type is the most popular.

Profile Area Chart In a *profile area chart*, the areas are arranged vertically and not horizontally as in an area chart. Otherwise, the profile chart corresponds to the area chart. As the following illustration shows, this is not the easiest type of chart to read.

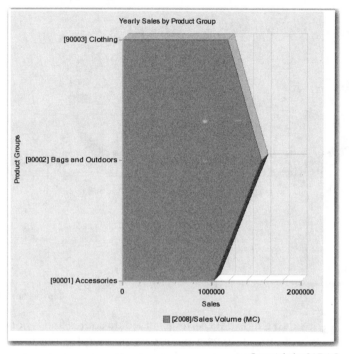

You can determine the line type in a profile area chart in the same way as for a profile chart.

Pie Chart The *pie chart* is definitely one that you can use frequently—it's basic, straightforward, and can have a dramatic effect if formatted correctly. In a pie chart, the proportional part of the elements of a data series are displayed in a whole. This chart type has only a single data series and is used primarily to highlight a particularly important element. As the following illustration shows, adding some depth to this chart can make it much more interesting. I also added another option, Explosion Offset, which separates the pie pieces. You can find this option if you use Refine and choose PIE properties in the overview section, and then increase the Explosion Offset in the properties section and separate the pieces to whatever spacing looks good to you. The preview will show you the adjustment dynamically as you change the settings. Note in the illustration that you can scroll across the screen and see the details for each of the pie pieces.

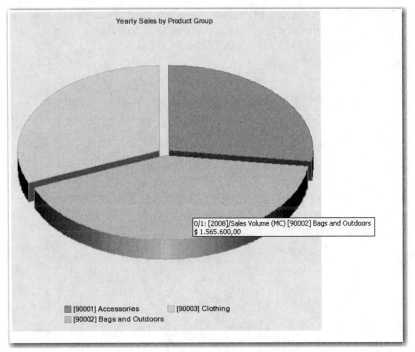

Yearly Sales by Product Group

0/1: [2008]/Sales Volume (MC) [90002] Bags and Outdoors
$ 1.565.600,00

[90001] Accessories   [90003] Clothing
[90002] Bags and Outdoors

A pie chart only reads a single data series from a data source and ignores all others. You can determine which series is to be used by choosing Pie | Series Index | *<number of table series>*. Another parameter you can easily set is how much of the drawing area your pie chart should take up. To do so, choose Pie | UsedSpace | *<value as percentage of drawing area>*.

Polar Chart   The *polar chart* is another specially formatted chart type that can be used in certain situations, but it doesn't really offer any advantage over and above the other, more readable chart types. In any case, it's an option and each category has its own value axis. The values of a data series are depicted as areas, as shown in the following illustration. As you can see, this chart type would have to be explained carefully to make sure that the business user is correctly interpreting the information. Looking at the results of this chart type, you would be hard-pressed to come up with the information from the report.

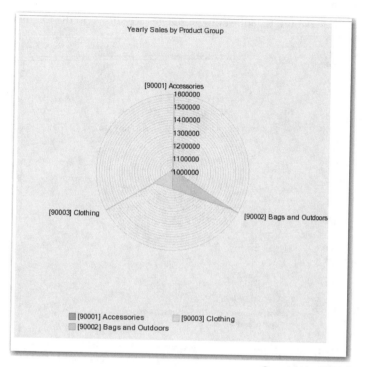

Yearly Sales by Product Group

A polar chart only reads a single data series from a data source and ignores all others. You can determine which series is to be used by choosing Polar | Series Index | *<number of series>*.

Speedometer Chart   Another one of my favorites is the *speedometer* chart type. A speedometer displays one or more key figures in the form of a pointer. The speedometer is divided into several value ranges, and the user immediately sees the value range in which the pointer is currently positioned.

A speedometer only displays one data column of the data provider. This is the basic speedometer with no color groups, but it is dramatic enough to catch your interest. In the case of the speedometer chart,

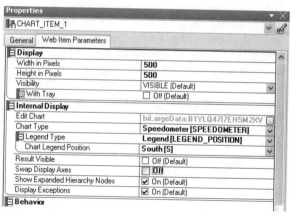

I typically turn off the parameter to Swap Display Axis since a swap of pointers with other values in this situation would not show correctly or make any sense. The Swap Display Axes setting in the Web Item Parameters tab of the WAD is shown here.

The results of these parameter and settings changes are shown in the following illustration.

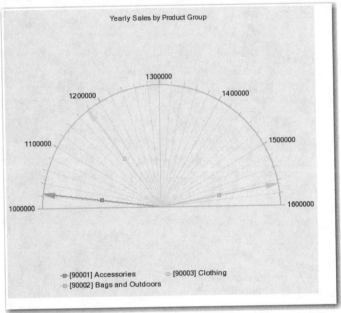

You can also determine which data column is to be displayed by choosing Speedometer | Data Index | *<number of data column>*. In terms of the display of the pointers, you can determine whether to display the categories as pointers rather than the data column by choosing Speedometer | Use Categories. You can also define the look and feel of the pointers—whether you want the arrow displayed or something else to take its place by using Speedometer | Show Arrows. Some of the other options in a speedometer are to add some color formatting, font changes, and background colors. In some cases with the different properties that you can use within the chart types some don't really work such as with speedometer chart types. You can change the dimensionality of the chart type but with the speedometer chart type nothing will happen since 2.5D and 3D are not possible. These settings are found in the Global Settings under Refine. An example of the color formatting is illustrated next.

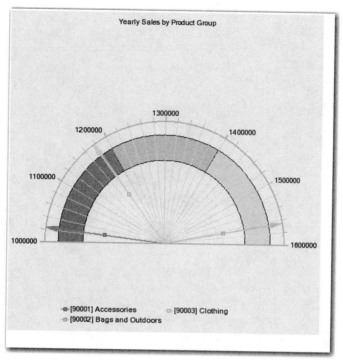

Split Pie Chart   The *split pie chart* is another favorite of mine. In a split pie chart, several data series are displayed per category as a pie segment, and are depicted in proportion to each other. For this example, we will go back to the data provider we used previously for the column chart type and have two key figures by year and see what this offers us. I like the display of the different sections, and if we add some dimensionality to this, it immediately looks close to being a finished chart. The next illustration shows an example of the end result.

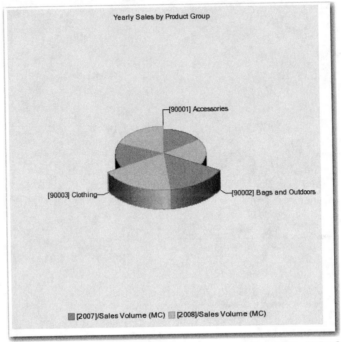

One of the other options of all the different free-flowing chart types, such as the pie and polar charts, is that they can be moved or rotated into different views. This is very useful if you are going to work with 2.5D or 3D shapes.

At this point, you likely are starting to get a feel for what the initial dashboard process would look like. If we were to incorporate several of these charts together into one dashboard, we could start blueprinting what we might want to present to the customer. I've taken some of these chart types and used a simple table to hold their format a bit more. This takes about 15–20 minutes and lays the foundation for a dashboard. An example of the initial configuration and the result is shown in the next illustrations. Although this example is limited to six charts, it is sufficient to help you understand the overall dashboard setup and architecture. I'm hoping that this will pique your interest for what is in the next chapter once we really get into formatting and designing your dashboards.

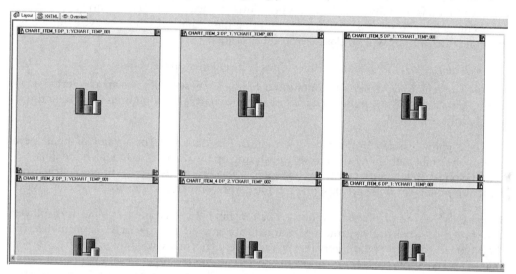

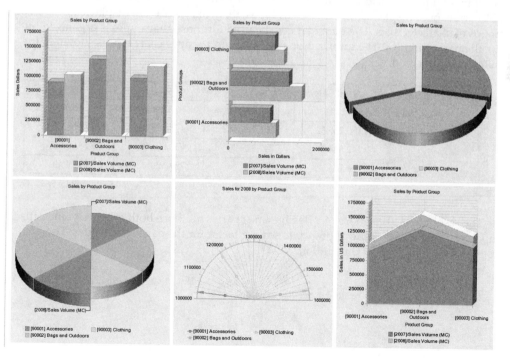

Class 2 Chart Types

Class 2 chart types include scatter charts, time scatter charts, histograms, and heatmaps. They are not necessarily more complex than the class 1 chart types but are more specific to certain situations than the class 1 chart types. Thus, in the case of class 2 chart types, we have a more defined set of data to use for building these charts. In this case, you build the table on which a chart type of class 2 is based as follows:

- The first data row contains the values to be entered on the X axis.
- The remaining data rows contain the Y values. These data rows are converted into data series. The number of data series in the chart is the total number of data rows minus 1.

The X value of a data point is always from the first data row. The Y value of a data point is from one of the remaining data rows, depending on the data series to which the data point belongs. The data providers for histograms and heatmaps need a different structure; the requirements for these are described in the corresponding sections for these chart types.

Scatter Chart   In a *scatter chart*, either the relationship between numeric values is displayed in several data series or two groups of numbers are entered as a row of XY coordinates. This chart type displays irregular intervals (clusters) and is normally used for scientific data so using these types of charts for business purposes requires a unique situation. Both axes of a scatter chart are value axes, so we would not necessarily use the scatter chart type to display something with a characteristic like Product Groups down the rows since this would not look correct once displayed. In other chart types, the X axis is used to display categories or groups of characteristics. The data that is to be used for those chart types is organized by month and key figures. The information used to build a scatter chart type is shown in the following illustration.

	Quarter. Calendar Year			
	1.2003	**2.2003**	**3.2003**	**4.2003**
Billed Quantity	170,250,32	171,406,182	172,765,649	171,685,760
Net Sales	742,344.30	747,329.80	753,021.96	748,078.47
Planned Sales	756,136	762,019	754,590	744,2760

The resulting chart is more of a flexible line chart type. Since both axes are values, it's important to be aware of the appropriate scaling factor for the particular values. The final result is shown in the next illustration.

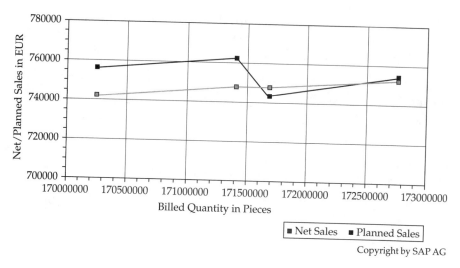

You can fill the areas between two points of a data series, almost as if the chart were an area chart. To do so, choose Scatter | Filled.

Time Scatter Chart   A subset of the scatter chart is the *time scatter chart*. The X value can be a date or time. The basic Chart Designer configuration screen for this chart type, shown next, gives you a hint that it is not meant to be used to show information by products or customers; rather, it is used for tracking and data analysis in a more value-driven approach. Notice the formatted Date approach to the X axis.

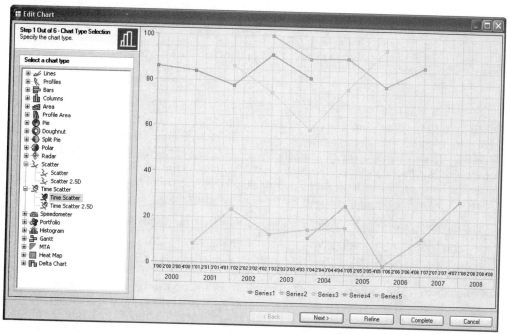

As you can see, the axes are both value driven and not category driven. Therefore, the data needs to be similar to the data used in the scatter chart type; the data provider for this example is shown in the following illustration.

	Time 1	Time 2	Time 3	Time 4	Time 5
Time	06:40:00	11:06:40	15:33:20	20:33:20	23:53:20
No. of Batch Processes	250.00	10.00	19.00	150.00	300.00

The results of applying the time scatter chart type are shown in the following illustration. The X axis is the time in hours and the Y axis is the number of batches processed.

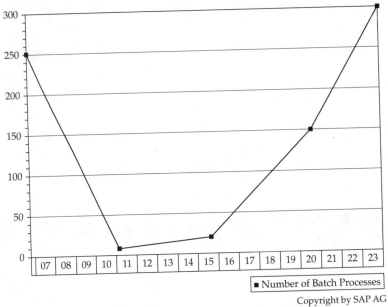

■ Number of Batch Processes

These types of charts are great for displays with date or time values. You can set up to three different time axes; for example, one for years, one for quarters, and one for months. To do this, choose Time Axis | Line | Line Type1 to Line Type3. You can also use Line Format1 to Line Format3 to specify the format in which the time values are to be displayed. You can use the properties Line Step1 to Line Step3 to set the intervals between time units. The following abbreviations are used for the time specifications:

D = day, Mon = month, Y = year, W = week, Q = quarter, H = hour, Min = minute, S = second

As in the former scatter chart type, you can fill the area beneath a data series by choosing Time Scatter | Filled. This might offer a more dramatic display of the information.

Histogram Chart   The *histogram* is used primarily for the graphic display of a series of activities. The frequency of a characteristic is displayed in a histogram (for example, the sales revenue for a product group). The frequencies are divided into classes, where each class corresponds to a column in the histogram. In a histogram, categories (classes) are entered on the X axis and the corresponding values are entered on the Y axis. The information for the histogram chart type is shown in the following illustration.

Product	Sequence	Net Sales
Paper Clip	1	362,643.23
Multi-Function Pen	2	576,034.09
Post-It Set	3	198,493.43
Biro	4	547,116.83
Mouse Pad	5	521,850.64
Business Card Holder	6	611,238.54
Coffee Mug	7	577,020.82
Candy Tin	8	535,852.04
Bottle Opener	9	433,939.79
Writing Pad	10	514,179.24
Fountain Pen	11	490,866.26
Automatic Umbrella	12	564,021.33

Unique ID   Value

Copyright by SAP AG

In this case, I had to do some adjustments to the X and Y axes to allow the data to be shown consistently across the chart. Even after these changes, understanding the results of this chart type is difficult, as shown next. Typically, you'll know when you need to use a histogram chart type because the data that you are trying to chart will not fit any of the other chart types and the histogram will be the only one that makes sense.

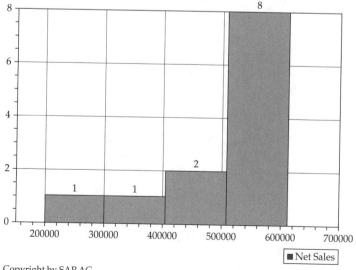

Copyright by SAP AG

Analyzing this information based on the data provider, we see that the sequence is on the Y axis and the sales data is on the X axis. The numbers within the chart are the number of sequences that are within that range, so the preceding histogram shows one sequence in the 198,000 to 300,000 range, one sequence in the 300,000 to 400,000 range, two sequences in the 400,000 to 500,000 range, and the remaining eight sequences from 500,000 to over 600,000. This is very similar to the clustering process in data mining, where items that are within a certain range are grouped together. To be displayed correctly, a histogram needs one data source with exactly the structure shown earlier. The first data column contains unique numeric values only; these do not need to be sorted. The second data column contains the values that are sorted into the classes of the histogram. Again, notice we are talking about two data columns and one category column. You can control the number of classes by choosing Histogram | Classes | *<required number of classes>*.

Heatmap Chart   The last class 2 chart type is the *heatmap*. This chart type is very unique in nature and with all the requirements needed in terms of a specific set of data we will talk through this one and show a sample of data required as well as the resulting graph. Heatmaps allow you to display large volumes of data compactly in a diagram. As in the histogram, the heatmap chart type groups information together in ranges of values, so this chart type is appropriate if you are not really looking for details but for patterns in the data.

You can display the values of two key figures compactly and independently of each other for a number of data series. The display is two dimensional:

1. Area (rectangle size) records the values of the first key figure (such as Billed Quantity).
2. Color (position in color ramp) records the values of the second key figure (such as Net Sales).

You can identify unusual values and trends easily and answer business questions such as "How do the sales figures in various distribution channels and product groups compare to each other?" An example of the data required for this chart type is shown in the next illustration.

Product Group	Bag & Outdoor		Accessories	
	Billed Quantity	Net Sales	Billed Quantity	Net Sales
Distribution Channel	Pcs	$	Pcs	$
EDI	16,551,490	215,536,876	79,298,050	214,482,973
Fax	24,955,409	336,593,498	125,809,073	328,978,177
Internet	15,690,502	211,184,935	80,488,755	208,231,891
Others	6,506,994	87,931,877	31,377,975	83,535,015
Phone	17,859,461	242,425,306	92,644,635	241,551,902
Overall Result	81,563,856	1,093,672,492	409,618,488	1,076,779,958

Product Group	Office		**Overall Result**	
	Billed Quantity	Net Sales	Billed Quantity	Net Sales
Distribution Channel	Pcs	$	Pcs	$
EDI	39,353,472	160,261,488	135,203,012	590,281,337
Fax	59,691,316	254,827,544	210,455,798	920,399,219
Internet	37,181,491	157,070,018	133,360,748	576,486,844
Other	15,195,978	64,238,884	53,080,947	235,705,776
Phone	43,503,122	183,924,137	154,007,218	667,901,345
Overall Result	194,925,379	820,322,071	686,107,723	2,990,774,521

Copyright by SAP AG

You build the report on which a heatmap is based with a table that must contain the following:

- Exactly two characteristics (such as Distribution Channel and Product Group). The first characteristic (Distribution Channel) can have up to 100 characteristic values (such as EDI, Fax), and thus determines the number of data series. The second characteristic (Product Group) can have various characteristic values (such as Bad & Outdoor, Accessories), and thus determines the number of categories for each data series.

- Exactly two key figures (data columns) for each category.

So, this is probably the most restrictive chart type we've encountered so far. The required query is very specific and a bit more involved to work with. The basic Chart Designer configuration diagram itself is intense, as shown next, and if your information or your requirements are not specific to the heatmap process, the chart will make very little sense.

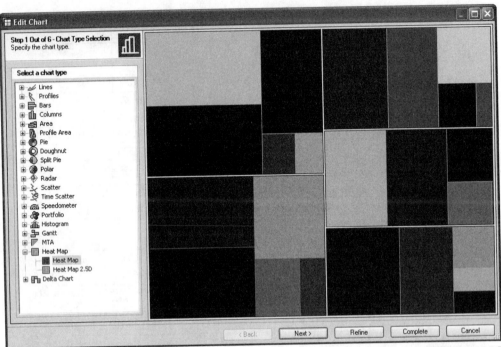

A diagram of what is happening in this chart is shown in the next illustration. You can see that you define a driver key figure, Billed Quantity in this example, that serves as the lead value for sizing the rectangles.

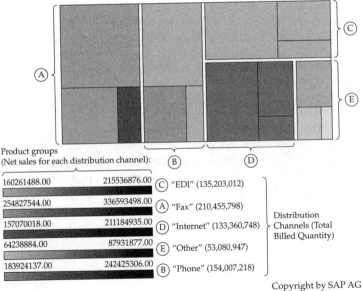

As previously mentioned, the two display dimensions are area and color. In the area dimension, the characteristic value Fax (Distribution Channel characteristic) results in the large square to the upper left of the heatmap, since its categories (Product Groups) have the largest Billed Quantity. The three categories are within this rectangle; each is represented as a rectangle proportional to its Billed Quantity. Therefore, your three Product Groups are defined by the three color sections within each of the groups. In the color dimension, the three product groups Bag & Outdoor, Accessories, and Office are differentiated by color based on the Net Sales for each Distribution Channel. For the Distribution Channel, the colors for the Bag & Outdoor and Accessories rectangles are similar, whereas the Office category, on the other hand, is easy to distinguish (compare to data provider). The good thing about this is that when you render the template, you can scroll over each of the rectangles to identify the values and, in this case, the Distribution Channels.

Class 3 Chart Type: Portfolio

The only chart type included in this class is the *portfolio*. Unlike the last chart type discussed, heatmap, the portfolio is a chart type you see all the time, particularly when dealing with financial information. For example, the *Wall Street Journal* and *USA Today* often use a portfolio chart to depict the ebb and flow of the different stock groups or industries for that week. These chart types identify groups that are growing and/or declining over the past X time frame. An example of the basic configuration screen for the portfolio is shown in the Chart Designer in the following illustration.

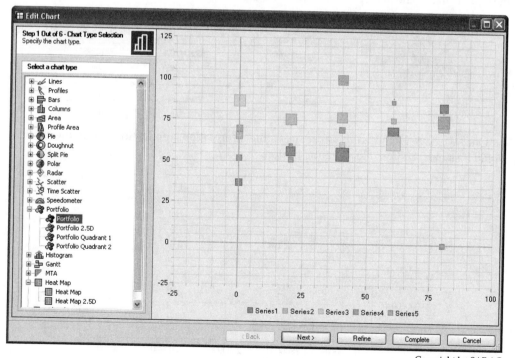

A portfolio displays the position of an object (enterprise, product, and so on) in a four-field matrix. The position of the object is defined using two dimensions and the X and Y axes depending on the movement of the overall amounts or values. So, the base of zero is moving to correct for some variance that is defined. Portfolios are used mainly in enterprise and product comparisons. A portfolio can be sorted, for example, like the products of an enterprise by their dimensions economics and strategic significance.

The most important aspect of this chart type is the construction of the underlying query to support it. Once you get this set up correctly, the final build of the chart itself is routine. You build the underlying table for a portfolio as follows:

- The first data column contains the values to be entered on the X axis.
- The second data column contains the values to be entered on the Y axis.
- The third data column is relevant for the bubble size.
- You can add further pairs of data columns to the table. The first data column of a pair always contains the Y values and the second data column the bubble size.

The X value of a data point is always defined from the first data column. The Y value of a data point is defined from the second data column, depending on the data column to which the data point belongs. The X and Y values together give you the center of the bubble. In the following example, the X axis is the Net Sales, Y is the Invoiced Quantity, and the bubble size as the average value—Sales/Quantity.

Product Group	Net Sales	Invoiced Quantity	Sales/Quantity
Accessories	2,158,051.18	820,857,004	2.63
Bag & Outdoor	1,931,710.05	153,849,431	12.56
Office	1,843,494.99	534,755,366	3.45

	X Values	Y Values	Bubble Size

Once we have identified the structure of the information, application of it to the chart would be similar to the following illustration.

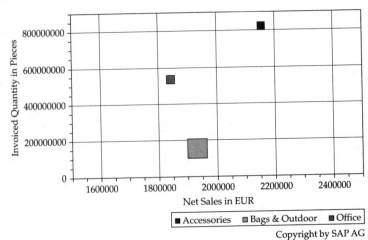

There are additional parameters that you can readjust, such as the form of the markers from a bubble or hexagon, by choosing Data Series Format | Default Data Series | Area Properties | MarkerShape. The field MarkerSize has no function for this chart type. You can change the marker size using the following approaches:

- If Portfolio | Size in Percent is not checked, the pixel size is calculated from the minimum and maximum values in pixels.
- If Portfolio | Size in Percent is checked, the pixel value is calculated as a percentage of the hypotenuse of the X and Y axes in the drawing area.
- Entries in the properties Portfolio | Minimum Value and Maximum Value.
- Checking the property Portfolio | Minimum Automatic or Maximum Automatic.

If you are formatting a single portfolio with a fixed size, use automatic calculation of the value range and deactivate the property Portfolio | Size in Percent. If you are formatting a portfolio whose size can change, use automatic calculation of the value range as well as the property Portfolio | Size in Percent. If you want to display multiple portfolios on a Web site with comparable scaling, enter a minimum and maximum value (for all portfolios). Finally, you can use the property Portfolio | Minimum Value to ensure that small markers remain visible.

Class 4 Chart Types

Class 4 chart types are useful for tracking and analysis of activities such as projects and processes. We are all familiar with the concepts of the two class 4 chart types, which are the familiar Gantt chart and the milestone trend analysis (MTA). These charts are designed to depict information dealing with dates and times as they relate to the process and progress through a project and either hitting milestones and/or tracking variances from the milestones required. One of the other areas in which I have some experience, the Finance module in SAP, has a fairly new component called the Financial Closing Cockpit. One of its major charting components is the use of a Gantt chart to track the period closing process in finance or controlling. The next illustration displays the initial configuration screen for a Gantt chart in the Chart Designer.

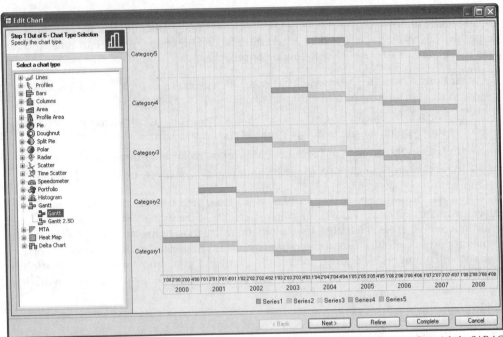

Gantt Chart   Specific to the *Gantt chart*, you can illustrate the time progression of projects and their substeps. You can also group these substeps in categories. The time is displayed on the X axis and the substeps and categories are displayed on the Y axis. If you created categories, all substeps are displayed separately for each category on the Y axis. You can display the time in days or you can use start and end times:

- Start Date
- Start Time
- End Date
- End Time

All combinations of start and end points are supported:

- Start Date & End Date
- Start Date & Start Time & End Date
- Start Time & End Time

If you select Start Time as the start point, the system uses the current data as the Start Date. If you select Start Date or End Date as the start point or end point, the system fills Start Time and End Time with the value 0:00. This is particularly important for the interpretation of end points in the Gantt chart.

As with class 3 chart types, the construction of the data provider is the most important part of the process. You build the table on which a Gantt chart is based as follows:

- The table must contain at least two data columns. The first column determines the start point; the second column determines the end point.

- In addition to the start points and end points, categories are also entered in the data columns. You must make at least one entry (data column) for the start point and end point for each category.

An example of this type of query is displayed in the following illustration.

Work Packages	Concept Creation		Specification		Solution Validation	
Project Steps	Start Date	End Date	Start Date	End Date	Start Date	End Date
Chart	01-25-2005	01-31-2005	02-20-2005	02-28-2005	03-20-2005	03-25-2005
Object Services			03-15-2005	03-20-2005	03-25-2005	04-06-2005
Web Runtime	03-01-2005	03-17-2005	02-26-2005	03-05-2005		
Overall Result	03-01-2005	03-17-2005	03-15-2005	03-20-2005	03-25-2005	04-06-2005

Copyright by SAP AG

The example illustrates a table for a Gantt chart; it contains three categories and no data for some start and end times. The substeps are the Project Steps: Chart, Object Services, and Web Runtime. The categories are the Work Packages: Concept Creation, Specification, and Solution Validation. Once this information is applied to the Gantt chart type, the final result would be something similar to the display in the following illustration.

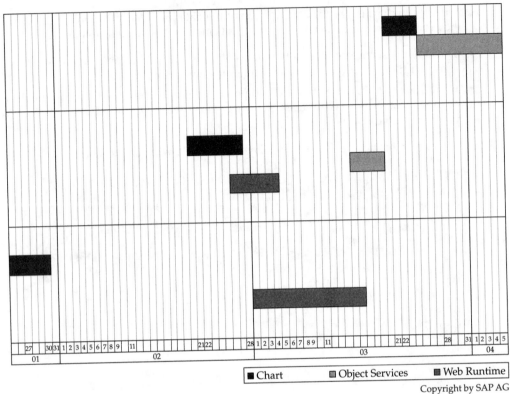

In the example, the categories Concept Creation, Specification, and Solution Validation are displayed from bottom to top on the Y axis. The substeps are included in accordance with the data in the underlying table, that is, only Chart and Web Runtime are included for the Concept Creation category because no data is specified for the Object Services substep. The start point and end points for the substeps are displayed on the X axis (month, day).

Milestone Trend Analysis Chart (MTA)   The other class 4 chart type is the *milestone trend analysis*, which enables you to monitor the contents of the project progression. Based on the data, you define the milestones and then can schedule appointments and display any deviations. The Y axis is defined as the target time axis with the scheduled milestones; the X axis represents the actual time axis. The appointments for project meetings (reporting times) are recorded on this X axis. In these project meetings, for each milestone, each owner is asked about the upcoming fulfillment date. The fulfillment dates named are entered into the chart using the meeting time. A forecast curve is produced for each milestone. If target and actual times coincide, the milestone for the scheduled time has been reached and the forecast curve runs horizontally. In the other cases, if the milestone is moved during the project meetings to a later time or earlier time, the forecast curve rises or drops, respectively.

You build the underlying data provider (query) for a milestone trend analysis in this manner:

- The table (query structure) must contain at least two data columns. The first column determines the reporting time; the second column determines the milestone.

- You can add further pairs of data columns to the table. The table can consist of 2, 4, 6, and so on, data columns.

Therefore, as your format, you would have within the columns specific projects— say, with two columns each, the first being the reported time and the second being the milestone time—and down the rows would be the actual milestone. This would give you the formatting required to fit the information required by the MTA template, shown here in the Chart Designer.

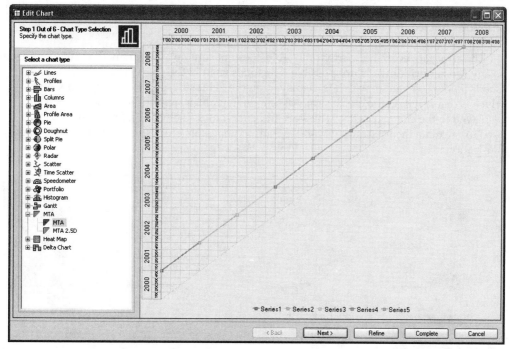

Copyright by SAP AG

The MTA can also be created without categories, which means it contains data series only.

Class 5 Chart Types

The final group, the class 5 chart types, comprises the delta chart and its variant waterfall chart. These chart types use the "flowing" concept to display information. You probably have seen or worked with this type of chart when the goal is to group together multiple sets of information, normally to offer some sort of range of information and display it graphically.

Component	Delta Chart	Waterfall Chart
Hierarchy in data table	No	Yes
Number of totals	2 (start value, end value)	2+n (start value, end value, and interim values, if applicable)

TABLE 6-3   Differences Between the Chart Types Delta Chart and Waterfall Chart

Delta Chart   A *delta chart* outlines the development of a total value by displaying various interim values. Important to note is that these interim values are not displayed as subtotals, but as deltas. The delta chart only deals with flat data tables; this means the interim values are individual items. If you have a hierarchical data table—that is, if the interim values are made up of multiple single items—the system automatically selects the waterfall chart variant to display the data. The differences between the chart types delta chart and waterfall chart are outlined in Table 6-3.

An example of a table for a delta chart is shown in Table 6-4.

The critical concern here is that the table does not contain a hierarchy (hierarchy nodes), so any further drilldown is not possible. The totals used in the chart are the items Cost of Goods Sold (start value), which is displayed on the debit side, and Revenue (end value), which is displayed on the credit side. All remaining values are interim values, which are displayed in the chart as deltas. The start and end values (including all interim values) are used to calculate the total sum (Overall Result). The results are displayed in the following illustration.

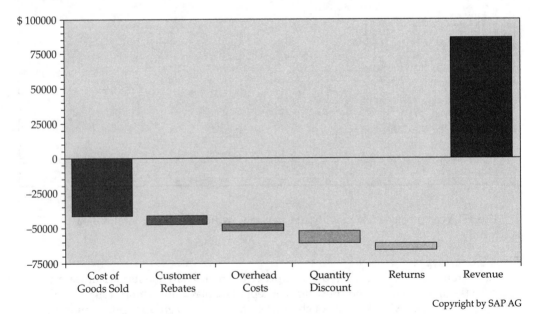

TABLE 6-4
Information for
Delta Chart

Profitability Line	Earned Amount
Cost of Goods Sold	−41,500.00
Customer Rebates	−5,700.00
Overhead Costs	−5,000.00
Quantity Discount	−9,050.00
Returns	−4,325.00
Revenue	87,000.00
Overall Result	21,425.00

This example includes the items Cost of Goods Sold and Revenue as totals (displayed at the two ends of the graph). The four interim values are displayed as deltas: Customer Rebates is therefore the difference between the previous value Cost of Goods Sold and the following value Overhead Costs, and so on.

Waterfall Chart   As I mentioned, a variant of this chart type is the *waterfall chart* and it is probably the one that we recognize as the more commonly used chart type. In terms of the data structure for this type of chart, we can have a number of different formats:

- The start and end values are always totals.
- The data table can be structured as a hierarchy. Individual interim values do not have any additional subsets—they are therefore not displayed as single items, but as hierarchy nodes. These nodes can be expanded.
- All interim values without subsets are treated as deltas.
- All interim values with subsets (that is, nodes) that cannot be expanded are treated as deltas.
- The last node in a hierarchy level (if used) is the total.

You can see that this information would fit well into the configuration format of the delta chart type. The following illustration shows the initial configuration screen used for the delta chart type. I've chosen the 2.5D display to give this view a bit of depth.

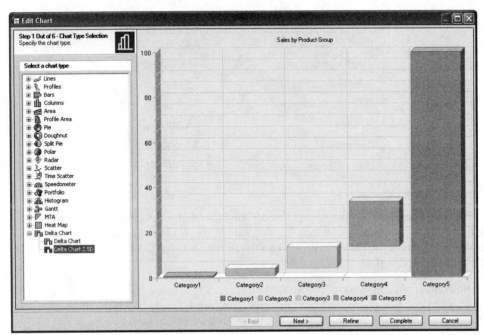

Copyright by SAP AG

In some cases where the waterfall format is required, some additional wrinkles may come into play. For example, if the report requirement is to include not only these start and end values but also averages and actuals, this doesn't quite fit into the chart type delta because of the additional requirements. So, to facilitate this, we use another chart type to mirror image the waterfall format and also support the addition of averages and actuals. An example of the type of data contemplated here is shown in the following illustration.

Customer Contracts	MINIMUM	AVERAGE	MAXIMUM		ACTUAL
A	40	50	20	A	65
B	35	60	35	B	72
C	50	67	40	C	105

Copyright by SAP AG

In this data set, we have Customer Contracts with the Minimum, Maximum, Average, and Actual information. With this set of data, we can develop a waterfall chart either with the delta chart type (making some minor adjustments) or by using a more basic approach and starting with a line chart type. If you work with the delta chart type, the approach is straightforward and you will see that the values for each of the groups fit nicely into the requirements. Going a step further and using the line chart type to format a waterfall chart, you would start in the Chart Designer with this type and in Step 3 of 6 you would change the individual series into Stacked Columns to generate the range format for the difference between the minimum and maximum, as shown in the following illustration.

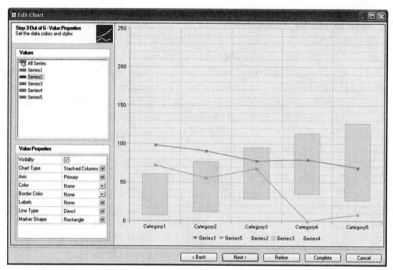

Copyright by SAP AG

The trick here is that once you are finished setting up your stacked columns, you can then go back and hide the sections of the stack that you don't want to see. This generates a waterfall view of the data using the line and stacked chart types. I've used this approach to show that even the more complex chart types can be imitated by using either two or more basic chart types that are available. Once you've configured these ranges, you can still keep the Actual and Average to display as the line chart. The following illustration shows the end result of this format.

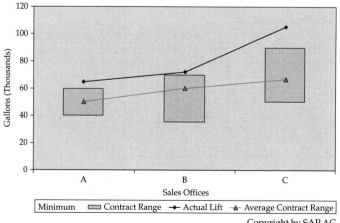

Copyright by SAP AG

As you can see, you have the floating ranges for Minimum (the lower edge of each of the floating boxes) and Maximum (the sum of the minimum and maximum numbers is the size of the box), the Average and Actual displayed as a line chart. This is a complex chart type but results in a very straightforward display of the data.

Formatting Charts Using the Wizard

This section explains the series of wizard steps that you go through to set up any of the chart types previously discussed. As with any of the objects within BI, there are some parameters and functions that are consistent across all the different chart types. If we look at those consistent parameters, we can cover about 75 percent of all the activities required to develop a chart. As I mentioned earlier, the great thing about this process is that it's very close to or the same as using the familiar chart options with Excel, and we have a wizard to help us move through the steps. The wizard helps you to format a chart in just a few steps. We've already reviewed all the chart types so that you can identify which one you need to use, which is the first step. You then specify a title, specify the number of data series and categories, specify the colors of the chart, and define the properties of individual series and of the axes. You can fully format your chart using the wizard. If you want to change further details in the chart, you can do so in the Chart Designer (using the Refine option) or by clicking Back in the wizard you can go back step by step until you get to the appropriate step and make the necessary changes. Understanding what chart type will work with what formatted query is a big help and will make this process much easier.

After you have added the Chart Web item to the WAD, you can start the wizard process.

Open the Chart Designer by double-clicking the Chart Web item. If you used the wizard the last time you used the Chart Designer, it is opened again with the wizard. Otherwise, click the Wizard button in the Chart Designer. The structure of the viewing window changes: The individual wizard steps with short descriptions and properties that you can change for each step are displayed to the left. The chart preview is displayed to the right. The chart preview changes according to the values you assign to the properties. This gives you an idea of how your chart will appear later on. The navigation process is straightforward; the bottom of the dialog box has Next and Back buttons to help you work through the wizard.

Step 1 of 6 – Chart Type Selection

For this sequence, we are going to use the basic columns chart type, so in Step 1 of the wizard expand Columns (click the + to its left) and choose Columns, as shown in the next illustration. Click Next.

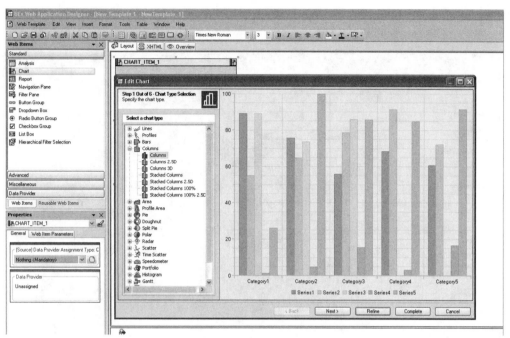

Step 2 of 6 – Texts and Data Selection

You can set values such as the following in the upper-left window:

- Define a title and subtitle for the chart.
- Specify labels for the axes.
- Assign a unit to the axes.

Make the following entries in the lower-left window:

- The number of series and categories as they occur in your data source. This is basically the number of groups that you might have in your data source. This does *not* affect the outcome of your chart and the actual values that appear. That is, if you set the number of series to 5 and your true number is 15, this will not eliminate or adjust the true number. This is for display purposes only in the preview so that you can get a good idea of what your chart will look like in the end.

- The Minimum Value and Maximum Value that correspond to your query. Again, the same comment as above applies. You don't need to know the exact Minimum and Maximum values. This is for preview display only.

What will happen is that no matter what number you set this to, after you execute your chart the initial time it will reset at the appropriate numbers based on the number of values in the report being used. Looking at our example, if we set both the Series Count and Category Count to 1, as shown here,

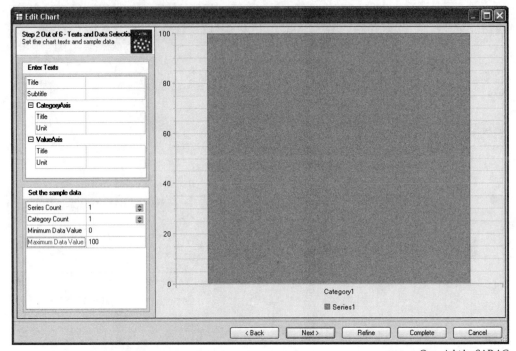

and then use the query that we worked with originally, which has more than one category, we can see that the chart will execute and show the appropriate number of series and categories—what was in the data source query. This can be seen in the next illustration—there are three categories in the query. Therefore, the original parameter that was set to one has now changed and is showing all three values.

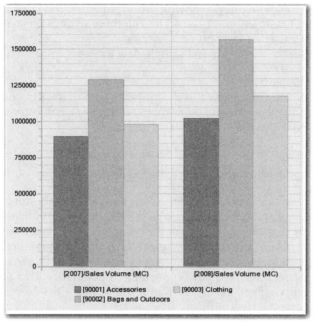

If we go back into the settings in this chart type, we can see that the system has reset the value for the Category Count to 5:

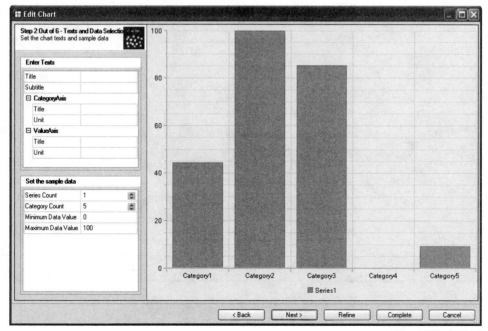

So again, these settings are for previewing the information, and not the true settings. You should look to estimate as close as possible with these settings for some of the more complex chart types but again, only preview specific.

After you have set the chart texts and sample data in Step 2, click Next.

Step 3 of 6 – Value Properties

In this step of the wizard, you can set specific properties for all rows in your chart or for individual rows (for all pie charts and polar charts: categories). For example, you can change the chart type for just one series or label just one series:

1. In the upper-left window, select All Series or select an individual series.

2. Change the properties for the selected series in the lower area of the window.

You can also change the color and border color, as well as the label for a series. The properties available depend on the chart type. In the following illustration, I changed a few of the settings to demonstrate the outcome of the changes. In this case, if we had more than one series, we would not be able to change these settings in detail, and this is the reason why you should try to get the number of series correct so you have that freedom (settings in the last step). In this case, I left the Chart Type setting to Columns, added a Secondary Axis, changed the Color, and changed the Labels from text to values. Click Next after you set the element colors and styles.

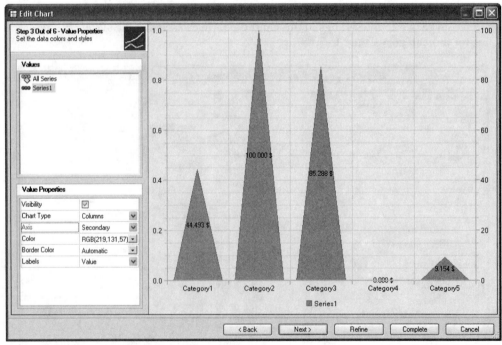

Copyright by SAP AG

Step 4 of 6 – Element Properties

In this step of the wizard, you can set specific properties that affect the background, the drawing area, or the legend. You can also modify the font for the chart title and chart subtitle.

- For example, you can set a color ramp in the background:

  1. Select Background in the upper-left window.

  2. Enter a Color and a Secondary Color. Specify a color ramp in the Gradient field.

  The color is a bit different in that once you set the color, the title of the color is a technical name rather than the actual color font. In any case, you will see the change in the color on the screen, as shown in the following illustration.

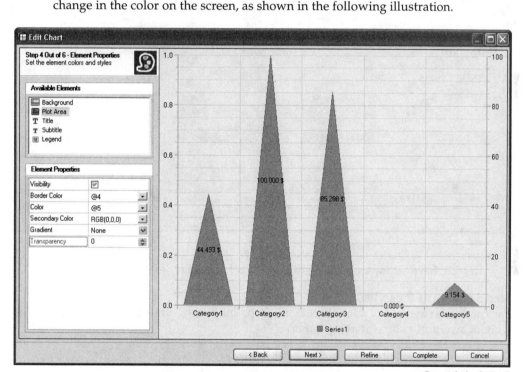

Copyright by SAP AG

- You can set the same properties for the drawing area and you can also set a transparency by entering a value between 0 and 100 in the Transparency field.

- If you select Title or Subtitle in the upper-left window, you can specify the font, orientation, size, color, and style.

- To change the properties of the legend, select the legend. In the lower-left window, you can specify whether the legend is to be visible (Visibility), whether you only want to display the legend (Alignment | Only Legend), and where the legend is to be positioned (Position | Left). In our example, I changed the Legend to be in the Background and at the Top, as shown in the following illustration.

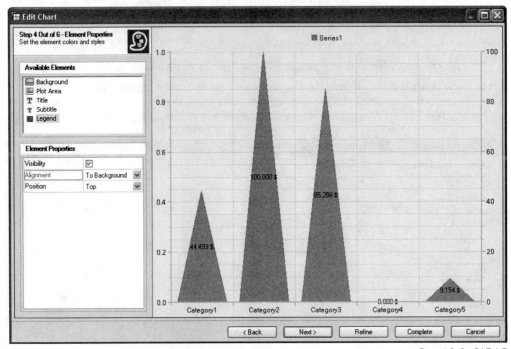

After you have set the axes property element colors and styles, click Next.

Step 5 of 6 – Axis Properties

You can format the axes of your chart in this step. The wizard omits this step for chart types without a vertical axis, such as a pie chart.

1. Select the required axis in the upper-left window.

2. Select the corresponding properties in the lower-left area.

If more axes are listed for formatting than are visible in the chart preview, the additional axes do not have the property Visibility. Select the Visibility field under the relevant axis to make it visible, and then format it as required. In our example, I've changed the Category Axis a bit to show some changes, as shown in the next illustration. In the Axis Properties portion of the screen, I've changed Position to Secondary, which moves the titles to the top of the screen from the bottom, and I've changed the Axis Type to Stacked, which adjusts the display of the titles and gives them the boxed, column-heading look.

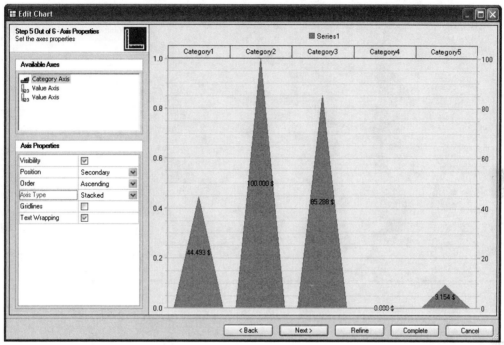

Step 6 of 6 – Completion

You close the wizard in the last step. You have the following options:

- Click Refine to continue working on the chart in Chart Designer. This will allow you to make further changes to your chart type. The Chart Designer in the Refine mode offers all of the same formatting options that we went through in the six steps all on the same page. Therefore, you can just click each item and the required parameters will appear in the lower portion of the screen, as shown next.

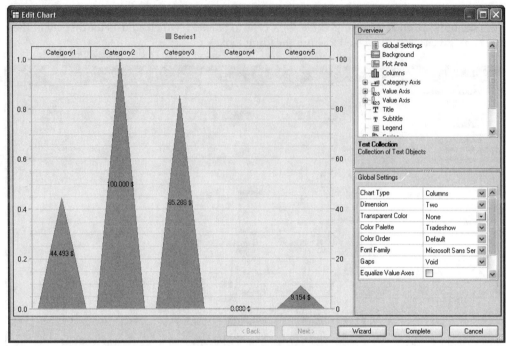

- Click Complete to save the formatted settings for the chart and return to the Web Application Designer.

You've completed your initial configuration of the columns chart type. As you can see, the wizard process is sufficiently straightforward that a business user, especially "superusers," could do this if they require adjustments to their settings. However, they would require authorization to access the WAD.

The settings are now saved with the Web item in the WAD. You can edit the chart and change your settings whenever required. If you edit a chart using the wizard, the wizard is opened again when you next edit the chart. You will go through this process several times before you get your chart to look exactly how you want it, so don't be disturbed if the initial display of your chart is not quite what you expected. This is as much an art as it is a science.

Defining Chart Properties

There are so many different formats, filters, and adjustments available for charts that we couldn't possibly get through them all individually in this chapter without it running hundreds of pages so we will focus on the ones that will help support you with the creation of dashboards and good reports. However, this section does discuss and give examples of many of the chart elements and their properties. It gives you menu paths in as much detail as possible for you to find the settings yourself. As we go through each of these elements and their properties, you'll start to get an idea of what each one can be used for and what importance it has, especially when you start to get into each of the element's properties, such as Area, Text, Border, and Background.

In this process of fine-tuning, it does not matter whether you have already modified the chart using the wizard or whether it still has the default settings, although you will find that there are different formatting parameters that you can only get to via the Chart Designer (Refine button) and not via the wizard.

A chart consists of individual elements whose properties you can change independently of one another. The element properties are layout settings such as color, font, and line settings, as well as logical changes in the chart such as setting the chart type (also for individual data series). All elements that you can change for the current chart appear in the list of elements in the right-hand window of the Chart Designer. Elements that are not supported for the current chart type are not displayed. The most important elements and their properties appear in Table 6-5. Note that some of these chart elements are only available for certain chart types, specifically the Layout element and the Data Series and Category element.

Chart Element	Properties
Global Settings	Chart type and dimensions, color settings for transparency, screen and data series, font, data gaps.
Layout	Position of chart in the plot area, position of title, subtitle, and legend.
Background	Color and pattern of background and border (that is, all the chart apart from the plot area).
Plot Area	Color and pattern of the plot area, the area on which the chart is drawn (without the axis label), and the frame around the plot area.
Bars, Columns, and so on (depends on chart type)	Position and layout of the chart type–specific properties.
Category Axis	Scaling, labeling, and layout of the category axis (only for charts with a category axis).
Value Axes 1 and 2	Scaling, labeling, and layout of the value axis (only for charts with relevant axes).
Title and Subtitle	Text, position, and appearance of the title and subtitle of a chart.
Legend	Position and appearance of the legend.
Series	Layout settings for a data series. For charts with multiple data series, different chart types can be assigned to the various data series here.
Points	Layout settings for individual data points.
Textures	Selection of texture images for formatting areas.
Data Series and Categories	For changes to label texts and creating trend lines.

TABLE 6-5   Chart Elements and Their Properties

Many of these chart elements are shown in the following illustration. When you click a specific element (Global Settings in this example), the properties of that element are displayed in the lower section of the screen.

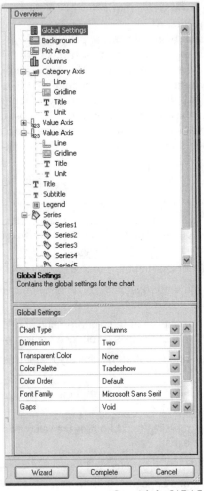

Copyright by SAP AG

So, the process is that you first select the element and then define the properties of the element. These properties, which are the lowest level of configuration, differ depending on the chart type you select. We will look at the basics of the important ones to see what we can accomplish by incorporating them into the charts.

To select the element of the chart type, you can either click the actual element in the chart preview (this element is then selected in the list of properties) or select the required element directly in the list of properties (the element is then selected in the chart preview so you can validate that it is the appropriate element). The latter, direct approach is recommend for complex charts with many small parts, because clicking the required element in the preview area can then be difficult.

NOTE *This process is being completed via the Chart Designer and not the wizard.*

An example is displayed in the following illustration. The Columns element is selected, and the properties and highlights in the preview are specific to the Columns attributes.

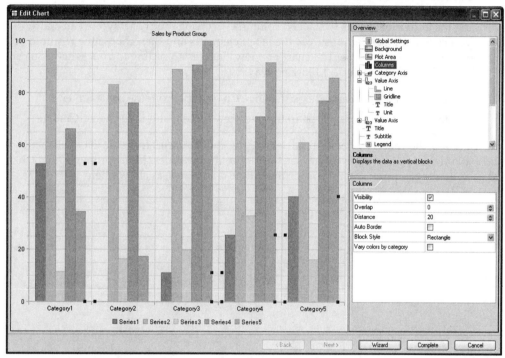

Copyright by SAP AG

You now can define one or more properties for each element. As previously mentioned, some properties are consistent across all chart types. They are listed here:

- Either/or properties that you select by clicking in the field; for example, Visibility.

- Properties with a predefined selection list that you select by selecting the required entry from the list; for example, Area Properties | Gradient | Horizontal.

- Numeric values of properties that you enter directly or increase/decrease using the arrow buttons next to the field; for example, Width | 4.

- Color values that you can select from the palette or enter as an RGB value (for example, RGB(89,133,182)), in HTML format (for example, #CF0082), or using the standard name, which is a bit trickier than the other two options.

As you can see, there are very few areas where you will be able to fill in some parameter manually, so there's not much you can do to damage the chart. You will need to experiment with these settings to get the appropriate format and view. Now that we have the formatting and font information complete we can move into some of the standard parameters found in the Chart Type itself.

Changing the Chart Type

A chart is normally displayed as a bar chart, but you can change the chart type for the entire chart. You can also combine multiple chart types in the same chart by changing the depiction of a single data series. For example, you can display the planned turnover of several subsidiaries and show the average current turnover as a line. This is the approach that we used in the previous section to format a waterfall chart by using line charts and then changing the individual series to stacked columns. To change the chart type of an entire chart, you choose Global Settings from the list of elements and then choose the required type from the field Chart Type. The chart preview changes according to your entry. You can also change the chart type in the following way:

1. Right-click the chart and choose Change Chart Type from the context menu.

2. Select the required chart type in the overview screen, and then choose Change.

To change the chart type of a single data series, choose Series from the list of elements and expand the node so that you can see the required data series. In the property field Chart Type, choose the required chart type for this single data series, as shown here.

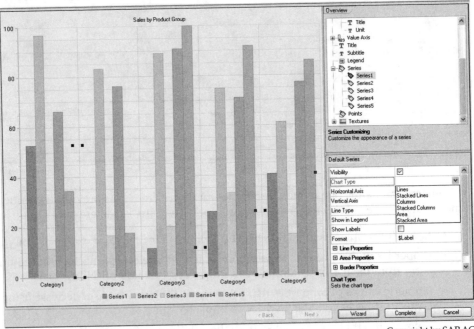

Changing the Size and Position of Chart Elements

The Chart Designer optimally places all elements of a chart in the chart area, taking all element properties that influence size and position into account. The position and size of elements are influenced by the following factors:

- Font size, and size and quantity of text for elements such as axis labels, titles, and legends.

- Space between individual elements.

- Automatic positioning of elements. This affects titles, subtitles, and legends (for example, the alignment of the chart).

- Manual positioning of elements. This affects drawing areas, titles, subtitles, and legends.

You can also define the minimum offset around an element. You can do this for axis labels, legends, and the entire drawing area. The Chart Designer takes the defined offset into account when automatically positioning all elements. To make this adjustment, select the required element and enter the appropriate value in pixels into the property Offset.

If you are looking to adjust the positions of the elements manually, you can do this via the WAD from the Properties tab in terms of the entire layout as we have done in the former section by changing the standard default from 300×300 to 450×450. You define the position of certain elements in relation to the chart size in the Chart Designer. You therefore define the position not using absolute measurements such as pixels or centimeters, but with percentage values. You always enter four percentage values for positioning (for top, bottom, right, and left). These values form an area that is reserved for the element in question.

You always calculate the percentage values for the positioning of an element from the left and top edges. The reserved area for the element in the following illustration begins at 25% and ends at 50% distance from the left edge. It therefore covers 25% of the horizontal chart area. The top edge of the element begins at 25% and the bottom edge ends at 37.5%. This means that the element has a height of 12.5% of the entire chart area.

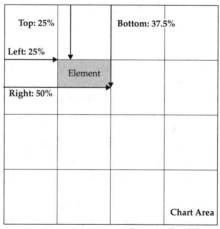

Copyright by SAP AG

To accomplish this process, choose Plot Area from the list of elements and then choose the required element. Once you are in the appropriate screen, deselect the field Automatic and then enter the percentage values into the fields Top, Left, Bottom, and Right, as shown in the next illustration. The element is moved to the required position as you make your entries. If the element is smaller than the area that you reserve for it, it is moved to the center of the reserved area. If you position the elements so that they overlap, they may hide one another. The sequence of elements from background to foreground is as follows: drawing area, title, subtitle, legend.

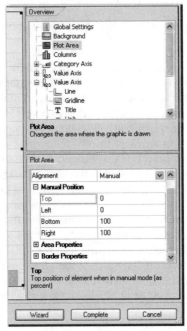

Copyright by SAP AG

Assigning Colors

You can also assign colors to text, lines, and areas. The Chart Designer provides you with many opportunities to select colors or use custom colors. For example, you can select colors from a color spectrum or select colors from a palette of predefined colors. The color's technical name is going to be difficult to understand, but as long as you can select the specific color from either of these two options, you are in good shape.

To work with the predefined color, enter the color as an RGB value. The RGB color definition mixes a color from the colors red, green, and blue, and uses the color values 0 to 255. For example, white has the RGB value 255,255,255, black 0,0,0, and red 255,0,0. Gray values have identical color values for red, green, and blue.

To work with the color as a hexadecimal value, enter the value with a leading number sign, #. This type of color entry is mainly used in HTML. In principle it functions like the RGB notation, but it uses hexadecimal values instead of the numeric values 0 to 255. Therefore, black is #000000, white is #FFFFFF, and red is #FF0000. You can use this color notation if you are already using color specifications in your intranet and want to use them in your chart (or the other way around).

You can also enter standardized color names for the 16 colors of the VGA standard palette and another 216 colors of the Netscape palette. The names are in English and are, for example, black (#000000), white (#FFFFFF) and red (#FF0000) in the VGA palette or deep pink (#FF1493) or pale green (#98FB98) in the Netscape palette. I recommend using one of the two preceding options (RGB or hexadecimal value) rather than trying to enter the name in English, because using the technical names is guaranteed to give you the color you want whereas entering the English word won't necessarily do so.

The final method is to assign values from the current color palette using direct entry. You can directly assign the 64 colors of the color palette by entering the values between @1 and @64. The numbers follow the entries in the palette row by row; for example, @1–@8 correspond to the colors from row 1 of the color palette, and @9–@16 correspond to the colors from row 2. Upon a changeover of palettes, the respective RGB from the assigned palette entry is used.

Selecting Color Values from the Palette and Spectrum   To select the color values from the palette and spectrum, select the element whose color you want to change and scroll to the property Color or Secondary Color. Click the arrow to the right of the field to open the color menu. The upper area of the color menu contains a spectrum of all the colors of the rainbow, and the lower part contains a palette of 64 predefined colors. To select a color from the color spectrum, position the cursor over the required color and click, or use the arrow button to move in the required direction. A small circle at the end of the cursor marks the selected area. The status bar at the bottom of the color menu shows you the corresponding RGB and hexadecimal values. To select a color from the color palette, click the required color field. The color is then assigned to the selected element.

Varying Color Values Using Transparency   You can also change the color of an area using the property Transparency. The transparency value specifies how solid a color is, or how much the background shows through. This allows you to create additional effects for the color of an area. Select the required area, scroll to the Transparency property, and specify the percentage value for transparency. Zero percent means no transparency, and 100% means completely transparent (background shows through).

Automatic Color Assignment   If you have no color preference, you can have the Chart Designer assign colors automatically. Just select the required element, scroll to a color property, and then select the option Automatic from the first line of the color menu. The Chart Designer only takes properties with the value Automatic into account when assigning colors automatically. Manual color assignments are retained.

Making Global Color Settings   Assigning colors can be very long and drawn out if you are going to go through each of the series or chart types to do this. If you would like, you can change the colors using a global approach, which will reduce the maintenance and effort. The Chart Designer has functions for changing the colors of your chart quickly, without changing each individual color setting of an element. Go to the Global Settings and then chose one of the standard color palettes and color order, as shown at right. This instructs the system to automatically set up the colors for you.

Formatting Areas

You can format the areas of elements either by changing the color or by assigning a pattern, a gradient, or a texture. You can change the following areas:

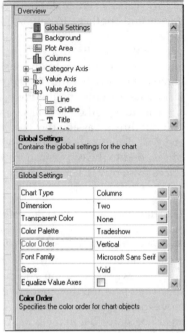

- Background of the chart and the drawing area
- Background of the title, subtitle, or legend
- Background of the axis label and title

To format an element's areas, select the element in the chart or choose one from the list of elements. Then in the property area, choose Area Properties and define the required area there. You can find settings for the background of the entire chart in the list of elements directly under Background.

When formatting the areas, these tips will help you to get through this process with a bit more consistency:

- When you select a pattern or a gradient, define both the color and the secondary color. By default, the secondary color is black (RGB 0,0,0). In this way, the second color is the color that emphasizes the pattern.
- Gradients begin with the primary color and change to the secondary color.
- You can choose either the pattern *or* the gradient *or* the texture. The order of the items in this list reflects the hierarchy: a texture has priority over a gradient, and a gradient has priority over a pattern and a simple color.

Using Textures

A texture is an image file that you can use to fill an area. The texture consists mainly of a pattern that can be placed next to and on top of itself repeatedly without the interface being visible. You can use any image file in the format BMP, JPEG, PNG, or GIF as a texture. This will allow you to add some header information or corporate logos to your chart. Remember that in this case, the logo will be a part of the chart rather than a part of the Web template. You can apply the logo to the Web template by using the Web item parameters found in the WAD.

To assign a texture, right-click Textures in the list of elements and choose Add Texture. Then browse to the required file in the file directory and click Open. The image file is now stored as a new texture and can be assigned to an area. To format an area with this texture, select the area, go to the Area Properties section, and then click the arrow to the right of Structure. Then select the actual texture that you would like to use. Finally, select one of the following parameters for the Texture Mode property (shown in the next illustration):

- **Tile**   The texture is placed next to and on top of itself until the entire area is filled.
- **Stretch**   The texture is stretched to fill the entire area.

- **Plain** The texture remains in its original size and is aligned to the top left-hand corner.

- **Center** The texture remains in its original size and is aligned to the center of the drawing area.

- **Fit** The texture is increased in size proportionally so that it is aligned to the left and fills the entire height of the area.

- **Center Fit** The texture is increased in size proportionally and placed in the center of the area.

Copyright by SAP AG

Formatting Lines

Lines outline colored areas (for instance, as edges of columns in a column chart) or stand alone as pointers in a speedometer chart. You can change the lines using color, format, or width. For lines that display data series in a chart, you can also define the line type (whether the line between data points is straight, curved, or incremented).

NOTE *As you can see by now, you follow a general procedure when defining chart properties in the Chart Designer. Identify the item that you will work on, identify the parameters that you can affect, and explore how and where they can be adjusted. You can also go into the system and see that you can find these settings fairly easily and the remaining settings for this object are straightforward.*

To change line appearance, select the element in which you want to format a line, look to the properties for the parameters, and change the appropriate settings for the line. The corresponding section in the chart is highlighted so that you can see what is going to be changed. Because the change itself is on a line and not on an area or object, you have to look closely to see the change appear on the screen.

You also can change the line type of a chart that has at least one data series of the type profile or line. You do this by selecting the property Data Series Format | *<name of data series>* and then choosing the entry from the Line Type list.

Formatting Axes and Gridlines

Most of the chart types have two axes: a value axis and a category axis. With most chart types, the values of a data series are plotted along the value axis and the categories along the category axis. Normally, the value axis corresponds to the Y axis and the category axis to the X axis. Three-dimensional chart types also have a third (Z) axis.

Gridlines (or orientation lines) are vertical and horizontal lines that divide up the drawing area. They improve the readability of the individual chart values. The list of elements tells you which axes are available in the chart. It is possible that two value axes are displayed there although only one is visible in the chart preview. This occurs if the second axis lacks the property Visibility.

Axes consist of the following elements: Lines (axis labels), Gridlines (axis scale), Title (title of the axis), and Unit (unit of measure identified on the chart). If you want, you can also make scaling, boundary level, and data sequence specifications in the properties of axes. As in all cases, the properties that you can define depend on the chart type you selected.

You can add an additional value axis to a chart with value and category axes. You can place individual data series of the chart on the second value axis. This can be useful if the value ranges of two data series are very different. If this is the case, you can set a different scaling factor for the secondary axis in order to balance the chart. If the list of elements contains the entry ValueAxis2, the selected chart type allows you to add a secondary axis. To do this, select the required value axis from the list of elements, make sure that the Visibility field is selected in order to display the axis on the chart, and finally choose the Secondary entry from the Position field (see the following illustration). This last option is very important or you will either have overlapping values on one axis or have inconsistent views of the primary information.

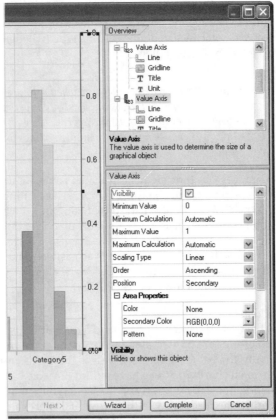

Copyright by SAP AG

Again, as you can see, this is configured in the Chart Designer setting Refine rather than in the wizard step-by-step process. The process of using the steps within the wizard approach will be displayed in an example later in this chapter.

Adjusting the Scaling of an Axis

The scaling factor of an axis influences the distribution of the data series within a value scale. There are four types of scaling: linear, logarithmic, root, and square. In most cases you will probably use the linear scaling factor, but it's good to know that there are other possibilities just in case. You can change the scaling factor for value axes, but not for category axes. It does not matter whether the X axis or the Y axis is the value axis. In the case of category axes in bar and column diagrams, you can select the property Variable Category Width to display the categories in different widths.

To change the scaling of an axis, click the required axis in the chart preview instead of selecting the corresponding entry in the list of elements. The enables you to identify better the position that you want to work on. Next, enter the minimum and maximum values in the fields. When entering value ranges, make sure that the values you enter tally with the values in your data sources. Values from data sources that are not in the range entered are not displayed in the chart later on. Selecting the fields Automatic Minimum and Automatic Maximum is recommended.

Changing the Position and Number of Tick Marks

This is one setting that I normally have the system automatically address, but you can change the number and position of the range symbols—tick marks. For value axes, you can define how many major and minor tick marks are displayed on the scale. To execute this configuration, click the required axis in the chart preview or select the corresponding entry in the list of elements. Then, in the property Gridline | Major Ticks | Major Tick Gap (shown in the illustration at right), enter an integer greater than zero, for example, 2. This specifies the interval at which major lines are displayed. You can also change the appearance of the tick marks in this element. This is also the case for category axes.

Another area where the positioning can be left up to the system is in the process of setting up the category labels. Work with the system defaults and make sure that the title that you will be using is consistent and functional. If you do decide to make changes manually, you can define on the category axes whether all category labels are to be displayed, or if not, which

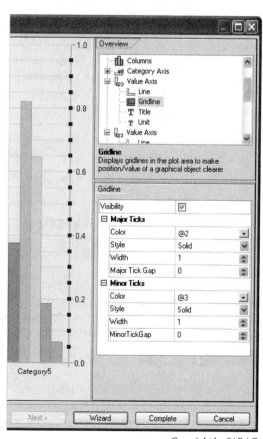

Copyright by SAP AG

labels you want to exclude. You can also change the position of category labels. This setup is fairly straightforward:

1. Click the category axis in the chart preview or select the corresponding entry in the list of elements.

2. In the property Category Axis | Axis | Category Gap, enter a value larger than zero to define how many categories should be skipped between each displayed category.

3. Select the property Category Axis | Centered if you want the category labels to be centered along the major tick marks.

4. Choose the option Secondary in the property Category Axis | Position to place the category labels on the opposite side of the chart. If the category axis is normally beneath the drawing area, it is now displayed above it. If it is normally to the left, it is now displayed to the right.

Formatting Texts

There are always numerous requirements where having a different format can make or break the chart and dashboard. Remember, the business user is the customer and the request to make a change to the formatted text is fairly straightforward versus some of the other components and feature. Some adjustments to formatted text within a dashboard is definitely helpful when it comes to the identification of critical pieces of information The areas within the formatting process in reference to Texts within the Chart Types included the chart title and subtitle, the axis title, axis label, and the legend belong to the texts that can occur in a chart. You can format the texts by changing the following properties:

- Font and font size
- Font color
- Font style (for example, italic)
- Position of the text field in the chart
- Alignment of the text

If you decide to set the font for all the texts in a chart at one time, you can just choose the Global Settings | Font property and select the font. The font that is set is valid for all the text elements that do not have their own text formatting—that is, for which the property Font is set to Automatic.

Alternatively, you can manually format text elements whose appearance should differ from that defined by the automatic and global settings. To do this, select the required text element, select the appropriate font, font size, and color, select the format, and then define the horizontal and vertical position and the direction of the text.

Formatting Data Series and Data Points

A data series consists of related data points. Each data series is uniquely identified by its own color or pattern. In a pie chart, only one data series is displayed. In other chart types you can display more than one data series. A data point is a single element of a data series. For example, a data point is displayed by a slice of a pie, a point or a bar.

You have a number of formatting options for data series and data points. Note that the preview window only shows sample data. You only see the actual data once it has been published. Change the preview window settings so that the number of data series and data points corresponds to the data provider. You can then meaningfully link a data series format to a data series. For chart types of class 1, the uppermost data series in the legend corresponds to the first table row, the next data series corresponds to the second table row, and so on.

To adjust the data display, you can reverse the format of the data and display the order of the data series or categories in reverse, thereby varying the impact of the chart. In a column chart that normally displays columns from bottom to top, columns are now displayed from top to bottom. To accomplish this, just use the Ascending or Descending setting in the property Order.

Plotting Data Series on a Secondary Axis   The ability to plot information on a secondary axis is critical for making comparisons. You will see that there are numerous situations where being able to display sales dollars and percentages of sales on the same chart is critical and more than likely a requirement. If the value ranges of data series vary considerably or if mixed data types are used, you can plot one or more data series to a secondary axis (Y axis). For example, you can plot the number of houses sold on the left Y axis (primary axis) and the average price on the right Y axis (secondary axis). To do this, you will, of course, need the data in the appropriate format in your report and also have two data series. To accomplish, first select the property Data Series Format and open the data series you want to edit (for example, Dataseries1). Then, depending on whether the horizontal axis or the vertical axis in your diagram is the value axis, select the value Secondary in the Horizontal Axis or Vertical Axis field.

Adding Data Labels   After you are finished with the previous task, you will want to add a data label to the axis. You can do this for all data series, a single data series, or a data point. Finding the appropriate location to set up the labeling can be a bit tricky. To add data labels to a single data series, select the property Series | Series 1 | Show Labels, whereby Series 1 stands for the series for which you want to add the label. Enter the content to be displayed on the label into the Format field. There are many possibilities that you can implement here using simple syntax. The formal syntax for the data label is {free text}{indicator} {0} [, | .] {0} {free text}, whereby the first position specifies if the value is absolute or a numeric percentage value or name of the field, the second position defines the number format, and the last position allows free text input for specifying the unit.

You can also enter a number format using zero and thousand separators or decimal points as required. Remember the following:

- Country-specific settings can influence the number format that is displayed.
- You can override the country-specific settings by using the separator $Sep.

Normally, two decimal places are used. If you use country-specific settings, then you can have a comma rather than a decimal place for the format. The same applies for the thousand separators—for example, 1000.00 in US formatting versus 1000,00 in EUR formatting.

Finally, the free text enables you to type in some additional information to be displayed. Remember to put the free text within for the display to work correctly. Some examples of free text follow:

- `"$Abs$Sep20,00"` EUR" gives the label `1234.5689` EUR for a value of 1,234.56 EUR.
- `"The percentage share is "$Percent0."` %" gives the label The percentage share is 25 %.

Adding, Changing, and Removing Trend Lines   You can visualize the trend of a data series using a trend line for a number of chart types. You can also extend the trend line past the data series in the chart in order to forecast future values and derive past values. There's very little that you have to do in terms of configuration. To see the options available, right-click the chart type and view the context menu.

There are the following types of trend lines:

- **Linear**   A linear trend line is an optimized straight line that is suitable for linear datasets. A dataset is linear if the pattern of data points resembles a line. A linear trend line normally displays a constant increase or decrease in values.

- **Logarithmic**   A logarithmic trend line is an optimized curve that is ideal if the rate of changes to the data first increases or decreases sharply and then stays nearly the same. A logarithmic trend line can use negative and/or positive values.

- **Potential**   A potential trend line is a curve. It should be used for datasets that compare measurements that increase with a certain rate (for example, the acceleration of a racing car in one-second intervals). You cannot add a potential trend line if your data contains null or negative values.

- **Exponential**   An exponential trend line is a curve that is used for data values that increase or decrease with an increasing tendency. You cannot add an exponential trend line if your data contains null or negative values.

- **Average**   The average value as calculated from multiple values. If there is only a small amount of data, large deviations in either direction can have a significant influence on the average.

- **Moving average**   This line smoothes out data fluctuations and can therefore show a trend or pattern more clearly. The moving average consists of a series of averages that are calculated from elements of the data series. A moving average uses a certain number of data points, computes their mean value, and then uses this mean value as a point in the curve.

- **Gaussian or normal distribution**   A method of statistics that records the frequency with which values are distributed within a value range. Normal distribution is particularly useful with histograms.

You can change all the properties of a trend line that you can define when you add the trend line as you can with any of the other chart types. So, you can adjust the color, the format, the display to 2D or 3D, and so forth. The chart types that offer you this option are the bar, area, line, portfolio, profile, profile area, column diagram or a histogram. You can also add a trend line to these chart types. Adding a trend line is fairly straightforward.

In the properties' Data Series, select the data series that you want to add to the trend line and then right-click the data series and choose Add Analysis Function.

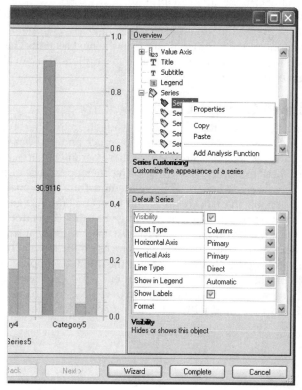

Copyright by SAP AG

Once you've set up the trend line, you can work with the formatting and display features in the same way as the actual columns and rows.

Rotating Charts   You can change the angle of the first segment of a pie chart, doughnut, polar chart, radar chart, or split pie chart, thus rotating the chart clockwise. This allows the developer to add some additional depth to this chart type.

1. Select the property *<Chart type>* | Starting Angle.
2. Enter the number of degrees by which you want to rotate the circle or rings clockwise. The first category at the top of the diagram begins with zero degrees, and the one at the bottom begins with 180 degrees.

Formatting 3D Effects

The final formatting option is to change the dimensionality of the chart type or the shape of the chart types. For column and bar charts, you can display the value ranges as rectangles, pyramids, cones, or cylinders, and for pie and doughnut charts, you can set the angle of inclination and the height of the pie segments or rings. The approach for both is the same. Go to Global Settings | Chart Type | Columns or Bars. Click the Dimension drop-down arrow and see how many options are available—normally there are either two or three. Return to the Overview section (top window) and choose a chart type, such as Columns. Go to the Block Style property and adjust from a rectangle to a cylinder or another shape.

We will see this in one of the additional charts in the next section. The same process can be used for all of the different chart types that have this option. You can also adjust the height and alignment of the different shapes.

Examples of Improved Chart Layout

You now are familiar with most of the parameters available in the chart type configuration. Yes, there are more, but those settings are not used as much and you can work through them as needed. In this section, we will use a number of these parameters to enhance some of the basic chart types. For these examples, we will improve the appearance of the charts in as few steps as necessary to create a good chart. This will demonstrate that you don't have to knock yourself out to produce good charts. Directing your time and effort on generating a dynamic, consistent, focused chart is much better than wasting your time and effort on a chart that has too many bells and whistles. If you go overboard on a chart with the formatting and colors, your customer will be distracted and not be able to focus on the tasks at hand.

As a refresher, the following illustration shows the initial dashboard presented earlier in the chapter. It's not a bad start, but it's not dynamic enough to get everyone's attention and drive a specific point home to the audience. For this, we need to enhance the charts to convey the message as directly and with as much impact as possible.

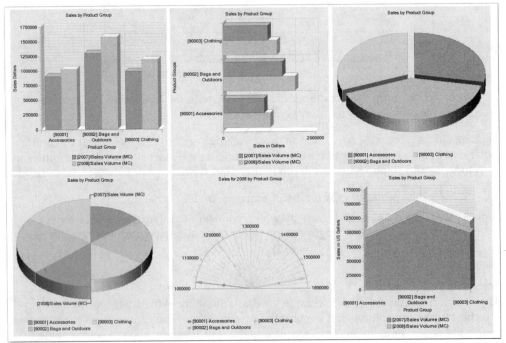

Now, what we don't want to do is overengineer the situation. There's a fine line between getting someone's attention and becoming overdramatic. We leave the drama to the reality TV series. We want the level of graphics that will grab someone's attention and hold it for long enough to convey the point.

Enhanced Configuration for a Column Chart

Let's start with the column chart. We can take the original chart and work with it. We know that the data is consistent and correct, which is about 70 percent of the battle. If the data is being displayed in the chart and showing the correct information, we can then work with the format and see if we can revamp it to make it more appealing and dynamic. You can use quick and simple settings to improve the standard display for column charts.

First, let's adjust the shape from a one-dimensional object to a 2D object and adjust from a rectangle to a cylinder, as shown next. To adjust to a 2D, just click on the 2D feature in the wizard first step. Once this is finished we will continue the formatting in the Chart Designer component of the wizard. This makes it more dynamic and jump out of the screen at the audience.

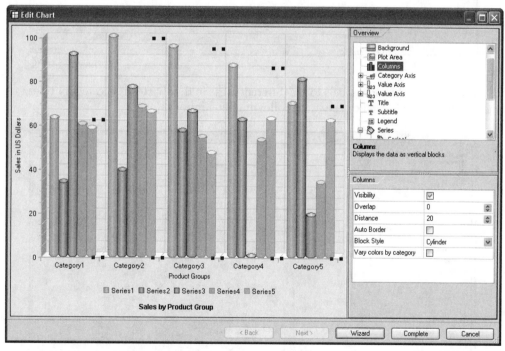

Copyright by SAP AG

We also can change the coloring to introduce two colors into each of the cylinders, as shown next. This is accomplished by using the Series 1 | Color and Secondary Color options. The trick here is to use the Gradient property to enhance the look and feel by using the Horizontal Center option.

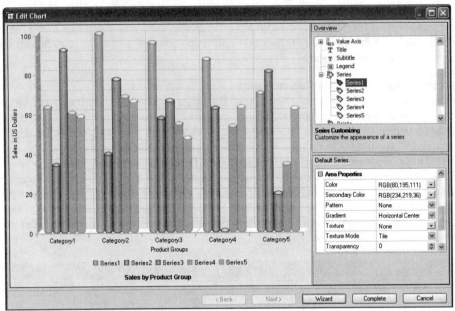

Now we can add some labels to the different areas in the chart—title, category titles, and value titles. This can be seen in the following illustration.

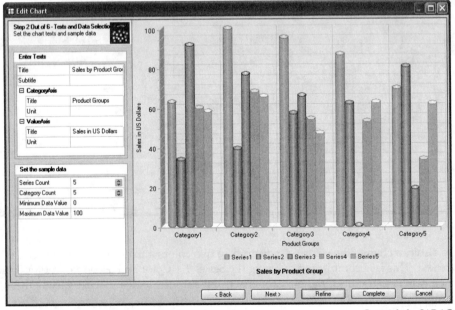

Also, remember that with this chart type, class 1, we normally turn on the SWITCH-MATRIX parameter to get the appropriate look and feel. Well, that's it for the basic formatting and adjustments, not that bad? And we've finished our chart for the columns. After just doing these minor changes, the final result is as shown in the following illustration. Not bad, and definitely good enough to publish. Of course, the colors will have to be validated with the corporate format, but overall this is a very good start.

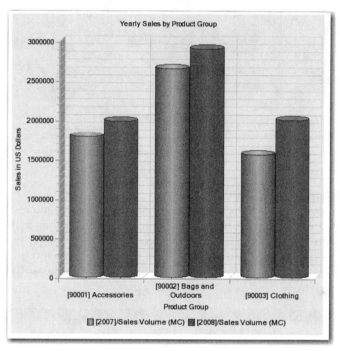

One setting deserves mention before we go to the next example: Swap Display Axis, which is found in the Web Items area and not in the chart type configuration. Depending on whether or not you have this turned on, the whole look and feel of the chart will change. The next illustration shows the results both of having that parameter turned on (shown on the left) and having it turned off. As you can see, this adjusts the entire display of the data and allows you to decide what look is best for your customer base. Both have different pros and cons, but overall they present the story very differently.

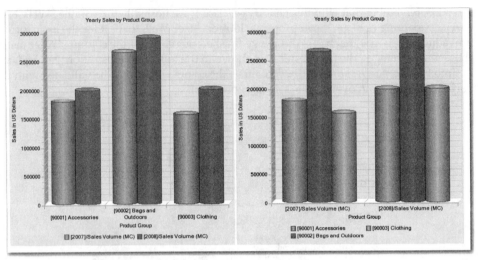

Enhanced Configuration for a Line Chart

To demonstrate enhancing the line chart type, we can take the same information we have in the other chart and switch from using yearly data to using period data. In the Chart Designer, change the chart type to Line and then go into the different series, Series1, 2, and 3, and adjust the format of the line and the marker. To help focus the business user on each line, we can change the color and the width of the lines and also increase the size of the marker, as shown here.

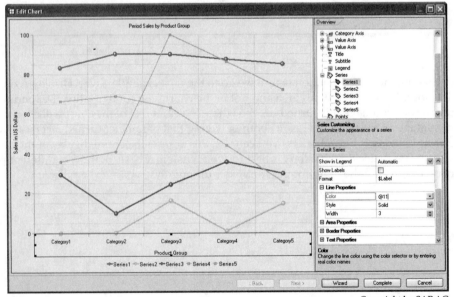

The preceding illustration shows the initial color setting. In the next illustration, the colors for the marker are adjusted so that we can show a circle with some depth to it. We have adjusted the primary and secondary colors.

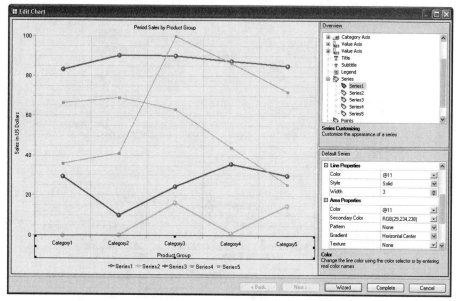

Finally we can change the Marker itself by adjustments made to the Circle and increase the size. This can be seen in the following illustration.

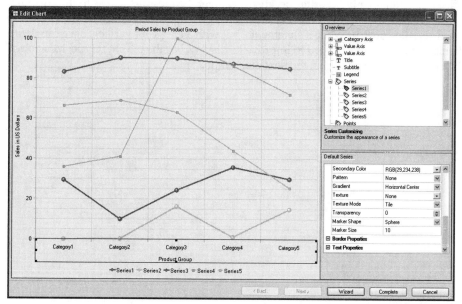

Add some additional titles to the axis and actual chart and your line chart is complete, as shown here.

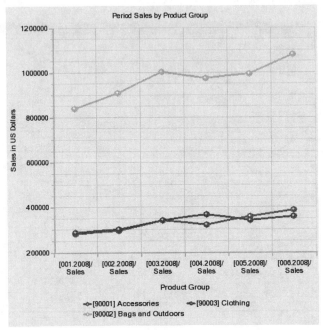

Copyright by SAP AG

Enhanced Configuration for a Pie Chart

The pie chart is one of my favorites because it can get the message across to the customer quickly and make the information very clear and concise. Sure, it doesn't offer any additional bells and whistles, such as what-if statements, but with a couple of variables, we can definitely work this one into any dashboard to improve its display. For the pie chart type, let's go with the 2D look and feel, as shown in the next illustration.

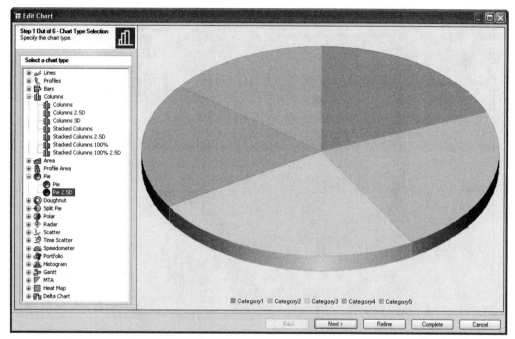

Now we just go into the pie chart type in the Chart Designer and go to the Pie overview screen and use the ExplosionOffset to expand the slices of the pie and separate them a bit to give some depth to the chart display. In that same process, we can change the look and feel of the actual slices with some enhancements to the coloring. We are using the primary and secondary colors with the gradient again in the Horizontal Position to give each of the slices some two-tone colors, as shown next.

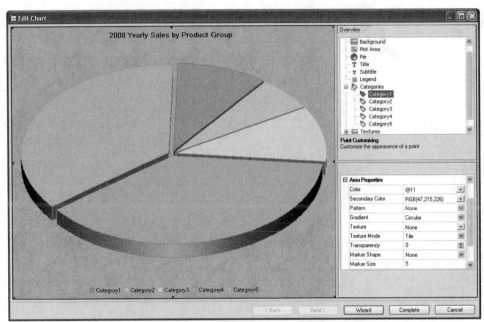

Add some texture to the background of the pie chart and then add some titles to the chart in the wizard and you get a result similar to that shown in the following illustration.

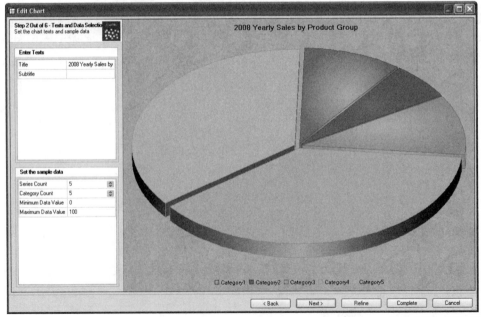

Once that is complete, we have our finished results. Again, the texture background and the colors used are changeable and will need to be approved by the corporate marketing department. We have now finished several chart types and used only about 6–8 steps each but the results are a very good and well-defined set of charts.

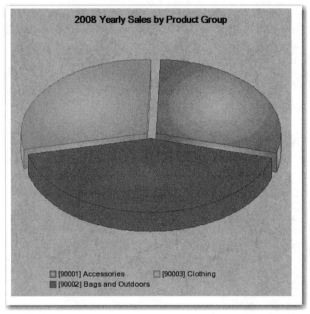

Now, for the final result, we take the three charts we have developed and combine them into a table in the BI WAD to see what some minor changes have done for this information. The results are shown in the following illustration. Compare what we had before and what we have now. This is definitely of the level to be published and distributed at a meeting and can be used for presentations and corporate management. The others were okay but not quite robust enough to catch the eye of the user and deliver the message about the corporate revenue. Now, with a little effort, we have a very good basis for a corporate dashboard.

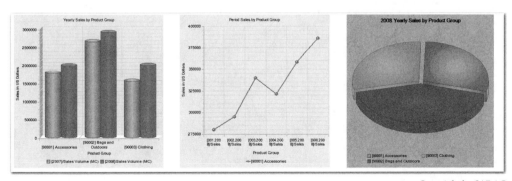

Enhanced Configuration for a Chart with Multiple Chart Types

In this situation we have a request for a chart type with multiple chart types incorporated into one. We can handle this request, but we need to ensure that the outcome will be consistent with the chart requirements. This is probably the most work—making sure that you are going to develop the chart that will be used rather than just brought out during corporate management reviews. In this case, we had to tweak the data a bit. Not that much, but this is a perfect example of the query and chart working together nicely.

The following is the illustration of the data that was used for this chart. All I did was to add the same key figure into the query twice and then, from the use of the query parameters, you are able to format the second key figure differently to show the % of Total Sales and also the cumulative result row. This can all be reviewed at a later date, but you can adjust basic data to be used to develop the next chart.

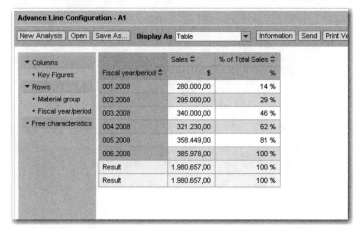

Copyright by SAP AG

We now have our two series: Total Sales and % of Total Sales. You will notice that I used the same formatting parameters that I did in the previous charts and combined that information into a single chart with multiple chart types. To start, we use the column chart type, and then in each of the series we choose a different chart type. This can be seen in the following illustration.

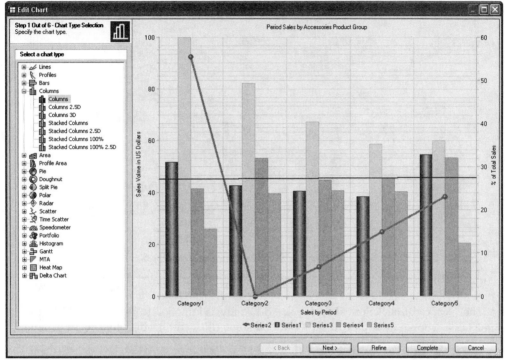

Then we went into each of the series and used what we learned before about the primary and secondary colors and the gradient approach to liven up the report. In this case we also use the Line Type in the second series to show the line chart type incorporated into the column chart, as shown in the next illustration.

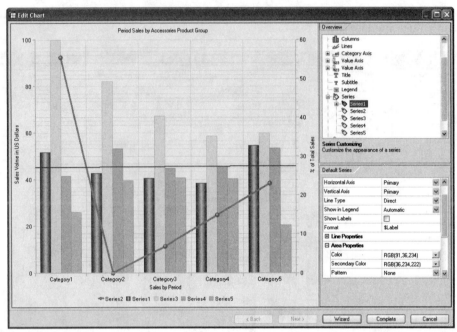

Then, we right-click Series1 and pick Add Analysis Function to get the trend line to show up, as shown next. Of course, we added some titles and headers for the information.

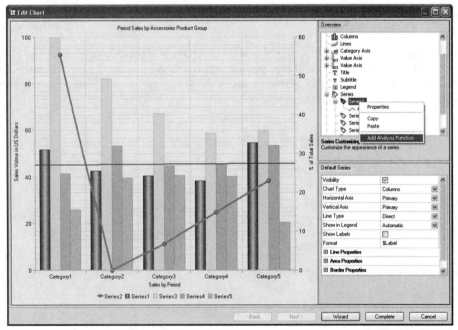

We finally add the second axis with some additional title text to identify the information quickly. This is illustrated next.

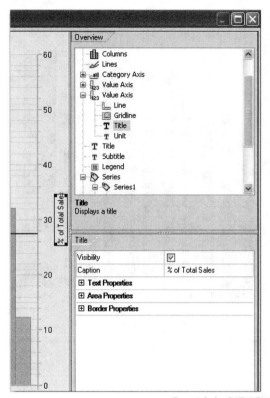

Copyright by SAP AG

The results are very cool. It's a great report with just enough key figures or KPIs to choose from. This will definitely offer the business users specific information to use during decision-making meetings. Here we have the total sales on one axis, % of sales cumulative on another axis, and the trend of the overall sales using the trend line functionality in the chart type.

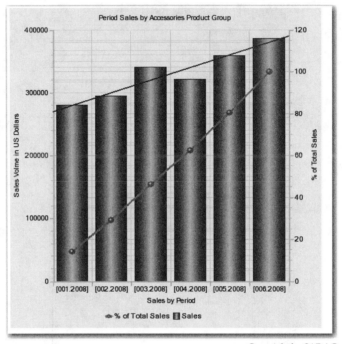

Configuration of Commands

The commands option within the WAD is not really a Web item, nor is it something that is available on its own. It's an additional component of a number of different Web items. During the configuration of a particular Web item, such as a Button Group, you would use a command. There are many different commands for both the Web reports and the planning process. There are over 50 of these commands and they are closely connected, but we will focus on just the Web-related commands to see what they can do for us in terms of improving the dashboard's functionality and final results. In the WAD, the command wizard is the main tool for creating commands from the Web Design API. You can use it to create commands easily by following a step-by-step procedure and include them in your Web template, enabling you to create highly individual Web applications with BI content. There are a number of approaches to making a command available in the Web template and dashboard that you are creating:

- Use the normal button format available.
- Create a hypertext link to execute a command process.
- Set up the command to be executed via a context menu.

Fortunately, the command wizard is available to guide you through the process. This means that manual entry of commands into Web templates is not required. In the command wizard, all of the parameters available for each command are listed so that they can also be set directly there. You also see a description for each command and each parameter directly in the command wizard. Many of the commands that are available are duplicates of the functionality that exists either in one of the other templates or in some form on the Web screens already in either a context menu from a right-click or from the standard Web template. Recall that we looked at some commands that are available in the standard template 0ANALYSIS_PATTERN in Chapter 1. Here we may go over some similar commands and they will sound redundant but are definitely unique.

Integration

The command wizard is part of the WAD and does not require any additional installation. You usually call the command wizard in the WAD from the Web item parameter Action (Command Triggered) (ACTION). You would normally look to use the commands with a Web item such as a Button Group. Within the Button Group you would click the Button configuration and within the Properties tab the Action - Command would be available. Numerous Web items allow you to access the command wizard. For example, if you insert a hyperlink into the Web template, you can also call the command wizard in the dialog box that follows by clicking the button next to the text-entry field.

You can create commands for data providers, planning applications, Web items, and Web templates. The command wizard provides you with two views for working with and creating commands:

- **Favorite Commands**   Includes all commands that you have marked as favorites.
- **All Commands**   Includes all commands that are available to you, sorted according to the various command groups.

As mentioned, we will focus on the commands for the Web type area rather than all of them. The configuration is reasonably straightforward, and the best example of this would be the standard default template that controls most of the initial Web Analyzer reports, 0ANALYSIS_PATTERN. We can see just about all of the different commands being used in that one template. We will take a look at one of them to show you the general pattern of setting up commands. Keep in mind that these commands are a bit more basic than the ones you would encounter if you were using the planning commands, where you are actually executing saves to data, calculations to be executed, and so forth. With the BEx reporting commands, we are basically executing a switch in the display of data that is currently available and offering a different view. The next illustration shows the 0ANALYSIS_PATTERN standard business content template, which controls many different reports.

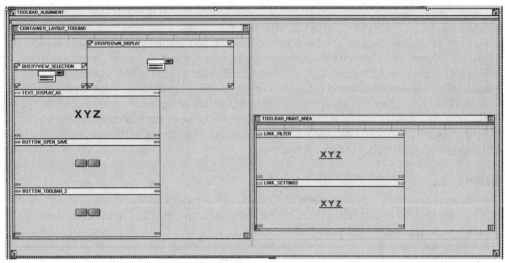

This template displays most of the commands that you see in the initial screen for each Web Analyzer report. As a quick example, if you were to execute just one of the basic reports, you would see all the commands on the toolbar, as shown here (and don't forget about the commands in the filters and settings portion of the report).

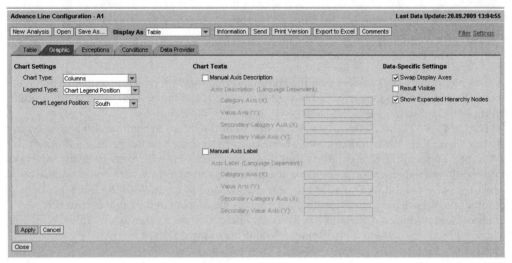

Commands for Web Items

Under Commands for Web Items, all the commands that you can use to change the status of a Web item are displayed. They are all available in numerous locations on the Web report, but the use of the command buttons will allow the business user to just click the button on

Parameter	Description
Target Web Item (TARGET_ITEM_REF)	You use this parameter to specify the Chart Web item for which the dialog is to be called.

TABLE 6-6   Command Parameter for Call Chart Properties Dialog

the screen. There are six different standard commands that you can use and apply to the Web items, described next.

Call Chart Properties Dialog

Using the Call Chart Properties Dialog command (OPEN_ CHART _DIALOG), you can call the Chart Properties dialog box at run time for a Web application. The parameter in Table 6-6 requires configuration within the process of setting up the command parameters when you insert the command.

For this first command, I will show you how to configure it. The configuration process for the other commands in the list is very similar, so you can go through and experiment with this process on your own.

Go into the WAD and use the Call Chart Properties Dialog command to display the Chart Properties. The initial step is to have a chart available, so we add a basic chart to this Web template, as shown next.

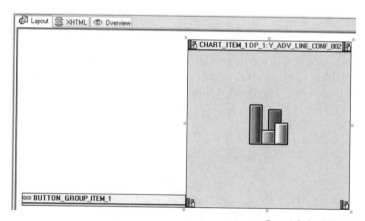

Copyright by SAP AG

Now we can see that we've added the button group to include the command above. This can be seen from the next illustration in the Edit Parameter screen.

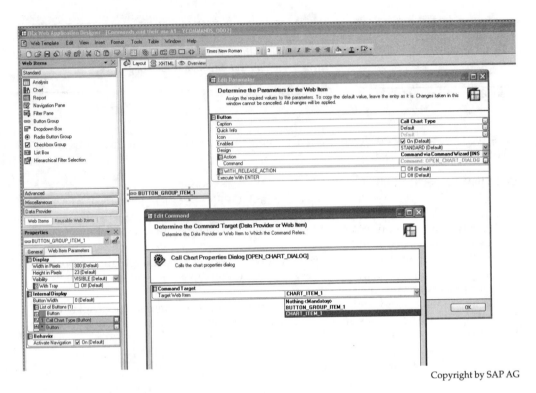

In this illustration you will see three dialog boxes, one for the button, one to assign the OPEN_CHART_DIALOG command, and finally the dropdown to attach the CHART_ITEM_1. The end result of this process is that we see the button for the Chart Type when we execute the Web report. This is shown in the following illustration.

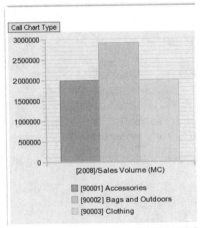

Finally, the result of clicking this button is shown in the following illustration. So, rather than having to use the context menu for the Settings area, we can use this button to make the process more transparent and direct for the business user. These are the types of items that will make your dashboards more functional and user-friendly.

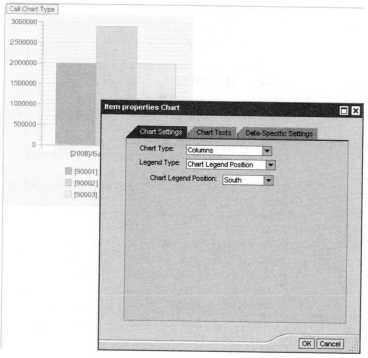

Copyright by SAP AG

Call Properties Dialog

The Call Properties Dialog command (OPEN_DIALOG_PROPERTIES_PANE) allows you to call the Properties dialog box to change the following elements at run time in a Web application: Web item parameters, properties of data providers, conditions, exceptions, characteristic properties, axis, data cells, and structure elements. Table 6-7 lists and describes the command parameters in the same sequence that they appear in the command wizard when you insert the command.

Setting Web Item Parameters

You use the Set Web Item Parameters command (SET_ITEM_PARAMETERS) to specify the parameters of a Web item at run time of a Web application. Table 6-8 lists and describes the command parameter in the command wizard when you insert the command.

If you select the Change Object Type (Standard) check box above the Target Web Item parameter, you make it possible at Web application run time to change to another Web item that you have selected under Type of Web Item.

Parameter	Description
Properties Set Definition (PROPERTIES_SET)	This parameter is used to specify the properties that can be displayed and changed in the Web application.
Properties Group Display (PROPERTIES_GROUP_DISPLAY)	This parameter is used to define how the properties are displayed in the Web application. The following options are available: Tab Pages (TABS) Headline (HEADLINE)
Properties Source (PROPERTIES_SOURCE)	This parameter is used to specify for which element the properties dialog is to be called: Web Item Parameters (ITEM_PROPERTIES) Data Provider Properties (DATAPROVIDER_PROPERTIES) Conditions (CONDITIONS_PROPERTIES) Exceptions (EXCEPTIONS_PROPERTIES) Characteristic Properties (CHARACTERISTIC_PROPERTIES) Axis Properties (AXIS_PROPERTIES) Characteristic Properties – Input Help (MEMBER_ACCESS_PROPERTIES) Characteristic Properties – Filter Values (FILTER_PRESENTATION_PROPERTIES) Data Cell Properties (DATA_CELL_PROPERTIES) Structure Element Properties (STRUCTURE_MEMBER_PROPERTIES) Properties of All Data Cells (ALL_DATA_CELL_PROPERTIES) Depending on the properties source you choose, there are a number of additional parameters that you need to set.

TABLE 6-7   Parameters of the Call Dialog Properties Command

Back to Initial State

Using the Back to Initial State command (BACK_TO_INITIAL_ITEM_STATE), you can restore a Web item in a Web application to its original state. If you use this command with the Web Template dialog box, the initial state is the display that existed when the dialog box was first opened. Table 6-9 lists and describes the command parameters in the same sequence that they appear in the command wizard when you insert the command.

Back to Previous State

Using the Back to Previous State command (BACK_TO_PREVIOUS_ITEM_STATE), you can return to the last navigation step for a Web item in a Web application. Table 6-10 lists and describes the command parameters when you insert the command.

Parameter	Description
Target Web Item (TARGET_ITEM_REF)	This parameter is used to specify the Web item whose parameters you want to define in the Web application.

TABLE 6-8   Parameter for the Web Item Parameter Command

Parameter	Description
Target Web Item (TARGET_ITEM_REF)	This parameter is used to specify the Web item for which you want to restore the state.
List of Target Web Items (TARGET_ITEM_REF_LIST)	This parameter is used to specify the list of Web items for which you want to restore the state.

TABLE 6-9 Parameters for the Back to Initial State Command

Set Status of Module

The Set Status of Module Command (SET_MODULE_STATE) allows you to activate or deactivate a module from Web item Analysis at runtime in a Web application. Depending on the settings in the module, this changes the standard display or the standard behavior of Web item Analysis. The parameters to set up this function are listed and described in Table 6-11.

Commands for Web Templates

These commands are also found in the standard Web template 0ANALYSIS_PATTERN. I think at this point a list of these commands will be sufficient. There is very little difference between these commands and what you read in the preceding "Commands for Web Items" section. Just as the name conveys, these commands are for the actual Web template, whereas the other commands were for specific parts of the Web items. The commands for Web templates that you can create with the command wizard are listed and described in Table 6-12, along with their parameters.

Commands for Data Providers

Under the commands for data providers, you can find a summary of all commands you can use to change the status of a data provider. You can use these commands to set filter values, set report-report interface (RRI) filters, reset displays with zero values, or change the navigational state of a data provider. There are over 50 different commands for data providers. We will be using some of them in our dashboards, so we will cover those specific commands in the following chapter when we use them.

Customization Using ABAP Classes

In some cases, the standard Web items and commands will not be sufficient and you will have to resort to creating customized commands and/or Web items. This practice was much more mainstream in the earlier versions of BI such as 2.1 and 3.0 because the Web functionality was very light, but now we have 100 percent more functionality and flexibility, so you should definitely look to use the standard components before you decide to create customized ABAP classes.

Parameter	Description
Target Web Item (TARGET_ITEM_REF)	This parameter is used specify the Web item for which you want to restore the state.
List of Target Web Items (TARGET_ITEM_REF_LIST)	This parameter is used to specify the list of Web items for which you want to restore the state.

TABLE 6-10 Parameters for the Back to Previous State Command

Parameter	Description
Target Web Item (TARGET_ITEM_REF)	You use this parameter to specify which Web item the command should relate to.
Alias (MOD_ALIAS)	This parameter contains the alias for the module. The alias makes it possible to identify a module, especially if more than one module is defined for a single Analysis Web item.
New Active State (NEW_ACTIVE_STATE)	You can use this parameter to activate or deactivate the module at run time. You can choose from the following parameters: • Active (ACTIVE/DEFAULT) • Inactive (INACTIVE) • Toggle (TOGGLE) By selecting Toggle at runtime, you switch the module from Active to Inactive or vice versa.

TABLE 6-11   Parameters for Set Status of Module Command

Command and Parameters	Description
Apply Personalization	Allows the use of Personalization in the Web template.
Delete Personalization	Deletes the Personalization settings in the Web template.
Save Personalization	This parameter is used to allow the business user to save their own personalization settings.
Save Bookmark	This parameter is used to create a bookmark for the Web application.
Add to Browser Favorites (ADD_BOOKMARK_TO_FAVORITES)	This parameter is used to specify whether the bookmark is to be added to the Web browser favorites or whether the bookmark ID is simply to be displayed as a message in the Web application.
Title (FAVORITES_TITLE)	If the parameter above is activated, this parameter is proposed as the title when users save the bookmark to their favorites. Users can accept or overwrite the proposal.
Load Bookmark	This parameter is used to start a Web application that was saved using a bookmark.
Bookmark (BOOKMARK)	This parameter is used to specify the technical name of the bookmark under which the Web application to be started was saved. You must have saved the bookmark using the Save Bookmark command.
Open in New Window (OPEN_IN_NEW_WINDOW)	This parameter is used to specify whether the Web application to be started is to be opened in a new browser window.

TABLE 6-12   List of Commands for Web Templates

Command and Parameters	Description
Start Broadcaster	This parameter is used to call the BEx Broadcaster. The current variable assignment and navigational state are passed to the Broadcaster.
Type of BI Object (START_OBJECT_TYPE):	This parameter is used to specify which BI object the Broadcaster is to start with. You have the following options: • **Current Web Template (EMPTY)** If you choose this option, the Broadcaster starts with the current Web template. • **Data Provider (QUERY_VIEW_DATA_PROVIDER_REF)** If you choose this option, you specify a reference to a data provider. The Broadcaster starts with the query view that is based on the data provider. • **Report (ITEM_REF)** If you choose this option, you specify a reference to a Report Web item. The Broadcaster starts with the report referenced in this Web item.
Start As Wizard (START_WIZARD)	This command is used to specify whether the Broadcaster is to be started as a wizard. If you want to start the Broadcaster as a wizard, you must also set the Distribution Type (DISTRIBUTION_TYPE) parameter. You can choose from the following distribution types: • Broadcast E-mail (MAIL) • Broadcast to Portal (KM_EXPORT) • Broadcast to Printer (PRINT)
Close Browser Window	This command is used to close the browser window at run time for a Web application. This command has no parameters.
Apply State	This command is used to display a copy of the current navigational state of a data provider.
Web Template (TEMPLATE)	This parameter is used to open a dialog to select the Web template into which you want to transfer a copy of the current navigational state of a data provider or Web item.
All Data Providers (ALL_DATA_PROVIDERS)	This parameter is used to specify whether you want to display in another Web application a copy of the current navigational state of all the data providers that exist for the Web template.
Data Providers (DATA_PROVIDER_REF_LIST)	This parameter is used to specify in list format the data providers whose navigational state you want to transfer to another Web template. You specify the individual data providers in the Data Provider parameter (DATA_PROVIDER_REF). Note that you must have already created all the data providers that you specify here for the current Web template.
All Web Items (ALL_ITEMS)	This parameter is used to specify whether you want to display in another Web application a copy of the current navigational state of all the Web items that are available in the Web template.

TABLE 6-12   List of Commands for Web Templates (*continued*)

Command and Parameters	Description
Web Items (ITEM_REF_LIST)	This parameter is used to specify in list format the Web items whose navigational state you want to transfer to another Web template. You use the Web Item (ITEM_REF) parameter to enter the various Web items. Note that you must have already inserted all the Web items that you specify here in the current Web template.
Open in New Window (OPEN_IN_NEW_WINDOW)	This parameter is used to specify whether you want to use a new window to display the Web application in which you want to display a copy of the current navigational state of a data provider or Web item.
Set Variable Values	This command is used to set variable values at run time for a Web application. Each of the variable values comes with its own list of values, including hierarchies, characteristic values, ranges, selection options, exclusion values, and inclusion values.
Variable Screen (VARIABLE_SCREEN)	This parameter is used to specify whether the variable screen is to be displayed. If you do not specify a value, the variable screen is displayed only if mandatory variables are not filled.
Variant (VARIABLE_VARIANT)	This parameter is used to enter a variant. You can start a Web application by using a variant or you can fill the variable screen with the values from the variant.
Variable Value (VARIABLE_VALUES)	This parameter is used to enter a list of individual variables. You need to set the following parameters for each entry in the list: Variable (VARIABLE) Variable Type (VARIABLE_TYPE) You can choose from the following variable types: Input String for Variable (VARIABLE_INPUT_STRING) Characteristic Value Variable (INFO_OBJECT_MEMBER_VARIABLE) Hierarchy Variable (HIERARCHY_VARIABLE) Value Set Variable (VALUE_SET_VARIABLE) Text Variable (TEXT_VARIABLE) Formula Variable (FORMULAR_VARIABLE) Binding Type (SELECTION_BINDING_VARIABLE) Web Item with Manual Input (ITEM_INPUT) Depending on the variable type you select, you must set additional parameters.
Open Variable Dialog	This command is used to display the variable screen at run time for the Web application. This command has no parameters.
Export Web Application	This command is used to export the Web application in a format that is identified in the export process. This can be an Excel document, PDF, or other formats.
Web Template (TEMPLATE)	This parameter is used to select the Web template that is to be used for the export.

TABLE 6-12   List of Commands for Web Templates (*continued*)

Command and Parameters	Description
Web Items (ITEM_REF_LIST)	You use this parameter to specify, in list format, the Web items that you want to export. You use the Web Item (ITEM_REF) parameter to enter the various Web items. You must have already inserted all the Web items that you specify here in the current Web template.
Export Format (EXPORT_FORMAT)	This parameter is used to specify the format in which you want to export the Web application. The following options are available: • Microsoft Excel (XLS) • PDF (PDF) • PCL (PCL) • Postscript (PS) • Microsoft Excel 2000 (XLS 2000) • CSV
Scaling Factor (LAYOUT_STRATEGY)	This parameter is used to specify the scaling for the export format: • **Fit to Page Width (FIT_HORIZONTAL)** The Web application is fit to the width of the page. • **Fit to Page (FIT_PAGE)** The Web application is fit to the size of the page. • **Poster (WALLPAPER)** The Web application is printed as a poster; individual areas of the Web application are printed on different pages.
Show Export Dialog (SHOW_EXPORT_DIALOG)	This parameter is used to specify whether to display an export dialog.
Paper Size (PAPER_SIZE)	This parameter is used to specify the format of the paper: • DIN A4 (DINA4) • Letter (LETTER) • Ledger 11 x 17 Inch (LEDGER) • Invoice 5.5 x 8.5 Inch (INVOICE) • Executive 7.25 x 10.5 Inch (EXECUTIVE) • A5 128 x 210 mm (DINA5) • A4-0 1682 x 2378 mm (DINA40) • A3 297 x 420 mm (DINA3) • A2-0 1189 x 1682 mm (DINA20) • A2 420 x 594 mm (DINA2) • A1 594 x 841 mm (DINA1) • A0 814 x 1189 mm (DINA0) • Broadsheet 17 x 22 Inch (BROADSHEET)
Paper Orientation (PAPER_ORIENTATION)	This parameter is used to specify the page orientation for the export format: • Portrait (PORTRAIT) • Landscape (LANDSCAPE)

TABLE 6-12   List of Commands for Web Templates (continued)

Command and Parameters	Description
Repeat Column Headers (REPEAT_HEADER)	This parameter is used to specify whether the header is to be repeated on each page of the export format.
Repeat Lead Columns (REPEAT_KEYCOL)	This parameter is used to specify whether the lead columns are to be repeated when you select the Poster scaling option.
Header Left (HEADER_LEFT); Header Center (HEADER_CENTER); Header Right (HEADER_RIGHT); and Footer Left (FOOTER_LEFT); Footer Center (FOOTER_CENTER); Footer Right (FOOTER_RIGHT)	These parameters are used to specify what is to appear in the location defined in the export format: • None (NONE) • Page Number (PAGENO) • Page of Pages (PAGEOFPAGE) • Date (DATE) • Date and Time (DATETIME) • Date, Time, and Page of Pages (DATETIMEPAGE) • Free Text (TEXT_CONTENT) If you select Free Text (TEXT_CONTENT), the text entry dialog appears.
Theme (BEX_THEME)	This parameter is used to select the theme.
Separator for CSV Export (CSV_SEPARATOR)	This parameter is used to set the field separator used when exporting to a CSV file.
CSV Field Delimiter (CSV_DELIMITER)	This parameter is used to set the field delimiter used when exporting to a CSV file.
UTF character representation (CSVENCODING)	This parameter is used to specify the character representation to export the data with. The following options are available: UTF-8 (UTF8) UTF-16 (UTF16)
Change Web Template	This command is used to change Web templates at the time of the Web application run time.
Web Template (TEMPLATE)	This parameter is used to select the Web template that you swap with the original Web template.
Display Web Template as Modal Dialog	This command is used to display another Web template as a modal dialog. This allows a specific template format to be passed at run time of the Web application. The basic saved format is a view of a Web template.
Width in Pixels (WIDTH)	This parameter is used to specify the width of the dialog.
Height in Pixels (HEIGHT)	This parameter is used to specify the height of the dialog.
Web Template (TEMPLATE)	This parameter is used to select the Web template that is to be displayed as a modal dialog.

TABLE 6-12 List of Commands for Web Templates (*continued*)

Command and Parameters	Description
Resize Automatically (USE_AUTOMATIC_RESIZING)	This parameter is used to specify whether the Width in Pixels and Height in Pixels parameters are to be used or whether the size of the dialog is to be adjusted automatically.
Close Current Web Template Dialog with Cancel	This parameter is used to close the modal template that you opened with the previous command. This command has no parameters.
Close Current Web Template Dialog with OK	This parameter is used to close the modal template that you opened with the previous command but it allows you to pass the settings to the current template. This command has no parameters.
Set Web Template	You use this command to start a different Web application using another window from the browser.
Web Template (TEMPLATE)	This parameter is used to select the Web template that you want to execute.
Open in New Window (OPEN_IN_NEW_WINDOW)	This parameter is used to specify whether the Web application to be executed is to be opened in a new browser window.
Back to Initial State	You use this command to restore your display to the original format. This command has no parameters.
Back to Previous State	You use this command to restore your display one step back. This command has no parameters.

TABLE 6-12   List of Commands for Web Templates (*continued*)

If necessary, Web designers and ABAP programmers can use the Custom Extension Web item to realize highly individualized Web applications. This Web item enables the display of information based on the current navigational state or the result set of a data provider. ABAP function modules can be used to read data from other sources and data from other SAP systems can be read using Remote Function Calls (RFC). In addition, the status of a data provider can be used as an input parameter when calling the ABAP function modules. You can use the Custom Extension Web item to render your own HTML, whether based on a data provider or completely freeform. In addition, you can use this Web item to insert JavaScript into Web templates. Some reasons why you would use a customized ABAP class and Web item might be

- Use of the current navigational state (including any variables) and/or the result set of one or more data providers
- Use of Web item parameters defined in the Web template; these parameters can be changed using commands
- Output of all information that can be called using ABAP and Remote Function Calls (RFC), such as information from databases or other SAP systems

Analysis Web Item: Using Parameter Modification

In some cases, you may want to adjust the Analysis Web item for specific formatting instead of using the standard default formatting. This is possible by using the Modification parameter in the Analysis Web item. You can find this option within the Internal Display in the Web Item Parameter screen. You can use the Modification parameter to change the default display and behavior. You can modify the table structure and the table cells. The Modification parameter provides modules whose use can be controlled using additional parameters. This function enables you to use similar options to those available in earlier releases with the Web Design API for Tables. Unlike the Web Design API for Tables, modifications enable you to make targeted changes to the display and behavior without any programming.

Making modifications to the Analysis Web item has some prerequisites. The main prerequisite is that the modules must be implemented in Java. The SAP Basis infrastructure in SAP NetWeaver 7.0 does not support any customer modifications or extensions to Java coding. Customers are therefore not able to develop their own modules for modifications to the Analysis Web item. In this case, SAP delivers a number of sample modules. You can use parameters to modify the display and behavior of these modules.

Summary

Wow, this has been another extremely busy chapter! It explained all the different chart types and all the formatting that's available for each chart type. One of the thoughts that I would like you to remember after this chapter is that there definitely are ways to accommodate many of your reporting requirements, and it's a matter of working with the toolset to figure out what can and can't be accomplished. I would venture to say that out of the numerous projects, spot consulting tasks, and OSS message requirements that I've run into, there's been a solution for over 95 percent of the customer needs using some formatting process within the WAD component and the Chart Web item. In my case, with the focus of BI using the new frontend of the BOBJ components, I will need to focus on becoming more acclimated to the nuances of these newer components, and I know that it will take some time to feel comfortable with the capabilities of these frontend user interfaces but this is the future focus of SAP BI. One of the significant differences between the BOBJ and BI reporting options is the ability of the business user to do more with the BOBJ reporting, which is more user friendly and business user oriented. This means that many of the backend tasks that we are exploring here with BI will become the responsibilities of the business users once the move to the BOBJ components is made. So, that being said, we already know that the BOBJ frontend reporting toolset will definitely cover 99.9 percent of all business user needs, meaning we just have to get as comfortable with those functions as we are with the WAD functions in the BEx Web Analyzer—basically, getting accustomed to the functionality of the individual system whether it is BOBJ or BI, but with different reporting toolsets to navigate and understand.

We also reviewed and developed some portions of a dashboard during our development of the different chart types. I pointed out how easy it is to get a working model of a dashboard up and running in very little time. This process will be expanded on in the next chapter and we will look to pull all of this together and develop the final version of the dashboards.

We also worked through some of the commands used in the reporting process, with the focus on just those commands that are used for the Web items, a basic set that affects the

Web items used in our reports. We will see in the next chapter that there are some additional commands from other command areas that we will use in our dynamic dashboards. Much of the command functionality is consistent with what you learned in this chapter, so you'll be able to easily work through those other commands without requiring much explanation.

One important takeaway from this chapter is that there is a ton of flexibility in the approach to creating a chart or configuring the parameters of a chart. You can work with almost any functional requirements in the WAD to accommodate the business user's needs. The chart types discussed in this chapter are taken directly from Excel functionality and are supported by a very slick HTML backend, so you can create these charts using mostly Excel functionality and then display them in the Web. The following chapter pulls together everything that we talked about here and in the previous chapters to build a dashboard using the SAP WAD and the BEx Web Analyzer.

Developing High-Impact Dashboards

This chapter covers the development of dynamic Web templates to be used in the dashboarding process for your company. We cannot possibly cover in one chapter all the concepts and topics related to the development of a dynamic dashboard because the subject matter is too expansive. In fact, it is so expansive that college degree programs are now offered specifically for dashboard design and development. Similarly, many approaches exist to designing corporate dashboards. My intention is to provide advice from the standpoint of developing dashboards for business users and the SAP BI system. Thus, I will share my own personal experience using the BI WAD component and explain how to organize Web templates to display the information as successfully as possible.

In this chapter, we will look at development of some dashboards and components of these dashboards within the BI WAD environment, but we will not just be grinding through template after template to fill this chapter with multiple examples. The focus here is on practical examples, not the conceptual approaches to dashboard development. There are numerous thought leaders in this field, and I'll leave the conceptual areas to them to discuss, including all the pros and cons of each of the different styles. My approach to this chapter is to explain how you can use the SAP BI WAD component to develop dashboards for business users that give them a tool consistent with the old adage "a picture is worth a thousand words."

Now one of my pet issues is the use of the word "dashboard"—is this an overused word or what? A dashboard is so many things now I can't keep count of how many different corporate dashboards there are—management, strategic, operational, human resource, etc. and it goes on and on. So for all of the times I will use the word "dashboard" I have to apologize now for those that are reading this and cringe over the use of that word and the widespread generic definition.

As we go through all of these different concepts and ideas we need to remember that everything that we discuss can be developed in the SAP BI system using the components of the WAD. Nothing that we discuss in the areas of development of a dashboard will require any other reporting toolset except for the WAD and the actual queries delivering the data. We will also look to make use, as much as possible, of the standard Web items and functionality. You should be able to say that you can develop these dashboards without the use of additional resources to develop XHTML or any other types of objects.

As a final note to this discussion as we go through these charts and displays we will not really be concerned too much with the color since in the context of this book we will need to communicate the use of color versus showing it. Interestingly enough this is a good thing for you to practice since if you can get your information and answers communicated to the business users by just using basic colors rather than all the colors under the sun then you're doing something that's worthwhile. I was never in favor of using multiple colors except for the requirements to be aligned with the corporate marketing requirements. Having too many colors will make you go cross-eyed if you're looking at the same screen each day; rather we just find the right amount of colors to be used and successfully communicate the information. I would rather err on the side of just the right number of colors but to each their own in the using of colors for emphasis. Just remember—don't go nuts on your dashboards with tons of colors that don't really help or mean anything critical. I can see someone using RED for a basic key figure or a non-critical KPI rather than some milder color.

Overview of the Development of Dashboards

In many ways, the whole field of delivery of the data via dashboards was first emphasized not by BI but by the use of SAP Strategic Enterprise Management (SAP SEM) and the Corporate Performance Management (CPM) component of that module. In BI we are really focused on getting the data from point A to point B as effectively and consistently as possible, then using the base reporting components to generate reports for display purposes. So the whole dashboard concept was the final reporting component developed. Sure, we have a great set of reporting tools and now with the acquisition of Business Objects that frontend is getting much more attention. But we primarily focused on actual reports either via the frontend of the BEx Analyzer (Excel based) or the BEx Web Analyzer (Web based). The idea of dashboard components really didn't start to get true attention until the WAD started to be used more aggressively and in conjunction with the Visual Composer the ability to generate and develop more effective dashboards was available.

But in the SEM-CPM area we had both the Management Cockpit and the Balanced Scorecard. So in SEM we really were looking to develop the display toolset for these management tools. In this area SAP is working with the concepts of Norton and Kaplan in the Balanced Scorecard area and those of Patrick George in the Management Cockpit area. That being said, some of my experience and approaches are probably going to be leaning toward their ideas when it comes to dashboards and their formatting and focus.

Now we will not be looking at the Balanced Scorecard process since this is more of a complete management component and a large portion of the focus of the Balanced Scorecard is not truly dashboard activities but more management processes both vertically and horizontally throughout the company. Where we will find some ideas of what a true dashboard should look like is in the area of the Management Cockpit in SEM. This component really got into the whole concept of visualization and display processes that occurred during the presentation of information. Not sure if anyone remembers but the initial concept of the Management Cockpit (MC) was having all of this information displayed in a room—Management Cockpit Room— and everyone would come to that room and be immersed into the key performance indicators

(KPIs) of the company and discuss topics around growth and profitability of the company. Well, the whole idea of having everyone in the same location at the appropriate time was a bit much and having a room dedicated to strictly dashboard metrics was not going to have a long life. So, after the first cycle of SEM-CPM at SAP the Management Cockpit room idea was dropped but not the actual dashboard process. If you remember, the MC consisted of Walls, Frames, and Views and in each case there was a consistency to the architecture. You will see the influence of these MC concepts a bit later in this chapter.

You will see that several different attributes are required to build a strong dashboard and that being able to configure the end result in the system is only one of them. You will find that pulling together all the aspects of a good dashboard requires as much skill in the areas of business logic and understanding as it does in the actual use of the WAD or other system products to create the final dashboard. My motto is KISS—keep it short and simple. The idea of creating a fancy dashboard with all the bells and whistles included will only distract you from actually building a good, sound dashboard that delivers what the business user needs—fast, accurate, and consistent data displays. You also don't have to reinvent the wheel and struggle from scratch with every dashboard. Use templates and other components that are already available and built, and don't worry about reusing a specific set of colors in the same dashboard; if you need to, go for it. Again, presenting everything in the dashboard in bright colors and different colors only distracts the business user and makes it harder for them to identify the important information. The fewer items that they have to digest and the more time they can take reviewing and investigating the data, the more productive they will be—and the less maintenance you will have for both the dashboard itself and the data. A dashboard with only one chart type often is more effective than a dashboard, that has everything under the sun on it—tachometers, split pie charts, dynamic meters, and cockpit-style formats with all the KPIs as indicators that you might see in a vehicle or airplane. Keep your focus on the goal and your dashboard will develop at the appropriate level for the business user needs.

In the latter part of this chapter we will focus on building a couple of dashboards to show examples of the concepts that we discuss but having developed several of them will give you an idea of what can be achieved using the WAD and all of the functions available in this toolset. We will focus on a couple—one in the sales area and another in an industry specific area. The reason for this is that once you decide on a particular toolset to build your dashboards, which could turn out to be something other than BI, I would hope that you can use some of the information obtained here to develop your dashboards using the other reporting tools. I'm talking as though there isn't another dashboard component in the reporting toolset with SAP but I'm sure that many of you have read about and probably are using, to some extent, the dashboarding component delivered by BOBJ. That reporting component would be the BOBJ Xcelsius. In either case, there are some similar features between the WAD and Xcelsius but once you decide to use either BOBJ or BI you'll start to focus solely on what you can accomplish with the chosen reporting software.

Process of Developing a Dynamic Dashboard

There are several specific task activities that are required for building a dashboard. We find that they are all important but one seems to always get short changed by timelines or milestones and then you're looking at an uphill battle with developing dashboards that will actually work for your business user. The one I'm talking about is requirements gathering.

Of the different tasks needed to accomplish the development including the actual configuration and reporting strategy development, the requirements gathering is, I believe, the most important but the one that gets reduced or cut depending on the milestones and Go Live timeframe. I've seen companies where the development of report specs have been delayed so long that you don't have any time to think about what the business user wants and needs, only the time to get the current task completed based on what has been given to you as basic requirements. Don't take for granted that the business user will give you everything that is required. They are not as expert as you are at knowing what the system can and can't do, so you need to question and enhance the business requirements so that the functional specifications can be valid. You need to take the appropriate time to develop the report specs required and work with the business users on the format and functionality required from the dashboard. You can also make suggestions on the dashboard format and this is where, I think, most dashboards go down the drain. We don't usually ask and push back on anything that the business user might want, even if the idea of a specific KPI in a dashboard might not be the appropriate location for it. There are a number of thoughts around the level of KPIs, what types of data are necessary, and so forth, and we'll talk about that in a bit.

You also need to make sure you focus on the actual requirements of the dashboard and the business needs, not on what the system is capable of doing or what unusual dashboard designs you can come up with. Potentially, you could develop and distribute to your business users something straight out of *Star Wars*, but if you don't deliver the information in the form required, your customers will not be happy. They might find all the interactive features (such as sliding bars and so forth) amusing at first, but that will quickly change if you failed to understand what their requirements are and how to present them. The rule of thumb is that if an item doesn't add value to the dashboard, you shouldn't add it. Over 75 percent of all charts found on a dashboard are column, bar, pie, and line charts, and these are supported by all major software systems. Don't add new functionality, such as an unusual chart type, simply because you want to see how it works. If you encounter something unusual about the business requirements, question the business users and you will probably find that you can fine-tune the specifics such that those requirements can be handled by a standard chart type. Don't worry about the system not being able to support the dashboard; unless someone specifically asks for a dashboard that looks like the interior of an aircraft cockpit, you should be in pretty good shape.

As a final comment around the development of dashboards as we mentioned we want to make sure we listen to the users whether they are the C-level management, operational level, or analysts from the business. What we don't want to do is develop dashboards that require a doctorate degree to understand and explain. I know we've all run into these types of dashboards that look great at first glance but the initial discussion around what each metric means and how to interpret them is painful and requires you to take notes for review so that you can read the statistical information.

NOTE *"C-level management" refers to corporate positions whose titles begin with "Chief"—CEO, CIO, COO, CFO, and so forth.*

We need to realize that the normal amount of time that each of these different levels of people have during the day to review and assimilate the information from these dashboards is anywhere from about two to three minutes for a C-level professional to about five to eight minutes for an operational management person and the difference has nothing to do with any sort of difference in knowledge base. It has to do with the types of data. The C level, they are looking to get the information that they need and then go manage and grow the business. They don't get the big bucks for sitting and taking hours out of their day to understand the metrics of their business. Their responsibilities are to run the business so the two to three minutes is all they can afford or their time is not being spent wisely. As for the operational management this person is going to have a more detailed dashboard with more specific information around the execution of their business processes and therefore will require more time to understand and probably start to dig deeper into the details and statistics behind the information. This could also link to having additional drilldown reports available linked to this dashboard or possibly drill-through reports that could be used. So, let's not take our time and develop a dashboard that makes you feel as though you're sitting for the SATs each time you go to read it.

Required Details of the KPIs

When it comes to actually developing KPIs, we need to approach this from several angles. But the first item of business is to define what a KPI is for your business users. Wikipedia, referencing F. John Reh, explains *key performance indicator* as

> …a measure of performance. Such measures are commonly used to help an organization define and evaluate how successful it is, typically in terms of making progress towards its long-term organizational goals. KPIs can be specified by answering the question, "What is really important to different stakeholders?" KPIs may be monitored using Business Intelligence techniques to assess the present state of the business and to assist in prescribing a course of action. The act of monitoring KPIs in real-time is known as business activity monitoring (BAM). KPIs are frequently used to "value" difficult to measure activities such as the benefits of leadership development, engagement, service, and satisfaction. KPIs are typically tied to an organization's strategy using concepts or techniques such as the Balanced Scorecard.

Well, that just about sums it up, right? We could, and people do, sit and battle over what a KPI is for hours on end. I've tried many times to get agreements around what KPIs are for a specific company with varying success. Have you ever tried to meet with your divisional managers and once you have them all in a room try to get a standard set of KPIs from them and then get some sort of agreement on what they are? You would spend your entire professional career trying to do something like that. Sure, each division may be selling some unique product line or have some exceptions to the rule in terms of KPI information but within a company there has to be some set of performance indicators that can be quantified so that we can take those and start to drive the business as a whole; then once those KPIs are defined, using the exceptions to the rule for each division to help drive, at a more granular level, the additional products or services that are key to that line of business. It gets even more difficult if the KPIs are linked to monetary gains and everyone has to agree not only on the KPI itself but on the calculations that are taken into account for the value of that KPI. Quite the show when it comes to that aspect of the KPI connection but this starts us into a discussion that is more associated to a Balanced Scorecard rather than a dashboard. So the dashboard is more of a display of information that has happened and hopefully helps us forecast what might happen in the future versus the basic idea of a Balance Scorecard where it is a management toolset that links everyone throughout the company against KPIs.

KPIs differ depending on the nature of the organization, the organization's strategy and the development level of the organization we are generating the dashboards for. They help to evaluate the progress of an organization toward its vision and long-term goals, especially toward difficult to quantify, knowledge-based goals. So, we need to get these defined and the critical document for this is the report requirements or functional requirements that should be developed initially by the business users. Don't let them off the hook by trying to help the process along; you will find yourself creating these documents with little or no help from the business. This is a self-defeating scenario. There is little chance that whatever you develop will be approved by the business user unless you're the business user also. It would be better for you that they reject the functional requirements immediately so that you don't waste your time developing some set of KPIs that are not agreed upon by the business and once you get the entire dashboard completed they realize that it's not giving them any indicators that are going to be helpful in their position. Definitely, get the business users involved by offering examples of the final result. Demonstrating the use of a dashboard and driving the need for this component to help your company survive will improve the results that you get from the business requirements document. If all else fails in getting the business requirements directly from the business user, then getting consensus sign off on the KPIs you've developed is a must. Do this either from the actual business user point of view or from the management level so that someone from the business has approved the use of these metrics before starting the process of configuration. I know the idea of getting consensus around metrics for one business user group from the management level just above seems a bit harsh but it's much better than having to reengineer everything that you've spent months on after you're done.

Requirements gathering doesn't end with KPIs. In my experience implementing BW/BI or SEM-CPM, I have seen very few companies work through the requirements gathering to the extent needed to develop a set of good requirements for the development of the dashboards. Typically, everyone does a great job up to the point of establishing the appropriate KPIs, but after that the requirements gathering stops. This is actually just the start of the process. After this level of information analysis, we have the whole area of architecture and display to follow through and understand. Developing a display component before you get more information about the KPIs is premature. You need to ask questions about positioning, priorities, and formatting. For example, the color schemes will be approved by the corporate marketing department, so that's not a big issue, but you need to understand if other colors within the dashboard should be softer or bolded. Following are the types of questions you need to pursue after you establish the KPIs. For example:

- Out of your list of metrics, what are the primary KPIs that the business can't do without?
- If you could have *only* one KPI, what would it be?
- What formats would work best for you (column charts, line charts, pie charts, bar charts, etc.)?
- What experience do you have with analysis using a scattergram, radar chart, and so forth?

If the answer to this question is that they've never used them, this gives you a good idea of what types of charts will work for your audience. Avoid using types of charts that are familiar to you or that look good to you but are probably not the ones that would make sense immediately to your business users.

- If you were looking at a display of information, where would you want your critical KPI to be located (top, bottom, left, or right)?

- If a list of values is being used for filters, what format would work best for you (radio buttons, dropdown list, check box, etc.)?

- Would you prefer to type in a specific value of a characteristic, such as "Region," or choose it from a list?

- How comfortable are you with analysis of two or three metrics on one chart, each with its own scaling?

    This means your chart would have different scaling factors running up the primary and secondary axes. Is that something that will be easy for the business user to think through or will it cause confusion? The concern is whether the metric would be too unusual and possibly be misread, potentially causing errors in decision making.

- If within your requirements you need additional drill-through reports, is this something that should be available via a context menu or a hyperlink directly on the dashboard screen?

I know some of these requirements sound like overkill but when we are developing a dashboard we are well past the fact that we are getting the appropriate data and information. This is all about displaying the data correctly, accommodating the business user with information, and reducing the total time that they spend on getting to the data and rather increasing the time they spend on analysis of the data. At this point take the time to diagram out an overview of what the dashboard will look like and socialize this throughout the business user community. This additional effort will make the sign off of the final product easier and more successful.

What Are the KPIs?

We talk about these things called KPIs quite a bit. Seems that everyone has some KPIs that they have to manage and need to understand the process of managing them during the business process. Again, on this topic there are is a ton of additional information and material that is available so I'll keep my discussion just to the comments that make sense to our topic here rather than going into too much conceptual information. There are a number of situations where the whole idea of KPIs needs to be revisited and reworded. Maybe we can call it something else so that we get a clear picture of what these indicators really are. I've reviewed some of my projects and identified some of the critical areas where we will have to focus during the process of developing the correct KPIs. One of my cardinal rules is that we try desperately to avoid having too many KPIs. I can't tell you the number of times where I've seen a dashboard overloaded with KPIs and you're constantly trying to manage one or the other of these different indicators. We all know that there are critical indicators that will make or break our businesses and we just have to find the right ones and make sense of them.

During a project with a vehicle manufacturing company, we were reviewing these different groups of indicators and found that the inclination was to look at all of the business outcome indicators rather than looking at the source indicators. After review, we found that one of the critical Key Performance Indicators is customer satisfaction. During our analysis we found a direct correlation between the customer satisfaction level and the sales of their vehicles in the next 4–6 month time frame. This was a great find since everything was driven (not a pun) by this analysis—sales, cost of goods sold, inventory levels, labor costs—and this impacted many other areas outside of just the revenue streams. With this additional KPI in their dashboards we were able to really get some good information to them that would proactively impact their bottom line rather than trying to influence the actual sales numbers other ways such as discounts, promotions, etc.

During these fact-finding workshops, you have to realize that you can only manage a specific number of KPIs. No one can manage 50 KPIs or even 30 KPIs, and even 20 would be a big challenge. You need to be aware of the total number of KPIs and make sure that there aren't so many that they work against each other in the process. For example, if you were increasing the emphasis of the overall worker productivity KPI, you might lower your rating on the KPI regarding employee satisfaction of their work environment. Having indicators that work against each other is a no-win situation. Normally within the company, these KPIs are tied to moves in positions, salaries, and bonuses, so the ability to identify just the correct few KPIs will be a very challenging process.

After you've narrowed down the list of KPIs to about 15 or so we can organize them into groups and headings. There are a number of groups that can be identified within KPIs. One area would be in terms of the role that you are responsible for and the KPIs applying to that role. If you are involved with management of a specific department, the KPIs need to be directed to just those activities and not be so wide-ranging that they encompass other areas that you don't have full control of during the Management by Objective (MBO) process. If my MBO and bonus depends on the Net Profit Margin, then I need to be able to affect the total sales *and* the costs involved. If I'm only responsible for Total Sales and I'm a sales person, then this is a fair KPI to be looking at during the year and to be gauged against.

Another area that we need to be aware of is the actual data that is being used in the calculation of the KPI. We need to try and make the indicator as transparent as possible so that we can make sure the business user has the ability to manage to that specific indicator. For example, if we use an MBO of sales, we want to make sure that it's consistent with the person's responsibilities. If we use a sales number that is calculated with adjustments made for all sales except for sales of specific products or promotional activities, we start to muddy the waters and now the Account Executives are trying to understand the details of the MBOs rather than doing their job, which is selling.

Several other aspects of KPIs are more obvious with regard to the development and validation. One is the fact that we have distinct types of indicators that separate measures into operational and strategic KPIs. I'm comfortable with the fact that we can focus our attention on the nature of the indicator and make sure we are not asking someone to achieve a strategic goal when all they can really do is influence an operational measure. Therefore, during the process of identifying KPIs and assigning them to individuals, we need to ask ourselves if these are KPIs that will affect the day-to-day activities of the person or are they KPIs that will affect the goals of the company. We see these two different groups of KPIs all of the time and should be very familiar with the differences.

Another aspect of KPIs is the data frequency involved. The individuals being managed by these KPIs should know the length of time they have to influence the direction and outcome of their personal MBOs. Time periods typically are defined directly in the dashboard as quarterly, daily, or yearly information.

Finally, we have some enhanced items that we see in the dashboards that I would like to point out. Sometimes, as I have mentioned, we get too caught up with all of the bells and whistles and the final result of the dashboard is something like a what-if scenario rather than an indicator or dashboard display. We need to make sure that we clearly separate the ability to create a set of KPIs from doing what-if analysis on the indicators versus a display of a KPI. It's all great to be able to shift percentages and values around to see what might be an outcome but to spend too much time over-analyzing the possible outcomes is not the best use of a business analyst's time. Rather than having them analyzing the actual information, we find some dashboards offering too many options to make comparisons that are meaningless in the scheme of things. Work the KPIs around doable measures and benchmarks and we will not have all of the what-if analysis going on. The what-if will be relegated to forecasting and planning rather than comparison of what was actually posted versus some random changes in levels.

You also need to be very aware of what types of information you deliver to the different groups. Most people immediately want to see the day-to-day information to do analyses. That is fine if they are doing operational KPIs, but strategic KPIs require more static, longer-term information. Business users who are responsible for driving the long-term growth of the company need monthly, quarterly, and yearly numbers, not daily information. You want to offer them a larger window to the data so that they can analyze trends and patterns without the distraction of new information arriving every 24 hours.

There are many more aspects of KPIs that we could delve into and analyze, but these are some of the issues that I've run into during my projects and workshops to gather KPI information.

Tips on Visualization of Dynamic Dashboards

In this section we will work through some ideas on the visualization that goes on with regard to dashboards. Now, I'm not going to say that I'm an expert in this area and there are definitely concepts that I will refer to that have some other more technical terminology and approaches but from my experience these are areas that we don't seem to work hard enough at to get right and be able to put yourself in the position of the business user and what they are actually looking at. From my perspective we need to get some external comments about the dashboards that we are building. This can definitely improve our approach to the final display of KPIs to the business. I'm also sure that there are other topics or areas where you might have run into issues and have come up with your list of to-do's when it comes to building the Web templates. Think about including some of the ideas about visualization offered in this section into your current list and keep them in mind as you go through your process. Also, these are not in any order of priority since I believe there is no dependency from one to another. They are separate issues that will come up as you go through your development. Just remember one thing as you work through this. We are trying to get our point across as quickly and as directly as possible and that is the real challenge. This is definitely one of my challenges. There are many times where I'm sure a particular topic could be addressed in a much more effective manner and after about two hours of conversation I'm still not getting to the point. Many of us have this issue and since we communicate and develop our ideas that way, we look at these dashboards the same way. They are just another way to talk to a topic for hours and hours and then finally get to the point. If we can narrow down the conversation and get to the point our skill sets in the area of dashboard development would increase at the same rate. So, rather than continuing to talk about these topics (following my own lead), let's get started.

Optimum Level of Information

One of the most common mistakes in dashboard development is to attempt to *squeeze as much into the screen as possible*. If we try to fit too much into one screen, it ceases to be a dashboard and becomes a visual bulletin board. If this is the result then what you have is someone that has to understand the navigational approach to reading the dashboard rather than analyzing the dashboard. So what we start to see is someone trying to expand the dashboard the correct way to see what they need and then start to focus on this specific issue such as looking at bullets, detailed data, and anything else we've decided to add to our dashboard over time rather than the true needs for our MBOs. The following illustration is an example of this effect. The actual metrics and the approach to displaying those metrics are good, but the developer started to add in hyperlinks at the bottom of the page, a To Do list or Action List, additional scroll bars since we couldn't get everything on the one screen, adding additional colors to highlight whatever is critical since everything is starting to get so tight that we really can't distinguish what is a KPI versus what is just information. At some point during the development we lost track of what the actual KPIs are that we initially used the dashboard to understand.

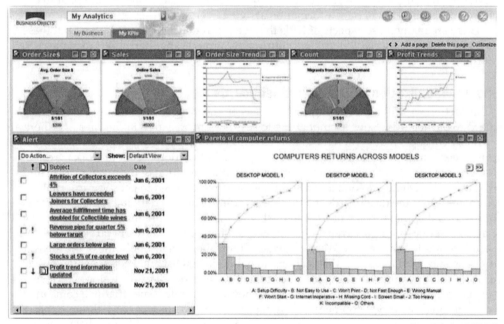

The following illustration shows another example of this issue. This dashboard started to get out of hand as soon as they started to *add colors*—and lots of them—to this display.

Then, with way too much already going on in this dashboard, they tried to push more into the screen by adding the *fancy buttons to the left side.*

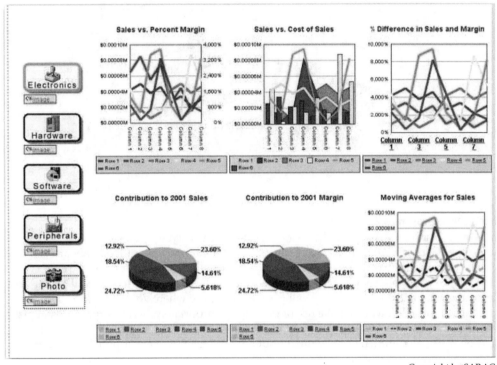

Five different chart types are included in the Web screens at the top of the dashboard. Assuming that the developer is able to get all of them to work appropriately, we encounter issues with spacing. The descriptions are not clear enough for us to understand what all the colors mean, and because there's not enough space, the titles have been reduced to being so small that we would have to have worked with this information over time to understand what each indicator is trying to tell us. Remember, you have a total of three to four minutes of the CEO's time to deliver the information needed to make decisions, so make the most of that time. This dashboard is too overloaded—too much information all at once, too detailed, and no central focus to the primary KPI that the developer is trying to communicate to the business user.

Information Blocked from the Initial View

In the following example, the developer has decided to use a 3D chart. Without a doubt, the chart looks very interesting, but due to the depth that the 3D adds to the chart, some information is *blocked from view.* In the very back of the 3D chart, you can't see the last column, so you really don't know whether that information is flat or has some activity that you just can't see. This situation could get worse as these columns move higher and start to block the middle of the screen. Other than that issue, I think that this chart would, with a little bit more work, actually drive the information home and give a very good focus to the KPIs, but we would have to adjust the format a bit to unblock the data, then add some titles and information to give this more structure.

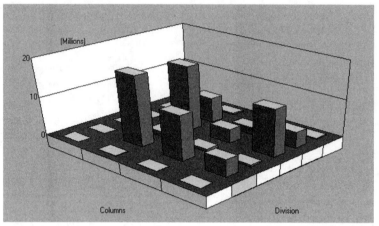

Using the Appropriate Chart Type

In the next example, we see that the dashboard developer tried to get a bit creative by using some of the normally *unused chart types*. Again, can you identify what this dashboard is trying to show you within 15 seconds of reviewing the information? I'm all for using the correct chart type in your dashboards, but trying to add the radar chart type (lower-right corner) to a dashboard where it doesn't add any value is wasting space where you could add some additional metric that would make use of the space appropriately. If you were to look at just that portion of the chart, you probably wouldn't understand the result of the information quickly. You could figure it out eventually, but it would take too long, especially if you have a tight window of time for analysis such as in the case of a C-level management user.

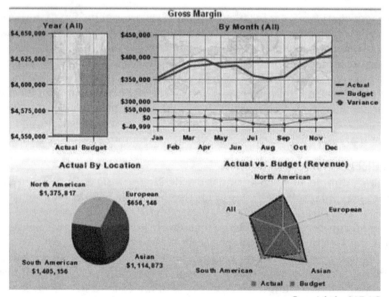

The pie chart to the left of the radar chart in the previous dashboard works just fine and is a perfect example of using the appropriate chart type to drive home your information and results to the business analyst. Another issue in this dashboard is to the top right in terms of the two line chart types. What is the *actual KPI*? Is it the actual versus budget gross margin profit or is it the variance? I like the fact that both are shown here, since we can get a look at the information used to create the variance, but whichever is the primary KPI should really be in a bolder color scheme and highlighted. It would seem, based on the positioning, that the basic information—Actual and Budget—represents the primary metrics and therefore should have the most room, but without some additional focus point, we can't really be sure. The top left of the dashboard includes another chart that is outlining yearly the Actual and Budget values. This one isn't immediately obvious but you figure it out pretty quickly. As you can see, the Actual total is the complete chart area and the Budget is embedded into that area with a darker color. My question is whether the scheme would be reversed if the Actual value was less than the Budget. That is, would the whole area be the Budget and the Actual be just a darker area? If that is the case, then this chart would start to get *confusing* because each month it could change format on the viewer.

As you can see as we go through these examples, one dashboard can have multiple issues that are not working correctly for the business analyst. As long as you're aware of these pitfalls in creating dashboards, you can understand where you might be challenged on your architecture and possibly why the business users are having difficultly working with the dashboards. I have seen companies invest tons of money into a dashboard approach to management and wind up having only 50 percent of their employees use it. The other 50 percent continue to download the information into Excel and create their own charts for analysis purposes. The goal of the dashboard approach is to eliminate this practice so that the analysts can focus on doing their jobs, which is to analyze the data, instead of gathering and formatting the data. As you've noticed, in this section I've been italicizing certain phrases or words to emphasize a point and catch your attention. This is exactly what you want to do with the dashboard. You want to *focus the user's eyes* on a certain portion of the information *first*, and then have them review the other KPIs. To do this, use some sort of change in the font or color scheme to highlight some specific portion of the dashboard.

Using Space Appropriately: One Screen vs. Multiple

One of my pet issues is the idea that we have agreed with the business and have too many KPIs without any push back and find ourselves with too many KPIs to put into one screen. Again, remember, only *one screen* makes up a dashboard. Make sure everyone knows that we can only have a certain number of KPIs or these metrics start to lose their identity in the mix. This next illustration shows this situation to a tee. Since the business user may want to have so many metrics we start using *scroll bars* to get everything on "one screen" even though with scroll bars it actually means that we have more than one screen. I would have been happier if they would have created some drill-through to more detailed information rather than having scroll bars to compensate for this problem. In addition to this there is also an additional tab page for even more metrics. Again, one of my pet issues—How many metrics can one person have and still do their jobs appropriately? Ten? Twenty? Thirty?

After more than 10–15 you start to drive the business user nuts since succeeding in one area might easily defeat you in another. In many cases, these KPIs start to work against each other and then you really have a problem if they are linked to bonuses and MBOs.

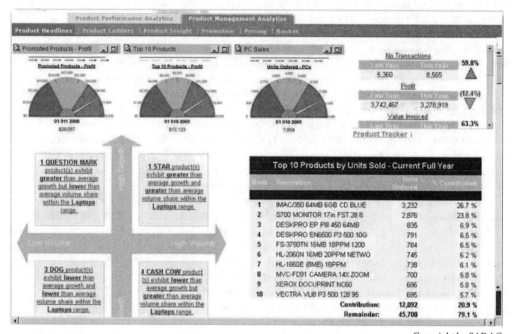

The preceding dashboard is a very good example of a developer having difficulty differentiating between a Balanced Scorecard approach and a dashboard concept; some information is specific to management processes, typically found in a Balanced Scorecard, and the other information is presented as a dashboard. There is so much information that the dashboard has scroll bars, additional tab pages, and links on each of the charts to more information. Even though this tab is labeled "Product Headlines," it presents much more than just the headlines. This dashboard is appropriate for a middle-management position or a business analyst and not for any C-level management groups.

Displaying the Appropriate KPIs with the Appropriate Chart Type

The next example shows the need to *understand what KPI* you are trying to present. The line chart presents a very clear, focused metric on the dashboard, but the title states "Actual to Budget Variance"—if you look at the chart, it is showing actual and budget values but no variance.

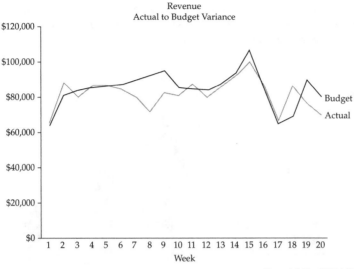

Revenue
Actual to Budget Variance

We either have to guess the variance or assume that overall the budget numbers are higher for the larger percentage of the time than vice versa and this is assuming that the KPI is the cumulative variance and not just the individual variances. I think the actual outcome of this metric is impossible to identify. What should be available is another line chart, or *only* a line chart, for the variance number itself. This would make life much easier for the business analyst. To really display the entire story you would need to have some other chart type since the variance looks like it will be both negative and positive.

The following illustration shows the use of filled-in circles for the chart type to make a point about operating costs versus revenue. This is a chart type doughnut with the center filled in to make it look like a solid format. This example has a couple of issues. First, once the operating costs get to be more than the revenue, the color scheme changes from a green background and brown filled-in area to a lighter-brown background and a darker-brown filled-in area. This should be the first clue that the chart type will not work appropriately with this metric display. The second issue is that expanding circles are used for the total amounts. Although the user can scroll over the areas to see the actual total numbers, to immediately get a feel for this information, the user needs additional context as to the proportion of size to amount.

Costs vs. Revenue

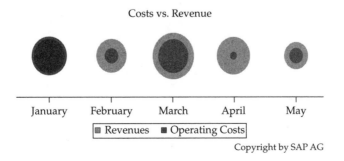

Let's take this information and use another chart type—yes, the boring column chart type. In the following illustration, we see the same information, but in this case we can easily identify what is going on in terms of total volume and amounts with revenue versus operating costs.

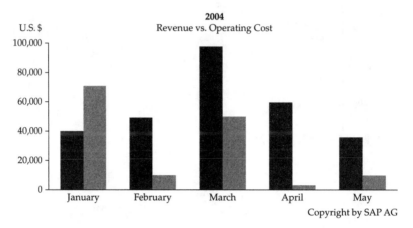

You can also see that even though the revenue was much lower in April than in March, the difference in revenue versus operating costs is about the same. Therefore, some fixed costs are probably in the operating costs to keep them at such a high level. You can also see that after about the $60,000 level, operating costs are going to start eating into margins due to the fixed costs (probably). This illustration shows how easy it is to get additional information out of this data using this chart type versus the other chart type, which you have to struggle just to read. Yes, the column chart type might seem very straightforward and boring, but the business user will thank you for its simplicity. They want to get the data quickly and effectively, not take a test in graphic design. So, use the *appropriate chart type* in your design.

Use of Colors and Spacing in the Dashboard

In the next example, the developers have gone wild with *bright* colors. You can't see this because the illustration is in grayscale, but the dashboard in this example is loaded with bold shades of red, green, and yellow. It also has way too many different chart types. In the presentation of these KPIs we need to decide on what the primary chart type would be and work with the functionality.

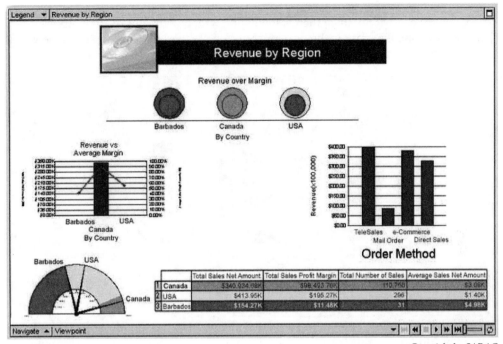

Having a total of five different chart types and presentation patterns on one dashboard is very complex for the business user to understand and interpret. Also notice the use of a very large space—relative to the amount of space we have to develop these dashboards—for a corporate logo. This is a waste of space. A large corporate logo is great in a presentation or a letterhead, but a business user who is looking at a dashboard for their own corporation doesn't need a reminder of what the corporate logo looks like. If your marketing group insists on the inclusion of the logo in the dashboards, try to persuade them into allowing a smaller corporate logo for the dashboards. Finally, the headings are way too big. The title Revenue by Region takes up about 25 percent of the entire dashboard. Your titles and corporate logos should be no more than about 10 percent of the total space you have to work with, if that. So, in this one dashboard, we've identified five different issues:

- Too much color is used.
- The colors are too bright.
- Too much room is given to the corporate logo.
- Too much room is given to the titles of the reports.
- Too many different chart types are included in one dashboard.

Take a closer look at these different dashboards from an outsider's perspective and see what the business user will see. I am a firm believer that if you really want to know whether your dashboard design is correct, you should show your dashboard to someone completely outside of that particular industry; if they can understand the information and offer some additional analysis of this information within about 30 seconds, then your dashboard is probably pretty good. If not, then there's something wrong with your display process.

In the following illustration, the developer decided to work with a 3D type of view and use very bright colors.

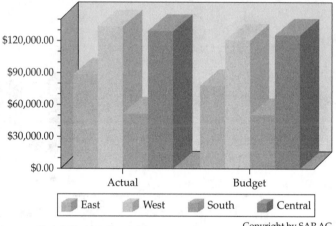

Copyright by SAP AG

The combination does offer some additional focus to the chart but doesn't really add anything of additional value from the analysis point of view. Also, some context is missing because Actual and Budget do not have any sort of corresponding time-period titles such as monthly, quarterly, or yearly. The primary reason I'm offering this chart type 3D column as an example is to show that it doesn't really add anything to the analysis of the data whether we are looking at a single, 2D or 3D format. In most cases there aren't really any cons of having one dimensional view versus another but it can be a bit distracting at times. One issue is that the additional graphics used might cause a performance issue, because all of those additional pixels' worth of display have to be pulled over into the chart and that with the use of colors we may want to use milder ones rather than shocking the business user with these multiple bold colors. You need to review and take into account the cons of any of these creative displays of the metrics because there is always a price to pay for having a highly graphical screen.

Use of Dynamic Graphics in the Dashboard

Hey, don't get me wrong about the use of dramatic dashboards, with the new BOBJ component to the BI frontend, we have components such as Widgets, Dashboard Builder, and Xcelsius that allow the display of the dashboards to look exactly like some of the previous examples and really have bold statements and displays. As a matter of fact, I've purposely not disclosed the information about the systems being used on some of the examples to show you that no matter what system you use—BOBJ, BI WAD, and so forth—it's not just the system that makes a dashboard but the overall architecture and formatting. You can create an excellent dashboard directly from an Excel spreadsheet. It wouldn't have all the bells and whistles, but it would definitely be functional and capable of supporting the data that you might see on dashboards. An example of a dashboard with dynamic graphics can be seen in the following illustration.

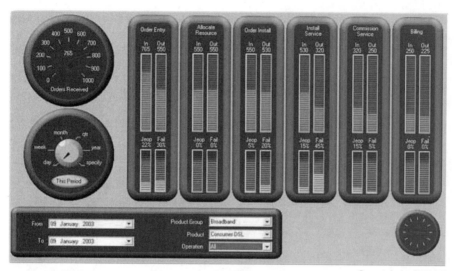

Copyright by SAP AG

This represents a true dashboard-type approach to displaying the KPIs. Personally, I think this example displays a few too many metrics, but that depends on the audience for this dashboard. For middle management, the total number of metrics seems right—very direct, consistent statistics, and a good format (possibly some wasted space). I'm more concerned about the additional filters at the bottom left. How many different combinations can the business user work with? I also don't see an easy component that would enable the business user to save the specific settings once they switch the combinations to the correct set. In other words, once a person has navigated to a particular set of Product Group, Product, Operation, and time frame, can they *save it as a variant*, reformat and save again, and so forth? This capability would enable the person to retrieve that particular combination much more easily based on a saved variant. Another question I might ask is whether this dashboard could have been presented using simpler column, bar, and line charts or did the business user specifically ask for something that actually looks like a car or aircraft dashboard?

At this point, having reviewed several examples, it's time to pause and reconsider what a business "dashboard" really is. It's not intended to be a video game, so it doesn't need to look like a racecar dashboard or something out of a Hollywood set. Rather, it is a display of critical KPIs in a single-screen format using charts and graphics and is intended to be easier to analyze than a report. Just give the high-level picture of the information and leave it at that. Having reviewed and worked with a number of different reporting systems, I understand the temptation to use all the dynamic and dramatic components to make a statement with the dashboard format, but giving in to this temptation usually results in an unmanageable dashboard that doesn't serve its purpose.

The dashboard in the next illustration is another example where the developer of this dashboard simply needed to step back and review the screen to identify the issue. If I look at the allocation of the space in this dashboard we've actually given additional space to the buttons for navigation and this space is very important in the dashboard since we are looking to make a statement with only one screen. The space given to the buttons could be used for additional information about the critical tachometers for # of New Customers, Revenue, Top-10 Revenue, and Order Value.

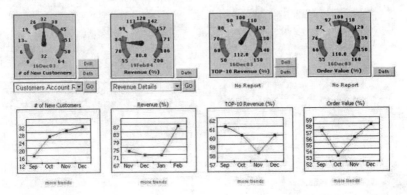

I like quite a bit about this dashboard; it's straightforward, presents the information in a very good display, and includes comparisons across the bottom charts. The viewer's attention is definitely drawn to the primary information with the colors across the top tachometers, but giving them more room and size would make the dashboard better. If this would happen the upper metrics would be the same as the lower charts you would embed with the buttons positioned at the bottom of the diagram so that the size would be exactly the same as the charts below. Also, instead of hyperlinks for "more trends," I would have a dropdown list with all the additional reports or charts available via the selection option.

Right Size and the Right Information Level

The following illustration is an example of a very good dashboard that follows most of the rules in terms of color, emphasis of the primary KPIs with additional colors and some dimensionality, and much better titles to identify exactly what we are looking at.

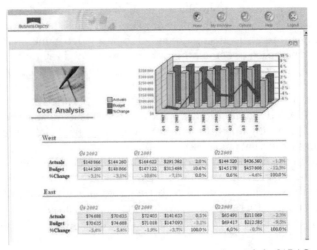

Starting at the top, the dashboard includes some good examples of metrics that give the business user both Actual and Budget and then the Variance or % change to give some perspective. Inclusion of the summary charts in the lower half of the dashboard is a good example of incorporating summary reports into the dashboard so that all the information in the *dashboard doesn't have to be presented as charts*. You don't have to force the information into a chart to allow it into a dashboard. If the data lends itself to a summary report and it works for your business user, go with the summary report.

What I do have an objection to in the preceding example is the amount of valuable space that the logo takes up—over 25 percent of the total space on the top area of the dashboard. If you have no other KPIs to present, then make the chart with the line and column chart types included bigger to fill the upper portion of the dashboard. The logo or picture file only needs to be large enough to get noticed for a moment, not to take up valuable real estate on the screen. In this case, it's not even a logo but a picture of some sort of accounting information that doesn't offer any value to the dashboard or the data. This could be relegated to a small portion of the upper bar chart area and the metrics could be given all the additional space. I would also caution about the 3D views of the data. There are no issues with the overlapping of the columns in this situation, but we can't guarantee that won't occur with all of the rolling data. We would just have to watch and see if this issue does occur.

Getting Too Graphical and Losing Focus on the KPIs

The next example, one of the more interesting displays, uses lots of JavaScript and graphical horsepower to execute the screen. I'm concerned with that aspect of this dashboard, but what concerns me more about this approach to a dashboard is the positioning of the data and the breakdown of the data.

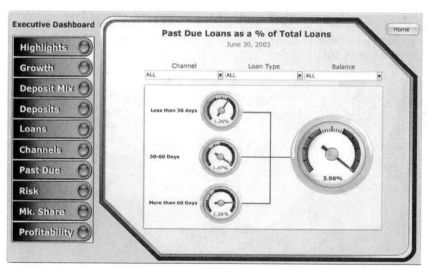

Apparently, the primary KPI is the large gauge on the right side of the screen. Okay, so *what is the metric represented here?*

If I look at all four gauges we see that the display is confusing. If I look at the middle three gauges and the information displayed I'm not sure of the process of positioning the values in the gauges. See, the three are not indexed the same. If that's the case, we need to have some sort of range showing in the gauge. Look at the top and middle gauges and we see that the color sections are different and that's OK since the good, middle, and bad sections may move, but if you look closely at the positioning of the arrows the top is 1.26% and that's leaning to the right whereas the middle gauge is 1.47% and it's completely over to the far right but the difference between the two doesn't fit the display spacing between 1.47 and 1.26. Same goes with the bottom gauge. Now the larger indicator shows that 3.98% is completely to the far right and in red. So what would have happened if it was a total of 5.90%? Would the gauge range expand to accommodate this difference? Or what is the maximum or highest total for these loans?

I also have to question the multiple options to change the data. I will assume that as we change the information on the left side, the gauges change to reflect the information according to the item highlighted. There seems to be too many KPIs available here and also too much in terms of short-term memory required for this to work. By that I mean that we are expecting the business analyst to remember everything about each of these indicators as they page from one to another. I would find that a bit difficult to do. There is just so much that your short-term memory can hold onto while moving through additional information. Then you are looking for the business analyst to take that remembered information and use that to integrate with other information to make a decision? I would find that more stressful rather than helpful. If you are going to have all of this information available, you need to figure a better way to show it. What you don't want to do is to "lose" the current information while looking at any other information. A better approach to all of this information would be tab pages since you can tab from page to page and not lose any of your information since you will not have to click a button and remove one set of data for another; just click from tab to tab and go back to another tab at any time. This is a situation where the display got the better of the person creating the dashboard.

The next example is a well-thought-out dashboard in terms of total information and good use of space, but the whole display and design is completely off. As an exercise, take a moment now to review the dashboard from a business analyst's point of view and jot down what you find wrong with it. As you read on, compare your list against my list of items.

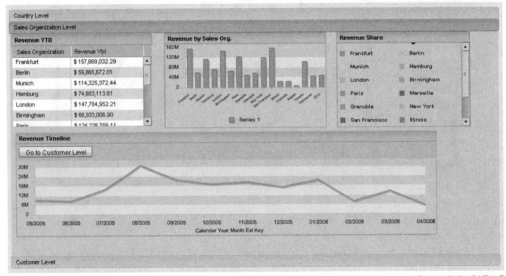

So first, if I look at this dashboard, the one area that I would really like to point out is the fact that the *color scheme doesn't match*. If you look at the screen on the far right you'll notice that it's identifying each of the sales organizations as a specific color. Now, if I look at any of the charts I don't see this color scheme anywhere. So that's our first issue and really the one that I wanted to highlight in this dashboard, but if we continue to review these screens we see a few more concerns.

Second, if I look at the different charts I can't really tell which ones are the primary KPIs. They are all in the same font and colors and there's nothing distinguishing one metric from the other in importance.

Third, in the upper-middle chart I'm wondering what is involved in the organizations of each of these Sales Orgs. I don't see that they are sorted alphabetically, or in priority of total sales, or by technical name. Basically they are listed randomly and the business analyst will have an issue with that setup.

Finally, I would also take note of the titles—titling something "Series 1" is not a title. So I've assumed that this is a graphical interpretation of Revenue YTD from the chart on the left but that's just an assumption and to do that assumption your business user will have to think about something else other than analysis of the data.

Again, remember our jobs here are to collect the data and present the data consistently so that the business analysts will do their jobs of analysis of the data. I will also assume that the lower chart has the primary KPIs since it takes up most of the room on the dashboard and we should focus on that one the most. Therefore, having to be able to identify the KPI itself quickly is critical. In this case the title again is not straightforward enough and needs to be cleaned up. I would also think that we need to have some sort of context to this information. Are the sales for this time period good, okay, bad? For that purpose we need to have some sort of benchmark—Planned Sales, Period to Period comparison, or something like that—to give the information more validity.

The Architecture of the Dashboard

Let's talk a bit about the best business practices when it comes to actually developing a dashboard. So far we've covered the mechanics of setting up a dashboard, the KPI process within a dashboard, and generally how to organize your information in a dashboard. Now we are going to discuss the architecture of the dashboard in a bit more depth.

We've seen a number of different chart types used in dashboards in this chapter, some different variations of dashboards including dynamic, interactive, and others that include every bell and whistle under the sun in them. If we look at the basics of a dashboard we find that there are some standard rules of thumb when it comes to how a person will review and assimilate the information from a dashboard. In the last section we talked about the number of KPIs that make sense based on the total number that a person can proactively work towards. Well, this falls nicely into the total number or KPIs that you should include in a basic dashboard. The number runs around 12–15 KPIs per dashboard display. What this means is that if I have more than 15 what I should be doing is looking to add a tab page or some other approach to stage the other KPIs for further review and not try and push all of the 25 plus KPIs into one screen or set up a scroll bar to move around and see all of the indicators.

Now, if we look at some of the basics of a dashboard we have a set of views that we can identify. A view is basically one set of indicators in a specific chart type. So, if I have sales by quarter in one screen—this is a view. Normally we look for only two but not more than four KPIs in one view. If there are more than this the business analyst will have difficulty identifying all of them and deciding what the outcome of the particular view is—so the question is how many KPIs per view before the business user has a difficult time deriving any information from the view? If you were to review some of the concepts of the founding fathers of dashboards they would suggest two to three KPIs per view and this is not bad since you can have six views per screen and that means that you can have a total of 12–18 KPIs on one screen. This is more than enough information for one business user to understand at one glance. Now, what do we do to move the business user's sight to where the more important indicator or information can be found—by the use of color or some other component that you can highlight or enhance to show some difference in one KPI versus all of the others? Use the format, fonts, colors, different chart types, or any other approach that you feel will make your critical KPI stand out and be noticed first. Some of the dashboard critics suggest that the eyes move the same way as your strong side hand—so if you are right handed your eyes will go right first, and vice versa if you are left handed. In my case, let's not let the individual make that choice. We can make it for them by use of dramatic objects in the dashboard. The amount of formatting is a tricky one. You don't want too little and you definitely don't want too much. Too little is not bad but your dashboard will come across as not complete or polished if you don't have enough highlights to it. If you have too much not only will it be distracting to the users but it may also cause an issue with performance of the dashboard. We don't want either so you will have to decide what the business user wants and go from there. Some would rather have chart types like columns and bars but others can't be without tachometers and other more elaborate objects.

As you go through the process of building a dashboard, look to integrate some of these ideas into your dashboards, keeping in mind (as always) that the executive who will be looking at a strategy dashboard has only about two to four minutes to review the dashboard, understand what the dashboard is presenting, assimilate the information, and be able to take that and use it to drive the growth and future of the company.

Examples of Effective Dashboards

If we look at one of the Web items we worked on in a former chapter we can start to really work through some of the ideas and concepts discussed in this chapter and see if we are following all of the important points while building a dynamic and focused dashboard. So, in the following illustration we can see the column charts that we used in the previous section and let's discuss what is going on within the chart. Now, the chart itself is in pretty good shape so let's also assume that we have agreed upon the KPIs so that our focus is on reviewing the finer points of the display and presentation.

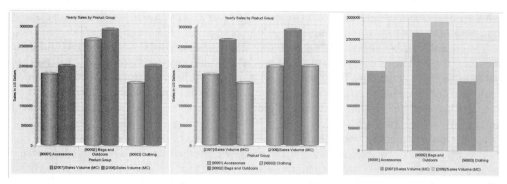

As a reminder, this illustration is a comparison of the three different column templates that we worked on in Chapter 6. Again, because the illustration is in grayscale, we can't really discuss the colors. Suffice it to say that one of the items you would evaluate is the color scheme for the columns, to make sure that it's effective.

Now there's a distinct difference between Chart 1 (far left) and Chart 2 (middle) in terms of presentation of the information. In your mind which approach will allow you to review this information easier and faster so that you can get back to actually running the business based on this analysis? From the two charts we can see that they differ based on the groups of information that are presented. Chart 1 has the groups based on the Product Groups and Chart 2 has the groups based on the Yearly Sales Volume. Same information in both charts but very different approaches to the analysis processes. I personally tend toward the formatting in Chart 1 since I can immediately see the information, understand the results, and based on the interpretation go out and execute a plan. I know that from year to year my sales have gone up for each of the Product Groups. Very straightforward, very direct and gets the information to the business user directly with very little effort on the business user's part to understand the formatting used in this dashboard. In terms of Chart 2 the grouping in Sales Volume is nice but what does that tell us and is it intuitive enough for our purposes? We can't immediately see that the sales from year to year went higher, we also can't tell or are we expected to realize that in each case the sales for each Product Group increased. We also can't really identify from the chart that the overall year-to-year sales volume has increased either. We can attempt to interpret the results but that means opening the door to interpretation and that's not a good thing when it comes to charts that you may find yourself explaining to the corporate world.

Even if we turn the tables a bit and suggest that this dashboard is looking to compare sales in the different Product Groups, will this allow us to suggest that Chart 2 is better at explaining the results than Chart 1? I guess we can give a slight edge to Chart 2 since the Product Groups are together rather than apart but that would still not give a decisive edge to Chart 2 versus Chart 1. Looking at Chart 1 we can still see that comparison very clearly and be able to identify the comparison between Product Groups very quickly and accurately.

So if the appropriate formatting and positioning is completed you will see that it can stand up to a number of views of the analysis.

The overall display and sizing is good for both charts. An initial suggestion would be to adjust the Y-axis. The grid goes from $0.00 to $3,000,000.00, but each Product Group has well over $1,000,000 in sales. The Y-axis could be scaled so that it starts at $1,000,000, which would simplify the charts. Another suggestion would be to move the "Product Group" title for Chart 2 so that the business user doesn't look down from the chart and wonder where the columns are for Product Group.

Now, consider the rightmost chart—Chart 3. It's format of the data is good and the positioning of the information is very similar to Chart 1 but the titles are a bit either nonexistent or scarce. So we don't have any titles up the sides or at the top. You can probably see that this is one dimensional versus the others that are two dimensional and that's OK even though some of the "wow" factor goes away without some tweaking of the colors but I'm not going to say that this is a bad chart template based on the fact that it's only one dimensional. Remember, the focus of these Web templates is the delivery of the information in a consistent and focused approach, not how many dimensions can we use to get the information displayed. So, all in all, we can see that with the basics that we talked about in the previous chapters we can build a useable and consistent Web item for a dashboard.

Before we get into the configuration details of a good dashboard, take a look at the example dashboard shown next, which clearly incorporates all the concepts discussed thus far. This dashboard was built using the SAP BOBJ component Xcelsius and sources the data directly from the BW system using BW queries and BOBJ Universes. Xcelsius has the capability to set up dashboards with every Widget imaginable in terms of graphics, such as tachometers, aircraft cockpits, and off-the-wall graphics, but here the use of the basic column and line chart types with some actual summary reports thrown in looks great.

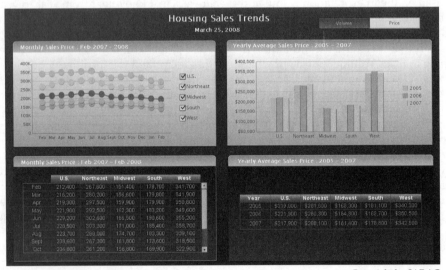

Copyright by SAP AG

Taking a closer look at this dashboard, we see that it has very focused metrics. It presents volume and pricing data for housing sales trends. The space has been used very well. For example, the check boxes for navigation on the line chart type have been incorporated into the display of the chart type. The titles are clear and direct and don't take up a lot of space; Housing Sales Trends comprises only about 5 percent of the total space available.

There is some scrolling in the lower-left report but that is very limited since in this case we are scrolling only 12 months at a time and therefore it will always be the same level of scrolling, which would not be the case if the rows were controlled by something like types of homes where the total number of rows might expand and contract. The yearly average sale price report is well positioned and consistent. We see that the metrics have been structured to between four and six depending on whether you define the use of years as another metric.

This dashboard is direct and focused—Monthly Sales Price and Yearly Average Sales Price with additional historic perspective based on information from 2005 through 2007, then details by Month for 2008. Again, in this case the color is used to identify the primary metrics—top two charts and then it draws your eyes to the lower two reports. I would have used a different background color so that the bottom two reports are not as minimized as they actually are due to the darker black against lighter black background.

The coloring that is going on is very basic, no highlights or fading activities and the scaling is clear and consistent. I believe that there should also be a third button at the top of this dashboard—Price, Volume, and Price/Volume Analysis since we can gather much more information if we integrated these two sets of metrics into an overall analysis but that would have depended on the report requirements and this would be second-guessing the development requirements. In that case, I would have offered an additional prototype dashboard with the additional button to draw the business user's attention to this possibility. Since we have about 4–5 metrics on each of the screens it would be reasonable to have an additional button for a total of 12–15 metrics for this dashboard. You can also see that there are only four boxes in front of the business analysts. This immediately gets the analyst what they need with no assumptions or guessing required by the analyst. This is a good, solid, well-designed dashboard and takes into account the needs of the business analyst and also of the BI system.

Now, let's take the lessons learned from the previous examples and apply them to another dashboard and dig into the details of the actual architecture in the WAD in the process. Remember, you first need to have your sources of data correctly formatted and ready to go for the different chart types that you will be presenting. So, you should have already decided on the chart types, reached consensus on the KPIs, and gotten the data sourced appropriately defined to make the configuration process easier and more focused on the design and display than on the data. Nothing is as frustrating as developing the entire dashboard and then executing it only to find that the information that you expected to see is not there. In this case, I'm going to adjust the format to scale into the thousands to help clear some space on the screen next to the Y-axis. The next illustration shows the same chart and chart type with different scaling. You can see that it's a bit clearer with the scaling turned on, but remember that you have to identify the change in the scaling factor somewhere in your titles. Also, remember that scaling might affect other charts in your dashboard, but as long as all the amounts are going to be scalable, then making the adjustment to the display is safe.

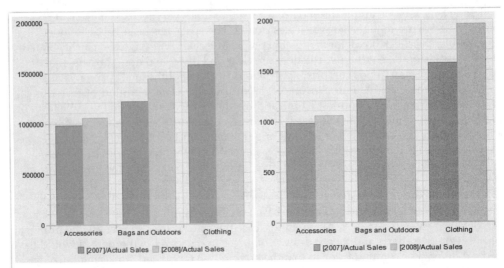

So, for this example I have a series of metrics that we will apply to a dashboard and integrate as many of the concepts we discussed as possible. My metrics are going to be Actual Sales, Cost of Goods, Incoming Orders, and Planned Sales, with a comparison between 2007 and 2008 information with a calculated value showing the Average Price/Unit and the Average Cost/Unit. In addition I'll be applying several parameters to each of the charts. Please refer to the previous chapter for additional details about the formatting and configuration of the queries that will support these types of charts. Initially I will scale everything to the thousands as we did in the previous example and also turn on the Swap Display Axis parameter for each chart type on the Web Item Parameter list. This can be seen in the illustration at right.

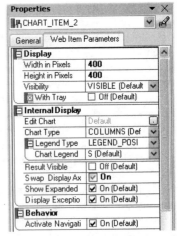

For each metric we will use suitable chart types but again the one thing that we will have a difficult time showing here is the color scheme. Just to say that in each case we have different colors for each of the series in the chart types. I will adjust the font level for the primary metric in the chart but I could have also changed the color to emphasize the primary metric. This dashboard will be straightforward in nature and what I mean by that is we will not focus on additional items within the dashboard such as variables, text, information, hyperlinks, etc., but look to generate a good, solid, consistent dashboard and leave the bells and whistles for further discussions within your company. These are parameters that should be identified in the requirements document and then prototyped for the business users. The next illustration is the finished product for our dashboard discussion. As you well know, there are many components to the development of a dashboard and what I've done here is to develop a dashboard that will tell the appropriate story and a bit more just so that the business analyst starts to ask additional questions and possibly decides that there are additional KPIs that they need over time and rather than these specific KPIs shown here, they may require adjusted information over time.

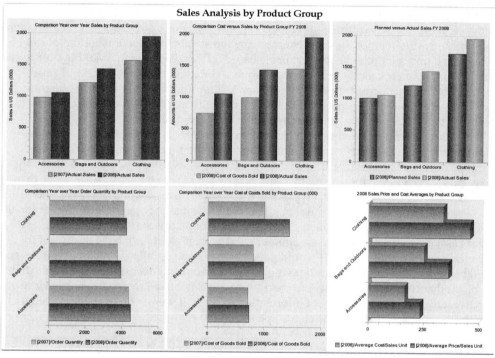

This dashboard is titled "Sales Analysis by Product Group" and for this example we will accept that the default information around the required KPIs for this dashboard is accurate. As you can see we have six KPIs with two key figures per view and a total of six views. If I do the mathematics correctly we are looking at 12 KPIs for the business analyst to assimilate at one time. This is a reasonable amount of information for the business user to assimilate. In this example we presented the high-level information and summary by year for all of the metrics. We could have added something in terms of a period analysis rather than a yearly analysis or we could also have set up something for a Year to Date analysis for 2009. These are excellent additions that could have been made and we could have added these additional metrics to this dashboard but as we mentioned before, we don't want to cram tons of metrics onto one dashboard. If there are more we either a) use a tab page to add additional layers to the dashboard and assign an appropriate title such as "Periodic Sales Analysis YTD 2009 by Product Group" and this would have all of the same indicators as the current view of this dashboard but at the period level rather than the yearly level, or b) use some sort of drill-through to get to the additional detailed analysis.

Let's look at this based on the discussion we had earlier in this chapter. In the case of clear titles and descriptions I think we can see that everything is well spelled out and consistent in nature. There are no assumptions that the user has to make in understanding what these metrics are talking about. If I were to give this to someone who didn't have any idea of what these metrics were all about they would be able to immediately identify the information and be able to make some specific statements about the Sales and Costs for the years 2007 and 2008. (As a matter of fact I did do this with two other consultants and ask them to explain to me what this dashboard was describing and within 20 seconds they were both able to explain at least three different components of this dashboard.) The color scheme is significantly different for the metrics across the top versus those on the bottom portion of the screen. If this color scheme was available based on this display you would be able to see that there is one metric that is graphically unique and that is 2008 Sales Price and Cost Averages by Product Group. This is the primary KPI for this dashboard. I've highlighted it both with colors and also with a 2.5D chart type rather than a one-dimensional display, to identify it to the business analyst as soon as they open the dashboard.

The titles and headers do not take up a disproportionate amount of space, and the information for the bar chart types is set to diagonal so that it doesn't use up excessive space for the Y-axis headings. Each chart that is identified as Sales or Costs is scaled to the thousandths to conserve the space otherwise taken up by the extra zeros. Also notice that the maximum for each of the chart types will increase as the total values increase, and in all cases the scaling on the Y-axis is the same. This offers the analyst one uniform format for all the charts across the top and another uniform format for all the charts on the bottom. In this case, if we had decided to use another chart type, it would not have improved the statistical analysis available but it would have given it some additional eye candy. We even could have used the column chart type for all the metrics, but I decided to incorporate the use of another chart type, and the line chart type would not have worked correctly since there is really no history or range of information to chart. If we were to use period versus year for the analysis, then the line chart type would have worked.

As for configuration, if you look at one of the views of the data, you can see what was necessary to configure these Chart Web items. Initially, I had to format the view and get it to display consistently—diagram directly over diagram, center the dashboard title, and so forth—and to do this I used my favorite initial approach: insert a table. Once I accessed the WAD, I inserted a table into the design work area and inserted six Chart Web items into each of the cells. As shown in the illustration at right, I set the table to a 3×3 format and, to make the charts consistent and eliminate the gap between the charts, adjusted the width to 75%.

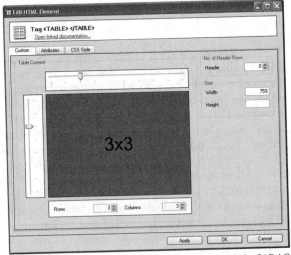

I typed the dashboard title into the middle space of the first row of the table and adjusted the font to bold and adjusted the texture and size of the typed header as shown in the next illustration.

Help													
‹›	Book Antiqua	▾	5	▾	**B**	*I*							

Overview

Sales Analysis by Product Group

: YSALES_BY_YEAR_001 (Sales by Year Tem		CHART_ITEM_4 DP_5: YSALES_COST_TEMPLATE_001 (Sales and		CHART_ITEM_3 DP

As for each of the chart types, I did several formatting adjustments, but all of the parameters are available directly from the Edit Chart Designer component. Initially I used the wizard to assign the titles to each of the axes and to the top of the chart. This is shown in the following illustration. It's important that you fill in all three titles—Category, Value Axis, and actual Title.

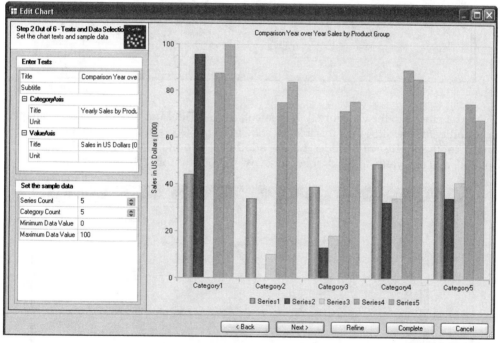

Once I finished in the wizard, I clicked Refine to enter the Chart Designer, shown next, to adjust the display parameter for one of the titles so that more room is available in the dashboard. I adjusted the format of the Block Style to Cylinder from Rectangle to give the columns more depth.

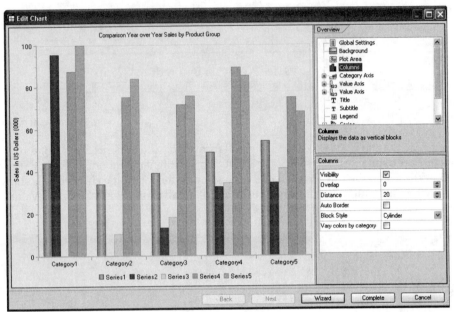

Next, I moved to the Category Axis element, clicked Title, and turned off the parameter for Visibility for the title along this axis, as shown next. This created more room for the statistics at the expense of the titles, but the additional information offered by the title wouldn't add any value to the dashboard anyway. I did this for each of the charts.

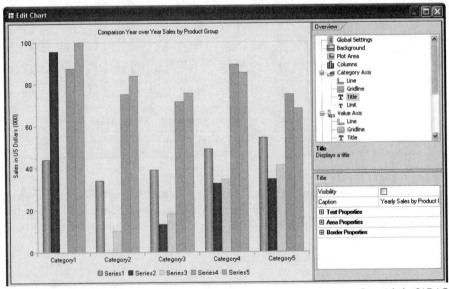

I then turned off all the gridlines for each of the charts. This clears up the background of each of the charts and helps visually identify the information. It also helps with increased performance of the whole dashboard. Another parameter I adjusted is the coloring of each of the columns. I used the same approach shown in the previous examples and used both the primary and secondary colors to enhance the depth and visual appeal and used the gradient to include the two levels of color onto each of the columns. These settings can be seen in the following illustration.

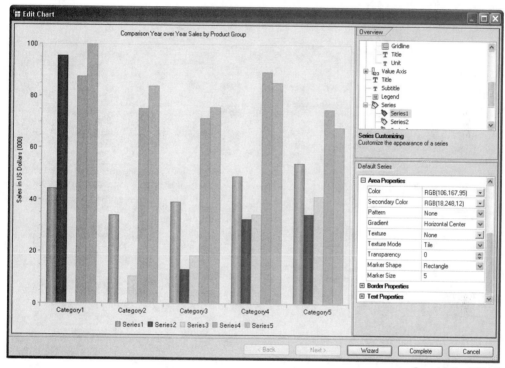

For the bar chart type used for the averages, I turned on the 2.5D view of the bars and adjusted the titles for the Y-axis to diagonal. To increase the display view of the information, I adjusted two parameters in the Web Item Parameters tab in the WAD. First, I increased the width and height of the pixels from the default 300 each to 400 each. Second, I used the parameter Swap Display Axis for each of the charts to make sure that the data structures can be formatted to the chart type.

After making these adjustments, the dashboard was complete. Although this dashboard doesn't have any "wow" factor, it does have a solid and consistent look and feel that would be very inviting to an analyst who just wants to be able to get the information they need from the KPIs to run the business and then work to improve those metrics.

Let's take a look at another dashboard, for Sales Analysis, shown next. In this case, the KPIs being used are more practical, meaning they include not only indicators that give us information about the results but also leading indicators that will help us in terms of growing a business. The KPIs include customer satisfaction, actual order value, and market share. With these types of leading KPIs, we can estimate the growth of the company and make critical decisions about its overall health. Again, the dashboard doesn't include large amounts of nonessential graphics or objects, enabling the business user to quickly understand the information and make the required decisions. The color scheme is basic, not bright and distracting. The KPIs use a very similar color scheme except the primary KPI, so that it attracts the business analyst's attention first. It is also a different chart type.

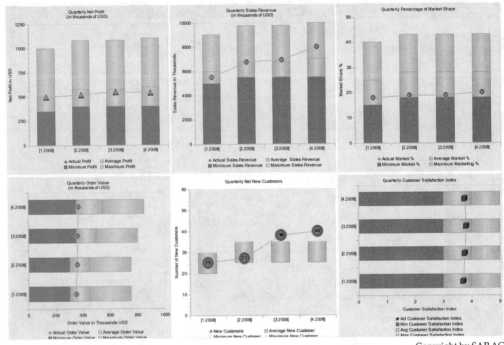

This dashboard incorporates several chart types—stacked column, waterfall, and stacked bar. These offer a good vehicle to illustrate the indicators well and drive home the results. The dashboard doesn't incorporate additional objects, such as List of Values; for example, we could have shown a series of regions with this information divided among them and offered a Radio Button Group to toggle between each of these different regions. We could also have set up variables or check boxes to help with this process. All these additional components are available and are fairly straightforward to incorporate into your dashboard. You will need to adjust the spacing for these different options and therefore possibly move from having 12 KPIs per screen to 10 KPIs, with the additional space allocated to either corporate logos or the components just mentioned. Basically, the enhancements that you can make to the dashboard process are limitless.

This Sales Analysis dashboard shows a series of indicators with formats that will help business users to understand and identify critical KPIs and immediately grasp the point of the information. Notice that we have switched to the *stacked* approach for this information due to its nature. Basically, there is only one actual value per view on this dashboard, and the other information is for analysis against planned information. So in this case, rather than having a dashboard with two lines—one for planned and one for actual information—we have *ranges* of information for planned or expected levels of each of the indicators. This will provide the business analysts additional information and enable them to compare the overall growth and progression of each of the indicators.

Which KPI business users are supposed to look at and understand immediately upon opening this dashboard should be clear; the overall structure of the lower-middle view is dramatically different from the others. The waterfall chart type displays this information in a manner that is unique but also very direct and focused. Business users can immediately see that there has been an increase in the overall progress of capturing new customers. The company has increased the number of new customers from 25 in the first quarter to 40 in the fourth quarter of 2008.

Now, additional information can be used to understand in more detail what 40 customers in Q4 means to us. If we were to have added an indicator around the total current customers and then a comparison between where we were versus where we are, that would be helpful. Also, the customer profitability would have added additional information of importance to this discussion. But we are looking to get specific information immediately to the executives and management so the critical number is the actual additional customers added. This immediately offers inherent information that we are moving to be more profitable since additional customers hopefully means that we will be seeing additional revenues from these new clients. We can definitely see that in Q1 we only had a net 25 new customers and therefore during the year we are doing a better job of looking for and adding to the new customer list. In any case, we can immediately see that the range that we would like to be in is the section of the range that is highlighted with color and is identified by the cylindrical shape. This can be seen in more detail in the following illustration.

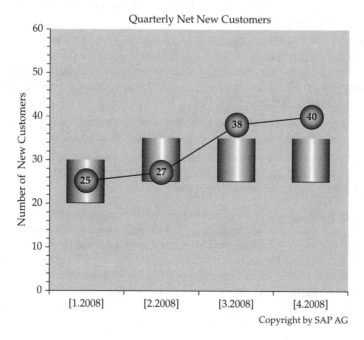

Quarterly Net New Customers

Copyright by SAP AG

In this dashboard view, the information is very clear—quarterly net new customers. Display of the actual number has been turned on so that the business analyst doesn't have to scroll over the information to see the total number per quarter, which is a time-saver for them. They can also see all four values at the same time, whereas with scrolling they would see only one value at a time.

Let's back away for a moment and review the entire Sales Analysis dashboard. There are certain items that we need to review and validate to ensure that we have incorporated as many best business practices as possible into this dashboard. So, if we look at each of the areas of formatting, we see several pros:

- All the titles and informational items on this dashboard are consistent. Therefore, once you understand one title and chart range information, you can understand the others. This reduces the amount of time required to get comfortable with each chart type and their individual titles and subtitles.

- All of the color schemes are the same. To achieve this, I created one template object and then just copied it to another object. I had to make additional changes and fixes to the copied object, but having a starting point saved time and ensured consistency.

- The total number of KPIs is 9 to 12—depending on the approach that you use to count them. We have six actual KPIs, but in addition we have the same three indicators for each and this outlines the ranges of Maximum, Average, and Minimum for each indicator. These can be classified as three additional indicators.

- The amount of graphics used is consistent with the required look and feel and will not affect the performance of the dashboard.

- Subtitles and titles are consistent for each of the charts. For the subtitle, if it's a stacked bar, the subtitle is below, and if it's a stacked column, the subtitle is to the left side of the screen.

- Business users can easily understand and focus on each of the indicators. I conducted my own test on this dashboard and asked several people who are not involved with BI to look at it for the first time and tell me what they think. Within the allotted 20 seconds per KPI, all were able to understand the information and give one conclusion from the overall dashboard.

- The scaling is consistent and everyone is scaled to the thousands rather than in some with different scaling factors. This dashboard has all at one scaling factor level.

- In each case, the business analysts used in the test case were attracted to the lower-level indicator first, and then started reviewing the other charts. This would validate the approach that I took to highlight the critical KPI.

As mentioned previously, the format of the query that supports this dashboard is as critical as what chart type is chosen to display this information. In this case we are using queries with four columns—Lowest Level, Average Level, Highest Level, and then the Actual itself. This will allow the series within the chart type to pick up the appropriate information by column. This drives home the need to have the correct query to support the correct chart type. Now the trick to developing this chart type is that the initial three column values of the queries need to be the differences rather than the total. So, your Lowest Level is the total amount used—in the case of Sales Revenue, it would be $500,000,000.00 (scaled in the graph). Now, the Average is actually $600,000,000.00 but in your InfoCube you are storing the difference or in the query you are calculating the difference—so the Average is actually $100,000,000.00. Using the average number of $100,000,000.00 and using the Stack option for the bar chart type you get the $600,000,000.00. You do the same for the Highest Level, and when it is presented on the chart, you get your correct sections for the ranges.

To configure this dashboard, I again started with a table in the WAD. I then added the required Web items—Column and Bar Chart types. Just remember that if you need to adjust the size of the table, you should use the option to reduce the size. This will help eliminate any spaces between the chart types. I've used 80% in this case to help structure the Web items as well.

Now the rest of the configuration for the stacked columns comes into play with the series formatting. Within the wizard, I assigned the chart type stacked columns and then switched to the Refine approach to get to each of the series to configure at that level, as shown next. Using the different shades of color helps emphasize the sections of the stack.

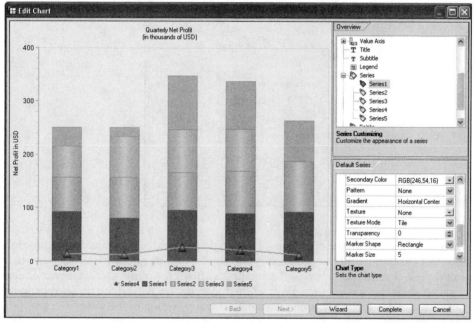

For Series4, I changed the look and feel via the Refine view to the line chart type and also adjusted the format of the Area Property. In this configuration, I adjusted several items, as shown in the next illustration:

- I changed the Chart Type to Lines.
- In the Area Properties, I adjusted the two colors—Color and Secondary Color.
- In the Area Properties, I adjusted the Marker Shape to Triangle.

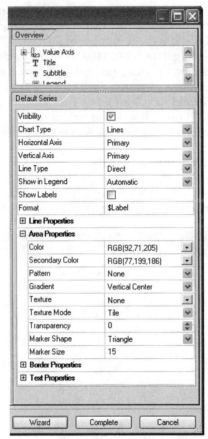

In the case of the waterfall chart type, I had to do a couple of additional configuration changes, but I used the same stacked column to start, and then just worked with the colors within the series to make them invisible, creating a "floating" center section. I created that type of chart in about five minutes. With a little touch-up, I achieved the finished product. The next illustration shows the configuration for the top section of the waterfall chart—I didn't really make the section invisible but rather made it blend with the background so that the color is the same as the background color. That's the trick.

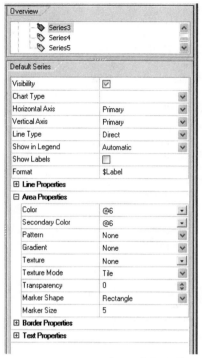

Copyright by SAP AG

To complete this, we can now look at Series4, which is the line chart type. In this case, I adjusted the look and feel of the line and marker itself. As shown in the following illustration, I enlarged the size of the marker so that the complete value can be seen within the object. I adjusted this to a size of 30, and chose Circle for the Marker Shape. Finally, I turned on the (visible parameter) Show Labels option. The important item here is to leave the Format field blank. This will allow the values to show up as absolutes rather than fighting with currency or unit of measure (UOM) signs.

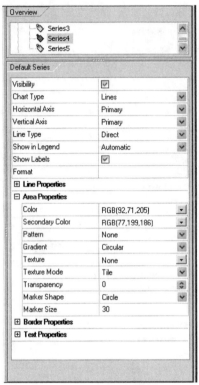

The additional configuration is very similar to that of the previous dashboard. All in all, this is a consistent dashboard and will accommodate many different requirements by your customers. Yes, you could get really fancy and add all the bells and whistles, even going as far as creating your own HTML that you type directly into the XHTML tab within the WAD. If you want items that consist of links to other formatting options that are not available within the WAD or links to other systems, you will have to use this functionality. All in all the WAD component of BI to help with the display of our KPIs within a dashboard format.

If we take this configuration and go just one step further using the Visual Composer (VC) toolset, we can see the finished results of a dashboard. Now this example has more dynamic visual appeal, but the basic information that you see is very similar to what we just developed from the WAD. The next illustration shows the finished product of a WAD-developed report in VC. You can see that this type of data is very similar to what we've reviewed, but now the "wow" factor comes into play.

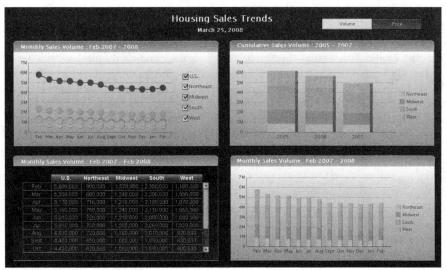

The shading of the chart background, different approaches to use of variables in the report, and just overall eye appeal is much better in this example versus what we just created in the WAD. We could easily have included the variables, radio buttons, navigation pane, and so forth into this dashboard, but you can see that this will be fairly straightforward. Look at this final dashboard closely and see what you think. I believe that this dashboard is a great example of what a true dashboard should look like. Be selective with what is incorporated into your dashboards. If your business user is interested in having what-if scenarios available on a dashboard, think about putting this type of chart type on a separate tab within your dashboard. This will make very clear what is required reading versus what is available to use for estimates.

Summary

In this chapter we looked at as much functional information as we did system information. The focus was as much on configuration of the dashboards as it was on the development of the concepts around the dashboards. I wanted it to be that way since we mentioned that building these dashboards is as much an art as it is a science. What's the saying—you need to *be* the dashboard—so that you can understand what and how to put everything into one frame and get everything out to the analyst, CEO, or production manager as quickly and as effectively as possible. Your main goal here is to support the business, not control the business. So, take this opportunity to make sure that all of the hard work that just went into the architecture of this critical information warehouse is going to be able to support the reports that are required. It's a challenge to do this right and make sure you're focused on the overall picture rather than the latest and greatest software system. I'm all for innovation and moving to the best system possible but not at the price of sacrificing the reporting process. We say this many times, information is the most critical resource that a company has after its human resources but for some reason we sometimes seem to lose track of that fact and before your focus comes back onto the goals of the company you're looking at a business situation like the history of Woolworths versus Walmart, or for those a bit younger the analogy would be something like the history of Circuit City and Best Buy.

We didn't overkill the actual configuration of the dashboards themselves since many of us have already worked on some sort of dashboarding and in some cases have developed more WAD templates than we could ever develop and display in this one chapter. Your particular dashboard will be successful well before you start configuration. It will be a success or failure based on the display process and development of the particular display depending on the requirements. There are numerous items within this chapter that I hope you use during the development of corporate dashboards, cockpits, billboards, or whatever the titles of these items will be in the next generation of BI, but the one primary point I would like to make is to question the business user in detail. You are the one that has the knowledge of what a dashboard can and can't do and what will display appropriately. But, if you ask many business users what they want, the answer is "everything" and, regretfully, that is what I see quite a bit—a dashboard that has *everything*.

Migrating 3.x to 7.0 BEx Web Reports and the WAD

This chapter takes us a bit off of the track in terms of building dynamic Web templates or dashboards but I believe it's important and there are many companies that are looking to either a) understand the process or b) find out what the pros and cons are for the migration of the BEx Web Analyzer and the WAD templates. This would be a great process to know and understand when talking with your customers. It's definitely a plus when you are looking at a transition project from a 3.x to a 7.0 system. This task—migration of reports, both the basic BEx Web Analyzer reports as well as the more advanced WAD reports—will allow you to get involved in another aspect of the whole BW/BI landscape. The basic concept and approach seems simple enough but as you well know, the devil is in the details and this is the case in some areas of migration of Web reports. We will be covering the process in detail for the Web-based reports—both basic and WAD templates—but we will not really go into too much detail around the migration process for the BEx workbooks since this is more on the BEx Analyzer side rather than on the Web side. I do realize that we can have workbooks in the Web and the requirements around migration of the workbooks may come into play. It's just that if we start to include this additional component in detail we then start to find ourselves talking about the migration of the Information Broadcaster, the BI Portal components, and other items not directly related to our discussion. There is some good documentation on each of these processes on some of the SAP-related Web sites as well as the help.sap.com Web site.

The critical part of this whole migration process doesn't really have anything to do with the system process but with the reporting strategy that your customer has adopted. If we get the right reports at the right time migrated, then everyone is happy, including the business users. This chapter is presented in three parts. Initially, we will discuss the overall migration activity. Next, we will examine the individual components involved in migration. Finally, we will work our way through the migration activity via a process-oriented approach.

Overview of the Migration Process

The migration process from 3.x to 7.0 for the Web-based reports is fairly straightforward. As long as you follow the steps in sequence, all should go well. If you skip steps or perform them out of sequence, you may run into issues with the migration process. If we look at the overall question of "why" to migrate reports from 3.x to 7.0, we have to look to the business user for the answer. The decision to migrate is definitely more of a business one rather than a technical one. With the current version in BI, a company can have all the backend functionality up on the 7.0 version objects but keep all the frontend components on the 3.x version. It may decide, simply because everything is working well in 3.x, that there are no additional business requirements to move forward with the migration process for the reports.

Companies that have implemented a version of BW prior to NetWeaver BI 7.0 and are evaluating whether to migrate have to consider both how they will implement the many new functions available and how existing objects will be migrated. The 7.0 components offer a ton of new functionality, and if a company wants to take advantage of these options, it has to migrate to the 7.0 frontend toolset. If you are experiencing too many gaps in reporting based on the functionality in 3.x, then migration to 7.0 is the way to go. If, on the other hand, you see that in some cases (for example, BEx workbooks) there is little or no gap between what the business user needs and what they currently have, then migration of these components would not be required. The great thing about the 7.0 platform is that it will support both versions of these reports at the same time, so you can migrate based on customer (business user) requirements and demands. You would just have to manage the process of accessing the reports and workbooks based on the version required to run them and avoid converting a report or workbook by mistake. This can present its own challenges, which we will talk about later in this chapter. The impact of the changes from 3.x to 7.0 to the reporting objects includes a complete change to the BEx Query Designer, queries, workbooks, Web templates, and additional new components such as the Information Broadcaster (new in the platform due to the fact that it is running against—Java rather than ABAP stack). Other objects, such as the use of structures in the queries and RKF and CKF functionality, have changed also.

With the BI 7.0 system, new tools and a new runtime process are available in the BEx Web Analyzer and BEx Analyzer. This critical change means that now the Web portion is running on the Java stack rather than on the ABAP stack. Figure 8-1 shows this process.

As you can see, the BEx Analyzer runs on the ABAP stack while the BEx Web Analyzer and all the new components run on the Java stack. This allows a distinct separation between the two sets of tools and offers the Web-based reports more flexibility and functionality. This also makes a change to the approach in terms of performance tuning and a different set of components to help with this effort. Within the BI 7.0 J2EE engine, a runtime layer is formed supporting the BEx Broadcaster, BEx Web, Integrated Planning, and Knowledge Management functions of the SAP Net Weaver 7.0 BI (2004S). Also, included in this architecture is the new Adobe Document service to support Web-based printing. With the NW BI 7.0 reporting component, new tools and a new runtime are available with all the frontend tools using the Web. At the same time, all the previous tools and the Web runtime from the BI 3.X are delivered in order to make sure that a step-by-step, business-driven transition is followed. It's important to note the following so that you understand some of the distinct differences between the two options:

- All the new frontend features are only available with the new NW BI 7.0 component.
- Objects created with the new 7.0 tools can no longer be edited with the 3.x BEx tools.
- The 3.x BEx tools are delivered to support editing of existing scenarios.

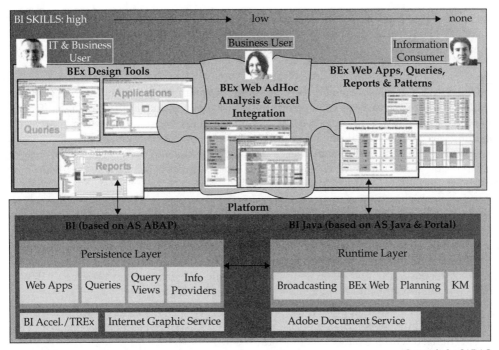

FIGURE 8-1 Platform used by 3.x and BI 7.0 reporting

- The 3.x BEx tools are usable on the new SAP NW BI 7.0 server. Therefore, you will have two sets of components that you can use directly from the same context menu.

- Conversion of 3.x objects is done on an "as needed" basis and no mass conversions are possible.

- Except for queries, converted objects are stored as new objects. Old objects are never automatically deleted.

- The recommendation is to make the change step by step, because further new features will only be made for the new tools.

- Generally speaking, once an object is converted, you will not be able to open that object with the 3.x components. Therefore, it is a good idea to create a copy of the existing objects just to have a backup during the migration.

As mentioned, NW BI 7.0 is shipped complete with both the BEx toolset for NetWeaver BI 7.0 and the BEx toolset for BW 3.5. To support these two toolsets, two distinct runtimes are delivered with the NetWeaver BI 7.0 system. The new BI toolset offers many new and important features, and these tools are the only ones that can be used with the new frontend functionality in BI. These tools are all members of the Business Explorer family and include the BEx Query Designer, BEx Analyzer, BEx Web Application Designer, and BEx Report Designer.

> **NOTE** *Since the BI system is delivered with both component reporting tools—3.x and 7.0—deactivating one of the two toolsets is an option. This will avoid any issues with opening a report in the incorrect frontend toolset and therefore possibly corrupting the report itself. Choosing this option requires some adjustments by your system support team.*

Objects that have been created with the new toolset cannot be further maintained with the BW 3.x toolset. In this case, SAP needs to supply this component (3.x functionality to run BEx Reports) to support customers that continue to use and maintain their existing reporting objects. The actual migration process for a reporting object takes place when a BW 3.x reporting object is opened using the relevant new BI tool and then saved. The details of the migration process are specific to the type of reporting object to be migrated. A summary of some important information follows:

- All existing SAP BW 3.x queries can be edited with the SAP NW 7.0 BEx Query Designer without further manual adaptation. Therefore, you can open any BW 3.x reports in the Query Designer in the 7.0 version without any additional configuration.

- After editing with the new tool, queries can no longer be edited with the SAP BW 3.x component, and this includes the 3.x BEx Query Designer.

- Any queries created or adapted with the SAP NW 7.0 BEx Query Designer will appear in the Open dialog box of the SAP BW 3.x tool but can't be opened or changed with the older version of the tools.

- Query views that were created using the 3.x functionality will still run after a query has been changed with the new BEx Query Designer and will also be available in the BEx Web 7.0 frontend without any migration. Therefore, query views will move over to the new 7.0 NW BI frontend tools automatically.

The BEx Query Designer is the solo tool in NW BI 7.0 that allows the creation and maintenance of query objects. The BI 7.0 version of the BEx Query Designer has been totally rewritten as a .NET Visual Basic application, complete with a redesigned user interface and numerous new features and capabilities.

The act of opening a BW 3.x query with the new BEx Query Designer and then saving that query will migrate it from the old version to the new BI version. Again, once this has occurred, it is no longer accessible by the BW 3.x BEx Query Designer. Interestingly, it will still be visible in the list of queries using the 3.x frontend component but will not be available to execute via this frontend.

Figure 8-2 shows the possible scenarios with both BW 3.x and BI versions of queries. Each version of the query can be opened, maintained, and saved using the respective version of the BEx Query Designer. During the process of migration, the object—queries in this case—will be saved with the same internal name but with a different version and possibly in a different table. Table RSZCOMPDIR contains a listing of query objects, their internal names, and their content release level. You can find this table by using one of the SE*xx* transaction codes in the system and normally the SE16 is available to most users. On a more detailed level, if you have a value of 100 or more in the Version field for a query, this indicates that the query has been migrated to the NW BI 7.0 version.

Checking the Version field is a very easy approach to track and manage the migration of the queries. Several SAP Notes are available that address the scenarios for backing up your

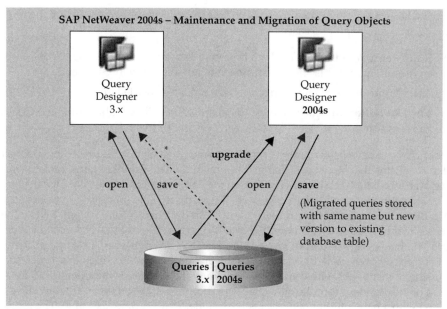

* Visible but cannot be opened

Copyright by SAP AG

FIGURE 8-2   BEx Query Designer—scenarios for migration

3.x queries before migration, and I would suggest using this backup process more for the workbooks than for the queries. In terms of the WAD templates, this migration process is a bit different in nature but the requirement for a backup query is not as critical as it is for the workbooks. The migration of HTML and XHTML is more forgiving than the migration of VBA. Also note that if you are converting a reusable component such as a variable, restricted key figure, or calculated key figure, all queries that use this component can be maintained only with the new BEx Query Designer. This can be especially important when you are looking to manage and migrate the reports on an as-needed basis. If you don't watch out for this, you may end up having to migrate all the reports prematurely.

As the preceding discussion indicates, the planning process for migration is important and critical to the business users. If you intend to restrict their access to either the new BI 7.0 toolset or the 3.x BW toolset, SAP Note 962530 will help you with this process. Basically, lock out everyone from using one or the other component so that no mistakes are made in the initial process. This will also be useful until everyone that is required to has had additional training on the new reporting components. Then, you can release the access as your company is rolling out the new frontend components and functionality.

In the case of the BEx Web Application Designer for NW BI 7.0, a complete redesign of the platform and the functionality has occurred. It has been redesigned as a .NET Visual Basic application and is delivered with numerous new features and functionality to enhance the Web-based reports in BI. Similar to the BEx Query Designer, SAP delivers a BW 3.x version to support the use and maintenance of existing BW 3.x Web applications. In the new version of the BEx WAD, additional Web items have been added and some of the 3.x Web items have been removed. This adjustment means that some rework of existing Web templates may be necessary when they are migrated to the NW 7.0 version. Following are some of the missing Web items that were popular to use:

- **Role Menu Web item**   This Web item can be transported into the BI 7.0 environment, but this specific approach is not a best business practice.
- **Alert Monitor Web item**   This has been replaced by the Universal Worklist (UWL).
- **The List option for query views**   This option is still available but in the Consumer Patterns component (see Chapter 2 for a review of this component).

Other changes have been made within the overall process, but the preceding are the more popular Web items that have been changed or replaced. With these changes, some rework of existing Web templates may be necessary once they are migrated to the NW 7.0 version. Also, the JavaScript functions and enhancements made with the Table Interface component of the WAD in BW 3.x will need to be manually adapted. In the next section, we will review the differences that may occur while migrating the WAD templates, with a basic example of the XHTML that is generated upon migration. If the BW 3.x Web template contains items that are not supported in the new BI 7.0 routine, they are removed in the migration process and new version of that object with comments explaining the reason for the change and the omission of the old item from the new template are inserted. When the new template is saved, it is stored with a new internal name and status in the separate database table. This leaves the original version of the Web template intact so that it can be migrated again, if necessary. The new version of the Web template will not be useable from the BW 3.x WAD. Figure 8-3 shows the different scenarios of the migration and maintenance of the BEx WAD.

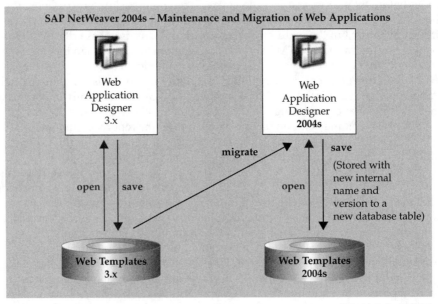

Copyright by SAP AG

FIGURE 8-3   Options for migration with the BEx Web Application Designer

The migration process for BEx WAD templates is very different from that for the BEx queries. You will use the migration tool in the NW 7.0 BEx WAD. This is an easy and quick approach to migrating existing WAD templates. Unfortunately, the migration tool will not convert some elements, such as JavaScript used to create tab pages in the older version or the BEx Web Designer API tables. These elements must be rebuilt using the standard delivered Web items in the BI 7.0 WAD. With this in mind, it may be an option in some cases, to rebuild the Web templates directly rather than rely on the migration tool. This probably is not going to be as intense a task as you might think, because many of the different objects that we had to build from scratch in 3.x are now standard delivered Web items in 7.0, such as the Tab Pages Web item and the command wizard option in BI 7.0.

Approach to Migration of Web-Based Reports

There are a number of different aspects that we need to understand around this process and the success of a migration is not only due to the system process but also relies on the business and political environment at each company. You will have to do a complete due-diligence process initially so that you will not fall into any of the potholes embedded in the business culture. This due diligence requires a round or two of meetings with all the different groups that will be affected by the migration. You should very carefully pull together a hierarchical list of the critical issues and challenges that you might encounter during a migration process. The migration process can be overwhelming without a list of items that you can check off as you complete them.

A good first step in the migration process is to clean up business users' Favorites folders. Business users tend to assign frequently used reports and other objects to their Favorites folders but fail to get them changed over to standard reports. The issue is that nothing in the Favorites folder is migrated. So, you need to find out which of these reports and objects lurking in the Favorites folders of each department, group, and team need to be moved over to a folder within a specific role so that they can be migrated. You also need to come up with a strategy for moving them, including the variants associated with them. You'll need to explain to business users which reports are candidates for being moved. For example, if a business user has 75 reports in their Favorites folder, you need to instruct them to identify and list the reports that are essential to performing their job. Then, you need to follow the company process for moving them to the appropriate role and folder. Getting business users to give up less than all their favorites is not as easy as it may seem, but with a little nudging and some time limits (always put a time limit on this task), everyone will come up with a list.

Great, you have completed your first task in the migration process. Now, you need to decide on which approach to use to do the migration. Following are some questions to consider:

- Go with a big bang approach and migrate everything in one session, or migrate the reports in phases?

- Migrate the reports of each department based on need or requirements, or start with the group that has the smallest list of reports and go from top to bottom via that approach?

- Start with the group that needs the most help with VBA or customized reports with numerous custom APIs or lots of broadcasting, or do this group last?

Whichever approach to migration you choose, make sure you establish some justification for it so that you have answers ready when users begin to question your timing. What I try to do is understand the client's needs and timeline and then look at several aspects that would make or break the client's project, and then I make the choice based on those criteria. There is not a strict rule for which approach to take, so it is more of an art than a science.

You need to make sure that you minimize complications in whichever approach you take; in other words, make the process as easy and as straightforward as possible. Avoid a migration where 50 percent of the reports for a department are migrated and the other 50 percent are still using the 3.x toolset for reporting. The user is bound to get frustrated and use the wrong toolset, creating even more issues. Take a step-by-step approach so that everyone can understand and feel comfortable with the migration process. Importantly, you must inform business users about the migration process beforehand. Conduct learning sessions, both formal and informal, where you demonstrate the functionality of the system so that the business users are comfortable with the change. Demonstrate the newer functions of BI 7.0 reporting, such as the additional flexibility of the Information Broadcaster, the use of calculations within the frontend of the Web report, or the numerous new functions in the Web template and what's behind each of the buttons on the screen—exceptions, conditions, all the key figure attributes, and so forth. In my experience, the more I demonstrate functionality and talk to the business users, the lower the total number of defects I have to deal with and the more directly I can work with business users to resolve problems.

If you have 100 business users who are migrating reports that they've been working with for years, you really need to train them on the new reporting functions thoroughly. This will definitely reduce the complications when going live and eliminate much of the lower-level complaints about the new reporting tools. You will definitely reduce the number of comments like "this reporting toolset doesn't work the same as my former frontend" or "this reporting component doesn't do everything that the other frontend did." If you demonstrate the functionality that has changed, you can avoid issues down the road. For example, there is a significant change to the process of inserting a query into a workbook. The 3.x version has a command on the context menu—Insert Query. In the 7.0 version, that option is gone and you have to follow specific steps to insert a query into a workbook. The reason for this is the use of the two different support stacks—ABAP and Java. In this case, demonstrate the multiple steps required. Following are some of the other changes you might consider demonstrating:

- In the BEx workbook, the use of the Insert Query function has been replaced with the use of the "design mode" toolbar to assign the different objects from the query into the workbook (for example, navigation pane, analysis grid, and information). A one-step process has changed to a six-step process.

- In the BEx query, the entire view has changed because the basic template has changed from a tab-based view to a button-based view.

- In the WAD template process, the Role Menu Web item has been eliminated and the Map Web item is only available in the WAD and not the BEx Web Query.

- The navigation process within the BEx Analyzer and the BEx Web Analyzer has changed. Training material will be needed to make the transition to the BI 7.0 environment consistent and straightforward.

To avoid confusion during the migration, make sure everyone in the company knows well beforehand when it is going to occur. This boils down to administrative activities mostly and all very critical. As you start to move closer to the go live date, make sure all users are aware of the timeline, and give them updates if anything is going to change. Also, in terms of planning the migration itself, try to make the reporting shift during a time when the business users have an opportunity to make sure they have everything they need to do their jobs. Try to do the migration over a weekend or during a slow time of the period. Avoid doing the migration right before a period closing or some other very important or critical activity. This will avoid confusion and make everyone proactive in their approach to the migration.

Another area to be aware of is compatibility issues or accidental migrations. Avoiding any additional concerns around these two aspects of the migration is important. In one instance, a project that I was involved with was going through a migration and for some reason the customer didn't realize that the new BI 7.0 system needed all of the functionality of the Java stack to be available and thought that the BI 7.0 system worked on the same or similar platform as the 3.x system did. So, there was little or no support for the Java stack issues and concerns. The BI portal was not set up appropriately for the migration and to accept the 7.0 IViews for the reports to be attached to the portal. You can avoid all these issues that deal with overall system capabilities by communicating with the client in the planning stage. For example, make sure that everyone has the appropriate version of Excel uploaded to their laptops so that there's no problems debugging any issues and you don't have to worry about inconsistencies in the basic Excel versioning.

Don't look to try and overkill the migration, meaning don't try to migrate all of your WAD templates, Web reports and all queries at once. There are very good reasons why you don't migrate some reports such as those that have large amounts of VBA or the business user is fine with what they have—3.x version, or the resources needed to deal with all of the fixes required for the migration are not available on a 100 percent basis but can only devote 50 percent of their time to the migration.

To summarize this section, make sure that you have a very good plan! This is the key to a successful migration. Make sure that you keep it simple and make everything as clear as possible to business users. Remember, your customers are the business users and management of the corporation, not the IT department. Their needs are quite different from an IT person who isn't concerned if they're looking at a list of information or a dynamic report. If you phase in the migration, you should be able to build on wins as each phase is rolled out. Ensuring that the initial phases are a success is very important so that word gets around how much more flexible and user friendly the newer system is for the business user. This will definitely make the remainder of your migration process easier and less stressful.

Migration Activities

Now we are going to look at each of the items that we need to migrate. In this section, we will work through the mechanics of completing the migration process. The different components that we need to deal with are the standard business content (SBC) to support the BI 7.0 objects, the WAD library, Web reports, the WAD templates and finally the variants. (Migrating variants tends to get the most attention from business users, which is understandable; if I were a business user who created numerous personal variants over years of using these reports, I would be very interested in making sure that I didn't have to redo all of my work.) These are the different migration activities and in the next section we will organize them into the appropriate step-by-step process so that the complete migration process will be successful. Each of these processes is fairly straightforward and can be done via a step-by-step approach. The BEx workbooks can be a bit tricky and challenging, but we will not go through the migration process for BEx workbooks because it's more of a BEx Analyzer issue than a BEx Web Analyzer issue. Thus it is beyond the scope of this book. If the project that you are involved with requires the migration of BEx Workbooks you may want to review the information found on the sap.help.com Web site.

Standard Business Content for Migration

Your initial focus should be on making sure that all of the standard business content (SBC) that needs to be migrated is activated. This is not that hard, and if you're used to activation of the SBC within BW, you will be able to very quickly collect these objects and then activate them. The following illustrations show some of this content in the display process within the SBC activation process. You can find the majority of the required SBC under the header BEx Web Template—and of course this is the 7.0 version, not the 3.x version, which is clearly marked on the SBC activation screen. To access these, go to the Administration Workbench and use the button on the left side of the screen BI Content. Then using the option for Object Types you can see the Web Templates and Items for both the 3.x and 7.0 versions.

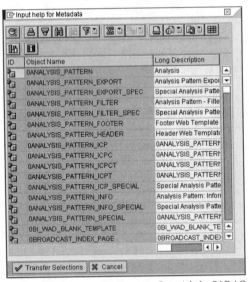
Copyright by SAP AG

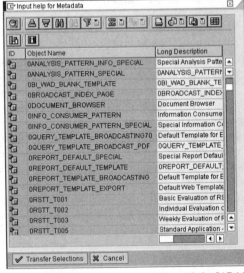
Copyright by SAP AG

Most of the required templates are listed together in the area of the 0ANALYSIS_PATTERN template. This, of course, is the root template for many different items, but as you can see, several other templates are necessary. Several of these templates are actually a part of 0ANALYSIS_PATTERN, such as 0ANALYSIS_PATTERN_EXPORT, which offers the format for the Export process in the standard Web template. There is one minor trick to this process

and it's something that you would
immediately find out once you execute your
WAD templates, since you would get either a
warning or an error, but it's available in the
SBC area and needs to be activated. Under the
3.x templates, you will find the final 7.0
template required. That is the template that
controls some components of the Information
Broadcaster. So, you have to expand Web
Template (Format SAP BW 3.x) to get this
one. The illustration shows the actual template
required—0BROADCASTING_TEMPLATE70.
Now, if you are not using the Information
Broadcaster, you do not need this template, but
depending on what you are accessing, you may
run into a warning that this specific template is
not active. So, activate it here and be done with
all of the SBC at once.

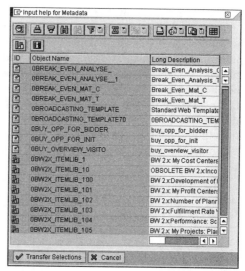

WAD Library

Migrating the WAD library items is another small but important task, because if you go
through this process and don't migrate these items initially, you will immediately get error
messages as you attempt to migrate the Web reports. You may or may not have used this
component, but it's always good to check and make sure that everything you need has been
migrated. If the functionality available in the WAD library has not been used, then nothing
further needs to be done in this section. The following illustration shows the WAD library,
which is a part of 3.x WAD and therefore has not been seen before in this book.

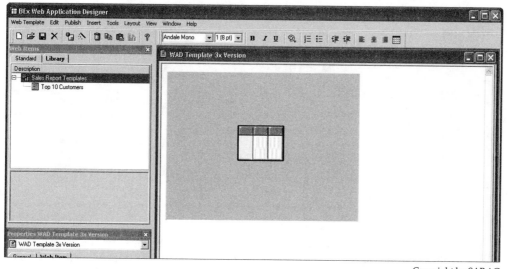

As you might know, the 3.x version of the Web reports did have a WAD library but the 7.0 version of the WAD doesn't have a "library." What it does have is a component called Reusable Web Items, and that is where the library objects are migrated to during this process. They are very similar in functionality and usability. So we would be migrating from the library to the Reusable Items. We will see that each component in the WAD has its very own approach to migration and its own toolset that is used to migrate. In this case, we will use an ABAP program to execute the migration. Using the program RSZW_ITEM_MIGRATION_3X_TO_70, we can move the library items to the Reusable Items list. The following illustration shows the program component after we use transaction code SE38 and insert this program into the execution field.

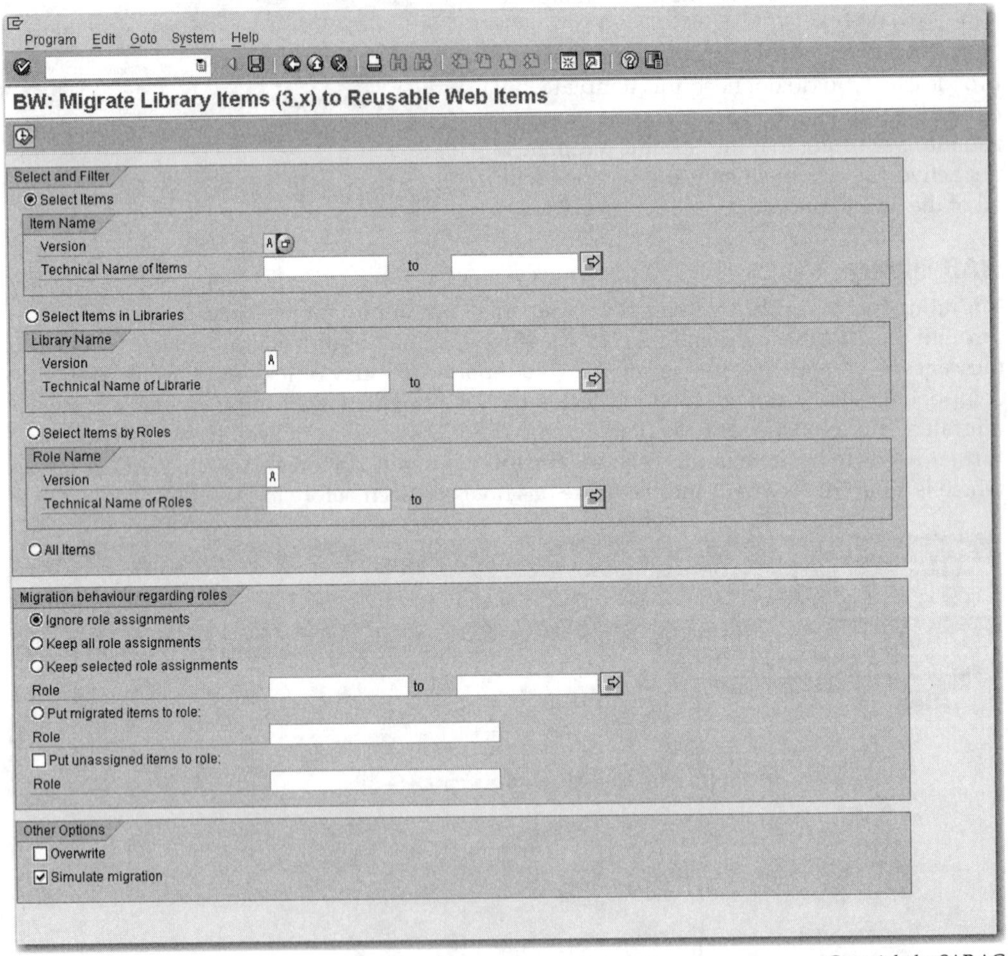

As you can see, this program allows us to migrate selectively based on filters, including by specific items, libraries, and roles, or by the All Items option. The bottom section of this program is important—identifying the behavior of the roles that are possibly assigned to these library items. You can realign the templates to different roles, ignore the role assignment, keep all role assignments, and other approaches. We normally want to see that everything is positioned as it was in the older version, so the second radio button, Keep All Role Assignments, is normally what you will see selected. I have not come across any issues with this step in the process and it has been fairly straightforward each time. Even if you choose to migrate all items, you shouldn't run into any errors or concerns.

Web Reports

Migrating Web reports is also fairly straightforward. The only issue that you may come across during the migration of the Web reports or queries is that you forgot to migrate one of them. This process is different from what you just did for the WAD library and the SBC activation. To migrate the Web reports, you have to use the Query Designer. There is no specific program or component, just the Query Designer for BI 7.0. All you need to do is open the 3.x query within the Query Designer 7.0 component and it will immediately migrate when you save it. So, let's take a look at the process in the system.

The following illustration shows the creation of a query in the 3.x Query Designer. As you can see, the process is not too complex, and the process is the same no matter what level of complexity a query may be.

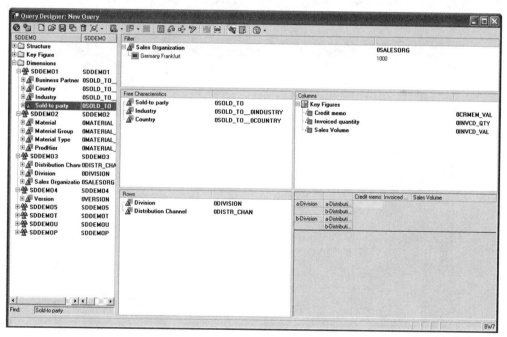

The next illustration shows the process for saving this query—the technical name YCUST_REPT_3X_Q001 has been assigned to it for identification purposes.

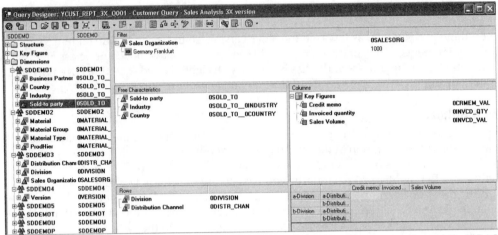

Copyright by SAP AG

Now we go to the 7.0 Query Designer and access this same query. The next illustration shows that we can see the same query within the 7.0 Query Designer even though we created it in 3.x.

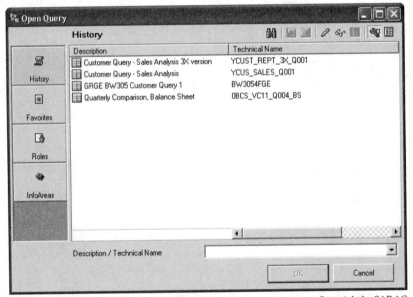

Copyright by SAP AG

Now we will open it in the 7.0 Query Designer and review the information. The next illustration shows the query within the 7.0 Query Designer. As you can see, the system realigns the characteristics and key figures in the appropriate fields, since the 3.x and 7.0 versions are quite different.

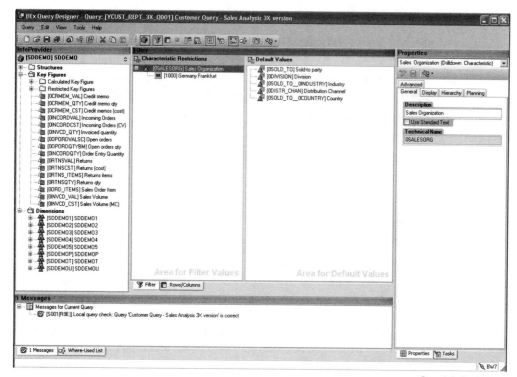

We now execute the query and confirm that the format is correct and the query actually does work in the newer environment. This is shown in the following illustration.

We then save the query within the new environment, as shown next.

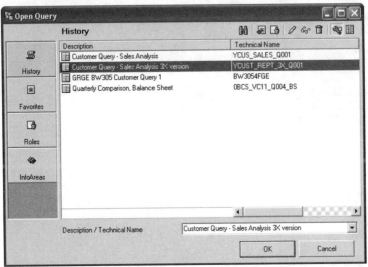

Now let's test the same query in the 3.x environment. As mentioned, this query will not be available in the older environment once it's opened and saved in the newer environment. This is shown in the illustration that follows. A notice is displayed in the older environment confirming that the query is actually a 7.0 version now.

WAD Templates

Now we turn our attention to the WAD templates. With the WAD templates, we encounter another approach to the migration process. In this case, we have a migration wizard, shown next, to help us through the steps.

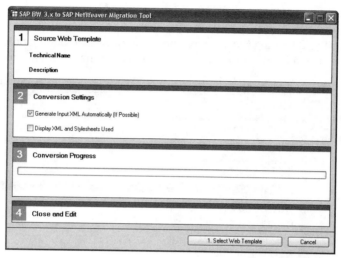

As you can see, this process has four steps, and this is where you will find out if all the previous steps have been completed correctly. If any have not been completed, you will get either a warning or an error at this step. You access this migration wizard via Tools | Migration Tool.

For purposes of demonstration, I've created a basic WAD template in the 3.x version of the component, shown in the following illustration. You can see that this is 3.x because it has the item library, which 7.0 doesn't have.

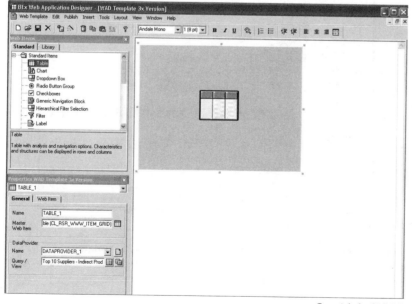

Now we'll step back into the 7.0 WAD to demonstrate the migration process. Before we start, we need to look and make sure we don't see the 3.x WAD template in the list of the 7.0 WAD templates. The following illustrations show the process of logging onto the 7.0 WAD and then doing a search for the 3.x version template within the 7.0 environment.

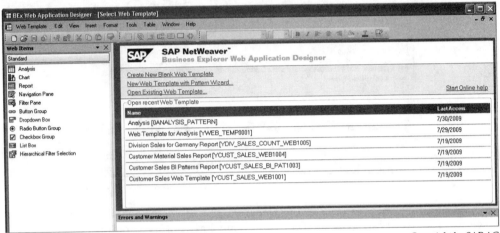

Go to the Open button in the top toolbar and click it to access the search dialog box. A search on the technical name of the WAD template returned no objects, as shown next.

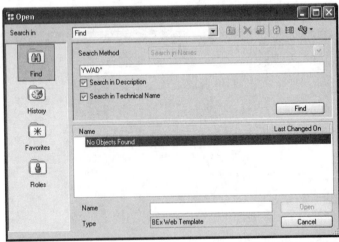

Now, we will start the migration process for these WAD templates.

Accessing the migration wizard and then doing the same search for the WAD template, the template from the 3.x environment shows up, as shown next.

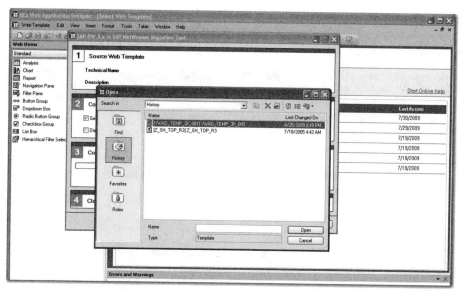

We executed the first step and the report is inserted into the migration wizard to be processed. As indicated by the Change button, in the first step, we could have gone into the WAD template and made a change to the template before the migration process if we wanted to adjust the description or some other parameters within the WAD template. Once we are through with Step 1, we can then execute Step 2. In this step, we identify whether we would like the system to generate the XML and all the other components of the WAD template, such as the graphics, different style sheets, and XHTML conversion. These options for both Step 1 and 2 are shown in the following illustration.

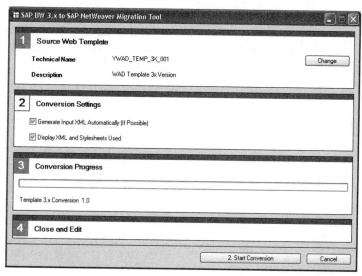

The conversion is executed in Step 3. If the template is successfully migrated, it will create its own URL and XSLT to use during the execution of the report. This is shown in the following illustration.

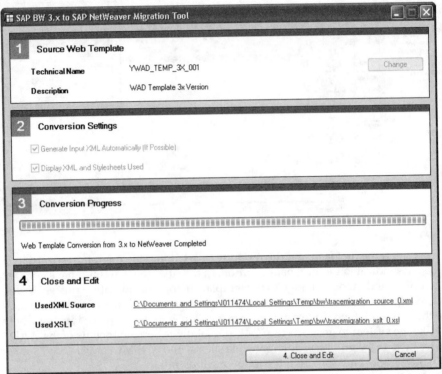

After the migration wizard is done with its job, we should be able to see the converted BI 7.0 template. The next illustration shows the end result. All components are identified and the template looks like it has been successfully migrated.

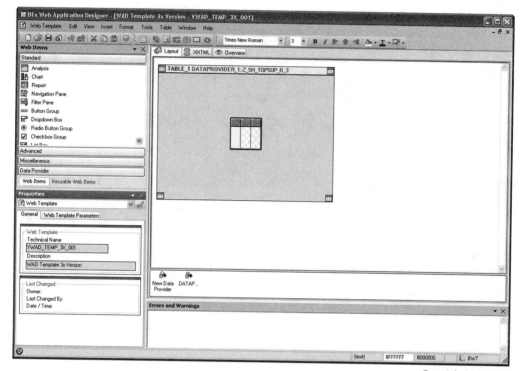

As you can see in the next illustration, the data provider came along with the template. If the query had not been migrated first, then during the migration process, you would have gotten an error or, at the very least, a warning.

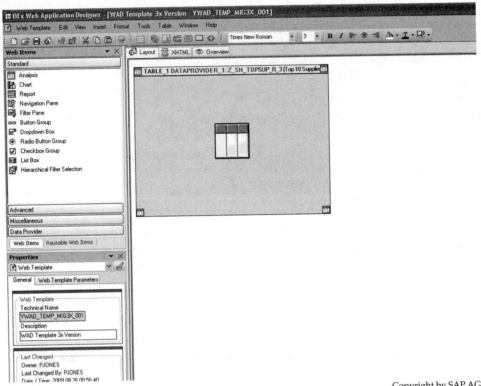

The result of executing the new report is shown in this illustration. As you can see, this report would need a little work or customization to make it look consistent and user friendly.

Let's also look at the XHTML that has been converted. The next illustration shows the format of the report before the conversion. Notice that the XHTML looks more like ABAP. If you look closely at the XHTML screen for the converted 3.x template and look down to the sixth row, you will see a prompt to call the ABAP process to access the CSS style sheet for the report background. It's the line with the CSS template that is different. As we know now the CSS style sheet is not used for the standard background. Now with the BI 7.0 we use the themes that are managed in the BI Portal for this task. During the conversion process, the wizard handles many different styles and formats and tries to convert all of them.

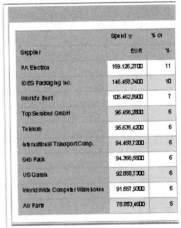

In this case, we see that the XHTML has not fully taken advantage of the ABAP programs that are used now and were not available a couple of years ago.

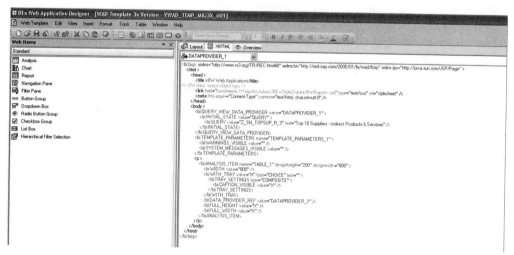

The next illustration shows the same Web item using just the 7.0 Web template. Notice that the whole approach to executing the XHTML is different. This is not to say that the migration process will not work for you, but you may find that the execution will be affected a bit. In this case, the CSS template is not there but a prompt to another location in the Web application is being executed.

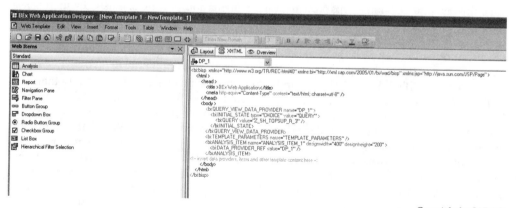

The next illustration shows what we can produce with a few very minor changes to the font sizes in the standard parameters for the Analysis Web item.

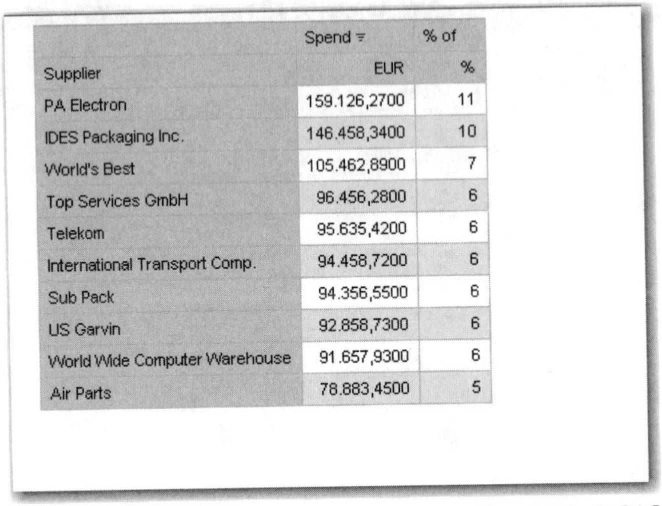

Supplier	Spend ⍨ EUR	% of %
PA Electron	159.126,2700	11
IDES Packaging Inc.	146.458,3400	10
World's Best	105.462,8900	7
Top Services GmbH	96.456,2800	6
Telekom	95.635,4200	6
International Transport Comp.	94.458,7200	6
Sub Pack	94.356,5500	6
US Garvin	92.858,7300	6
World Wide Computer Warehouse	91.657,9300	6
Air Parts	78.883,4500	5

Copyright by SAP AG

After this step, it would be very important to review and execute as many of the WAD templates as possible to test the newly converted queries.

Variants

After finishing the previous steps, you are, for all intents and purposes, finished with the basic migration process. However, in most cases, you still need to migrate the variants, which are closely related to reporting. Business users create variants to make it much easier to access specific information based on the values that are saved. Migrating these variants sometimes is a critical piece of the migration process, so you need to understand how to do it.

Currently within NW BI 7.0 SPS08 and SPS09 there is no existing functionality that enables you to migrate query variants to and from the NW BI 7.0 runtime and the SAP BW 3.x runtime in NW BI 7.0. In order to fully understand how BEx query variants work, you need to understand the different places that variants can live within NW BI 7.0. Upon execution of a complete upgrade to NW BI 7.0 from SAP BW 3.x your query variants are still technically stored as ABAP variants and therefore reside within the VARI table. A program was delivered by NW BI 7.0 that enables you to migrate these variants into a separate data store, RSR_VARIANT_XPRA. This separate data store is technically the RSRVARIANT table. This newer SAP BW 3.x query variant data store exists only within the SAP 7.0 BI environment and is where query variants for the SAP BW 3.x runtime are stored.

In terms of variants and the creation of them, we have to be on a specific SP to have both the BEx Analyzer and the BEx Web Analyzer variants available. To have both the ability to use and create the local and global variants for both components we need to be on SPS12. The query variants that are created within this new runtime are stored technically in the RSRPARAMETRIZA table as personalization settings.

NOTE *To be able to create both local and global variants within the two different toolsets—BEx Web Analyzer and BEx Analyzer—you should be on at least SPS12. On a lower SPS than this, you will be able to create both local and global variants on the BEx Analyzer but only the local variant on the BEx Web Analyzer.*

So to recap, there are three different data stores available in NW BI 7.0:

A. SAP BW 3.x Runtime = VARI

B. SAP BW 3.x Runtime within NW BI 7.0 = RSRVARIANT

C. NW BI 7.0 Runtime = RSRPARAMETRIZA

In order to migrate variants from tables for A to tables for B you can utilize the ABAP program RSR_VARIANT_XPRA. In order to migrate query variants from data store B to data store C or vice versa you will utilize another migration program. You need to initially import the transport available that has this specific migration component included. Make sure you review the process within your system so that you do not write over existing programs within your system. Once you are done importing the SBC transport with the programs installed, you then go to transaction code SE38 or SA38 and run the program Z_MIGRATE_VARIANTS. Once you have executed this program, you see the execution screen shown in the following illustration.

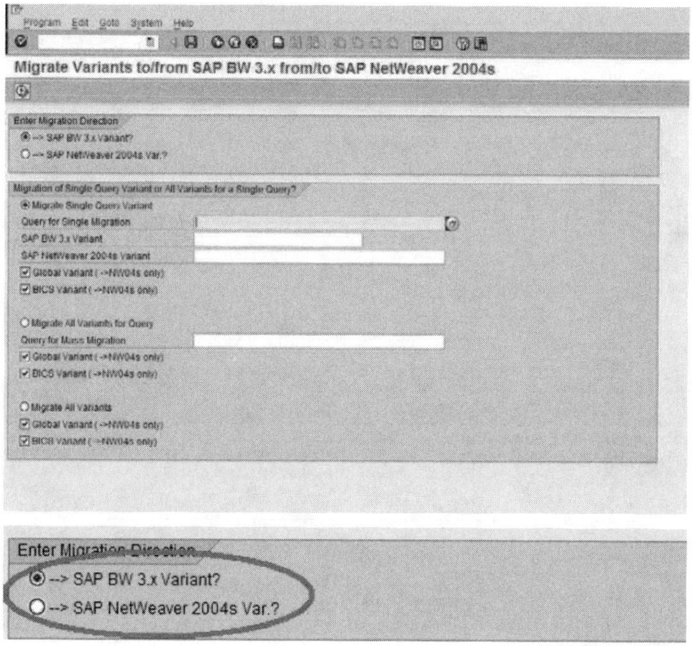

This program allows you to migrate from and to 3.x and 7.0. It also offers filtering so that you don't have to migrate all the variants if you don't want to. After you execute this program, you will see that the variants desired are now available in the RSRPARAMETRIZA table and available for 7.0 reports.

But let's step back just a bit and review this variant situation. If you migrate all the variants, then you won't have them available for any 3.x reports that may be left. So, you need to make sure that these reports are the ones that are affected and none of the variants are being used in any other capacity, such as a global variant on a process chain. If you look at the tables for both the 3.x and the 7.0 variants, you will see a big difference in the storage of these two sets of values. The illustrations that follow show the process of accessing the 3.x variant table RSRVARIANT to see the list of variant values that are available. Remember, the variants saved for the 3.x version are set up in an ABAP format. Therefore, these variants are coming more from the BEx Analyzer side than from the BEx Web Analyzer.

The next display is for the 7.0 variant table RSRPARAMETRIZA. You can see that this is very similar, but in the follow-up illustrations you will see that the values are stored in

XHTML rather than in ABAP format. This allows the BEx Web Analyzer to create the variants—both global and local.

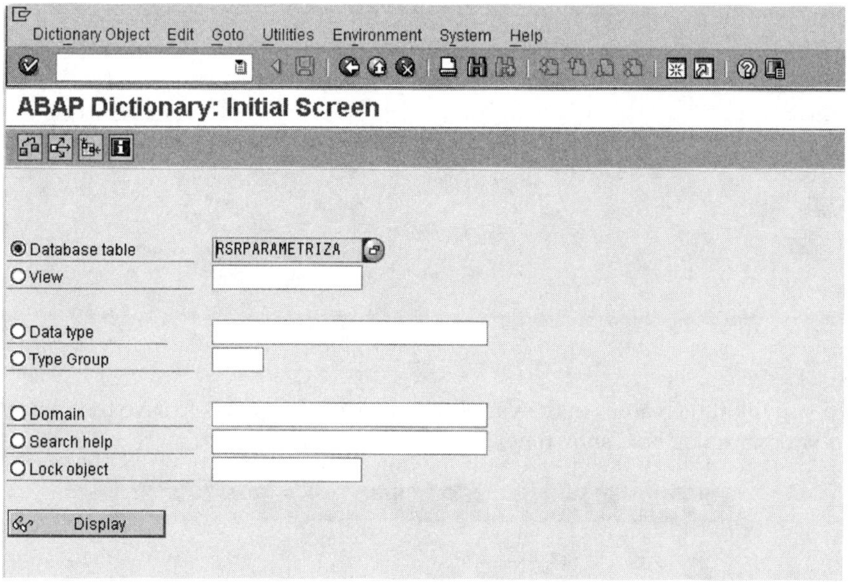

Copyright by SAP AG

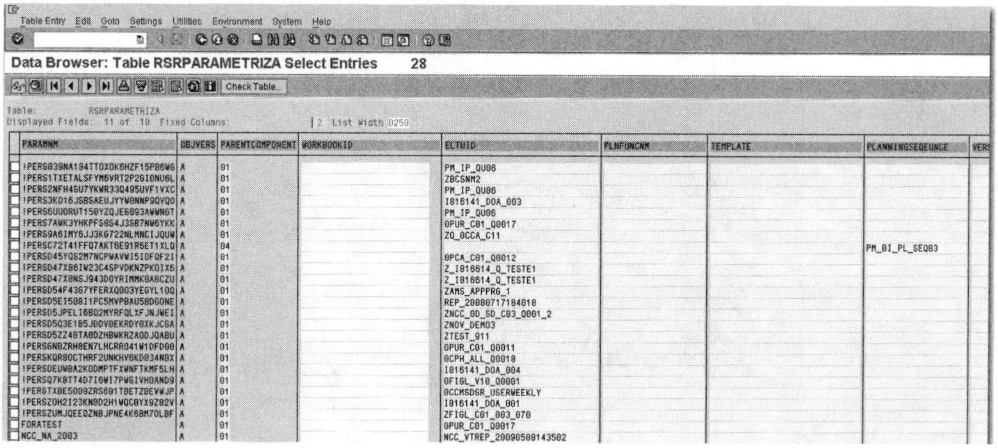

Copyright by SAP AG

Let's look at a very basic variant that is created. From the Web side, you can now create a variant so that your business users can be responsible for this process, and you will probably only allow them to create local variants—variants that they set up for themselves and that can't be used by anybody else. If you decide to allow global variants, once these variants are available, they are available for all business users.

Start by creating a variant from the Web. The following illustration shows the variable screen used to create the variant.

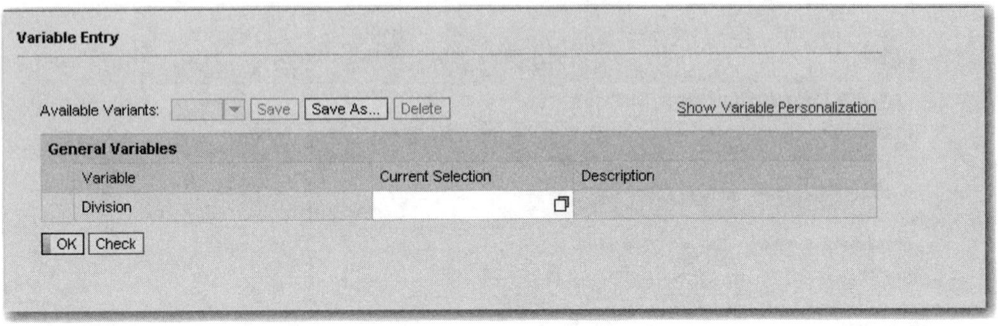

Copyright by SAP AG

Once you fill in the values in the variable screen, click Save As to save the variant using the Save Variant dialog box, shown next.

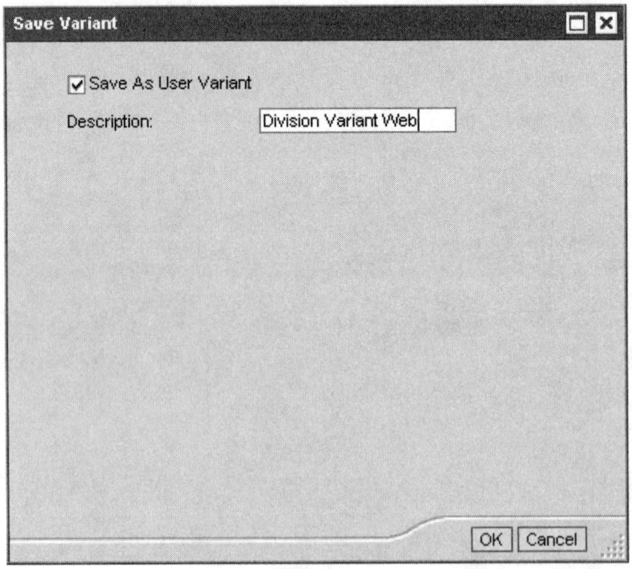

Copyright by SAP AG

The Save As User Variant check box is checked by default. If you leave that turned on, you will create a local variant. If you deactivate that parameter, your screen will change a bit and allow you to enter a technical name for the variant, as shown next. This variant will then be a global variant.

If you leave the box checked to create a local variant, all you need to do is enter a description into the field, as shown in the illustration.

If we go into the RSRPARMETRIZA table we see that it is storing the one variant created by me as indicated in the following illustration.

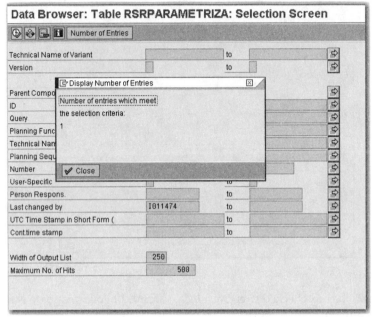

If you look at that one variant and how it is stored, you will notice that a technical name has been assigned to it, as shown in the following illustration. The system automatically assigns this technical name, and it's more of an encrypted number than a true technical name. Also notice that the values of the variant are stored in an XHTML string rather than an ABAP field. This allows the creation of these variants on the Web as well. So, during the migration process, the older version variants are switched from an ABAP format into an XHTML format.

If you step over into the BEx Analyzer, you can also use the same variants created in the BEx Web Analyzer, as shown in the following illustration.

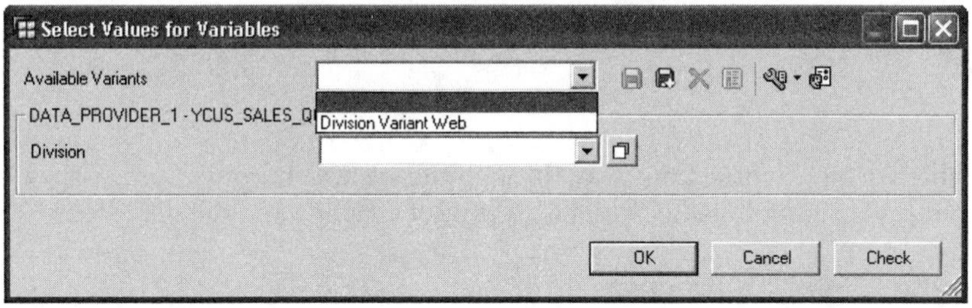

Copyright by SAP AG

If you create a global variant and fill in the Technical Name field, you still get an assignment into the RSRPARMETRIZA table, but it will look just a bit different. The next two illustrations show the creation of the global variant and the table with the different variants that are available for display. You can identify the two types of variants by looking at the User-Specific column on the far right of the screen. This field contains an X if the variant is user-specific and therefore a local variant. If the field is not checked, the variant is a global variant and available to all users of this query. Also notice that the technical name of the variant is quite a bit different. The global variant has a true technical name, whereas the local variant has the longer, system-generated technical name. There are a number of differences between the local and global variants, but one important difference is that global variants can be used in scheduling processes, such as background job runs and Information Broadcaster settings, whereas the local variants, due to the nonconforming technical name, can't be used in scheduling processes because you can't assign them to the job.

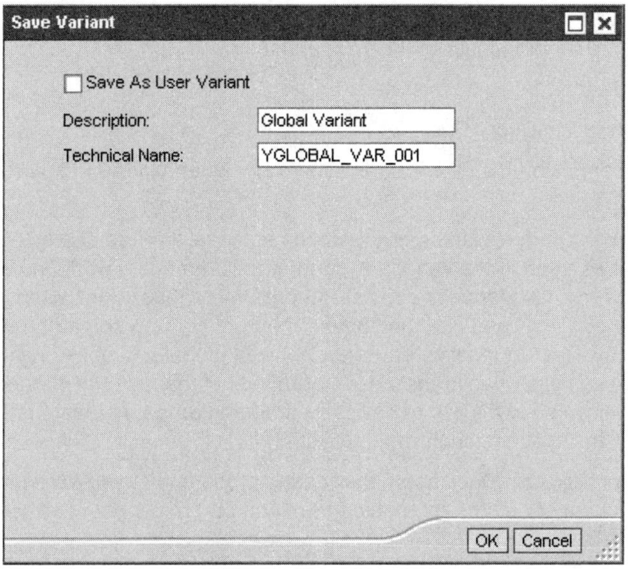

Copyright by SAP AG

Data Browser: Table RSRPARAMETRIZA Select Entries   1

Technical Name of Variant	Version	Parent Component of Variant	ID	Query	Planning Function	Technical Name of a Template	Planning Sequence
YGLOBAL_VAR_001	A	01		YDIVISION_001			

Table: RSRPARAMETRIZA
Displayed Fields   11 of 16   Fixed Columns: 2   List Width 0250

Now that we have worked our way through the system migration process, we can look at combining everything together to set up a project timeline and detailed steps.

Steps in the Migration Process

We have discussed and reviewed all the components that are involved in the migration process specific to the WAD templates and BEx Web reports. Now let's take a look at the process based on a step-by-step approach. The tables in this section list the sequence of steps involved in the different phases of a migration project. Before you perform any of these activities, remember to activate the required standard business content objects so that you don't have to worry about it during the rest of the migration.

The first phase is the migration of the queries. You need to take care of this first so that once the WAD templates are migrated, they can link up directly to the appropriate queries. Table 8-1 lists the general steps involved.

The next objects to be migrated are the Web Application Designer templates. Table 8-2 gives an outline of all the specific activities.

Step	Description of the Task
1	List the technical names of the queries that will be migrated.
2	Access the BEx Query Designer in the 7.0 version.
3	Find the queries that are to be migrated.
4	Open the query in the Query Designer and save it.
5	Execute the query using the new 7.0 BEx Query Designer; via the BEx Web Query execute option.
6	Once you execute the query and navigate using some of the free characteristics and varying the values used in the variables, confirm that the query works as expected. (For example, check that navigation is consistent, determine that values used in the variables filter the query correctly, and use the context menu to confirm some of the functionality is working correctly.) Test at least three different navigational processes against each query migrated. (For example, change the values of the variables, use the context menu of either the characteristics or key figures to navigate, drag and drop a characteristic into the report, execute Export to Excel and confirm the results.)
7	Document in a "Migration Document" the testing process that you experienced. This migration document should be the outline or migration project plan to track the progress of these migration tasks.

TABLE 8-1   Steps in the Migration of BEx Web Queries

Step	Description of the Task
8	Close the query and execute a check in the Query Designer to confirm the configuration is consistent. Document this result.
Steps If Migration Fails (the Query Save Generates Error Messages)	
1	Review errors and execute an attempt to self-correct the error by using the context menu on the error message.
2	If Step 1 works and the error is identified and corrected, check that the query is consistent and executes correctly.
3	If the error persists, open a help desk ticket to fix the issue and cc the responsible person for this query to update them on the activities or whoever is identified as the responsible person in the migration process.
4	If the error is fixed, go to Step 5 in the preceding list and continue through the migration process.

TABLE 8-1   Steps in the Migration of BEx Web Queries (*continued*)

Step	Description of the Task (Migrate the WAD Library)
1	Migration of the WAD Library to the Web Reusable Item folder is required prior to migration of the WAD templates, so execute ABAP program RSZW_ITEM_MIGRATION_3X_TO_70 to accomplish this step of the migration. This is a backend program to execute; therefore, a specific person will execute this and confirm that the library items have been migrated consistently. This program should be run in simulation mode first and confirmation that all library items migrate correctly and can be accomplished first.
2	Execute the actual migration of the Web library items. Once this is completed, send an e-mail or other form of communication to everyone involved in the migration process to inform them that migrating WAD templates is now possible and they can start the process.
3	Validate that a 7.0 folder has been created for each library item.
4	Document this activity in the Migration Document in the WAD worksheet or the documentation approach that you have identified.
Step	**Description of the Task (Migrate the WAD Templates)**
1	Confirm that the BI portal for the system is available. This is required for the support of the 7.0 WAD templates by the Java stack.
2	Identify if there are any Web items that are not supported in the 7.0 version; that is, Role Menu, AD Hoc Item, Alert Monitor, Hierarchical Item. Document this in the Migration Document. There are some objects that can be migrated to 7.0 from 3.x that are not standard, such as the Role Menu. This is not a best business practice but is available if required. As always, before you make the decision, answer the question, "Why should I continue to use a 3.x version object and can I work with a standard object to accomplish the same results?"

TABLE 8-2   Steps in the Migration of WAD Templates (*continued*)

Step	Description of the Task (Migrate the WAD Templates)
3	Identify if there are any customized objects in the WAD templates such as custom Java, table lookups, and so forth. Document this in the Migration Document.
4	Access the 7.0 Web Application Designer.
5	Migrating the WAD templates is different from migrating both the workbooks and queries. This is not an executable where you open the template and save. Instead, this is an executable process. Once in the 7.0 WAD, go to Tools I Migration Tools. The actual process is described earlier in the chapter, in the section "WAD Templates."
6	The dialog box for the migration process appears—SAP BW 3.x to SAP NetWeaver Migration Tool. In Step 1 of the migration wizard, click the Select Web Template button to access the 3.x WAD templates.
7	In the Open dialog box, find the WAD template that will be migrated and open it.
8	Once the WAD template is identified by the migration wizard, you can, if necessary, click Change in Step 1 to change the template.
9	Click the Start Conversion button. This is the conversion settings check box in the migration wizard.
10	The migration wizard will build the XML-formatted version of the WAD template and execute it in Step 3.
11	Confirm in Step 4 that a successful migration has occurred by clicking Close and Edit to close the template.
12	After the successful migration, execute the WAD template and navigate through a series of executables. This should be no less than three different navigational steps to confirm the functionality of the WAD template is working (for example, change the values of the variables, use the context menu of either the characteristics or key figures to navigate, drag and drop a characteristic into the report, execute Export to Excel and confirm the results).
13	Document in the Migration Document the testing process that you experienced.
14	Close the WAD template and execute a check in the Query Designer to confirm the configuration is consistent. Document this result.
	Steps If Migration Fails (WAD Template Does Not Convert Successfully and Error Message Is Generated)
1	Confirm the type of error message (such as "Web item not consistent with 7.0 version," etc.).
2	Identify if the error is Java stack related and if it can be corrected immediately or if the error message needs basis support.
3	If additional support is required, enter a help desk message via e-mail and cc the responsible person for this task or if the process is to open a help desk message, then initiate the process.
4	If the error can be corrected, re-execute the conversion program to see whether the migration is successful.

TABLE 8-2   Steps in the Migration of WAD Templates (*continued*)

Because the technologies that support the 3.x and 7.0 WAD templates, respectively, are completely separate but support the same template in both 3.x and 7.0 the WAD templates can be migrated multiple times.

The process of migrating BEx workbooks is outlined in Table 8-3. We haven't worked through a detailed analysis of the migration strategy for workbooks in this chapter, but this step-by-step process will give you some ideas and topics to discuss and review before you start the migration process with your BEx workbooks. It is important to review the extent that complex programming was done in the BEx Workbook such as VBA and complex macros.

Step	Description of the Task (Initial Steps for Workbook Migration: System Setup)
1	Open an Excel spreadsheet and go to the option toolbar and using the context menu go to Tools I Macros I Security. Make sure that the security option is set to Low. This will allow basic VBA to be migrated along with the workbook.
2	Still in the Security dialog box of the Excel spreadsheet, turn on the option Trusted Publishers by checking the box Trusted Access to Visual Basic Project.
3	Close the Security dialog box and proceed with the migration process. If these two steps are not completed, the workbook migration will fail.
Step	**Description of the Task (Migration of the BEx Workbooks)**
1	Confirm that the workbook you are migrating exists by finding the description of the workbook to migrate.
2	Check if there are any nonconforming objects—that is, VBA programs—in the workbook. Document this in the Migration Document. As previously mentioned, if there is complex VBA in the workbook, it would be safe to create a copy of the workbook prior to migration so that a consistent backup is available.
3	Open the BEx workbook in the 7.0 version of the BEx Analyzer. A message will appear confirming that this workbook will be converted to 7.0 upon opening.
4	Confirm that there are no messages generated with errors (see the bottom status bar line for messages—access them by double-clicking them).
5	If the migration is successful, execute the workbook and execute several navigational steps. Also vary the values entered into the variable screens to confirm that the workbook is consistent and valid.
6	The testing process should be at least three different navigational processes. Document the results in the Migration Document (for example, change the values of the variables, use the context menu of either the characteristics or key figures to navigate, drag and drop a characteristic into the report, execute Export to Excel and confirm the results).
7	Close the workbook and exit the workbook itself. Then reopen the workbook and execute with different parameters to validate the consistency of the format. Document this process in the Migration Document.
8	Close the workbook to complete the migration.

TABLE 8-3   Steps in the Migration of BEx Workbooks (*continued*)

Steps	Steps If Migration Fails (Workbooks Present Issues Due to Amount of VBA Assigned to Each Workbook)
1	Identify the error message if possible (such as "VBA was not converted," etc.) and review if it can be fixed immediately.
2	If the error can be fixed, continue with the migration steps. If not, document the error and open a help desk message and cc the responsible person.
3	Since the workbook can be re-migrated, execute the migration process again.
4	If the errors can't be corrected, then decide whether the workbook should be migrated at this time and if resources are available to rebuild the portion of the workbook that has been corrupted.

TABLE 8-3   Steps in the Migration of BEx Workbooks (*continued*)

Summary

This chapter provided a basic review of the overall migration process and concepts in the NW BI 7.0 frontend, from the high-level discussion of the concepts down to the very detailed discussion about how to migrate the report variants. Migration definitely poses some challenges, the hardest of which is the initial discussion of why and what reports should be migrated. The normal thought would be to immediately think that all reports, both the Web and the Analyzer reports and workbooks, should be migrated since the backend is going to 7.0 and the directive for configuration in the BI 7.0 might be that all architecture is to go with 7.0 and question the reason for any 3.x configuration (except for the required 3.x configuration around certain datasources and infosources such as inventory datasources). This approach would be foolhardy and cause quite a bit of frustration and confusion. So, after this initial reaction, you should sit down and develop a reporting strategy for the actual reports that you will migrate. We didn't really get into the migration of the BEx Analyzer queries or workbooks, so you will need to do some further research on that side to decide what to migrate. Just remember about the VBA within the workbooks and test the migration with the VBA first before you move forward with your entire workbook group. You may find that you need an additional resource to help with the fixes on the VBA programs that have been used or you may decide that a phased approach is better due to the additional work required. Now that this critical decision was made we then worked through all the basic steps and some more advanced steps for the migration process.

The success of your migration process really depends on the business users' reaction to all the new functionality and the changes to the old functionality that will affect how they work. The decision and process of migrating the Web-based reports is a bit more straight forward than the decision about migrating the BEx Analyzer side, but in both cases the migration process should work nicely, and with the appropriate amount of testing and training, you will have a very successful process.

9

CHAPTER

Integration of SAP BusinessObjects Components into the BI Environment

This chapter discusses the current and future components of the BI reporting frontend. The current BI reporting tools have been around for 10–12 years in one shape or form. A significant leap in functionality occurred from the 2.x version to the 3.x version in both the BEx Analyzer and the BEx Web Analyzer. Another significant jump in functionality occurred from the 3.x version to the 7.0 version, including improvements in documentation, Web reporting, formatted reporting, BI portal integration, Excel integration with the BEx Analyzer, the use of distribution methods for reports, and authorizations.

The next phase in SAP technology evolution is the integration of the BI NW Reporting components with the BusinessObjects (BOBJ) components. This is a similar process that we went through for the Planning and Consolidations process where we started out with SEM-BPS (Strategic Enterprise Management-Business Planning and Simulation) and moved to BI-IP (Business Intelligence-Integrated Planning), then we moved to BPC (Business Planning and Consolidation), which was an integration of the old OutlookSoft software. So, we are going through integration between the components of BI that are very familiar to us and the components of BOBJ that we need to get comfortable with and familiarize ourselves with as soon as possible. These components consist of the combination of Business Objects (BOBJ) and the SAP Business Intelligence and its platform (NetWeaver). If I look at the actual components we will be discussing they are the BusinessObjects Web Intelligence (WebI), Crystal Reports, BusinessObjects Xcelsius, and the BusinessObjects Explorer. These are the current official naming conventions for each. This integration has been going on for awhile now and we are definitely well into the integration of each of these components directly onto the NetWeaver platform that we are all very used to at this point. As with all new components we will be experiencing some growing pains on the way but shortly all of these frontend reporting options will be fully integrated into the SAP BW or BI platform.

NOTE *At the current time the SAP BusinessObjects components listed here are the SAP standard. In the near future the addition of the SAP BusinessObjects component Pioneer will be used for an Excel-based reporting component. At the time of this publication the recommendation from SAP is to use the BEx Analyzer for Excel-based reporting requirements.*

This chapter is intended as an overview of the BOBJ components. It does not provide details about the configuration or design of reports or dashboards, but instead gives you a feel for the functionality, positioning, and features of each component. When you do decide to move forward with the BOBJ components, the overview provided in this chapter should make the detailed configuration easier.

Overview of the Integration and Positioning Process

The entire group of BusinessObjects frontend tools is currently called the SAP BusinessObjects portfolio (or BOBJ for short). This group includes the SAP BusinessObjects Explorer (formerly SAP BusinessObjects Polestar), SAP BusinessObjects Web Intelligence (WebI), SAP BusinessObjects Xcelsius, and Crystal Reports. These naming conventions are subject to change as SAP makes adjustments to the functionality or repositions certain tools.

With any new functionality in the SAP space, our first concern is how the changes affect our road map and strategies moving forward with the overall SAP process. With all the new frontend components, figuring out what component does what and where the overlaps in functionality exist is a bit of a challenge. But the big question in most shifts such as this, where an entire reporting frontend is shifted from the BEx approach to the BusinessObjects approach, is why? In this case, the question has a number of answers, and we will discuss a few from the system and business user point of view.

With the acquisition of Business Objects in 2007, SAP has made a shift that combines best-in-class business and industry applications with best-in-class solutions for business users. To integrate these two components, SAP Business Suite and the SAP BusinessObjects solutions, SAP has used the NetWeaver Business Warehouse (BW) Enterprise Data Warehouse (EDW) platform. For customers that have invested in BW, this has been considered the fundamental building block for their enterprise business intelligence (BI) capabilities. This gives the business users access to additional capabilities and tools that will allow them to extend and deliver business intelligence to almost any part of the organization. As in many cases with new functionality and toolsets, some companies have had little or no exposure to the new BOBJ components and need guidance and assistance for integrating the "new" products into their existing NetWeaver and BW landscape and also understanding of the going forward road map for SAP integration.

Two primary cases need to be addressed when planning an implementation of BusinessObjects solutions as an additional reporting component to the BW system. The first is the case where a new implementation of BW 7.0 is being deployed, or an older version of BW is being upgraded. At the simplest level, the migration of key business functionality from current systems and platforms to BW 7.0 makes maintaining the status quo with regard to BI capabilities a challenging process because current interfaces will begin to change as data moves over time from existing platforms to BW 7.0. Existing data extraction and loading processes, report templates, and most every other facet of the current reporting and analytical capabilities throughout the enterprise will likely require maintenance on functionality at some point during the rollout or migration. Beyond the simple "the interfaces will change" argument, however, a widely accepted best practice for ECC (and by extension, BW) rollouts is that organizations should not simply re-create their respective existing collections of reports to accompany the new environment but instead—even taking risk and complexity factors into consideration—any ECC and BW implementations should be viewed as an opportunity to rationalize the end-to-end BI framework and adopt an updated approach to reporting and analytics; one guided by the increasing need for timely, actionable, high-value insights for decision making and in support of work processes and operational reporting.

In the case of a BW implementation, BW or BI typically provides the catalyst for the organization to review its BI process and build on and deploy a new generation of BI capabilities. In most cases, the implementation will touch all corners of the enterprise. Further, by design, BW is architected around multiple components to achieve the best possible balance between uniformity, consistency, and flexibility, with individual business units or functional areas given a certain degree of flexibility to tailor the information and system to their particular business needs. This multiple-component approach is widely recognized as a best practice to serve multiple business groups and users across a large, complex enterprise; not only in the transactional realm, but also in the informational and analytical realms and concepts. The point is that although there are always multiple approaches that could be implemented for customers, a key factor to defining the overall strategy is the need to support multiple business user groups across the company. As the saying goes, information, and therefore BI, is one of the most critical factors in the success of your company and growth in this economic environment.

Another closely related principle to the preceding ones is the necessity to follow sound migration practices as the current "as-is" state slowly evolves to the future "should-be" end state. Migration best practices often involve components such as interim bridges and "reverse bridges" between legacy and new components; the "sprucing up" of existing components that—even though they will eventually disappear—need to be enhanced for a short duration to support iterative migration; and thorough integration and interface testing. In many cases, this "short period of time for support" turns into years of effort and needs to be looked at in this light. The business needs to develop a road map and work to be as consistent and practical as possible, but there are some situations that come up that will not allow the business to follow that particular road map. A case in point is the current (2008–2010) economic environment, in which many companies have had to redirect their attention to other, more critical issues in terms of driving sales and growth simply to survive. So, the BI process and projects are then moved from six months to two years in scoping and if these bridges for the current/future view of the reporting strategy are not consistent throughout your company, you will be dealing with other survival issues including the ability to generate useable reports.

One of the points I made in the migration chapter (Chapter 8) is that you look at new functionality and components with an eye on how this will support our company and not jump from the frying pan into the fire by just adding an additional layer of reporting components to a system that may need some help and is possible broken. It looks great for a time but the issues are still there, just the reports look better and more dynamic. But the underlying data and consistency issues are still there. So, an enterprise's pursuit of a new era of business intelligence and the resulting timely, actionable, high-value business insight should take advantage of leading-edge core technologies and products but at the same time, the mission-critical nature of what business intelligence should be necessitates being careful and methodical when implementing leading-edge BI products, components, and capabilities, as well as their associated architectures.

BI strategy and architecture teams have a duty to look critically at selected core technologies, products, product families, and architectural frameworks to develop an overall BI architecture and BI road map that is heavily driven by existing, proven technologies and at the same time can support and architecturally evolve toward technologies that are in the pipeline. Most importantly, the teams should be looking to match technologies and products with the BI strategy and documented needs from the business users and community. For example, if it is found that most business processes and analytic needs can easily be satisfied now and in the future by batch-oriented data, the BI strategy and architecture teams should not recommend that real-time data flows dominate the BI architecture. Basically, the recommended solutions should be neither over-architected nor under-architected with regard to likely current and future business needs and requirements.

"Business intelligence" means different things to different people and in a very similar way the concept of a "dashboard" has evolved—locking down a definition of a dashboard is as difficult as getting one definition for business intelligence. All of us have come to understand it in different ways, and we have been witness to customers where we only discovered well into the meeting that when we used the phrase "BI," one group was talking about a particular product, whereas another group was talking about it in terms of a concept or knowledge area. If such confused conversations are taking place even among business users or groups in the same company, implementers should be very aware of the likelihood that both our customers and other members of the project team have had no prior exposure to the SAP BusinessObjects solutions, and how we have conceptualized business intelligence.

Components of SAP BusinessObjects (BOBJ) for Reporting

I have found that during the process of getting acquainted with the numerous components of BOBJ that I was having difficulty understanding where each one fits. I'm sure it was the same issues that I faced with BI before but I'm guessing that the confusion was so long ago that I forget that there was any. So I initially needed to understand where each one of the components fits into the landscape before we can start to understand the functionality, flexibility, and configuration of each. As we mentioned, we will be looking at each of these components at a very high level and even though the configuration of the required source of data to each of these is critical, we will not be looking at items such as Universes or Data Federator in SAP BusinessObjects. Yes, these are critical and in most cases required before we can build any of the reports from tools such as Web Intelligence or Xcelsius but the development and process of configuring a BusinessObjects Universe is for another book. As a matter of fact, and you are probably tired of me pointing this out, but the configuration and development of the full set of these BusinessObjects reporting components would definitely fill another book. So, we need to align each of these components based on their functionality and use, and then discuss some additional basic information around each component.

What we want to avoid, and what is the underlying point from the previous discussion, is that the implementers of the BOBJ project should be aware that they may be in a BI "green field," and it can be useful to schedule a meeting with various stakeholders to discuss some common terms and approaches. The last thing anyone wants is to find out deep in the project that the customer "didn't know what they signed up for" or "didn't understand what it was we were going to deliver." These discussions should be a fact-finding process and a development of a practical BI approach. There are other aspects of the project that a meeting of this nature would benefit and allow everyone to flush out questions that may not have been considered by the stakeholders such as basic project type activities and milestones.

- **Define report requirements** Discuss the requirements gathering process. Instead of asking general questions such as "Which reports do you want, and what should be in them?" ask specific questions such as "What are you trying to achieve?" and "What are your business goals?"

- **Explore ad hoc querying** This may be an entirely new concept to some customers, and universes (semantic layer for the sources of data for the BOBJ-BI components) that are made available for such ad hoc activity should be designed with the end-users in mind. The universes should be easy to use and should cover a particular business process.

- **Discuss security** Many times the customer is only thinking about data security, which is governed by existing roles and security inside BW. However, none of that covers which universes and reports are visible to which users and groups, or which rights a user has in the InfoView portal (component used for business user viewing of reports, very similar to the BI portal) and what actions they can and cannot perform. This could mean ad hoc querying, as opposed to only viewing or refreshing reports, but would also include the ability to export report contents or schedule particular reports for their own business area or department.

- **Plan scheduling and report distribution** Most customers have not yet considered this in detail, so as the consultant, you need to be able to articulate what the options are and how scheduling may help reduce the load on BW during peak hours if a lot of users need to access the same report and information. Not every report has to be run interactively, which is a key point to make with customers.

- **Discuss report design and visualization (including dashboards)** Many things are possible, but the selected approach should be what is best for appropriate information delivery in the given use case. On the other hand, those who are most comfortable in BEx might need additional time with all the different possibilities and options available in BOBJ. You should have a comprehensive discussion about what makes sense in report design, which metrics comprise good items to display on dashboards, and which ones do not. Again, this means that dashboard and report design needs to line up with business goals—a novel idea but one that seems to escape many developers as they go through the process of developing these busy dashboards.

All of these points are still quite tactical. However, they will help to set the stage for the project, and in many cases the customers will not understand what they are getting until they see the first reports and dashboards, a point at which it is probably too late to make substantial changes. You can mitigate this risk with an upfront rapid scoping session and/or a pilot implementation. The advantage to this approach is that, fundamentally, it tends to be business focused rather than IT focused, and it aligns with a simpler implementation. Realize, though, that "fudged" demos on static data can leave customers with an impression that the complete implemented solution will be more responsive and faster than is realistic. Nevertheless, it can certainly help to provide the customer with a hands-on visualization of what things will look like in a full implementation.

In all cases, there should be a point to doing business intelligence, just as there was a reason for a customer to invest substantially in products and services to put a BI framework in place. That is, BI should be part of a larger business strategy to enable more efficient, consistent, and targeted use of information assets captured in the SAP systems, legacy systems, and other relevant business data. A lot of reporting is very tactical, whether it is operational reporting or regulatory and from an industry perspective, that is not really considered "Business Intelligence," but rather a simple representation of only its most basic components. We need to move the corporation to the next level, which is to encourage further analysis and provide ad hoc querying capabilities beyond a set of standard reports. Ideally, though, a BI strategy ties such analysis in with existing or new business processes, where BI plays a role both in discovery (Q&A) and monitoring the effect of policies and business initiatives.

Most customers will have some sort of BI strategy defined. Even exclusively operational reporting will have a thought behind it. In many cases it is directly related to a business initiative that is very specific, while in other cases it may be a desire to really change the organization and its business processes. It may not be always highly sophisticated, and if that is the case, you should help refine it further and propose a solution based on experience, as well as the customer's business needs. Recognize that customer resources will usually have done their research, but may misrepresent certain product features or misunderstand concepts that are very familiar to experienced consultants, so always clarify what they mean with what they say.

Formulate the strategy and seek approval from the customer. Where possible, try to get buy-in for a Business Intelligence Competency Center (BICC) to make sure there is a group that functions as a guardian of the BI solutions and applications post-implementation. The BICC members should not only drive best practices and system governance, but also ensure that the actual implementation aligns with the BI strategy. The BICC over time should help refine the strategy and drive it to ever further sophistication. We have all seen this process go astray with all of the other system-specific activities around the go-live and the post-go-live processes including critical issues with performance, business user additional needs, or just running out of budget or time but please look to drive this effort so that the BW system and the BI concepts can continue to proactively impact the corporation. We have to keep in mind the critical position of information within our corporations.

It is very important that you educate the business user or your customer on using the right tool for the right job, as the wrong choice is more likely to lead to implementations that fall short of the initial success criteria. You will have to manage not only which tool is more appropriate, but also the expectations with the customer, and what current product capabilities need to be considered when guiding the tool choice. Even if the right choice is made, diverging expectations or lack of support for certain features may still lead to problematic implementations. It is also clear, and this is the normal process with all new products, that a number of product changes have been, or are in the process of being enhanced, so all of these elements need to be taken into account when deciding on the right tool for the job at hand. The SAP BusinessObjects components have some well-established guidelines on selecting tools based on both the existing customer landscape and business user information or what SAP calls a "use case scenario." In the process of analyzing the various categories of issues reported by the companies and business users—apart from identified certain product issues—the analysis shows some classifications that clearly indicate incorrect tool choices, which lead to misaligned expectations of the solution.

Choosing the Right Tool for the Right Job

Now we can look at the different tools within this set to see what works where, so that we can identify and recommend the appropriate tool for the job. With the SAP BusinessObjects suite of BI solutions, several options enable organizations to bring BI to all business users. With the current components available, we have a bit of a mix in toolsets—most with a significant background with BusinessObjects and one aligned with the SAP BI reporting component and this group of reporting components will be the best business practice approach until the development of SAP BusinessObjects Pioneer product is available. These reporting options are

- BusinessObjects Explorer
- BusinessObjects Web Intelligence
- BEx Analyzer (Web and Excel)/Voyager/Pioneer
- Crystal Reports
- Xcelsius

As mentioned in the last section, SAP takes a use case–driven approach to determine which products are best to use for each business requirement, and then recommends that other consultants and businesses take a similar approach. When looking at the existing BW footprint at SAP customers, the following are the general guidelines for what constitutes the right tool for the right job:

- For information exploration where BW is in place, SAP BusinessObjects Explorer NetWeaver Version (that is, SAP BusinessObjects Polestar + SAP BW Accelerator) is the tool of choice.

- For casual, ad hoc reporting and analysis and general interactive reporting where BW is in place, Web Intelligence with OLAP universes is the first choice.

- For OLAP analysis where BW is in place, the BEx Analyzer (Web and Excel) client remains the tool of choice until the availability of the SAP BusinessObjects Pioneer. Voyager was the BusinessObjects component that was similar to the BEx Analyzer but should really not be concerned as an alternative. In the future, the preferred solutions for OLAP analysis will be based on the Pioneer project as a replacement for BEx Analyzer and Voyager.

- For formatted or production reporting from either BW or directly from ERP (ECC), Crystal Reports is the tool of choice.

- For dashboarding and visualization where BW is in place, the choice would be a combination of Xcelsius with Query as a Web Service (QaaWS) or LiveOffice as a connection layer.

As part of the requirements gathering in project preparation, it is strongly recommended to apply use cases to each of the requirements. That is, by not only capturing what the business needs are and how we plan to address them (as part of the project), but also including how reports and dashboards are delivered and consumed, we discover how end users will use the information that is provided to them. With this process in place it will help us further understand the nature of the requirements and functionality each business user needs. This will also help us determine which tool to use, as well as help us with our design approach. By not only considering the needs and requirements of the business user, we can also identify the reporting toolset that will satisfy their needs. As you can see, the process is twofold. First, identify the actual functional requirements, and then identify the reporting component that will satisfy those requirements. The following sections include both a basic background of the product use and the guidelines for mapping required end-user capabilities to the BI platform, starting with an overall baseline approach, as depicted in the illustration.

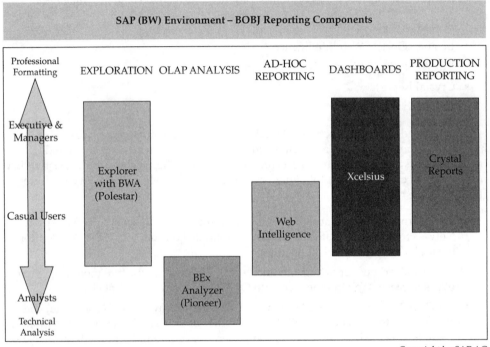

SAP (BW) Environment – BOBJ Reporting Components

Copyright by SAP AG

Again, the positioning of these components will really help you to conceptualize the BusinessObjects product. The preceding diagram shows the functionality across the top and the business user groups down the left side. Some of these tools overlap user groups, such as BusinessObjects Explorer and Xcelsius, but overall you can see what situation fits what tool. This should help you to identify the configuration approach and the implementation process. In a normal business use case, we would look at the process rather than the actual system component, and then work toward the appropriate tool that fits the situation. For now, we are going to look at the specific components of the BOBJ reporting toolset and include the use case information within each of these discussions. I find this approach more vertical and not horizontal enough for the business but it works for us in this book environment.

As we all look to migrate from our current reporting format to the newer format we always try to compare the newer items with the previous items and in this case I will also offer some comments to this effect in the areas that are really trade-offs such as the Crystal Reports versus Report Designer area but overall we will try to just outline the overall functionality. Also, in this case attempting to match reporting component to reporting component would be inconsistent with the approach that the business should take in terms of identifying the correct reporting functionality. Each should be viewed on their own value and functionality to the business. Now you can see that getting into too much detail would take us into another completely different avenue and the chapter would end up being twice the size. Just the configuration alone of the WebI would take about 200 pages to describe in detail and we haven't really even talked about the User Interface, which in this case is the InfoView. So the discussion will be high level and brushing over the functionality. As we always say, the devil is in the details, so using this section as an initial very general discussion of each component and then using other more detailed documentation to understand all of the complexities is a prudent approach.

Web Intelligence (WebI)

The Web Intelligence reporting toolset is one of the more recognized components of the BOBJ group. This section highlights the features of the WebI reporting tool and also gets into some of the configuration details. Now, remember, having a new reporting component will not mean that we are going to reinvent the wheel but using another toolset—BOBJ— rather than the SAP BI, we will be able to offer all of the same functionality plus some additional bells and whistles. So, as we go through this process, we will see some very similar activities that we've seen with the WAD or the BEx Web Analyzer. Just that they will possibly use different terminology and access them in a different manner.

In this case, we'll look at some additional details of the integration between the NetWeaver BW system and the BOBJ frontend toolsets, just to give you a general sense of how it works. In general, the Web Intelligence component has two main connectivity options for BW:

- OLAP universes
- Relational universes via SAP BusinessObjects Data Federator

If you look at a best business practice for the WebI, you will see that the suggested approach is via the use of OLAP universes with BW, as this will be the most widely implemented solution within the existing SAP customer base. The following diagram of the architecture shows that the OLAP universe can be supported by a direct link to the actual InfoProvider, such as the InfoCube or the MultiProvider. The preferred approach is to use the BEx query (in this case, the query is created as a definition using the BEx Query Designer and will probably never really be run for any business users as a report); this approach is preferred for several reasons, one of which is the ability to use calculated key figures (CKFs) and restricted key figures

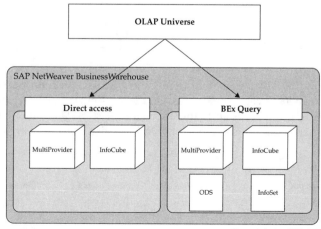

Copyright by SAP AG

(RKFs) that are created in the query definition. Since these are not found in the Infocube, the direct access method would not have access to these formulas.

Note the differences between the InfoProviders that can be directly linked to the OLAP universe and the ones that can be accessed via the BEx query. After the linkage between the two systems is complete, you need to understand what the mapping process is for the different objects within the BEx query. Table 9-1 shows a list of BW query elements and how they are used in an OLAP universe.

As you can see, the OLAP universe maps many objects within the BEx query to "classes," and this mapping is used in the creation of the actual WebI query. As an example of this, the following illustration shows a BW query in the BEx Query Designer.

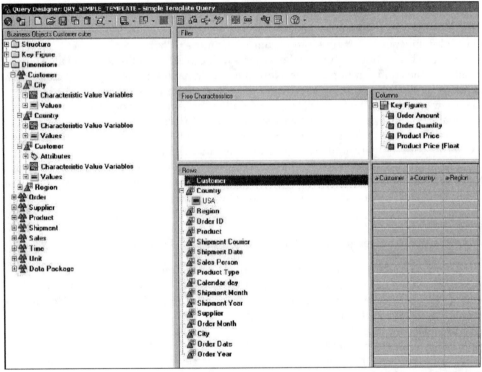

The Rows area of this query includes several characteristics, and the Columns area includes several key figures. On the left side, the actual cube structure is shown with the cube dimensions and different characteristics. The symbol for dimensions has three triangles and the symbol for characteristics has one triangle. If we focus on one portion of

BW Query Element	OLAP Universe Element
Cube dimension	Class.
Characteristic (incl. Time and Unit)	A class with dimension and detail objects (detail objects for key and description).
Hierarchy	A class containing a dimension and detail objects for each hierarchy level.
Calculated key figure (CKF)	Measure element in a class named key figures (information about the calculation is not available via the universe but the CKF is available to be used).
Restricted key figure (RKF)	Measure element in a class named key figures (information about the restriction is not available via the universe but the RKF is available to be used).
Key figure	Measure element in a class named key figures.
Navigational attribute	A class with dimension and detail objects (detail objects for key and description).
Display attribute	Each display attribute becomes a detail object underneath the related dimension object.
Query filter	Filters will be applied to the underlying query but are not visible in OLAP universe.
SAP variables	Query filter as predefined object, which can be optional or mandatory.
Custom structure	Dimension object.

TABLE 9-1 BW Query Elements and Corresponding OLAP Universe Element

this query, we see the characteristics, dimensions, and variables for the customer dimension, shown in the following illustration.

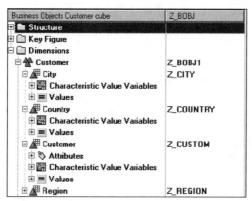

Copyright by SAP AG

In the next illustration, you can see what happens to these objects when translated or mapped into the OLAP universe. The dimension is Customer (technical name Z_BOBJ1) and the characteristics are City, Country, Customer, and Region. The illustration at right shows the result when an OLAP universe is built on top of such a BW query.

You can see that the cube dimension from BW results in a class in the OLAP universe (for example, dimension Customer). In addition, each characteristic in the query results in a class with dimension and detail objects. Level 00 objects represent the aggregated view on this characteristic, representing the "All" member from the underlying cube.

In terms of the display attributes of a BEx query definition, we see that they are detail objects within the OLAP universe. If we look at this in more detail, we see that display attributes are InfoObjects that are logically assigned or subordinated to a characteristic. For example, the characteristic Customer has two attributes, Phone Number and Fax Number. In SAP reporting tools, the

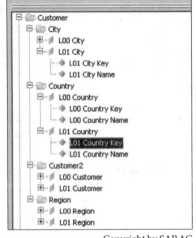

display attributes can only be used in combination with the actual characteristic, which means the attribute Phone Number can only be shown in the SAP reporting tool in combination with the characteristic Customer. In addition, characteristics can be defined as navigational attributes in the BW cube, which then makes these attributes available for navigational purposes in the reporting tools; navigational attributes are treated identically to a characteristic. This can get a bit confusing to both the developers and also for the OLAP universe so the universes differentiate between the two and the functionality of the display versus navigational attributes goes with these objects over to the OLAP universe. The following illustration shows a BW query in the BEx Query Designer. The row structure includes a characteristic Customer with four display attributes: Geographical Height, Postal Code, Sector Code, and Area Code. In addition, the BW query contains three navigational attributes in the rows: Regional Code, Postal Code, and Area Code.

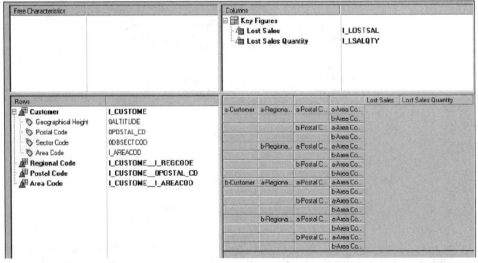

When we build an OLAP universe on top of this BW query, it results in the elements shown in the following illustration. The cube dimension from BW results in a class in the OLAP universe (for example, dimension Customer, not to be confused with the characteristic Customer). As mentioned, each characteristic in the query results in a class with dimension and detail objects. Level 00 objects represent the aggregated view on this characteristic representing the "All" member from the underlying cube (characteristic Customer resulting in a class Customer2 with dimensions L00 Customer and L01 Customer). Also notice that each navigational attribute in the query results in a class with dimension and details objects (navigational attribute Postal Code resulting in a class Postal Code with dimensions L00 Postal Code and L01 Postal Code).

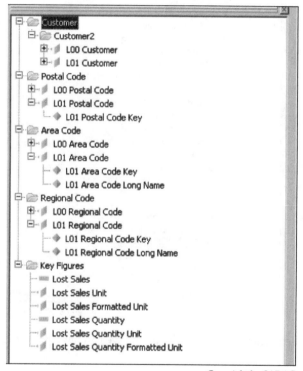

Copyright by SAP AG

The next illustration shows the display attributes from characteristic Customer and how these display attributes are treated in an OLAP universe. Each display attribute for the characteristic results in a detail object for the corresponding dimension objects in the universe.

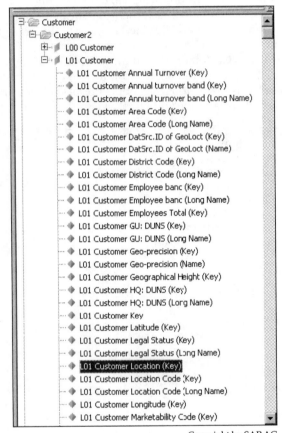

In terms of the key figures used in a BW query, we can have up to three different sets of information:

- Numeric value of the key figure
- Unit or currency information
- Formatted value, representing the user-specific formatting

The illustration here shows the result of two key figures in the OLAP universe. Each key figure is represented with a measure object in a class Key Figures. In the case where the key figure is configured in BW with a unit, an additional dimension object will be added representing the unit information. The "Formatted" value represents the numeric value formatted as a string value, following the user-specific formatting settings.

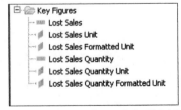

This gives you some idea of the linkage of the BW query to the OLAP universe. Once this process of creating an OLAP universe is complete, we can step into the Web Intelligence Rich Client and create the report by dragging and dropping the information into the appropriate columns and rows. The following illustration shows the initial screen for the Web Intelligence Rich Client. Once you start working in this environment, you will find that a number of functions and tasks are similar to those in the BEx Query Designer in terms of formatting and display options. All of the components are found in similar navigational processes as the BEx Query Designer—either in the right-click context menu or in the top toolbar, where you click and choose what you need to work on.

Once you have created the report, you will have developed an ad hoc analysis component that you will be able to navigate and slice and dice on to generate multiple different views of the data, with the option to save each of the views for later analysis. This is the primary ad hoc reporting and analysis product for casual business users in the BOBJ components. Web Intelligence is a complementary tool to leverage outputs, for the casual and business user, that might have been derived from a deeper analysis achieved in BEx Analyzer. If we look at the overall reporting strategy and identify the areas and requirements that the WebI can fulfill, we have a fairly well-defined list.

First, this component allows the business user to have a combination of ad hoc reporting and analysis primarily directed to the casual user. Second, as with all BOBJ products, Web Intelligence is a self-service process and therefore reduces reliance on the BW IT department. Third, this reporting tool also allows multiple sources of data, both SAP and non-SAP, to be integrated into the same reporting display. Fourth, all the functionality available in the BEx Web Analyzer is available in the WebI component, such as the ability to schedule and publish reports to a distribution list of users, and the ability to modify a report on-the-fly on the Web, save it, and then review or refer back to it in the future. Fifth, Web Intelligence also has all the user-friendly navigation capabilities that the BEx Web Analyzer has in terms of drag-and-drop navigation, context menu functionality, and the ability to switch information into a better format for the analyst. Sixth, it also allows the creation of reusable calculations (creating CKFs and RKFs on the fly). All of these components look at the actual information in the report, but in addition to these functions, Web Intelligence also has the ability to allow the business user to change the format of the report on the fly, adjust charts and table format, add conditions and exceptions, and adjust the positioning of all of these objects within the report. Again, if we compare (and we really shouldn't compare the functionality directly) the capabilities and uses for the WebI with either the BEx Web Analyzer or the BEx Analyzer, we see that we have much of the same functionality and more. It's just a matter of getting used to the actual process of doing these different tasks in the BOBJ environment.

To round out this discussion, let's look at some reports that are generated from the WebI format. In this illustration, the resulting report shows the information in a similar column format as you've seen before and, as mentioned, you would be able to make adjustments as necessary.

	California	Colorado	DC
2001	Colorado Springs	Colorado Springs	Colorado Springs
2001	Los Angeles	Los Angeles	Los Angeles
2001	San Francisco	San Francisco	San Francisco
2001	Washington	Washington	Washington
2002	Colorado Springs	Colorado Springs	Colorado Springs
2002	Los Angeles	Los Angeles	Los Angeles
2002	San Francisco	San Francisco	San Francisco
2002	Washington	Washington	Washington
2003	Colorado Springs	Colorado Springs	Colorado Springs
2003	Los Angeles	Los Angeles	Los Angeles
2003	San Francisco	San Francisco	San Francisco
2003	Washington	Washington	Washington

The next illustration extends the information into the development of a chart to display the data. As you can see, the ability to develop and use dimensional charts is available in the WebI component.

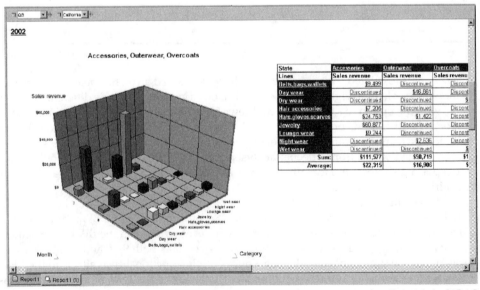

There are many other examples for the Web Intelligence reporting tool for BOBJ including variables, alerts, conditions, filters, and other parameters but these are just a few to offer some basic samples.

Xcelsius

Xcelsius is the component with all the bells and whistles for dashboarding in the BOBJ environment. This toolset really takes the whole dashboarding process to another level. It has all the functionality that is required for a dynamic dashboard and it is very easy to use and understand. Now, that being said, it still requires that we configure the underlying source of data correctly so that the different indicators available can read the appropriate information. Xcelsius 2008 is a visualization tool for creating interactive visual models based on highly aggregated data sets. It uses a point-and-click design time environment that can easily be used by business users. No programming skills are necessary for creating Xcelsius 2008 visualizations, but knowledge about dashboarding is still a requirement.

The following illustration shows the initial workbench for the Xcelsius product. As you can see, the object—Bar Chart—has been dragged and dropped into the worksheet. Notice to the right side of the screen you can see that very similar questions are being asked for the development and configuration of this chart type as were asked for the WAD. We've seen this information when we looked at the bar chart in the WAD component. So, what comes around goes around and as I mentioned nothing that you learn from the development of the chart types in the WAD will go to waste. The information such as subtitles, titles, categories, and so forth are the same and should be treated the same. The different categories of charts and types are found on the left side of the screen.

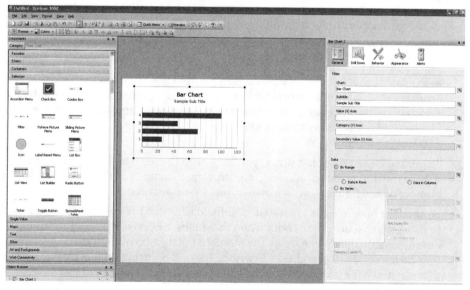

Copyright by SAP AG

One advantage that Xcelsius has over the WAD is that it offers additional types of objects, some of which are shown on the left side of the preceding illustration. You can see that the ease with which you can use a Selector or a Tachometer, and its dynamic and robust displays separate the Xcelsius from WAD functionality. This component is very user friendly and is positioned to be used by the business users as well as the power users to develop the dashboards on the fly. As you can see, there is plenty to review and discuss when it comes to the configuration using Xcelsius, but for this general introduction, we are going to look at some of the possible results that you can achieve with Xcelsius. Also keep in mind that configuring an interactive "what if" statement is much easier in Xcelsius than using the WAD and Integrated Planning (IP), and can be accomplished by the business user rather than the BW IT department.

All the features that are available in the other components are also available via Xcelsius, such as live data connectivity to KPIs, the ability to leverage the Excel modeling component (as shown in the preceding illustration, the worksheet can be an Excel worksheet), and, once you develop the dashboard, the ability to embed a dashboard into any Microsoft Office application, including PowerPoint presentations. You can display the developed dashboard via a portal, whether a BI portal or a corporate portal, and integrate SAP and non-SAP data into one dashboard. The integration of the SAP and non-SAP data still requires IT department assistance in most cases, but the integration of the data is much easier to work with and complete. When you are in the process of deploying Xcelsius for the enterprise, other considerations need to be taken into account in addition to all the guidance for OLAP universes and Web Intelligence. This is due to the fact that the OLAP universe is predominantly used as the backend for Xcelsius dashboards via the Query as a Web Service (QaaWS) component.

With Xcelsius, you need to use specific best practices to ensure they do not overload the Flash engine (component that allows the Xcelsius to function with dynamic displays and interactive activities), thus jeopardizing a fast response time for the live dashboards. End users of dashboard applications typically have little patience for poorly performing dashboards, so it is critical that you bear in mind the following best practices:

- Make sure that you pull in only the data that you absolutely need and must display in the dashboard. Xcelsius dashboards run within the Flash engine inside the browser, which is not designed for aggregating data, performing large mathematical calculations, or processing large data sets that require a large amount of memory. The guideline for data volume is to try to keep your data set ideally to 500 rows, 5,000 rows maximum.

- To guarantee fast response times, you may need to create highly specific BEx queries to base the universes on, and keep the universes small; or at the very least, keep the number of key figures low to increase query performance.

- Be smart in how queries are initiated. If the dashboard has multiple tabs, try to pull in data for subsequent tabs only when those tabs are accessed. Running all the queries on initial load can delay the moment the dashboard first displays, which may be longer than an end user is willing to wait. Splitting the queries up between tabs can make the dashboard far more responsive.

- Push aggregation down to BW. This is a proven and industry-standard strategy to keep the data sets small and make queries run fast. Expectations around the response of dashboards are very different from refreshing operational reports.

- Where a live query is not feasible, LiveOffice is a good option. However, the LiveOffice documents should also be optimized to ensure good dashboard performance.

- Ensure that you are on the latest patch levels for Xcelsius, BusinessObjects Enterprise (BOE), and BW. A number of product issues have been enhanced, so the latest Fix Packs provide all the resolutions for issues identified earlier. The Fix Packs are synchronized and rely on each other, so it is not sufficient to only patch the BOE servers or the BW system alone.

So, let's look at some examples of the results of using Xcelsius. This is where you really see the difference between the WAD and Xcelsius. The following illustration shows a finished dashboard generated by Xcelsius functionality.

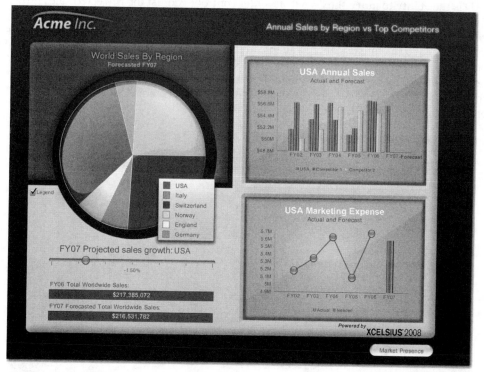

Copyright by SAP AG

This dashboard uses all the different concepts and rules described in the previous chapters:

- The title of the dashboard is very straightforward—Annual Sales by Region vs Top Competitors.

- All the information fits on one screen, so the business user doesn't have to scroll to see additional information. Although we do have additional information included in this format such as future sales growth, we don't have to navigate around the screen to display. We can review the current actuals, then navigate to or execute a what-if analysis directly from the present screen.

- Very direct chart types enhancements are used. The dynamic component of this is that we can really see the difference in the coloring and highlighting that are available in this dashboard.

- The chart at the bottom right has a very interesting approach to showing the current actual sales versus the forecast sales. The same information is displayed using two different chart types in the same chart. It actually works in this case and shows a dramatic difference between the actual data and the forecasted data. This uses the concept that we talked about to draw the business users, attention to the critical KPI first before viewing the remaining information.

All in all, this is a very direct, easy-to-read set of KPIs being displayed as a dashboard.

The one additional function that is available using Xcelsius but not available with the WAD is the ability to move the "what-if" slider control to adjust the projected sales growth and see the information onscreen automatically adjust to the change. With the WAD and even the VC there is some functionality to allow us to execute this type of what-if analysis, but compared to the functionality available in the BOBJ components, these options are only about 75% of the level of interaction and this requires additional effort by the BI IT team to configure. In Xcelsius the functionality is standard for this component. You can see in the following illustration, the projected sales growth has been adjusted to 10.50%, with a corresponding shift of all the indicators.

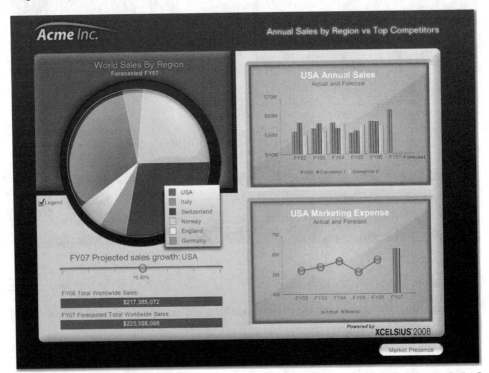

The following illustration demonstrates how the use of all the additional functionality available in Xcelsius can start to get us into trouble. As you can see, within this dashboard, we have the ability to show the forecast using the chart type radar. Can you figure the forecasted sales information within 20 seconds? It is possible but not as easy as in the previous dashboard.

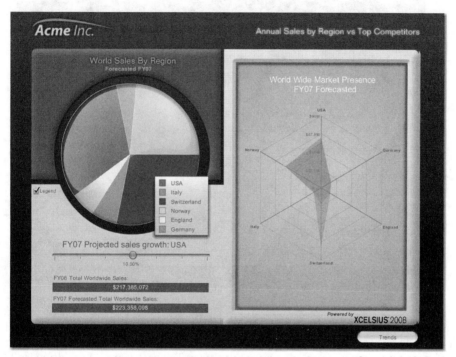

Copyright by SAP AG

Even in this case, the ability for the chart type to shift with the changes using the what-if process is unique. The following illustration shows the result of moving the slider from 10.50% to 22.50%.

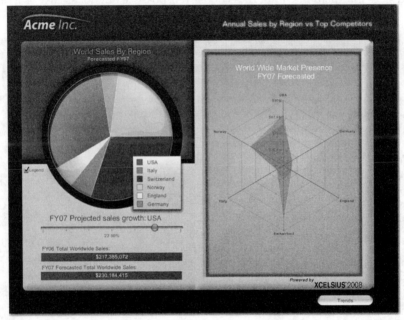

Copyright by SAP AG

The following illustration shows another example of what Xcelsius can do. The dashboard has three KPI screens and, instead of scroll bars, buttons are available at the top of the screen to support quick switching from one screen to another. The background formatting isn't too appealing, but if this is what the company is looking for, this can be done either in Xcelsius or using the WAD.

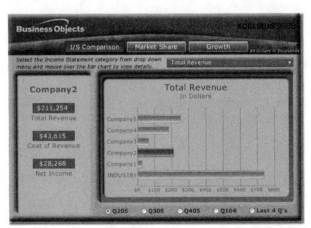

Copyright by SAP AG

As for the actual dashboard, you can see that each quarter is displayed individually, but the rightmost button enables the business user to see all four quarters in one screen. Clicking the Growth button at the top displays information for all four quarters for revenue growth. This changes the dashboard from three KPIs into a very straightforward dashboard with only one KPI—Total Revenue—and on the side three summarized values for Total Revenue, Cost of Revenue, and Net Income. This changes depending on what bar you click, and that information will show up on the left. Even though this dashboard has only one KPI, it demonstrates the ability to make a very basic dashboard useful and dramatic. Each of the other two buttons also shows a basic chart type—one displays a pie chart and the other displays a line chart, as shown in the following two illustrations, respectively.

Copyright by SAP AG

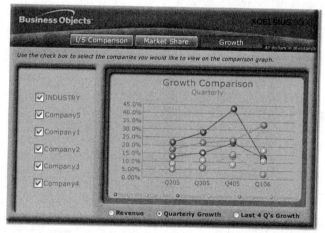

Copyright by SAP AG

The final example, shown next, is a very different type of dashboard, a complete what-if calculator. The title is Financial Analysis Calculator. Therefore, it doesn't display any actual or real data to do any comparisons. This is to be used only for extrapolations and forecasting models.

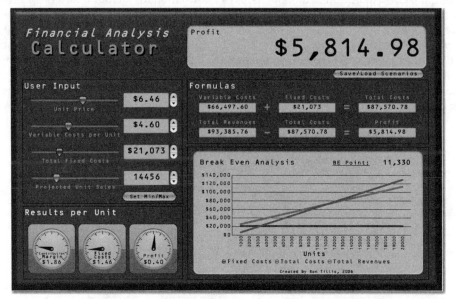

This is a very useful tool and, in the appropriate scenario, can be used to generate extremely valuable information to the overall inventory planning and budgeting process. In this case, none of the indicators are set and all can be adjusted and flexed to whatever positions the business analyst wants to review. As you can also see, the main goal of this analysis is to review the final Profit value, which takes up the most room on the dashboard and therefore should be the critical piece of information that we gather from this analysis.

Crystal Reports

Of all the tools within the BOBJ-BI environment, none is as recognizable as Crystal Reports, which has been available for quite some time. My initial introduction to Crystal Reports was around 2000, when SAP BW was using this as a preferred third-party tool. After its initial owner, Crystal Decisions was bought by Business Objects in 2003, the partnership between Crystal and SAP didn't expand as initially thought and the development of the integration between Crystal and SAP stopped. With the acquisition of Business Objects by SAP in 2007, we are back to using the functionality and formatting of the Crystal Reports toolset to help with the standard formatted reports.

Having worked with both the Report Designer in SAP BI and Crystal Reports in BOBJ, I believe SAP is definitely moving in the right direction. Crystal Reports is a very robust reporting system and can definitely satisfy your needs when it comes to generating standard, formatted reports for governmental agencies, and any required reports for stakeholders. If I were to look at just one item for comparison—the ability to use changes that have been made to the underlying query that supports the formatted report—I would immediately give the nod to Crystal Reports. When business users talk about Crystal Reports we talk mostly about the formatted reporting coming from this component. Several layers of integration make up Crystal Reports, but the other components deal with the user interface, server setup for distribution of reports, and other activities that allow users to share the formatted reports.

Crystal Reports is designed to work with your database to help you analyze and interpret important information. Crystal Reports makes it easy to create simple reports, and it also has the comprehensive tools you need to produce complex or specialized reports. Crystal Reports is designed to produce the required reports from both SAP and non-SAP data sources. The ability to log on and quickly get up and running with Crystal Reports is enhanced by built-in report wizards to guide you step by step through building reports and completing common reporting tasks. Crystal Reports has many of the same functions (such as formulas, cross-tabs, subreports, and conditional formatting) that most other reporting toolsets have, but the primary difference between Crystal Reports and the others is the formatting functionality.

The following illustration shows the initial worksheet or designer for Crystal Reports.

As you can see, the SAP menu offers Open Report, Create a New Report from a Query, Start BW Query Designer, and other options, but the goal normally is to develop a formatted report that can be distributed using another component of Crystal Reports—Crystal Server—to a specific group. Normally, these stakeholders are looking for a very nicely formatted report with information that can be shared externally. The look and feel of Crystal Reports hasn't changed much since I initially worked with it eight years ago. The additional functionality that allows you to use a wizard to start your build and guide you through the process should put you in pretty good shape immediately upon starting the process. As with any new system, you will need some time to bone up on some of the features and also how to navigate within the Crystal components rather than having to search and experiment with the parameters while trying to make your deadline for report requirements.

So, let's take a look at some results of using Crystal Reports and compare some of the features with, say, Report Designer. I've found that working with Crystal Reports is much easier than working with the Report Designer. Again, I'm a firm believer in the SAP BI toolsets, but as soon as you start to work with each of the reporting components, you will immediately see the differences. In the following illustration, you can see that even Crystal Reports can get into the dashboard mania.

This example shows the use of indicators, line chart types, pie chart types, and parameters that are changeable on the fly (click the name and the data changes to that specific person). This is a very nice dashboard, with well-positioned information and a focus on specific information. Dashboarding is not something that everyone using Crystal Reports is looking to do, but it is possible and very straightforward to complete. The hierarchy to the left of the chart also enables you to switch the information to a specific country. Executing this process changes the look of this report but it will still have the look and feel of a dashboard rather than a formatted report. You would be correct in saying that this is not the best business practice, to use Crystal for dashboarding, but the specific activity to focus on in this case would be that we have a structured layout that can be used and distributed. Again, can this be developed and distributed by using Xcelsius—definitely—and would it take on a more complete look—probably.

The following illustration shows a more typical view of a report generated from Crystal Reports. Even though we still have some graphics included in the overall report, the information is formatted in a specific manner for delivery.

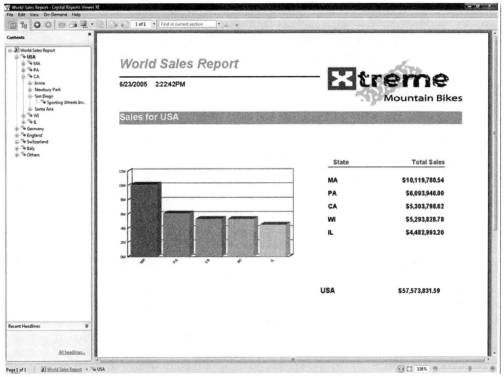

By using the navigation pane to the left, as you access information from different regions, the format of the report will not change but the displayed data will reflect the appropriate region. In this case, the basic column chart type is used to stress the total sales for this company. This report is ready to be printed or distributed to others and is of sufficient quality to be presented to company management. Crystal Reports is fully integrated with the full Microsoft Office suite and can use the integration between a Word document and a PowerPoint presentation to share information and dynamic results. So, you can set up a PowerPoint presentation only once and, depending on the data required, it will be updated and refreshed in the PowerPoint presentation at the same time as the Word document is updated.

Using Crystal Reports you can also take the final results from a Crystal Report and export them using PDF, Excel, or Word. This can be a real time-saver because you don't have to reformat a report that was developed in Word and export the results into an Excel spreadsheet.

In this case, the flexibility of Crystal Reports doesn't end with creating reports—your reports can be published in a variety of formats, including Microsoft Word and Excel, e-mail, and even over the Web. Advanced Web reporting lets other members of your workgroup view and update shared reports inside their Web browser. In addition, Crystal Reports saves time because all the features are very user-friendly and you can develop a report similar to the one displayed in the previous illustration in a matter of minutes without any training.

Basically, the features of Crystal Reports include the ability to generate formatted reporting, use static or dynamic data feed reports, offer printing in just about any format, and all of this with a very professional and complete report that can be distributed in multiple different methods, and can also incorporate both SAP and non-SAP information.

BusinessObjects Explorer

This is the newest component in the SAP BOBJ-BI suite. SAP BusinessObjects Explorer takes the place of SAP BusinessObjects Polestar. SAP renamed BusinessObjects Polestar to BusinessObjects Explorer to clearly describe the value it provides. BusinessObjects Explorer, accelerated version for SAP NetWeaver Business Warehouse, brings together intuitive information search and exploration combined with high performance and scalability made possible by SAP NetWeaver Business Warehouse Accelerator (BWA).

One of the main issues encountered with the other reporting toolsets was the inability to manipulate both structured and nonstructured data quickly. The combination of BusinessObjects Explorer and BW Accelerator resolves this issue. Using BusinessObjects Explorer, the business user can work with information on the fly and generate results for questions that are being asked at that time. In this way, the analyst doesn't need to wait for the BI IT department to pull together the information into a query or universe. The only requirement at this time is that all data must be either SAP BW data or non-SAP data, not a mix of the two. In the future, this component will be able to navigate against both types of data at the same time, but for now it must be either one or the other.

Using the BW Accelerator, SAP BusinessObjects Explorer is able to link directly to the BW InfoCubes, without the additional layer of either universes or BEx queries, and search through the information at very fast speeds. In some of the implementations of the BW Accelerator that I've been involved in, we have experienced increases in query performance from several minutes to pull the data and display to several seconds to generate the report. If the performance of the BW Accelerator directly against a reporting component is similarly impressive, your query will definitely perform much faster than in any other reporting component within the BOBJ suite. Power users, who understand the structures of the underlying BW data sources (BW InfoCubes), use SAP BusinessObjects Explorer to create Information Spaces, which are sets of contextually related objects selected directly from an SAP BW Accelerator index enabled for Explorer. New Information Spaces need to be indexed once, in order to generate the metadata required by the Explorer search engine. This is a very similar process that occurs using the BW Accelerator outside of the Explorer for performance improvements against BEx queries. Because BW Accelerator indexes are consumed directly, the values visible to users are always the latest, up-to-date values on the underlying BW InfoCube. Information consumers and analysts search and explore Information Spaces to create personal exploration views of the data and can then distribute the information across a group of analysts to develop additional information to help drive business for their corporation.

The functionality available with the BOBJ Explorer is not quite the same as the other reporting tools since it is used primarily for analysis and the sorting of data mining information, there are few formatting and context menu functions to work with. Accessing BOBJ Explorer is similar to accessing a search engine screen on the Internet, while other reporting tools present you with a selection of reports for execution. Most of the basic functions are available, such as generating reports and queries, using charts and graphics to display the information, and some navigational functions, but the primary goal of the Explorer is to allow you to obtain information and answers at the speed of thought. Parameters exist to allow the distribution of the data, but over and above that, the information is displayed as is for analysis.

Using BusinessObjects Explorer, you can query on terabytes of data and generate an answer for a customer immediately while you are on the phone with that customer and not have to get back to them with decisions on product cost, price, and shipping information. With this reporting tool, your business analysts can discuss areas of concern and get answers for questions immediately and not have to go through the process of getting a change request from the BW IT department. If this reduces the workload on the BW IT group, that is another benefit. Because business and power users can obtain information immediately, they can develop their own reports and test the information immediately. This requires a user interface that is user friendly and easy to work with, which is a trait of all the BOBJ products.

Summary

The rollout of the BusinessObjects reporting components is in its early stages. SAP is developing some extensions to these components with items such as Pioneer to support more detailed analysis and other enhancements in the integration of these reporting toolsets and the NetWeaver platform. All in all, you will have your choice of either or both sets of reporting objects. The support for the older-version BI reporting tools—WAD, BEx Web Analyzer, BEx Analyzer, Report Designer, and others—will continue through 2014 at least, after which these reporting features will be available but may not have as much support. SAP has already ceased further development of these components, but support is still available. In any case, understanding the differences and features that you get with both sets of components is important, and even if you decide not to go any further in the use of or configuration of any BusinessObjects components, it is important to understand each and where it fits into the SAP landscape.

You will find that SAP is moving to incorporate these components into many of its other product lines that are supported by NetWeaver platforms such as the BPC component. In BPC the integration will take place with all of the BOBJ reporting tools, which will support Excel functionality and have access to all of the Microsoft Office suite including the ability to integrate and use Excel, Word, and PowerPoint dynamically. If you are a BW/BI consultant in the SAP and Web environments, you really have no choice but to learn how to use these additional tools. The final versions of the reporting objects will be hybrids of the best of each company—SAP and Business Objects—and offer significant best business practice reporting components and processes.

Index

X